1000
CHAIRS

© 2005 TASCHEN GmbH
Hohenzollernring 53, D–50672 Köln
www.taschen.com

Original edition:
© 1997 Benedikt Taschen Verlag GmbH
© 2005 for the works by Salvador Dalí:
Salvador Dalí, Foundation Gala-Salvador Dalí/
VG Bild-Kunst, Bonn
Le Corbusier: FLC/VG Bild-Kunst, Bonn
© 2005 for the works by Gunnar Aagaard
Andersen, Richard Artschwager, Herbert Bayer,
Peter Behrens, Till Behrens, Max Bill, Georges de
Feure, Douglas Kelley, Lazar Markowitsch
Lissitzky, Robert Mallet-Stevens, Roberto
Sebastian Matta Echaurren, Ludwig Mies van der
Rohe, Charlotte Perriand, Jean Prouvé, Richard
Riemerschmid, Gerrit Rietveld, Otto Wagner,
Stefan Wewerka, Frank Lloyd Wright: VG Bild-
Kunst, Bonn

Edited by Simone Philippi, Susanne Uppenbrock,
Cologne
Design: Mark Thomson, Samantha Finn, London
Cover design: Sense/Net, Andy Disl
and Birgit Reber, Cologne
German translation: Klaus Binder,
Jeremy Gaines, Frankfurt/Main
French translation: Jacques Bosser, Paris

Printed in China
ISBN 3-8228-4103-X

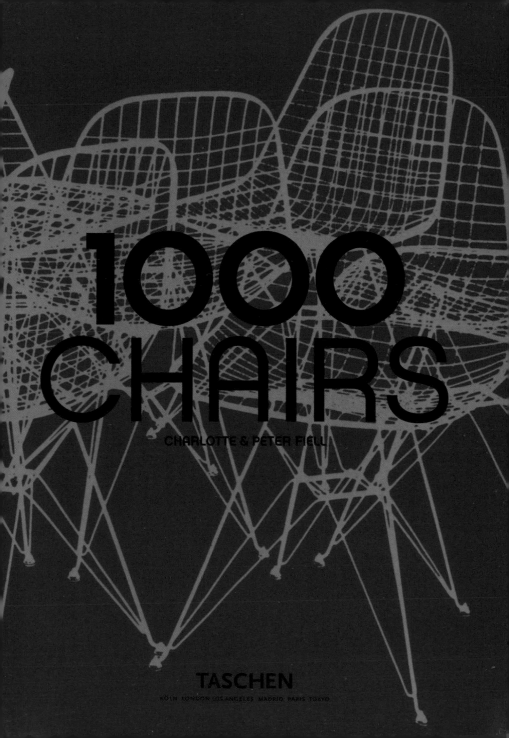

1000 CHAIRS

CHARLOTTE & PETER FIELL

TASCHEN

KÖLN LONDON LOS ANGELES MADRID PARIS TOKYO

Contents Inhalt Sommaire

"The connections, the connections. It will in the end be these details that give the product its life."[1]
"Eventually everything connects – people, ideas, objects, etc., ... the quality of the connections is the key to quality per se."[2]

Charles Eames, 1961

1. Frederick S. Wright Gallery, University of California, *Connections: The Work of Charles and Ray Eames,* UCLA Arts Council, Los Angeles 1976, p. 48

2. J. & M. Neuhart & R. Eames, *Eames Design: The Work of the Office of Charles and Ray Eames,* Harry N. Abrams, New York 1989, p. 266

The Chair: Design Diversity and the Nature of Connections

The concept of connections is intrinsic to design and nowhere more so than in the design of chairs. No other type of furniture offers the possibilities of making and facilitating connections in the same way or to the same extent. Because of this, more effort and more resources have been invested in the creation of chairs by more people over a longer period of time than any other type of furniture. Indeed, apart from possibly the automobile, the chair is the most designed, studied, written about and celebrated artefact of the modern era.

The success of a particular chair has always depended on the quality and range of the connections it makes, or which the designer is able to make through it, while addressing a specific need. At the functional level, a chair makes physical and psychological connections with the individual sitting in it through its form and use of materials. At the same time, it may embody meanings and values which connect with the user at an intellectual, emotional, aesthetic, cultural and even spiritual level. On another level again, fundamental connections are made between the structural components inherent in a chair's design. A chair can also connect visually and/or functionally with the context in which it is to be used, including other objects and styles. More broadly, chair design is connected with different ideologies, approaches to making, and economic theory. Farthest reaching of all, however, are the connections which a chair, its designer and, indeed, its manufacturer make with society at large – through the potential universality of the chair's appeal and the environmental impact of its manufacture, use and eventual disposal.

Over the last 150 years, the evolution of the chair has paralleled developments in architecture and technology and reflected the changing needs and concerns of society to such an extent that it can be seen to encapsulate the history of design. As George Nelson pointed out in 1953, "every truly original idea – every innovation in design, every new application of materials, every technical invention for furniture – seems to find its most important expression in a chair".[3] In our times, this is nowhere more apparent than in the development of better per-

3. **George Nelson,** *Chairs,* Whitney Publications Inc., New York 1953, p. 9

forming, more ergonomically refined chairs. The highly competitive office seating market, in particular, demands continual technical advances, as it is increasingly driven by tougher health and safety legislation and corporate specifiers ever more mindful of the welfare of their workforces.

Achieving a good solution to the problems posed by the chair is a complex and challenging proposition, even though, over its long history, its function as an aid to sitting has remained virtually unchanged. Chairs support people of all different shapes and sizes for different lengths of time and for different purposes, whether it be eating, reading, resting, waiting, writing or office tasking. Furthermore, each sitting position is invested with its own degree of social significance and set of conventions, including orthopaedic constraints. In most cases, the chair must adequately support the weight of the sitter at such a height that the legs hang down and the feet touch the floor. In this conventional sitting position, the weight of the head and torso is carried down to the bones of the pelvis and hip. The timeless problem associated with this physical relationship is that however much a chair seat may be softened, the pressure of the bone will eventually be felt on the flesh of the buttocks as uncomfortable. Ultimately, this results in the user having to change position – something which is done on average every ten to fifteen minutes. Indeed, the more exactly a chair is formed to give "ideal" static support and posture to the average human frame, the more it guarantees discomfort and, thereby, psychological stress for people with non-standard anatomies or those who do not wish to assume that particular posture. It is probably safe to say, therefore, that while the facility for correct lumbar support is important, especially in office seating, it is not as crucial as the chair allowing the user to move their legs freely and to make frequent adjustments of posture. For more healthful sitting, a chair should thus facilitate freedom of movement and encourage a variety of postures while providing flexible continuous support.

Beyond the technical considerations of sitting and how well users can physically and psychologically connect with specific forms according to different functional contexts, chairs are also designed and acquired for reasons to do with symbolic content, aesthetics and fashion. Of all furniture types, chairs especially serve to bolster egos and demonstrate "taste", while revealing their owner's socio-political viewpoint and real or would-be social and economic status. To this end comfort, practicality and economy have often been sacrificed in favour of the representation of decorative styles, radical design agendas and/or the selfexpressive impulses of designers.

The extraordinary diversity of chairs created since the mid-19th century has

Steel tubes, foam springs, and covers have been so developed technically that we can create forms which were unthinkable just a few years ago. Personally, I'd like to design chairs which exhaust all the technical possibilities of the present in which I also live.

Verner Panton, 1985
A. L. Morgan, *Contemporary Designers,* St. James Press, London 1985, p. 471

... the once humble chair has emerged – for the time being, at least – as a thoroughly glamorous object ...

George Nelson, 1953
G. Nelson, *Chairs,*
Whitney Publica-
tions Inc.,
New York 1953, p. 7

largely been due to the fact that, owing to the variety of the intended functions of the chair and the anatomic variability of users, there are no ideal forms. There can be many excellent solutions at any one time to the different contexts of use. While the profusion of designs for a specific function may share numerous similarities, at the outset what fundamentally differentiates one from another is the extent to which the designer has viewed function as either the purpose and goal or the subject of the chair. Whether the preference in approach has been weighted towards utility or aesthetics, the primary object of chair design remains the same – making connections – and over the last 150 years there have been innumerable interpretations of how best to achieve this. More often than not, the creation of a meaningful solution involves a process which not only takes into consideration intended function, appropriate structure (including deployment of materials) and aesthetics, but also method of manufacture, nature of the market, ultimate cost and proposed appeal. Different chairs emphasise different combinations of connections according to the priorities of their designers and the needs and concerns that are being addressed at different times.

As the preoccupations of society change, so too do designers' and manufacturers' responses to them. What may be viewed as a rational solution in one period, therefore, may be viewed as exactly the opposite in another. While some designs strive for and achieve an authority which leads to varying degrees of longevity, even those deemed "classic" have a limited functional and aesthetic appeal. Just as tastes change, so too other factors, such as expectations of comfort, vary from period to period and between different cultures. The inherent ephemerality of design, therefore, also accounts for the myriad solutions to the different functional contexts of the chair.

Although there is never one right answer to any given type, some chairs have had an enormous impact on the course of furniture design, for example Marcel Breuer's B3 Club chair ("Wassily") of 1925, Alvar Aalto's "Paimio" No. 41 chair of 1931–1932, Charles and Ray Eames' moulded plywood chairs of 1945–1946, and Joe Colombo's 4860 chair of 1965. These highly innovative designs were born of the search for better, more effective connections – a search which, more than anything else, has progressed design theory and brought a succession of important advances in technical processes and materials applications, from tubular metal to moulded plywood to injection-moulded thermoplastics. Theoretical and technological progress has, historically, not only invigorated interest in chair design but also fuelled the diversity of alternative solutions.

Architects have always been closely associated with chair design through their abilities to solve problems of structure and to make and exploit connec-

Introduction

tions. In the quest for greater unity of design, architects such as Charles Rennie Mackintosh (1868–1928), Frank Lloyd Wright (1867–1959), Alvar Aalto (1898–1976) and Carlo Mollino (1905–1973) included chairs within their artistic schemes for interiors and buildings. But as the manufacture of chairs moved away from the domain of the craftsman towards that of the industrial process, architects were also ideally positioned, with their background knowledge of engineering, to pioneer innovative chair designs within the constraints of modern manufacturing technology. Chair design has especially appealed to architects, for through it, more easily than with architecture, they have been able to communicate their design philosophies in three dimensions. According to the British architect Peter Smithson, writing in 1986: "It could be said that when we design a chair, we make a society and city in miniature. Certainly this has never been more true than in this century. One has a perfectly clear notion of the sort of city, and the sort of society envisaged by Mies van der Rohe, even though he has never said much about it. It is not an exaggeration to say that the Miesian city is implicit in the 'Mies' chair."[4] As a potentially mass-produced and thereby more accessible microcosm of the ideological aspirations of the architect, the chair has allowed some architects to make connections with far more people than would ever use or even view their buildings.

Throughout its history, chair design has become increasingly connected with the industrial process. In parallel with this, it has also become an increasingly complex and disparate area of activity. This is the result above all of the introduction of office systems furniture in the late 1960s, such as Herman Miller's revolutionary "Action Office II" of 1968. Systems furniture not only transformed the office landscape, but also paved the way for the massive growth of a market which its appearance utterly redefined – contract office seating. Since then, chair design has been sharply divided between the contract market, which is informed by technology, and the domestic market, which is governed by a plurality of tastes and a particular susceptibility to the evanescence of fashion. With more than 50 % of all employed people now working in offices in some countries[5] and requiring appropriate seat furniture, the office seating market clearly represents the single most important area of chair design. It is dominated by a handful of multinational manufacturing companies which employ sophisticated systems of production resembling those used in the automotive industry. The chairs they produce demand huge investments to develop and must be regarded as highly specialised pieces of ergonomic equipment. Often, these chairs are designed as seating programmes, such as Mario Bellini and Dieter Thiel's "Figura II" of 1994. Here, basic office task chairs can be upgraded through to executive versions with

A comfortable position, even if it were the most comfortable in the world, would not be so for very long ..., the necessity of changing one's position is an important factor often forgotten in chair design.

Eero Saarinen, 1948
M. Page, *Furniture Designed by Architects*, Whitney Library of Design, New York 1980, p. 208

4. **A. Bruchhäuser**, *Der Kragstuhl*, Stuhlmuseum Burg Beverungen, Alexander Verlag, Berlin 1986, p. 86

5. **John Pile**, *Furniture: Modern & Postmodern/Design & Technology*, John Wiley & Sons, Inc., New York 1990, preface to the second edition p. VIII. Pile has quoted this figure, "according to various (American) statistical studies".

the addition of extra adjustment functions, luxury options and different backrest heights. Office chair programmes not only embrace a wide range of uses, but can also function as a means of conveying status in the workplace.

The contract and especially the domestic seating markets have traditionally consisted, for the large part, of products considered mainstream both in their origin and their intended appeal. Mainstream chair design is conservative in its outlook and driven by cost more than anything else. While chairs that maximise economy above all else may achieve success through providing some functional satisfaction for the user and good sales for the manufacturer, they are usually less successful in other areas such as quality, durability, value for money, flexibility of function, overall performance, and aesthetic value. Mainstream chairs are rarely innovative beyond matters of cost and can be seen historically as largely derivative of the various advances made by the avant-garde.

The work of the avant-garde has traditionally made up only a small percentage of the contract and domestic seating markets, yet its influence over the course of chair design has been enormous. From the mid-19th century and even earlier, the chairs created by the avant-garde for specific domestic interiors had an impact far beyond the realms of the affluent minority who could afford them. Generally, this was achieved through their reproduction in contemporaneous design journals such as *The Studio*, *Dekorative Kunst* and *Domus* and their inclusion in exhibitions such as the 1902 International Exhibition of Modern Decorative Art, Turin. But the avant-garde historically also designed chairs for public buildings, as did the architect Otto Wagner for his Austrian Post Office Savings Bank of 1904–1906 in Vienna and – from around the turn of the century in particular – for a few progressive manufacturers, such as Jacob and Josef Kohn of Vienna. These chairs, too, were often given wider exposure through publications and design exhibitions, with the result that they, like their avant-garde domestic chair counterparts, were widely imitated. The effect of the avant-garde on mainstream chair design became even more pronounced as elements of the avant-garde moved away from a somewhat elitist outlook on design towards a more democratic viewpoint, nurtured by the possibilities offered by industrial mass production.

In pioneering the vast majority of the most important innovations in chair design, the avant-garde has often, inevitably, been tempered by the realities of the market, especially when working within the industrial process. When the avant-garde has gone too far beyond what is generally agreed to look good or be worth aspiring to at any given time – too far ahead of what the majority of people understand – it has remained on the fringe until, in some instances, more widely held tastes and attitudes catch up with it. Many members of the avant-garde, however, have preferred to work outside of industry and design chairs for an appreciative few. Those who have chosen to operate within the constraints of industry and the demands of the market have generally been driven by the desire to make more and wider ranging connections.

Our selection for this survey of the chair begins in the early 19th century because it was at this time, with the advent of industrialisation, that the first attempts were made to shift the chair from the realm of the crafted object to that of the designed product. New technologies and materials processes provided the chair with the potential to be produced in quantity, while systemised methods of manufacture demanded the simplification of form and structure. With this necessary reductivism, the chair began to demonstrate some of the important themes – such as revealed construction, truth to materials, and a trend towards lightness – that were embraced by later designers and the pioneers of the Modern Movement in particular. Examples of other types of seat furniture, such as stools, sofas and chaises longues, have been included because they set a variety of precedents, many of which had a direct bearing on the design of chairs.

The examples we have selected are virtually all products of the avant-garde. Whether the result of mechanised production or traditional craftsmanship, what they have in common – and what sets them apart from the vast majority of other chairs – is their powerfully argued rhetoric. Beyond matters of function and structure, the fundamental worth of chairs, past or present, lies in their communication of attitudes, ideas and values. The persuasiveness of a chair depends on the clarity of its rhetoric. The clearer the argument, the more likely it is that connections will be made, either consciously or subconsciously, and it is the quality of these connections, more than anything else, that determines the ultimate success of a chair.

The tubular steel chair is surely rational from technical and constructive points of view; it is light, suitable for mass production, and so on. But steel and chromium surfaces are not satisfactory from the human point of view.

Alvar Aalto, 1940
The Museum of Modern Art, *Alvar Aalto: Furniture and Glass,* The Museum of Modern Art, New York 1984, p. 7

Charles Eames, 1961
1. Frederick S.
Wright Gallery, University of California,
Connections: The
Work of Charles and
Ray Eames, Los Angeles: UCLA Arts
Council 1976, S. 48
2. J. & M. Neuhart
& R. Eames, Eames
Design: The Work of
the Office of Charles
and Ray Eames, New
York: Harry N.
Abrams 1989, S. 266

Stahlrohr, Schaumstoffpolster und Bezüge sind technisch so weit entwickelt, daß wir heute Formen schaffen können, die vor einigen Jahren noch unvorstellbar waren. Was mich angeht, so möchte ich Stühle entwerfen, die alle technischen Möglichkeiten der Gegenwart, der Zeit, in der ich lebe, ausschöpfen.

Verner Panton, 1985
A. L. Morgan,
Contemporary
Designers, London:
St. James Press
1985, S. 471

»Die Verbindungen, die Verbindungen. Zuletzt sind es diese Details, die einem Produkt Leben verleihen.«[1] »Zuletzt verbindet sich alles – Menschen, Ideen, Objekte, usw., ... die Qualität der Verbindungen ist der Schlüssel zur Qualität überhaupt.«[2]

Der Stuhl: Vielfalt des Designs und die Verbindungen

Auf das Konzept der Verbindungen kommt es an. Das gilt nirgends mehr als für das Design von Stühlen. Kein anderes Möbel bietet derartige und derart viele Möglichkeiten, Verbindungen herzustellen und zu vereinfachen. Darum haben die Menschen auch in die Herstellung keines anderen Möbelstücks so viel Anstrengungen und Ressourcen investiert wie in die von Stühlen, und dies schon über einen sehr langen Zeitraum hinweg. Tatsächlich ist der Stuhl – abgesehen möglicherweise vom Auto – das Industrieprodukt der Moderne, das die Designer am meisten beschäftigt hat; keines wurde genauer untersucht, über keines wurde mehr geschrieben, keines wurde begeisterter gefeiert.

Stets war der Erfolg eines Stuhlentwurfs abhängig von der Qualität und dem Charakter der Verbindungen, die dieser bzw. der Designer mit diesem Stuhl stiften kann, indem er auf ein bestimmtes Bedürfnis eingeht. Von seiner Funktion betrachtet, schafft ein Stuhl durch seine Form und die verwendeten Materialien eine körperliche und eine psychologische Verbindung zu dem, der auf ihm sitzt. Gleichzeitig vermag ein Stuhl Inhalte und Werte zu verkörpern, die ihn mit seinem Benutzer in intellektueller, emotionaler, ästhetischer, kultureller und vielleicht sogar spiritueller Hinsicht verbinden. Auf einer anderen Ebene wiederum gehen die konstruktiven Elemente des Stuhls und seine spezifische Formgebung grundlegende Verbindungen ein. Ein Stuhl kann sich zudem visuell und/oder funktional mit seiner Umgebung und den dort vorhandenen Objekten und Stilen verbinden. Darüber hinaus ist die Formgebung von Stühlen verbunden mit verschiedenen Ideen, Herstellungstechniken und ökonomischen Konzepten. Am weitesten jedoch reichen die Verbindungen, die ein Stuhl, sein Designer und natürlich auch sein Hersteller mit der gesamten Gesellschaft stiftet – einfach durch seine potentielle Universalität und durch den Einfluß, den er durch seine Herstellung, seinen Gebrauch und seine schließliche Entsorgung auf die Umwelt ausübt.

Im Verlauf der letzten 150 Jahre vollzog sich die Evolution des Stuhls und seiner Formen im Gleichklang mit den Entwicklungen in Architektur und Technik, und sie spiegelt damit die sich wandelnden Bedürfnisse und Interessen der Gesellschaft so präzise, daß man seine Geschichte als eine Art Designgeschichte im Kleinen betrachten kann. Darauf hat George Nelson 1953 mit der Bemerkung hingewiesen, daß »jede wahrhaft schöpferische Idee – jede Innovation im Design, jede neue Verwendung von Materialien, jede technische Erfindung in der Möbelherstellung – ihren bedeutsamsten Ausdruck in einem Stuhl gefunden hat".[3] In unseren Tagen läßt sich dies nirgends klarer ablesen als an der Entwicklung von immer funktionaleren und ergonomisch durchdachteren Stühlen. Insbesondere der von einem scharfen Wettbewerb bestimmte Markt der Bürositzmöbel verlangt permanent technische Neuerungen; eine Tendenz, die noch verstärkt wird durch immer strengere Gesundheits- und Sicherheitsverordnungen, aber auch durch eine Unternehmensführung, die zunehmend bewußter auf das Wohlergehen der Arbeitskräfte achten.

3. George Nelson, Chairs, New York: Whitney Publications Inc. 1953, S. 9

Die Funktion eines Stuhls als Sitzhilfe ist in der langen Geschichte des Stuhldesigns mehr oder weniger gleich geblieben, und trotzdem ist es eine vielschichtige und herausfordernde Aufgabe, überzeugende Lösungen der Probleme zu finden, die mit dem Design eines Stuhls verbunden sind. Stühle müssen in Körperbau und Größe ganz verschiedenen Menschen Stütze und Halt geben, und dies unterschiedlich lange und bei den verschiedensten Tätigkeiten: beim Essen, beim Lesen, beim Warten, beim Schreiben, am Arbeitsplatz im Büro. Darüber hinaus hat jede Sitzposition auch eine bestimmte soziale Bedeutung, ist besetzt mit bestimmten Konventionen und muß orthopädischen Ansprüchen genügen. Gewöhnlich muß ein Stuhl das Gewicht des Sitzenden genau so hoch halten, daß seine Beine herabhängen und die Füße gerade den Boden berühren können. In dieser konventionellen Sitzhaltung ruht das Gewicht von Kopf und Oberkörper auf den Becken- und Hüftknochen. An diesem Problem, das mit unserem Körperbau zusammenhängt, hat sich nicht viel geändert; ganz gleich, wie weich gepolstert ein Sitz sein mag, am Ende wird man den Druck der Knochen in den Hinterbacken als etwas Unbequemes empfinden. Also muß der Sitzende irgendwann seine Position verändern; dies geschieht etwa alle zehn bis fünfzehn Minuten. Und darum wird ein Stuhl, je sorgfältiger er als »ideale« Stütze und Halt für den menschlichen Knochenbau und seine Statik ausgeformt ist, zwangsläufig Unbehagen produzieren, körperliches Unbehagen zunächst und dann auch psychischen Streß für alle die Menschen, deren Körperbau den standardisierten Maßen nicht entspricht oder die sich in einer bestimmten Haltung nicht wohlfühlen. Also läßt sich wohl mit Gewißheit sagen, daß es, bei aller Bedeutung, die insbesondere bei Bürositzmöbeln der korrekten Stütze für die Wirbelsäule zukommt, dennoch wichtiger ist, daß Sitzende ihre Beine frei bewegen und ihre Haltung immer wieder verändern können. Für ein gesundes Sitzen muß ein Stuhl Bewe-

... der einstmals so bescheidene Stuhl hat sich – zumindest in unserer Zeit – zu einem durch und durch glanzvollen Gegenstand gemausert ...

George Nelson, 1953
G. Nelson, Chairs, New York: Whitney Publications Inc. 1953, S. 7

Eine bequeme Haltung, und sei es die bequemste der Welt, bleibt nicht lange bequem ... Die Notwendigkeit, die Körperhaltung zu ändern, ist ein entscheidender Faktor, der im Stuhldesign häufig vergessen wird.

Eero Saarinen, 1948
M. Page, Furniture Designed by Architects, New York: Whitney Publications Inc. 1980, S. 208

gungsfreiheit gewähren, eine Vielzahl von Sitzhaltungen ermöglichen und dabei kontinuierlich und flexibel Halt bieten.

Aber abgesehen von solchen technischen Überlegungen zum Sitzen und unabhängig von der Frage, wie gut die Benutzer mit den Formen körperlich und psychologisch zurechtkommen, die aus den jeweiligen funktionalen Zusammenhängen erwachsen, werden Stühle auch für Anlässe entworfen und aus Gründen erworben, die von eher symbolischer Bedeutung sind und mit Geschmack und Moden zu tun haben. Unter allen Möbeln ist es wiederum der Stuhl, der am häufigsten dazu benutzt wird, das Ego zu stützen und »Geschmack« zu demonstrieren, womit Stühle immer auch die sozialen und politischen Einstellungen ihrer Besitzer, auch deren gesellschaftlichen und ökonomischen Status demonstrieren: sei es der tatsächliche, sei es der Möchte-Gern-Status. Aus diesem Grund wurde die Bequemlichkeit immer wieder repräsentativen oder dekorativen Zwecken, radikalen Designzielen und/oder dem Selbstverwirklichungsdrang von Designern geopfert.

Daß seit der Mitte des 19. Jahrhunderts Stühle in so außergewöhnlicher Vielfalt geschaffen wurden, hat damit zu tun, daß es – wegen der mannigfaltigen Funktionen eines Stuhls und wegen der anatomischen Vielgestaltigkeit der Benutzer – keine ideale Form für einen Stuhl oder Sessel gibt. Zu jeder Zeit kann es, bezogen auf den jeweiligen Gebrauchskontext, viele gute Lösungen geben. In der Überfülle von Entwürfen für eine spezielle Funktion wird man zahlreiche Ähnlichkeiten feststellen; was sie aber voneinander unterscheidet, ist die Frage, ob der Designer Funktion eher als Zweck betrachtet, der erfüllt werden muß, oder mehr als das, was ein Stuhlentwurf zum Ausdruck bringen soll. Gleichgültig jedoch, ob er in seinem Vorgehen mehr Gewicht auf Nützlichkeit oder auf Ästhetik gelegt hat, am Ende geht es beim Entwerfen eines Stuhls immer um dasselbe: nämlich darum, Verbindungen zu schaffen. In den letzten 150 Jahren hat es unzählige Antworten auf die Frage gegeben, wie dies am besten zu erreichen sei. Fast immer gehörte zur Entstehung eines richtungsweisenden Prototyps ein Prozeß, bei dem nicht nur die gewünschte Funktion, eine entsprechende Konstruktion (und auch die entsprechenden Materialien) und die Ästhetik eine Rolle spielten, sondern auch Herstellungsverfahren und -kosten, Marktbedingungen, Endpreise und das gewünschte Produktappeal. In ihrer Verschiedenheit zeigen Stühle, auf wie viele Weisen sich derartige Kriterien kombinieren lassen, entsprechend den Zielen der Designer sowie den Bedürfnissen und Interessen, die in jedem einzelnen Fall berücksichtigt wurden.

So wie sich die Vorlieben einer Gesellschaft ändern, so ändern sich auch die Reaktionen von Designern und Herstellern auf gesellschaftliche Anforderungen.

Was zu einer bestimmten Zeit als vernünftige Lösung gelten konnte, ist später vielleicht genau entgegengesetzt beurteilt worden. Einige Designer haben nach vorbildlichen und richtungsweisenden Lösungen gesucht und diese auch gefunden, was dann zu mehr oder weniger ausgeprägter Langlebigkeit geführt hat, doch selbst diese als »Klassiker« geschätzten Entwürfe haben nur eine begrenzte Wirkung aufgrund ihrer Funktionalität oder ihrer Ästhetik. So wie sich der Geschmack wandelt, so ändern sich auch andere Faktoren, etwa die Ansprüche an den Komfort, mit jeder Epoche, und sie variieren auch innerhalb der jeweiligen Kulturen. So haftet jedem Entwurf auch etwas Flüchtiges an. Und dies führt wiederum zu den zahllosen Erscheingsformen, in denen sich dieses Sitzmöbel in verschiedenen Gebrauchszusammenhängen präsentiert.

Auch wenn es für keine angestrebte Lösung nur ein einziges richtiges Resultat gibt, so haben einige Stühle doch eine enorme Wirkung auf das Möbeldesign gehabt, so etwa Marcel Breuers Klubsessel B3 »Wassily« aus dem Jahr 1925, Alvar Aaltos für das Sanatorium Paimio entworfener Stuhl Nr. 41 (1931/1932), Charles und Ray Eames' Formholzstühle (1945/1946) und Joe Colombos Stuhl 4860 (1965). Diese avantgardistischen Entwürfe entsprangen der Suche nach besseren, effektiveren Verbindungen – einer Suche, die mehr als alles andere die Designtheorie vorangetrieben hat und immer wieder Fortschritte in Herstellungstechnik und Materialverwendung brachte, vom Stahlrohr bis zum geformten Schichtholz und zum Thermoplast-Spritzguß. Diese Fortschritte in Theorie und Praxis haben, wenn man die Gesamtentwicklung betrachtet, nicht nur das Interesse am Stuhldesign belebt, sondern zu einer Vielzahl unterschiedlicher Formen geführt.

Architekten hatten zum Stuhldesign immer eine besondere Beziehung, denn sie besitzen die Fähigkeit, konstruktive Probleme zu lösen und Verbindungen zu schaffen und zu benutzen. Bei ihrer Suche nach einem übergreifenden Design haben Architekten wie Charles Rennie Mackintosh (1868–1928), Frank Lloyd Wright (1867–1959), Alvar Aalto (1898–1976) und Carlo Mollino (1905–1973) Stühle in ihr künstlerisches Programm für Gebäude und Innenräume einbezogen. Auch als die Herstellung von Stühlen aus dem Bereich des Handwerks in den der industriellen Fertigung verlagert wurde und es darum ging, unter den Bedingungen moderner Produktionstechnik neue Stuhlentwürfe zu entwickeln, befanden sich die Architekten mit ihren ingenieurwissenschaftlichen Kenntnissen in einer ausgezeichneten Position. Stuhldesign hat Architekten immer wieder fasziniert, denn leichter als in der Baukunst konnten sie hier ihre Entwurfs- und Gestaltungskonzepte in dreidimensionaler Form vorführen. Zu diesem Thema hat der englische Architekt Peter Smithson 1986 geschrieben: »Man könnte sagen,

Der Stahlrohrstuhl ist in technischer und konstruktiver Hinsicht gewiß vernünftig; er ist leicht, für die Massenproduktion geeignet und so weiter. Doch vom menschlichen Standpunkt aus betrachtet sind Oberflächen aus Stahl und Chrom unbefriedigend.

Alvar Aalto, 1940
The Museum of Modern Art, Alvar Aalto. Furniture and Glas, New York: The Museum of Modern Art 1984, S. 7

4. **A. Bruchhäuser,**
Der Kragstuhl,
Stuhlmuseum Burg
Beverungen,
Berlin: Alexander
Verlag, 1986, S. 86

wenn wir einen Stuhl entwerfen, schaffen wir eine Gesellschaft und eine Stadt en miniature. Sicherlich ist dies noch nie so deutlich gewesen wie in diesem Jahrhundert. Man bekommt eine ganz klare Vorstellung von der Art Stadt und der Art Gesellschaft, die Mies van der Rohe im Auge hatte, wenn er selbst sich dazu auch nicht weiter geäußert hat. Es ist keine Übertreibung zu sagen, daß die Mies-Stadt im kleinen im Mies-Stuhl enthalten ist.«[4] Als potentielles Massenprodukt und damit als problemlos zugänglicher Mikrokosmos ihrer weltanschaulichen Vorstellungen hat der Stuhl so manchen Architekten die Möglichkeit gegeben, Verbindungen zu weitaus mehr Menschen herzustellen als sie Bewohner oder Bewunderer für ihre Bauwerke gefunden hätten.

Im Verlauf seiner Geschichte ist das Stuhldesign zunehmend in den Prozeß von Industrialisierung und industrieller Fertigung eingebunden worden. Parallel dazu hat sich das Stuhldesign zu einem immer komplexeren und vielfältigeren Tätigkeitsfeld entwickelt. Hierzu hat, vor allem anderen, Ende der 60er Jahre die Einführung von Büro-Systemmöbeln beigetragen, beispielsweise von Herman Millers revolutionärem »Action Office II« von 1968. Systemmöbel haben die Bürolandschaft nicht nur völlig verändert, sondern sie bahnten dem massiven Wachstum eines Marktes den Weg, der sich mit ihrem Erscheinen und der daraus resultierenden Auftragsproduktion völlig unstrukturiert hat. Seither hat das Stuhldesign zwei verschiedene Wege genommen: einerseits die Auftragsproduktion, geprägt von der Herstellungstechnik, andererseits das Design für den häuslichen Bereich, in dem die Vielfalt des Geschmacks und die Flüchtigkeit der Moden regieren. Wenn heute in einigen Ländern mehr als die Hälfte aller Arbeitnehmer in Büros arbeiten[5] und angemessene Sitzmöbel benötigen, dann wird verständlich, warum der Büromöbelmarkt die wichtigste Sparte des Stuhldesigns darstellt.

5. **John Pile,** Furniture: Modern &
Postmodern/Design & Technology,
New York: John Wiley & Sons 1990,
Vorwort zur 2. Auflage, S. VIII, Pile
zitiert diese Zahl
»nach verschiedenen (amerikanischen) Statistiken.«

Er wird von einer Handvoll multinational operierender Hersteller beherrscht, die mit hochentwickelten Produktionsverfahren arbeiten, welche durchaus an die Fertigungsstrategien der Automobilindustrie erinnern. Die Entwicklung der Stühle, die dort produziert werden, verlangt gewaltige Investitionen, und diese Produkte können als hochspezialisierte, ergonomische Büroausstattungen betrachtet werden. Häufig sind diese Stühle als Teile eines ganzen Sitzmöbelprogramms entwickelt worden, so etwa Mario Bellinis Stühle oder »Figura II« von Dieter Thiel (1994). Basismodelle dieser Stühle für den Büroarbeitsplatz können durch besondere Verstellmöglichkeiten, Ausstattungsoptionen und unterschiedlich hohe Rückenlehnen aufgewertet werden. Bürostuhl-Programme decken nicht nur einen weiten Nutzungsbereich ab, sondern können auch als Mittel fungieren, mit dem der Status eines Arbeitsplatzes zum Ausdruck gebracht wird.

Auf dem Büromöbelmarkt, aber auch bei den Sitzmöbeln für den privaten Bereich dominieren traditionell Produkte, die von ihrem Ursprung wie auch von der intendierten Ausstrahlung her als »mainstream« betrachtet werden. Das Design solcher Produkte für den Massengeschmack ist konservativ und vor allem von Kostenfragen bestimmt. Stühle, die unter dem Druck der Preisökonomie produziert werden, können durchaus erfolgreich sein, weil sie dem Benutzer ein Minimum an Funktionalität und dem Hersteller gute Verkaufszahlen garantieren; wenn es aber um Qualität, Strapazierfähigkeit, Preis-Leistungs-Verhältnis, Flexibilität und Funktionalität, Charakter und Schönheit geht, schneiden sie schlecht ab. Solche Stühle sind, abgesehen von den niedrigen Kosten, selten innovativ, und sie können im Kontext der Designgeschichte mehr oder weniger alle als Ableitungen aus avantgardistischen Entwürfen betrachtet werden.

Die Avantgarde hat sich mit ihren Arbeiten immer nur einen kleinen Anteil am Büro- und Wohnmöbelmarkt sichern können, auch wenn ihr Einfluß auf die Entwicklung des Stuhldesigns enorm gewesen ist. Seit der Mitte des 19. Jahrhunderts und bereits früher entfalteten Stühle, wie sie von Avantgardisten für ein ganz bestimmtes Interieur geschaffen wurden, eine Wirkung, die weit über den Kreis der wohlhabenden Minderheit hinausging, die sich solche Möbel leisten konnte. Dies war möglich durch die Publizität, die ihnen damals tonangebende Zeitschriften wie *Das Atelier, Dekorative Kunst* und *Domus* oder ihre Präsentation auf Ausstellungen wie der Internationalen Ausstellung Moderner Dekorativer Kunst (1902 in Turin) verschafften. Aber avantgardistische Designer haben Stühle und Sessel auch für öffentliche Gebäude entworfen, so etwa der Architekt Otto Wagner für das Wiener Postsparkassenamt (1904–1906) oder – vor allem von der Jahrhundertwende an – einige innovative Hersteller wie Jacob und Josef Kohn aus Wien. Auch diese Stühle wurden durch Publikationen und Designausstellungen häufig in weiten Kreisen bekannt, mit dem Ergebnis, daß sie, wie ihre avantgardistischen Pendants, vielfach imitiert wurden. Der Einfluß der Avantgarde auf das Massenprodukt Stuhl und dessen Formgebung nahm zu, als einige der avantgardistischen Architekten und Designer ihre elitären Auffassungen aufgaben und eine eher demokratische Vorstellung von Formgebung entwickelten; den Anstoß dazu gaben die Möglichkeiten, die sich mit der industriellen Massenproduktion boten.

Bei ihrer Pionierarbeit, mit der sie die Mehrheit der Verbraucher für die bedeutenden Innovationen im Stuhldesign gewinnen wollte, wurde die Avantgarde zwangsläufig immer wieder durch die Realität des Marktes behindert, besonders wenn sie für die industrielle Fertigung arbeitete. Wenn sich die Avantgarde-Designer zu weit von dem entfernten, was zu einer bestimmten Zeit allgemein als

Die großen Möbel der Vergangenheit, von Tutanchamuns Thron bis zum Chippendale-Sessel, sind stets eine konstruktive Einheit gewesen.

Eero Saarinen, 1953
M. Page, Furniture Designed by Architects, New York: Whitney Publications Inc. 1980, S. 209

schön und akzeptabel galt – und was die Mehrheit der Zeitgenossen ansprach –, blieben solche Entwürfe in der Schublade, bis Zeitgeschmack und Einstellungen sich gewandelt hatten. Viele Avantgardisten haben ihre Entwürfe jedoch lieber unabhängig von der Industrie für einen kleinen Kreis von Bewunderern geschaffen. Wenn Designer bewußt unter den einengenden Bedingungen von industrieller Fertigung und Marktbedürfnissen arbeiteten, haben sie dies getan, weil ihnen vor allem daran lag, engere und weitreichendere Verbindungen herzustellen.

1000 Chairs – unsere Auswahl beginnt mit dem frühen 19. Jahrhundert, denn damals, mit der aufkommenden Industrialisierung, wurden die ersten Versuche gemacht, den Stuhl aus dem Bereich des handwerklichen Objekts in den des bewußt gestalteten Industrieprodukts zu holen. Neue Techniken und Methoden der Materialverarbeitung ließen den Stuhl zu einem Möbel werden, das in großen Stückzahlen produziert werden konnte. Gleichzeitig erzwangen systematisierte Fertigungsprozesse eine Vereinfachung der Formen und Konstruktionsweisen. Mit dieser notwendigen Reduzierung wurde der Stuhl zu einem Demonstrationsobjekt für die zentralen Themen, mit denen sich Designer und insbesondere die Pioniere der Moderne von da an beschäftigten: Sichtbarkeit der Konstruktion, Materialtreue und die Tendenz zur Leichtigkeit. Beispiele für andere Typen von Sitzmöbeln, wie z. B. Hocker, Sofa und Liege, sind ebenfalls aufgenommen worden, weil hier eine Vielzahl von Prototypen geschaffen wurde, von denen viele eine direkte Wirkung auf den Entwurf von Stühlen hatten.

Die von uns ausgewählten Beispiele sind praktisch alle Schöpfungen der Avantgarde. Ob Produkt mechanisierter Fertigung oder traditioneller Handwerkskunst, was ihnen gemeinsam ist und was sie von der großen Menge anderer Stühle unterscheidet, ist ihre kraftvoll vorgetragene Rhetorik. Abgesehen von Funktion und Konstruktionsweise liegt der eigentliche Wert von Stühlen, ob ehemaliger oder zeitgenössischer Produktion, darin, daß sie Einstellungen, Gedanken und Wertvorstellungen vermitteln. Die Überzeugungskraft eines Stuhles hängt ab von der Klarheit seiner Rhetorik. Je klarer die vorgetragene Aussage, desto wahrscheinlicher ist, daß bewußt oder unbewußt Verbindungen entstehen, und schließlich ist es mehr als alles andere die Qualität dieser Verbindungen, die über Erfolg oder Mißerfolg eines Stuhlentwurfs entscheidet.

« Les connexions, les connexions. C'est finalement ce type de détail qui donne au produit son existence. »[1]
« Tout finit par se connecter – les gens, les idées, les objets, etc., ... la qualité des connexions est la clé de la qualité en soi. »[2]

Le siège, diversité du design et nature des connexions

Le concept de connexions est inhérent à la notion même de design et plus encore de design de sièges. Aucun autre type de meuble n'offre en effet autant de possibilités de créer et de faciliter des connexions du même genre ou de la même importance. C'est d'ailleurs la raison pour laquelle beaucoup plus de créateurs ont consacré davantage d'efforts et de moyens à la création de sièges qu'à n'importe quel autre type de meuble, et cela pendant une plus longue période de temps. En fait, mis à part éventuellement l'automobile, le siège est l'artefact le plus étudié et le plus célébré, l'objet du plus grand nombre d'ouvrages et de créations de notre temps.

Le succès d'un siège a toujours été lié à la qualité et à la variété des connexions qu'il engendre dans sa réponse à un besoin particulier. Sur le plan fonctionnel, à travers sa forme et ses matériaux, le siège met en œuvre diverses relations physiques et psychologiques avec l'individu qui s'y assoit. Dans le même temps, il peut représenter des significations et des valeurs qui le relient à son utilisateur à différents niveaux : intellectuel, émotionnel, esthétique, culturel et même spirituel. À un autre niveau encore, des connexions fondamentales s'établissent entre les composants stucturels appartenant à la conception du siège. Ce dernier peut également entrer en relations visuelles et/ou fonctionnelles avec le contexte dans lequel il est utilisé, y compris avec d'autres objets et d'autres styles. Plus largement, le design de sièges est connecté à toutes sortes d'idéologies, de procédés de fabrication et de théories économiques. Plus globales encore restent toutefois les connexions qu'un siège, son designer et bien sûr son fabricant établissent avec la société dans son ensemble, à travers l'universalité potentielle de l'attrait exercé par le siège, de l'impact de sa fabrication sur l'environnement, de son usage et de sa destruction éventuelle.

Au cours de ces 150 dernières années, l'évolution du siège a connu des développements parallèles à ceux de l'architecture et de la technologie. Ils reflètent le changement des besoins et des intérêts de la société dans une telle mesure que

Charles Eames, 1961
1. Frederick S. Wright Gallery, University of California, Connections : The Work of Charles and Ray Eames, UCLA Arts Council : Los Angeles, 1976, p. 48
2. J. & M. Neuhart & R. Eames, Eames Design : The Work of the Office of Charles and Ray Eames, Harry N. Abrams, New York, 1989, p. 266

Tubes d'acier, suspensions en mousse et recouvrements ont connu une telle évolution technique que nous pouvons désormais créer des formes impensables il y a quelques années encore. Personnellement, j'aimerais concevoir des sièges qui épuisent toutes les possibilités de l'époque dans laquelle je vis.

Verner Panton, 1985. A. L. Morgan, Contemporary Designers, St. James Press, Londres, 1985, p. 471

3. **George Nelson,**
Chairs, Whitney
Publications Inc.,
New York, 1953,
p. 9

... l'humble chaise de
jadis se transforme –
du moins actuelle-
ment – en un objet
profondément
séduisant ...

George Nelson, 1953
G. Nelson, *Chairs*,
Whitney Publica-
tions Inc., New York,
1953, p. 7

l'on peut considérer que l'histoire du siège illustre à elle seule toute celle du de-sign. Comme George Nelson le faisait remarquer en 1953 : « Toute idée authenti-quement originale – toute innovation en matière de design, toute nouvelle utili-sation de matériaux, toute nouvelle invention technique destinée au mobilier – semble trouver son expression la plus forte dans un siège. »[3] À notre époque, cela n'a jamais été plus évident que dans le développement de sièges sans cesse plus performants et de plus en plus ergonomiques. Le marché très concurrentiel du siège de bureau, en particulier, est en permanence à l'affût de progrès tech-niques, et il est de plus en plus soumis à une réglementation plus stricte concer-nant la santé et la sécurité, ansi qu'à des acheteurs toujours plus sensibles à la qualité de leurs conditions de travail.

Trouver une solution adéquate aux problèmes posés par le siège est une aventure complexe et une véritable gageure même si la fonction d'aide à la posi-tion assise est restée virtuellement inchangée au cours de l'histoire. Les sièges sont destinés à toutes sortes de morphologies, pour des durées variées et des objectifs différents, qu'il s'agisse de manger, de lire, de se reposer, d'attendre, d'écrire ou d'effectuer un travail de bureau. Par ailleurs, chaque position assise possède une signification sociale particulière et se rattache à un ensemble de conventions, y compris des contraintes d'ordre orthopédique. Dans la plupart des cas, le siège doit soutenir correctement le poids de son occupant à une hau-teur telle que ses jambes reposent naturellement et ses pieds touchent le sol, le poids de la tête et du torse étant reporté sur les os du bassin et des hanches. L'éternel problème posé par cette relation physique reste que, quel que soit le rembourrage du siège, la pression de l'os finit par se faire sentir sur le fessier et devient inconfortable. Ceci conduit finalement l'utilisateur à changer de position, ce qui se produit en moyenne toutes les dix ou quinze minutes. Plus un siège est conçu pour offrir un soutien statique et une posture « idéale » à une ossature hu-maine moyenne, plus l'inconfort paraît inévitable qui va imposer un stress psy-chologique à ceux qui ne possèdent pas cette anatomie standard ou ne souhai-tent pas adopter la posture suggérée. Cependant, il est probablement juste de dire que si la présence d'un support lombaire correct est importante, en particu-lier pour les fauteuils de bureau, elle demeure moins indispensable que la liberté, pour l'utilisateur, de remuer facilement ses jambes ou de changer fréquemment de position. Une bonne assise doit donc permettre la liberté de mouvement et toute une variété de postures, tout en offrant un soutien souple et continu.

Au-delà des considérations techniques sur la manière de s'asseoir et sur la façon dont les utilisateurs peuvent physiquement et psychologiquement se connecter à des formes spécifiques en fonction des différents contextes fonctionnels donnés, les sièges sont également conçus et acquis pour des raisons qui tiennent au contenu symbolique, à l'esthétique et à la mode. Parmi tous les types de meubles, le siège est un moyen privilégié de mettre en valeur son ego et d'afficher son « goût », tout en révélant son point de vue sociopolitique ainsi que son statut social et économique, réel ou souhaité. Dans ce dessein, le confort, les aspects pratiques et l'économie ont souvent été sacrifiés à la représentation de styles décoratifs, à des programmes de design radicaux et/ou aux impulsions de designers soucieux de s'exprimer.

L'extraordinaire variété des sièges créés depuis le milieu du XIXᵉ siècle tient largement au fait qu'il n'existe pas de forme idéale, tant est grande la diversité des fonctions attendues et des anatomies des utilisateurs. Pour chaque époque donnée, on peut trouver de nombreuses bonnes solutions à divers contextes d'utilisation. Si la profusion des modèles conçus pour un usage spécifique peut présenter de nombreuses similarités, la différenciation finale et fondamentale se juge à la façon dont le designer a évalué la fonction : est-elle l'objectif ou le sujet du siège ? Que la préférence ait été accordée à l'utilité plutôt qu'à l'esthétique, le but essentiel d'un siège reste le même : créer des connexions. Au cours de ces 150 dernières années, d'innombrables interprétations de la meilleure méthode pour y parvenir ont vu le jour. Le plus souvent, la mise au point d'une solution sensée implique un processus qui non seulement prend en considération la fonction visée, la structure appropriée (y compris la mise en jeu de matériaux) et l'esthétique, mais également la méthode de fabrication, la nature du marché, le coût final et un élément de séduction. Différents sièges peuvent mettre en valeur diverses combinaisons de connexions selon les priorités de leurs designers et les besoins et intérêts exprimés suivant l'époque.

Au fur et à mesure que les préoccupations de la société changent, les réponses des designers et des fabricants évoluent. Ce qui peut être considéré comme une solution rationnelle à une période donnée sera évalué de manière opposée à un autre moment. Tandis que certains modèles parviennent à imposer une autorité qui leur confère une longévité plus ou moins grande, les modèles jugés plus « classiques » possèdent un attrait esthétique ou fonctionnel limité. Si les goûts changent, il en va de même pour d'autres facteurs comme le besoin de confort, qui varie d'une période à l'autre et d'une culture à l'autre. L'aspect intrinsèquement éphémère du design explique ainsi la myriade de réponses apportées aux différents contextes fonctionnels du siège.

Bien qu'il y ait plusieurs solutions à une problématique donnée, certains sièges ont exercé un énorme impact sur le cours de l'histoire du design de mobilier : citons comme exemple le fauteuil club B3 « Wassily » de Marcel Breuer

Une position confortable, même la plus confortable du monde, ne le reste pas très longtemps... la nécessité de changer de position est un facteur important, souvent négligé par les designers de sièges.

Eero Saarinen, 1948 M. Page, *Furniture Designed by Architects*, Whitney Library of Design, New York, 1980, p. 208

(1925), le « Paimio n° 41 » d'Alvar Aalto (1931–1932), les sièges en contreplaqué moulé de Charles et Ray Eames (1945–1946) et le modèle 4860 de Joe Colombo (1965). Ces styles extrêmement novateurs sont nés de la recherche de connexions meilleures et plus efficaces, recherche qui, plus que tout autre raison, a fait progresser la théorie du design et a entraîné une succession de progrès importants dans les procédés techniques et les utilisations de certains matériaux, du tube de métal au contreplaqué moulé jusqu'aux plastiques thermoformés ou moulés par injection. D'un point de vue historique, les progrès théoriques et technologiques ont non seulement revitalisé l'intérêt porté au design de sièges mais également nourri toute une diversité de solutions alternatives.

Par leur capacité à résoudre les problèmes de structure et à créer et exploiter des connexions, les architectes se sont toujours intéressés de très près au design des sièges. En quête d'une unité de conception toujours plus grande, des architectes comme Charles Rennie Mackintosh (1868–1928), Frank Lloyd Wright (1867–1959), Alvar Aalto (1898–1976) et Carlo Mollino (1905–1973) ont conçu des sièges dans le cadre de leurs projets artistiques d'architecture et d'aménagements des intérieurs. Lorsque la fabrication de sièges passa du secteur de l'artisanat à celui de l'industrie, certains architectes, formés en ingénierie, détenaient la position idéale pour explorer des designs novateurs qui respectaient les contraintes des technologies modernes de fabrication. Par ailleurs, le design de sièges a particulièrement attiré les architectes car ils y trouvaient un moyen souvent plus accessible que la construction pour communiquer leur philosophie de la création en trois dimensions. L'architecte britannique Peter Smithson écrivait en 1986 : « On peut dire que lorsque nous dessinons un siège, nous créons une société et une ville en miniature. Ceci n'a certainement jamais été aussi vrai qu'au cours de ce siècle. Nous avons une idée parfaitement claire du type de ville et du type de société envisagés par Mies van der Rohe, même s'il ne s'est jamais beaucoup exprimé sur ce sujet. Il n'est pas exagéré de prétendre que la cité de Mies est implicite dans le fauteuil de Mies. »[4] En tant que produit fabriqué en grande série et donc plus accessible, microcosme des aspirations idéologiques des architectes, le siège a permis à certains d'entre eux de se faire beaucoup mieux connaître que par leurs travaux architecturaux.

Tout au long de son histoire, le design de sièges s'est de plus en plus rapproché du processus industriel. Parallèlement, il est devenu un domaine d'activité de plus en plus complexe et diversifié, en particulier grâce à l'introduction du concept de « système » dans le mobilier de bureau à la fin des années 60, comme, par exemple, le révolutionnaire « Action Office II » d'Herman Miller

4. A. Bruchhäuser, *Der Kragstuhl*, *Stuhlmuseum Burg Beverungen*, Alexander Verlag, Berlin 1986, p. 86

(1968). Les systèmes ont non seulement transformé le bureau paysager, mais ont également préparé la voie à l'expansion d'un marché que leur apparition allait contribuer à redéfinir : celui du siège de bureau. Depuis, la conception de sièges s'est nettement répartie entre un marché d'entreprises, nourri de technologie, et un marché domestique dominé par une plus grande pluralité de goûts et particulièrement sensible aux phénomènes de mode. Avec plus de 50 % des actifs travaillant aujourd'hui dans un bureau dans certains pays[5], et nécessitant un mobilier adapté, le marché du siège de bureau représente à l'évidence la part la plus importante du design de sièges. Ce marché est contrôlé par une poignée de fabricants multinationaux qui appliquent des procédés de fabrication élaborés, assez proches de ceux de l'industrie automobile. Les sièges qu'ils produisent nécessitent d'énormes investissements et relèvent dorénavant d'équipements ergonomiques extrêmement spécialisés. Souvent, leurs modèles sont conçus dans le cadre de programmes complets, comme le « Figura II » de Mario Bellini et Dieter Thiel (1994). Dans ce cas, le simple fauteuil de bureau peut être traité en version améliorée grâce à quelques fonctions supplémentaires de réglage, des options de luxe et un choix de différentes hauteurs de dossier. Les programmes de sièges de bureau couvrent un large éventail d'usages tout en prenant en compte le statut hiérarchique de leur utilisateur.

Les deux grands marchés du siège ont traditionnellement consisté, pour une large part, en produits considérés comme « courants » à la fois par leur origine et par l'intérêt visé. Essentiellement soumis à des impératifs de coût, le design de ces sièges courants est d'apparence conservatrice. Si ces sièges accordent une valeur suprême au prix de revient et peuvent apporter quelques satisfactions fonctionnelles à leurs utilisateurs et commerciales à leurs fabricants, ils sont habituellement moins convaincants dans d'autres domaines comme la qualité, la durabilité, le rapport qualité-prix, la polyvalence, la performance en général et l'esthétique. Ils innovent rarement au-delà de leur prix et peuvent être considérés, historiquement, comme le résultat des divers progrès réalisés par l'avant-garde.

La production avant-gardiste n'a en effet traditionnellement représenté qu'un faible pourcentage des deux grands marchés, bien que son influence sur le cours du design de sièges ait été déterminante. Depuis le milieu du XIXe siècle, voire plus tôt, les sièges créés par l'avant-garde pour des résidences spécifiques ont excédé un impact qui a largement excédé le cadre des minorités aisées qui pouvaient se les offrir. Généralement, leur notoriété était due à leur publication dans des magazines de design contemporains comme *The Studio*, *Dekorative Kunst*, *Domus*, et à leur exposition dans des manifestations comme l'Exposition interna-

5. **John Pile**, *Furniture: Modern & Postmodern/Design & Technology*, John Wiley & Sons, Inc., New York, 1990, préface à la seconde édition, p. VIII. Pile cite ce chiffre «d'après différentes études statistiques (américaines)».

Le siège en tube d'acier est certainement rationnel du point de vue de la technique et de la construction; il est léger, adaptable à la production en série, etc. Mais les surfaces d'acier et de chrome ne sont pas satisfaisantes d'un point de vue humain.

Alvar Aalto, 1940
The Museum of Modern Art, Alvar Aalto : *Furniture and Glass*. The Museum of Modern Art, New York, 1984, p. 7

Les grands meubles du passé, de la chaise de Toutankhamon à celle de Chippendale, se sont toujours distingués par leur unité structurelle.

Eero Saarinen, 1953
M. Page, *Furniture Designed by Architects*, Whitney Library of Design, New York, 1980, p. 208

tionale d'Art décoratif moderne de Turin (1902). Mais l'avant-garde a également créé des sièges pour des bâtiments publics, comme Otto Wagner pour la Caisse d'Épargne de la Poste autrichienne à Vienne (1904–1906) et, en particulier au tournant du siècle, pour quelques fabricants ouverts aux idées nouvelles comme Jacob et Josef Kohn, Vienne. Ces sièges furent également présentés dans des publications et des expositions de design, ce qui leur valut, comme pour les modèles avant-gardistes destinés à la maison, de nombreuses imitations. L'effet de l'avant-garde sur la conception du siège courant s'affirma encore davantage lorsque certains de ses représentants s'éloignèrent des aspects quelque peu élitistes de leurs projets pour embrasser un point de vue plus démocratique, alimenté par les possibilités qu'offrait la production industrielle de masse.

À l'initiative de la plus grande partie des innovations majeures, l'avant-garde a dû, inévitablement, tenir souvent compte des réalités du marché, en particulier lorsque la fabrication était industrielle. Quand elle s'est trop éloignée de ce qui était généralement considéré comme de bon goût ou de valeur pour l'époque – trop en avance par rapport à ce que la majorité des acheteurs potentiels pouvaient comprendre – elle est restée marginalisée jusqu'à ce que, dans quelques cas, l'évolution du goût et des attitudes ne la rejoigne. De nombreux membres de ces mouvements avant-gardistes ont cependant préféré rester à l'écart de l'industrie et travailler pour des amateurs éclairés. Ceux qui choisirent de créer en tenant compte des contraintes de fabrication et des attentes du marché ont généralement été motivés par le désir de générer des connexions plus nombreuses et plus riches.

Notre sélection d'exemples pour cette étude consacrée aux sièges commence au début du XIXᵉ siècle car c'est de cette époque, avec l'avènement de l'industrialisation, que datent les premières tentatives de tirer le siège du domaine de l'artisanat pour en faire un objet de design. De nouvelles technologies de traitement de matériaux permirent de produire des modèles en grand nombre tandis que des méthodes de fabrication systématisées entraînèrent la simplification de la forme et de la structure. Avec ce réductionnisme obligé, le siège commence à illustrer quelques-uns des thèmes importants comme la structure apparente, l'honnêteté dans l'utilisation des matériaux et la tendance à la légèreté, qui seront repris par des designers ultérieurs et en particulier par les pionniers du mouvement moderne. Quelques exemples d'autres types de sièges comme les tabourets, les canapés et les chaises longues ont été pris en compte parce qu'ils constituent des précédents, dont la plupart eurent un rapport direct avec le design de sièges.

Les modèles que nous avons sélectionnés appartiennent virtuellement tous à l'avant-garde. Que ce soit le résultat d'une mécanisation de la production ou d'une fabrication artisanale, ils ont en commun — et c'est bien ce qui les distingue de l'écrasante majorité des autres sièges — une rhétorique puissamment argumentée. En dehors des critères de fonction et de structure, la valeur fondamentale de ces sièges, passés ou actuels, tient à ce qu'ils communiquent des attitudes, des idées, des valeurs. La séduction d'un siège dépend de la clarté de sa rhétorique. Plus le discours est clair, plus les connexions se produisent, consciemment ou inconsciemment, et c'est bien la qualité de ces connexions, plus que tout autre facteur, qui détermine, au final, le succès d'un siège.

Samuel Gragg

Chair c. 1808

Bent ash and hickory construction with painted decoration | Gebogene Esche und Hickory, aufgemaltes Dekor | Frêne et hickory cintrés, décor peint

SAMUEL GRAGG,
BOSTON, 1808–1820

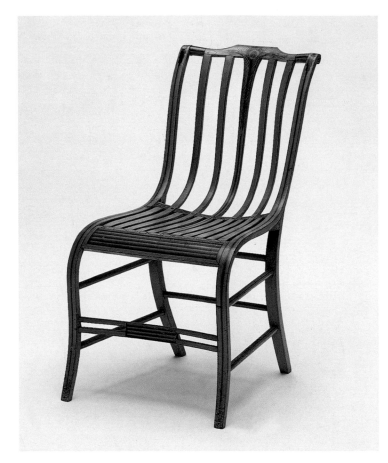

Predating Thonet's research into the bending of solid wood by some 40 years, Gragg received the first of several patents in 1808 for his revolutionary bent wood chairs. Described by him as "elastic", these solid wood designs afforded more comfort than traditional seating.

Bereits 1808, etwa 40 Jahre vor Thonets Versuchen mit formgebogenem Buchenholz, erwarb Gragg das erste von mehreren Patenten für seine revolutionären Bugholz-Stühle. Diese Entwürfe aus Massivholz, die er selbst als »elastisch« bzeichnet, waren bequemer als traditionelle Sitzgelegenheiten.

Précédant de près de 40 ans les recherches similaires de Thonet, Gragg dépose en 1808 le premier de ses multiples brevets révolutionnaires pour des sièges en bois cintré. Qualifiés par lui-même d'«élastiques», ces modèles en bois massif offraient un confort supérieur à celui des sièges traditionels.

Karl Friedrich Schinkel

Armchair
c.1820-1825

Painted, cast-iron constuction with wrought iron rods / Gußeisen und schmiedeeiserne Stäbe, lackiert / Fonte peinte et barreaux en fer forgé

KÖNIGLICHE EISEN-
GIESSEREI SAYNER-
HÜTTE, NEAR
NEUWID
(REISSUED BY TECTA)

▼ **Karl Friedrich Schinkel**
Bench, c. 1820–1825

KÖNIGLICHE EISEN-
GIESSEREI SAYNER-
HÜTTE, NEAR
NEUWID
(REISSUED BY TECTA

Cast-iron chairs were produced in significant quantities from the mid-18th century, but it was not until Schinkel's constribution to this field that such economy of form and efficiency of production was achieved.

Seit Mitte des 18.Jahrhunderts wurden Gußeisenstühle in großen Stückzahlen produziert. Erst durch Schinkel erhielten diese Stühle schlichtere Formen, die effizienter zu produzieren waren.

Des chaises en fonte sont produites en quantités importantes dès le milieu du XVIIIe siècle, mais il faudra attendre Schinkel pour arriver à un tel degré de perfection dans l'économie des formes et l'efficacité du processus industriel.

Michael Thonet

Chair, Model No. 14, 1859

Bent solid and laminated beech construction with woven cane seat | Rahmen aus gebogener, laminierter und massiver Buche, Sitzfläche aus Rohrgeflecht | Hêtre cintré massif et contre-plaqué, siège canné

GEBRÜDER THONET, VIENNA, FROM 1859 to PRESENT

▼ **Michael Thonet**
Boppard chair II
1840–1842

MICHAEL THONET, BOPPARD

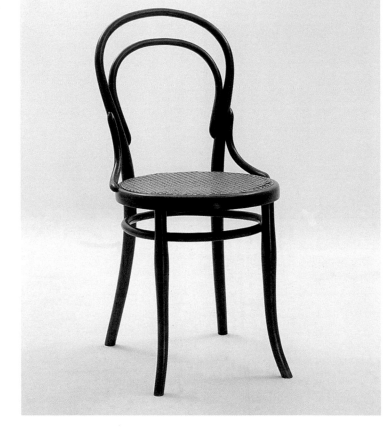

The result of extensive experimentation during the late 1850s into the bending of solid wood, the No. 14 chair remains one of the most successful industrial designed products of all time. The simplified form of the chair was developed by Thonet as a means of achieving his goal of mass-production : by 1930, 50 million examples had bees sold worldwide.

Der Stuhl Nr. 14, das Ergebnis langjähriger Experimente mit dem Bugholzverfahren während der späten 1850er Jahre, ist bis heute eines der erfolgreichsten industriellen Produkte aller Zeiten. Die reduzierte Form hat Thonet

Michael Thonet

Armchair
Model No. 14, c. 1859

Bent solid and laminated beech construction with moulded plywood seat | Rahmen aus gebogener, laminierter und massiver Buche, Sitzfläche aus geformtem Sperrholz | Hêtre cintré massif et contreplaqué

GEBRÜDER THONET,
VIENNA, FROM
c. 1859

▼ Michael Thonet
Chair, Model No. 4,
c. 1848

GEBRÜDER THONET,
VIENNA FROM
c. 1859

entwickelt, um seinem Ziel der Massenproduktion näherzukommen. Bis 1930 waren bereits 50 Millionen Exemplare des Nr. 14 verkauft worden.

Aboutissement de plusieurs années d'expérimentations sur le cintrage des bois massifs à la fin des années 1850, le modèle n° 14 reste l'un des produits industriels les plus célèbres de tous les temps. Sa forme épurée fut mise au point par Thonet pour faciliter la production en grande série. En 1930, 50 millions d'exemplaires en avaient été vendus dans le monde entier.

Unknown

Rocking chair,
Model No. 1, c. 1862

Bent solid beech with
woven cane seat and
back, leather straps |
Rahmen aus gebo-
gener, laminierter und
massiver Buche,
Sitzfläche aus
Rohrgeflecht, Leder-
riemen | Hêtre massif
cintré, siége et dossier
cannés, sangles de
cuir

GEBRÜDER THONET,
VIENNA FROM
c. 1866

▼ Unknown
Rocking chair,
Model No. 7500
c. 1880
GEBRÜDER THONET,
VIENNA

Virtually unknown in Continental Europe, the rocking
chair (an Anglo-American invention) was popularized by
the No.1. With its sweeping design, this chair suggests
movement even when stationary. The No. 17, like other
Thonet chairs, was designed in component form for
later assembly. Perhaps unwittingly, its design pays
homage to both the prefabrication and the geometry of
Joseph Paxton's Crystal Palace. (Bent Wood and Metal
Furniture: 1850 – 1946, The American Federation of Arts,
New York, 1987, pp. 221/2)
Der Schaukelstuhl, eine Erfindung der englischsprachigen
Welt und in Kontinentaleuropa praktisch unbekannt, wurde
erst mit dem Schaukelstuhl Nr. 1 populär. Mit einem ge-
schwungenem Design drückt dieser Stuhl selbst dann Bewe-
gung aus, wenn er in Ruhestellung bleibt. Der Stuhl Nr.17
wurde, wie andere Thonet-Stühle, aus vorfabrizierten Ein-
zelteilen zusammengebaut. Der Entwurf ist, möglicher-

Michael Thonet

Chair, Model No. 17,
c. 1862

Bent solid beech and
solid beech frame
with woven cane seat
and back | Rahmen
aus gebogener,
laminierter und
massiver Buche,
Sitzfläche und
Rückenlehne aus
Rohrgeflecht | Hêtre
massif cintré, châssis
en hêtre massif, siége
et dossier cannés

GEBRÜDER THONET,
VIENNA FROM
c. 1862

▼ Thonet catalogue,
1911, showing the
chair Model No. 17
and others

weise unbewußt, eine Hommage an Konstruktionsweise
und Geometrie des von Joseph Paxton entworfenen Kristall-
palastes.
Virtuellement inconnu en Europe continentale, le fauteuil à bascule (invention anglo-américaine) fut popula-
risé par ce modèle n° 1. Ses volutes suggèrent le mouvement, même au repos. À la différence des autres sièges
Thonet, le n° 17 était fabriqué en pièces détachées, pour
un assemblage ultérieur. Involontairement peut-être,
son dessin rent hommage à la fois aux principes de la
préfabrication et á la géométrie de l'étonnant Palais de
cristal de Joseph Paxton.

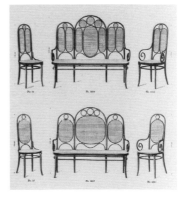

Dante Gabriel Rossetti

Rossetti,
c. 1864–1865

Ebonised, turned oak
construction with red
painted detailing and
woven rush seat |
Rahmen aus ge-
drechselter, schwarz
gebeizter Eiche mit
rot lackiertem Dekor,
Sitzfläche aus Binsen-
geflecht | Chêne
noirci, rehauts peints
en rouge, siège en
jonc tressé

MORRIS & CO.,
LONDON, FROM
c. 1865

▼ Morris & Co.
showrooms at
449 Oxford Street,
London

A reinterpretation of a Regency design, the Rossetti chair exemplifies "Art Furniture" – simple designs by well-known artist-designers which became popular in the latter half of the 19th century.

Als Neuinterpretation eines Entwurfs im Regency -Stil ist dieser Armlehnstuhl von Rossetti ein typisches Beispiel eines »Künstler-Möbels«. Einfache Entwürfe von bekannten Künstlern wurden in der zweiten Hälfte des 19. Jahrhunderts sehr beliebt.

Interprétation d'un modèle Regency, ce fauteuil de Rossetti illustre le mouvement « mobilier d'art » qui proposait des modèles simples signés d'artistes ou de designers célèbres, et qui fut très en vogue au cours de la seconde moitié du XIXe siècle.

attributed to Ford Madox Brown

Sussex, c. 1864–1865

Ebonised, turned wood construction with woven rush seat | Gestell aus gedrechseltem, schwarz gebeiztem Holz, Sitzfläche aus Binsengeflecht | Chêne noirci, siège en jonc tressé

MORRIS & CO., LONDON, c. 1864–1940

▼ Morris & Co. catalogue, c. 1910

The "Sussex" chair is generally credited to the painter Ford Madox Brown, who discovered its antique archetype in a shop in Sussex. It has, however, also been attributed to William Morris.

Der »Sussex«-Stuhl wird allgemein dem Maler Ford Madox Brown zugeschrieben, der den altertümlichen Archetyp dieses Entwurfs in einem Geschäft in Sussex aufstöberte. Der Stuhl ist aber auch schon William Morris zugeschrieben worden.

Ce fauteuil « Sussex » est généralement attribué au peintre Ford Madox Brown, qui s'inspira d'un modèle ancien trouvé dans une boutique du Sussex. Il a également été attribué à William Morris.

Christopher Dresser

Armchair, c. 1880

Ebonised wood construction with turned elements / Rahmen aus schwarz gebeiztem Holz, teilweise gedrechselt / Bois massif noirci, pièces tournées

CHUBB & SONS FOR ART FURNISHERS' ALLIANCE CO., LONDON

▼ Christopher
Dresser
Chair, c. 1880

CHUBB & SONS FOR ART FURNISHERS' ALLIANCE CO., LONDON

Inspired by the art of Japan and ancient Egypt, Dresser was a leading design reformer. This chair, with its Oriental references, opposes the decorative excesses of the Victorian era.

Inspiriert durch die Kunst Japans und des alten Ägyptens wirkte Dresser als führender Design-Pionier. Mit seiner Anlehnung an fernöstliche Formen war dieser Stuhl ein Angriff auf den überladen-dekorativen Stil der viktorianischen Zeit.

Inspriré par l'art du Japon et de L'Égypte ancienne, Dresser fut l'un des grands réformateurs des arts décoratifs. Ce fauteuil, aux références orientalisantes, s'oppose aux excès décoratifs de la période victorienne.

Thomas Jeckyll

Chair, 1876

Painted cast iron
construction |
Lackiertes Gußeisen |
Fonte peinte

BARNARD, BISHOP &
BARNARD, NORWICH

Thomas Jeckyll designed the Japanese Pavilion for the Philadelphia Centen-
nial Exhibition of 1876 and was one of the foremost Aesthetic Movement
designers. This eclectic chair and matching benches were used as seating
for Cambridge Station, England.

*Thomas Jeckyll, einer der führenden Designer des Ästhetizismus, entwarf den Ja-
panischen Pavillon für die Jahrhundertausstellung von 1876 in Philadelphia. Der
hier gezeigte eklektische Stuhl und dazu passende Bänke dienten im Bahnhof
von Cambridge, England, als Sitzgelegenheiten.*

Thomas Jeckyll dessina le pavillon japonais de l'Exposition du Centenaire,
organisée à Philadelphie en 1876, et fut l'un des principaux créateurs du
mouvement esthétique. Ce siège éclectique, avec bancs assortis, fut utilisé à
la gare de Cambridge, en Angleterre.

Ernest Gimson

Chair, c. 1895

Beech construction
with woven rush seat /
Gestell aus Buche,
Sitzfläche aus
Binsengeflecht /
Hêtre, siège en jonc
tressé

GIMSON & BARNSLEY
WORKSHOP,
PINBURY

▼ Ernest Gimson's
workshop at Pinbury
Mill, c. 1894

▼▶ Page from
Ernest Gimson's
sketchbook, c. 1886

Unknown

Rocking chair,
c. 1820

Cherry construction
with woven leather
seat | Rahmen aus
Kirschholz, Sitzfläche
aus geflochtenen
Lederstreifen |
Cerisier, siège en cuir
tressé

MOUNT LEBANON
SHAKER COMMU-
NITY, NEW LEBANON,
NEW YORK

▼ **Unknown**
Child's highchair,
c. 1870

MOUNT LEBANON
SHAKER COMMUN-
ITY, NEW LEBANON,
NEW YORK

The furniture created by Gimson shares an aesthetic purity with
Shaker designs. Both are imbued with a vernacular honesty
derived from superlative craftsmanship and the elimination of
extraneous detail.

Die von Gimson entworfenen Möbel teilen den ästhetischen Puris-
mus von Shakerentwürfen. Beide zeichnen sich durch eine schlichte,
regional orientierte und funktionale Formgebung aus, die von
hervorragender Handwerkskunst und dem Verzicht auf überflüssige
Details bestimmt werden.

Le mobilier de Gimson se rapproche par sa pureté esthétique
des modèles Shaker. Fidèles à l'esprit d'authenticité vernaculaire, ils sont réalisés à la main avec le plus grand soin et sont
exempts de tout détail superflu.

François-Rupert Carabin

Chair, 1896

Carved mahogany construction | Rahmen aus geschnitztem Mahagoni | Acajou sculpté

FRANÇOIS RUPERT CARABIN, PARIS

Hector
Guimard

*Chair for the dining
room of the Maison
Coilott, c. 1898–1900*

Walnut frame with
leather- upholstered
seat | Rahmen aus
Walnußholz, Sitz-
fläche mit Leder-
polster | Noyer, siège
rembourré

Both Carabin and Guimard fully exploited the expressive potential of carved wood and in doing so continued a French tradition that can be traced back several centuries.

Sowohl Carabin als auch Guimard haben die Ausdruckskraft von geschnitztem Holz bewußt eingesetzt und damit an eine jahrhundertealte französische Tradition angeknüpft.

Carabin et Guimard exploitèrent tous deux pleinement le potential expressif du bois sculpté. Ce faisant, ils poursuivaient une tradition française vieille de plusieurs siècles.

Georges de Feure

Sofa for the 1900 Paris Exhibition

Gilt ash frame with fabric upholstered seat, back and sides | Rahmen aus vergoldeter Esche, Sitzfläche, Seiten und Rückenlehnen gepolstert mit Stoffbezug | Frêne doré, siège, dossier et côtés

SIEGFRIED BING, L'ART NOUVEAU, PARIS

► **Georges de Feure**
Salon, on display at the 1900 Paris Exhibition in S. Bing's Pavilion

Inspired by organic plant life and the delicacy of French Rococo, this sofa, which was created for Siegfried Bing's boudoir at the Art Nouveau Pavilion (Paris Exhibition, 1900), epitomises Art Nouveau – a style which ironically denied historic stylistic influences.

Von floral-organischen Formen und von der Raffinesse des französischen Rokoko beeinflußt, ist dieses Sofa beispielhaft für den Jugendstil und dessen ironische Brechung historisierender Stile. Geschaffen wurde es für Siegfried Bings Boudoir im Pavillion de l'Art Nouveau (Weltausstellung Paris 1900).

Inspiré de motifs végétaux et du délicat style rococo français, ce canapé, créé pour le boudoir de Siegfried Bing au pavillon de l'Art nouveau (Exposition universelle de Paris, 1900), illustre le style Art nouveau qui refusait tout influence historique.

Louis Majorelle

Chair, c. 1900

Mahogany frame
with gilt bronze
mounts and sabots |
Rahmen aus
Mahagoni, Beschläge
und Fußmanschetten
aus vergoldeter
Bronze | Acajou,
éléments de décor et
sabots en bronze

LOUIS MAJORELLE,
NANCY

▼ **Louis Majorelle**
Armchair, c. 1900

LOUIS MAJORELLE,
NANCY

The most visually delicate of all Majorelle's designs, the unusual abstract organic form of the chair's back most probably symbolises the Tree of Life.

Das ungewöhnliche abstrakt-organische Muster der Rückenlehne symbolisiert wohl den Lebensbaum – einer der anmutigsten Entwürfe von Majorelle.

Une des créations les plus délicates de Majorelle, la forme organique curieusement abstraite du dossier de cette chaise symbolise probablement l'arbre de vie.

Hector Guimard

Chair, c. 1900

Carved pear frame with tooled leather-upholstered seat and back | Rahmen aus Birnenholz, geschnitzt, mit geprägtem Leder bezogenes Sitzpolster | Poirier sculpté, siège et dossier en cuir repoussé

▼ **Hector Guimard**
Chair for the "Salle Humbert de Romans", c. 1901

The popularity of Guimard's Art Nouveau designs was such that the term "Style Guimard" was coined. His swirling organicism was perhaps best expressed in his cast iron designs for the entrances to the Paris Métro. *Guimards Jugendstilformen wurden so populär, daß man direkt von einem »Stil Guimard« sprach. Seine verschlungene organische Formgebung kam in den gußeisernen Eingängen der Pariser Metro am besten zur Geltung.* La popularité des modèles Art nouveau de Guimard fut telle que naquit l'expression « style Guimard ». Son caractère organique s'exprime avec un bonheur particulier dans les entrées du métro parisien.

Eugène Gaillard

Chair for the dining room in Siegfried Bing's "L'Art Nouveau" Pavilion at the 1900 Paris Exhibition

Walnut frame with tooled leather-upholstered seat and back with brass studs | Rahmen aus Walnußholz, geschnitzt, mit geprägtem Leder bezogenes Sitzpolster und Rückenlehne, Ziernägel aus Messing | Noyer, siège et dossier en cuir repoussé, clous de laiton

SIEGFRIED BING,
L'ART NOUVEAU,
PARIS

▼ **Eugène Gaillard**
Dining room interior for the 1900 Paris Exhibiton

Exhibited at the Paris Exhibition of 1900, this chair embodies the idea of decorative form – each functional element appears almost to melt into the next, giving the design a visual coherence and fluidity.

Dieser Stuhl, auf der Pariser Weltausstellung von 1900 präsentiert, verkörpert, was dekorative Konstruktion sein kann – alle funktionalen Elemente scheinen miteinander zu verschmelzen, womit dieser Entwurf optisch geschlossen und zugleich fließend wirkt.

Présentée à l'Exposition universelle de Paris en 1900, cette chaise incarne l'idée d'une structure décorative, chaque élément fonctionnel semblant se fondre dans le suivant, donnant au dessin sa cohérence visuelle.

Émile Gallé

**Side chair for the
Maison Hannon,
1902**

*Carved beech frame
with upholstered seat |
Rahmen aus Buche
geschnitzt, gepolsterte
Sitzfläche | Hêtre
sculpté, siège
rembourré*

▼ **Emile Gallé**
Chair for the Maison
Hannon, 1902

Better known for his designs in glass, the decorative
floral elements of Gallé's chairs are highly reminiscent
of the raised cameo detailing of his exquisite vases.
*Den Namen Gallé verbindet man eher mit Glassobjekten.
Es verwundert deshalb nicht, daß die floralen Formen seiner Stühle an die reliefartig geschnittenen Glasdekors seiner
edlen Vasen erinnern.*
Plus connu pour ses travaux de verrier, Gallé se sert ici
de motifs décoratifs floraux qui rappellent le style de
camée de ses vases raffinés.

Antonio Gaudí
y Cornet

**Armchair for the
Casa Calvet,
c. 1898–1900**

Carved oak
construction /
Rahmen aus Eiche
geschnitzt / Chêne
sculpté

▼ Antonio Gaudí y
Cornet
Chair for the
Casa Calvet,
c. 1898–1900

Designed for a specific site, this chair was part of a
greater decorative scheme. Gaudi's interpretation of Art
Nouveau was more robust and stylistically abstract than
that of his French and Belgian counterparts.
*Gaudí entwarf diesen Stuhl für ein bestimmtes Interieur
als Element eines umfassenden dekorativen Programms.
Gaudis Interpretation des Jugendstils war schnörkelloser
und strenger als die der Franzosen und Belgier.*
Conçu pour un intérieur précis, ce siège faisait partie
d'un projet décoratif global et ambitieux. L'interprétation gaudienne du style Art nouveau est plus vigoureuse
et stylistiquement plus abstraite que celle de ses
confrères français et belges.

▲ Antonio Gaudí y
Cornet
Casa Battló,
Barcelona, 1906

45

Carlo Bugatti

Cobra chair for the Turin Exhibition, 1902

Decorated vellum over wood body with hammered copper section | Mit Pergament bespannter Rahmen aus Holz, Rückenlehne mit gehämmerter Kupferplatte | Vélin décoré sur châssis en bois, éléments décoratifs en cuivre martelé

CARLO BUGATTI, MILAN

▼ **Carlo Bugatti**
Snails Room at the International Exhibition of Decorative Arts, Turin, 1902

The "Cobra" chair was shown at the 1902 Turin International Exhibition of Decorative Arts and ensured Bugatti a reputation as a highly eccentric and idiosyncratic designer.

Der »Cobra«-Stuhl wurde zum ersten mal in Turin auf der Internationalen Ausstellung für angewandte Kunst von 1902 gezeigt. Er sicherteBugatti seinen Namen als äußerst exzentrischer und eigenwilliger Designer.

Ce modèle « Cobra » fut présente à l'Exposition inernational des arts décoratifs de Turin en 1902. Il assura à Bugatti une réputation da créateur excentrique et original.

By the 1900s, Bugatti's style had become more inspired by Orientalism. With their tassels and intricate inlay, his designs from this period appear to have been smuggled from some exotic harem.

Nach 1900 wurde der Stil Bugattis immer stärker durch orientalisierende Formen beeinflußt. Mit ihren Quasten aus komplexen Intarsien wirken seine Entwürfe aus jener Zeit, als seien sie aus einem exotischen Harem herausgeschmuggelt worden.

À partir de 1900, le style de Bugatti s'inspire de plus en plus de l'orientalisme. Avec leurs franges et leur décor complexe, les modèles de cette période semblent tout sortis d'un harem.

Carlo Bugatti
Bench, c. 1900

Part-stained wood construction inlaid with vellum, brass and pewter and adorned with tassels | Rahmen aus Holz, teilweise gebeizt, Intarsien und Verzierungen aus Pergament, Messing und Zinn, mit Quasten geschmückt | Bois teinté incrustations en vélin, cuivre, étain et franges

CARLO BUGATTI, MILAN

▶ **Carlo Bugatti**
chair, c. 1902

CARLO BUGATTI, MILAN

◀ **Carlo Bugatti**
Chair, c. 1895

CARLO BUGATTI, MILAN

Henry van de Velde

Bloemenwerf, 1895

Walnut frame with
leather seat | Rahmen
aus Walnußholz,
Sitzfläche mit
Lederpolster | Châssis
en noyer, siège en cuir

SOCIÉTÉ HENRY VAN
DE VELDE, IXELLES
FROM 1895

▼ Henry van de
Velde
Dining Room,
Bloemenwerf House,
Uccle, near Brussels,
c. 1896

In 1900, van de Velde moved from Belgium to Germany, where he practised his "anglicised" version of Art Nouveau. As an important design theorist, as well as a prolific designer, his chairs can be seen as realisations of his desire for functional objects that could exist beyond stylistic convention.

Im Jahr 1900 übersiedelte van de Velde von Belgien nach Deutschland; dort schuf er seine »anglisierten« Jugendstilarbeiten. Als bedeutender Designtheoretiker und als produktiver Praktiker verfolgte er das Ziel, funktionale Objekte zu kreieren, die jenseits aller stilistischen Konventionen Bestand haben sollten: Dafür stehen auch seine Stühle und Sessel.

Henry van de Velde

Havana, 1897

Oak frame with buttoned leather-upholstered seat and back and brass sabots | Rahmen aus Eiche, Rückenlehne und Sitzfläche mit durchgeknöpftem Lederpolster, Fußmanschetten aus Messing | Châssis en chêne, siège et dossier en cuir captitonné et rembourré, sabots en laiton

▼ Henry van de Velde
Bodenhausen arm-chair, 1897–1898
(Batik upholstery by Jan Thorn-Prikker)

En 1900, van de Velde quitte la Belgique pour l'Allemagne où il crée cette version anglicisée de l'Art nouveau. Important théoricien et créateur prolifique, il réussit à réaliser des sièges illustrant un désir de fonctionnalisme libéré de toute convention stylistique.

Henry van de Velde

Armchair for the hair-dressing salon Haby, 1901

Mahogany frame with leather upholstered seat, back and sides | Rahmen aus Mahagoni, Seiten, Sitzfläche und Rückenlehne mit Lederpolsterung | Châssis en acajou, siège, dossier et côtes rembourrés en cuir

SOCIÉTÉ HENRY VAN DE VELDE, IXELLES

▼ Henry van de Velde
Hair-dressing salon Haby, Berlin, 1901

While van de Velde rejected superfluous decoration and praised progressive British furniture design for its "systematc discarding of ornament", his chair designs nevertheless maintained a decorative quality and visual rhythm, through their swelling and tapering forms derived from highly abstract plant life.

Van de Velde verwarf alles überflüssige Dekor und lobte die englischen Möbel wegen ihrer »konsequenten Ablehnung des Ornaments« als fortschrittlich. Dennoch zeigen seine Stühle und Sessel mit ihren anschwellenden und sich wieder verjüngenden Formen, als Abstraktionen aus der Pflanzenwelt entwickelt, dekorative und rhythmische Qualitäten.

Henry van
de Velde

*Chair for the dining
room of the
Münchhausen
apartment, c. 1904*

*Beech frame with
woven cane seat |
Rahmen aus Buche
Sitzfläche aus
Rohrgeflecht | Châssis
en hêtre, siège canné*

HOFMÖBELFABRIK
SCHEIDEMANTEL,
WEIMAR

▼ Henry van de
Velde
Rocking chair, 1904

HOFMÖBELFABRIK
SCHEIDEMANTEL,
WEIMAR

Si van de Velde rejetait tout décor superflu et louait
l'avant-garde britannique pour son «rejet systématique
de l'ornement», ses modèles de sièges n'en affichent
pas moins une qualité décorative et un rythme visuel à
travers leurs forms tantôt renflées, tantôt fuselées, inspirées de motifs végétaux abstraits.

Bernhard Pankok

Armchair for a ladies' room, 1900–1901

Carved mahogany frame with upholstered seat and back | Rahmen aus Mahagoni, geschnitzt, Sitzfläche und Rückenlehne gepolstert | Châssis en acajou sculpté, siège et dossier rembourrés

VEREINIGTE WERK-STÄTTEN FÜR KUNST IM HANDWERK, MUNICH

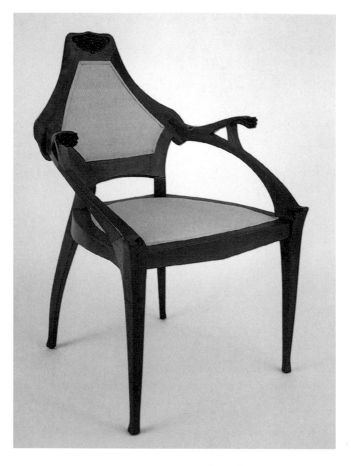

▼ Bernhard Pankok Furniture for a bedroom, exhibited at the "Deutsche Kunst-Ausstellung" Dresden, 1899

VEREINIGTE WERK-STÄTTEN FÜR KUNST IM HANDWERK, MUNICH

Like Endell, his Munich colleague Pankok also incorporated organic carving in his chair designs, instilling them with a certain sculptural quality.
Wie Endell arbeitete auch sein Münchner Kollege Pankok mit organischen Schnitzereien bei seinen Stuhlentwürfen, was diesen eine gewisse bildhauerische Qualität verleiht.

Tout comme son collège de Munich Endell, Pankok recourait à une sculpture organique pour créer ses modèles de chaises, ce qui leur conférait une certaine qualité plastique.

Bruno Paul

Armchair, 1901

Stained maple frame
with leather-
upholstered seat and
back section | Rahmen aus Ahorn,
Sitzfläche und
Rückenlehne
gepolstert | Châssis en
érable teinté, siège et
dossier en cuir
rembourré

VEREINIGTE WERK-
STÄTTEN FÜR KUNST
IM HANDWERK,
MUNICH

This chair design belongs to a set of furnishing for a
salon which Paul presented at the first Munich Exhibition of Art Handicrafts in 1901. The rear view shows the
chair frame's visible construction.

*Dieser Stuhlentwurf gehört zu einer Salongarnitur, die Paul
auf der ersten Ausstellung für Kunst im Handwerk 1901 in
München präsentierte. Die Ansicht von hinten zeigt die
außen sichtbare Konstruktion des Stuhlrahmens.*

Ce modèle de siège fait partie d'un ensemble de salon
que Paul présenta à Munich lors de la première exposition consacrée à l'artisanat d'art 1901. On notera la
structure apparente du châssis.

Josef Maria Olbrich

Armchair for the 1900 Paris Exhibition

Oak frame with upholstered seat and back | Rahmen aus Eiche, Sitzfläche und Rückenlehne gepolstert | Châssis en chêne, siège et dossier rembourrés

HOFMÖBELFABRIK
JULIUS GLÜCKERT,
DARMSTADT

▼ Joseph Maria Olbrich
"Darmstadt room", exhibited at the 1900 Paris Exhibition

Shown for the first time at the Paris Exhibition in 1900, this chair was a part of the "Darmstadt room" and thus one of Olbrich's first designs as a member of the Darmstadt Artists' Colony.

Erstmals auf der Weltausstellung 1900 in Paris gezeigt, gehört dieser Stuhl als Bestandteil des »Darmstädter Zimmers« zu den frühesten Entwürfen Olbrichs als Mitglied der Darmstädter Künstlerkolonie.

Présenté pour la première fois à l'Exposition universelle de Paris en 1900, ce siège fait partie d'un des premiers mobiliers crèes par Olbrich, alors qu'il étail membre de la colonie d'artistes de Darmstadt.

Josef Maria Olbrich

Armchair for the guest room of the Villa Friedmann, 1898 – 1899

Mahogany, leather-upholstered seat, brass sabots / Mahagoni, Sitzfläche mit Lederpolsterung, Fußmanschetten in Messing / Acajou, siège en cuir rembourré, sabots en laiton

▼ Josef Maria Olbrich
Chair for the guest room of the Villa Friedmann, 1898–1899

Olbrich was still in Vienna when he designed this armchair in 1898/1899 for the Villa Friedmann in Hinterbrühl near Vienna. Its form and decoration clearly express the artistic ideals of the Vienna Secession.

Noch zu seiner Wiener Zeit 1898/1899 entwarf Olbrich für die Villa Friedmann in Hinterbrühl bei Wien diesen Armlehnenstuhl, der in seiner Form und Ornamentik das künstlerische Vokabular der Wiener Secession klar erkennen läßt.

Olbrich était encore à Vienne (1898/1899) lorsqu'il dessina ce fauteuil pour la Villa Friedmann, à Hinterbrühl. Sa forme et son ornementation illustrent clairment l'expression artistique du style de la Sécession viennoise.

Peter Behrens

Armchair for the dining room of the Behrens House, *1900–1901*

White varnished poplar wood, leather-upholstered seat | Rahmen aus Pappel, weiß lackiert, Sitzfläche mit Lederpolster | Peuplier vernis blanc, siège en cuir rembourré

HOFMÖBELFABRIK
J. D. HEYMANN,
HAMBURG

▼ **Peter Behrens**
Chair for the dining room of the Behrens House, 1900 – 1901

HOFMÖBELFABRIK
J.D.HEYMANN,
HAMBURG

Presented at the 1901 exhibition "A Document of German Art" on Darmstadt's Mathildenhöhe, Behrens designed a private residence, the Villa Behrens, which he developed and furnished down to the very last detail. He designed a set of white-lacquered chairs for the dining-room, with the tone matching the underlying white hue of the room. The upholstered seats were originally drafted in red to harmonize with the ruby-red feet of a specially created set of drinking glasses. The design and look of the chairs are reminiscent of the "Bloemenwerf" chairs by Henry van de Velde for his villa in Uccle near Brussels.

Anläßlich der Ausstellung »Ein Dokument deutscher Kunst«, 1901 auf der Darm-
städter Mathildenhöhe gezeigt, entwarf Behrens ein Wohnhaus, die Villa Beh-
rens, die er bis ins letzte Detail selber gestaltete und ausstattete. Für das Speise-
zimmer entwarf er einen Satz weißlackierter Stühle, die auf den weißen Grund-
ton des Raumes abgestimmt waren. Die ursprünglichen roten Sitzpolster
harmonierten dagegen mit den rubinroten Füßen der speziell angefertigten
Trinkglasgarnitur. Formgebung und Ausstrahlung der Stühle erinnern an die
»Bloemenwerf«-Stühle Henry van de Veldes für dessen Wohnhaus in Uccle bei
Brüssel.

▲ **Peter Behrens**
Dining room in the
Behrens House,
Mathildenhöhe,
Darmstadt, c. 1901

C'est à l'occasion de la première exposition d'art organisée en 1901 sur la
Mathildenhöhe de Darmstadt, que Behrens conçut la Villa Behrens, une habitation qu'il dessina et aménagea lui-même dans ses moindres détails.
Pour la salle à manger, il imagina une série de chaises laquées en blanc, as-
sorties à la teinte dominante de la pièce. En revanche, les coussins à l'origine rouges s'harmonisaient avec les pieds rouge rubis des verres fabriqués
spécialement pour cet ensemble. Le façonnage et la force d'expression de
ces sièges évoquent les chaises « Bloemenwerf » d'Henry van de Velde, qui
furent créés pour la maison de Uccle, prés de Bruxelles.

Peter Behrens

Wertheim chair,
1902

Oak frame with
woven rush seat |
Rahmen aus Eiche,
Sitzfläche aus
Binsengeflecht |
Châssis en chêne,
siège en paille tressée

ANTON BLÜGGEL,
BERLIN

These furnishings for a dining room formed part of an exhibition at the Wertheim department store, Berlin. Its strict design abandons the Art Nouveau idiom and is typical of Behrens' later work.

Diese Speisezimmereinrichtung wurde auf einer Ausstellung im Warenhaus Wertheim, Berlin, gezeigt. Seine strenge Formgebung löst sich von der Formensprache des Jugendstils und wird typisch für Behrens' weiteres Werk.

Lors d'une exposition dans l'entrepôt Wertheim à Berlin, Behrens participa à l'aménagement d'une salle à manger. Le façonnage rigoureux du mobilier se détache du style Art nouveau et va désormais caractériser l'œuvre de Behrens.

◄ ▲ **Peter Behrens**
Dining room, exhibited at the "Ausstellung für moderne Wohnungskunst",
Berlin, 1902

59

Richard Riemerschmid

Chair, 1905

*Oak frame with upholstered seat |
Rahmen aus Eiche,
Sitzfläche gepolstert |
Châssis en chêne,
siège rembourré*

DRESDNER
WERKSTÄTTEN FÜR
HANDWERKSKUNST,
DRESDEN

▼ **Richard Riemerschmid**
Armchair, 1900

J. FLEISCHAUER'S
SÖHNE, NÜRNBERG

▼► **Richard Riemerschmid**
Living room, c. 1902

Richard Riemerschmid

Armchair, 1905

Mahogany frame with upholstered seat | Rahmen aus Mahagoni, Sitzfläche gepolstert | Châssis en acajou, siège rembourré

DRESDNER
WERKSTÄTTEN FÜR
HANDWERKSKUNST,
DRESDEN

▼ Richard
Riemerschmid
Armchair,
1906–1907

DRESDNER
WERKSTÄTTEN FÜR
HANDWERKSKUNST,
DRESDEN

Influenced by the British Arts & Crafts Movement, Riemerschmid's simple, unornamented designs were the result of a synthesis of traditional forms with a functional urban elegance.

Von der englischen Arts & Crafts-Bewegung beeinflußt, entwickelte Riemerschmid schlichte, schmucklose Formen, die eine Synthese von traditionellen Formen und funktionaler städtischer Eleganz darstellen.

Influencés par le mouvement Arts & Crafts britannique, les modèles sobres et sans ornement de Riemerschmid résultaient d'une synthèse de formes traditionnelles et d'une élégance fonctionnelle toute urbaine.

Charles Rennie
Mackintosh

*High-backed chair
for the Rose Boudoir,
Turin Exhibition,
1902*

White painted oak
frame with stencilled
decoration on
upholstered seat and
back | Rahmen aus
Eiche, weiß lackiert,
Sitzfläche und
Rückenlehne gepol-
stert, Bezugsstoff mit
Schablonenmalerei |
Châssis en chêne
peint en blanc, décor
au pochoir, siège
rembourré

Designed for the Mackintosh Rose Boudoir in 1902, this extraordinary chair epitomises the ethereal and symbolic characteristics of "The Spook School".

Diesen außergewöhnlichen Stuhl entwarf Mackintosh als Bestandteil des »Rose Boudoir« 1902. Er ist beispielhaft für den ätherischen Symbolismus der soge-nannten »Spook School«.

Conçu pour le « Rose Boudoir » de Mackintosh en 1902, ce siège extraordi-naire exprime tout le caractère éthéré et symbolique de la « Spook School ».

◀ Charles Rennie
Mackintosh &
Margaret
Macdonald-
Mackintosh
The Rose Boudoir,
International
Exhibition of
Modern Decorative
Art, Turin, 1902

Charles Rennie Mackintosh

Lug chair for Hous'hill, 1904

Stained oak construction with mother-of-pearl inlay and upholstered seat and back | Rahmen aus Eiche, gebeizt, Perlmuttintarsien, Sitz und Rückenlehne gepolstert | Chêne teinté, incrustations de nacre, siège et dossier rembourrés

FRANCIS SMITH, GLASGOW

▼ **Charles Rennie Mackintosh**
Blue Bedroom, Hous'hill, Nitshill, Glasgow, c. 1905

The vernacular vocabulary of the Lug chair, designed for the Blue Bedroom at Hous'hill, contrasts sharply with the formal geometry of the Orient-inspired "Hill House" chair – a truncated version of which Mackintosh also designed for the Blue Bedroom.

Charles Rennie Mackintosh

Hill House chair,
1904

Ebonised oak
construction |
Rahmen aus Eiche,
schwarz gebeizt |
Chêne noirci

ALEX MARTIN,
GLASGOW

Die traditionelle Formensprache des Ohrensessels, entworfen für das Blaue
Schlafzimmer in Hous' Hill, steht in starkem Gegensatz zur formellen
Geometrie des fernöstlich inspirierten »Hill House«-Stuhls – eine vereinfachte
Version des Stuhls, den Mackintosh ebenfalls für das Blaue Schlafzimmer
entwarf.

L'expression très simple de ce siège à oreilles conçu pour la chambre bleue
de Hous'hill contraste de façon marquée avec la géométrie formelle de la
chaise d'inspiration orientale de « Hill House », dont une version tronquée a
également été dessinée pour la chambre bleue.

Adolf Loos

Chair for the Café Museum, c. 1898

Stained, bent beech frame with woven cane seat | Rahmen aus gebogener Buche, Sitzfläche aus Rohrgeflecht | Châssis en hêtre cintré teinté, siège canné

JACOB & JOSEF KOHN, VIENNA, FROM C. 1899

▼ Adolf Loos
Café Museum,
Vienna, c. 1900

Evolutionary rather than revolutionary, the Café Museum chair demonstrates Loos' distrust of innovation for its own sake and his belief that it was better to improve upon established successful designs.

Als eher evolutionärer denn revolutionärer Entwurf zeigt der Stuhl für das Café Museum die Abneigung, die Loos gegenüber Innovationen um der Innovation willen hegte, und zugleich seine Überzeugung, daß es besser sei, eingeführte und bewährte Entwürfe zu verbessern.

Plus proche d'une évolution que d'une révolution, la chaise du Café Museum illustre le peu d'intérêt que Loos accordait à l'innovation en soi et sa conviction qu'il valait mieux améliorer des modèles reconnus et réussis.

Otto Wagner

*Armchair for the
1900 Paris Exhibition*

Red-stained beech
frame, upholstered
seat, back and
armrests, brass
sabots| Rahmen aus
rot gebeizter Buche,
Sitzfläche, Rücken-
lehne und Armlehnen
mit Stoffpolster,
Fußmanschetten aus
Messing | Châssis en
hêtre rouge teinté,
siège et dossier
recouverts, sabots en
laiton

Although similar in form to his designs for "Die Zeit" (1902) and the
Austrian Post Office Savings Bank (1905–1906), this design by Wagner,
with its originally stitched textile and upholstered back, is more luxurious
and less utilitarian.

*Obwohl er formal den Entwürfen für »Die Zeit« (1902) und die Österreichische
Postsparkasse (1905–1906) ähnelt, wirkt dieser Stuhlentwurf wegen des ursprünglich bestickten Polsterstoffs für die Rückenlehne luxuriöser und nicht so
streng funktional.*

De forme similaire aux œuvres réalisées pour « Die Zeit » (1902) et pour la
Caisse d'Épargne de la Poste autrichienne (1905 – 1906), ce modèle de
Wagner au tissu imprimé en sérigraphie et aux accoudoirs rembourrés est
cependant plus luxueux et moins utilitaire.

Josef Hoffmann

Armchair, 1899

Mahogany frame with leather-upholstered seat and brass sabots | Rahmen aus Mahagoni, Sitzfläche mit Lederpolster, Fußmanschetten aus Messing | Châssis en acajou, siège en cuir rembourré, sabots en laiton

ANTON POSPISCHIL,
VIENNA

The form of this chair is highly zoomorphic and suggestive of muscular tension. The powerful curves of the back legs in particular evoke the impression of an animal poised to take flight.

Dieser Sessel wirkt äußerst zoomorph und vermittelt den Eindruck gespannter Muskelkraft. Die Anmutung eines sich zum Sprung sammelnden Tiers bewirken mit ihrem mächtigen Schwung vor allem die hinteren Beine.

La forme de ce fauteuil, qui suggère une tension musculaire, est légèrement zoomorphe. Les courbes puissantes des pieds arrière, en particulier, évoquent un animal prêt à bondir.

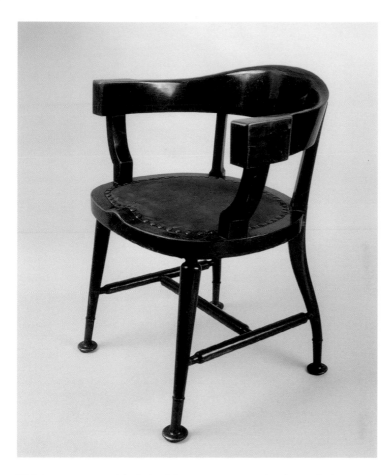

Adolf Loos

Armchair, c. 1899

Mahogany frame with upholstered leather seat and brass sabots | Rahmen aus Mahagoni, Sitzfläche mit Lederpolster, Fußmanschetten aus Messing | Châssis en acajou, siège en cuir rembourré, sabots en laiton

J. BOHN, VIENNA

With its ornament solely derived from its structure, this chair, which strongly resembles Hoffmann's designs, echoes Loos' belief that "Ornamentation is a waste of effort and so a waste of good health." (Adolf Loos, *Ornament und Verbrechen*, 1908)

Bei diesem Stuhl ist das Dekor allein aus der Konstruktion abgeleitet, darin ähnelt er dem Entwurf von Hoffmann, und ist ein Echo auf Loos' Überzeugung, der »Ornament als Verbrechen« betrachtete: »Das Ornament ist eine Verschwendung von Energie und darum vergeudete Gesundheit.« (Adolf Loos, »Ornament und Verbrechen«, 1908)

Avec un caractère ornemental uniquement issu de sa structure, ce fauteuil ressemble fortement à certains modèles d'Hoffmann et fait écho à la conviction de Loos pour qui, « L'ornement est un gaspillage d'efforts et donc une perte d'énergie. » (Adolf Loos, *Ornament und Verbrechen*, 1908)

Otto Wagner

Armchair for the telegraph office "Die Zeit", 1902

Stained, bent beech frame with woven "Eisengarn" cord seat and upholstered back section, aluminium fittings and sabots | Rahmen aus gebogener Buche, Sitzfläche aus Eisengarngewebe, Rückenlehne gepolstert, Fußmanschetten und Beschläge aus Aluminium | Châssis en hêtre cintré teinté, siège en tressage de corde « Eisengarn », dossier à section rembourrée, sabots et garnitures en aluminium

JACOB & JOSEF
KOHN, VIENNA,
FROM C. 1902

▼ Otto Wagner
Reconstruction of the "Die Zeit" facade

▲ Otto Wagner
Stools for the telegraph office "Die Zeit", 1902
JACOB & JOSEF KOHN, VIENNA

Otto Wagner

Armchair for the boardroom of the Austrian Post Office Savings Bank, 1905–1906

Bent solid beech and laminated wood frame with upholstered seat, aluminium fittings | Rahmen aus gebogener, massiver und laminierter Buche, Sitzfläche gepolstert, Fußmanschetten und Beschläge aus Aluminium | Châssis en hêtre massif et bois contre-plaqué, siège rembourré et garnitures en aluminium

JACOB & JOSEF
KOHN, VIENNA,
FROM C. 1906

▼ Otto Wagner
Stool for the main banking room of the Austrian Post Office Savings Bank, c. 1906

JACOB & JOSEF
KOHN, VIENNA

Wagner's chair and stool designs are exceptional for their modernity. The aluminium fittings are not just decorative, but also protect the furniture where it is most sensitive.

Wagners Stuhl- und Hockerentwürfe zeichnen sich durch ihre Modernität aus. Die Beschläge aus Aluminium fungieren nicht nur als Schmuck, sondern schützen die Möbel auch an ihren empfindlichsten Stellen.

Les projets de chaises et de tabourets de Wagner se distinguent par leur modernité. Les ferrures en aluminium ne font pas seulement fonction d'ornementation mais protègent également les meubles aux endroits les plus sensibles.

71

Koloman Moser

Armchair for the main hall of the Purkersdorf Sanatorium, 1902

Painted beech frame with wickerwork seat | Rahmen aus Buche, weiß lackiert, Sitzfläche aus Korbgeflecht | Châssis en hêtre teinté, siège en vannerie

PRAG-RUDNIKER KORBWAREN, VIENNA (REISSUED BY WITTMANN)

Used in the entrance hall of the Sanatorium designed by Hoffmann, this chair's cubic form and restricted use of colour typify the Secessionist style and anticipate the geometric abstraction of the Modern Movement.

In der Eingangshalle des von Hoffmann entworfenen Sanatoriums aufgestellt, verkörpert dieser Stuhl durch seine kubische Gestalt und den sparsamen Einsatz von Farbe den Stil der Secessionisten und nimmt die geometrische Abstraktion der Moderne vorweg.

Utilisé dans l'entrée du sanatorium dessiné par Hoffmann ce fauteuil illustre par sa forme cubique et son économie chromatique le style sécessionniste, et annonce l'abstraction géométrique du mouvement moderne.

▲ **Josef Hoffmann**
Main hall of the
Purkersdorf
Sanatorium, c. 1906

Josef Hoffmann

Armchair for the Wittgenstein apartment, 1904

Black stained oak frame rubbed with chalk, leather-upholstered seat | Rahmen aus Eiche, schwarz gebeizt, Poren weiß eingerieben, mit Leder bezogene Sitzfläche | Châssis en chêne teinté noir cérusé, siège en cuir rembourré

WIENER WERKSTÄTTE, VIENNA

▼ **School of Josef Hoffmann**
Adjustable chair, c. 1905

Hoffmann's stained oak chair embodies the Wiener Werkstätte's craft ideals and predilection for geometric patterns. A contemporary photograph shows the chair with a seat cushion.

Hoffmanns Sessel aus gebeiztem Eichenholz verkörpert das handwerkliche Ideal der Wiener Werkstätte und auch deren Vorliebe für geometrische Muster. Eine zeitgenössische Photographie zeigt den Stuhl mit einem Sitzkissen.

Les sièges en chêne teinté de Hoffmann incarnent l'idéal artisanal des Wiener Werkstätte et leur prédilection pour les motifs géométriques. Une photographie contemporaine montre ce siège équipé d'un coussin réglable.

Josef Hoffmann

Chair, Model No. 330, 1902

Bent solid beech and bent laminated wood frame with internal upholstery and metal fittings | Rahmen aus gebogener, massiver Buche und laminiertem Holz, eingearbeitete Polsterung, Metallbeschläge | Châssis en hêtre massif cintré et bois contre-plaqué cintré, rembourrage et garnitures en métal

JACOB & JOSEF
KOHN, VIENNA,
c. 1902–1916

▼ Josef Hoffmann
Dining room,
c. 1904

The No. 330 and its armed version the No. 330/F appeared on the cover of J. & J. Kohn's 1909 catalogue. As part of the firm's upholstered line, it is likely they were mainly intended for domestic use.

Die Stühle Modell Nr. 330 und Nr. 330/F (mit Armlehnen) erschienen auf dem Umschlag des Firmenkatalogs von J. & J. Kohn aus dem Jahr 1909. Sie gehörten zum Polstermöbelprogramm des Unternehmens und waren vor allem für den Wohnbereich konzipiert.

Le n° 330 et sa version fauteuil n° 330/F parurent sur la couverture du catalogue J. & J. Kohn de 1909. Appartenant au mobilier rembourré de la firme, ils étaient principalement destinés à un usage domestique.

Josef Hoffmann

*Armchair, Model
No. 728/F,
1905–1906*

Stained, bent solid
beech frame with
moulded laminated
wood seat and turned
beech elements |
Rahmen aus geboge-
ner Buche, Sitzfläche
aus geformtem
Schichtholz, gedrech-
selte Verbindungs-
elemente | Châssis en
hêtre massif cintré
teinté, siège en bois
contre-plaqué cintré
et éléments en hêtre
tourné

JACOB & JOSEF
KOHN, VIENNA

▼ Jacob & Josef
Kohn, sales cata-
logue, 1916, Suite
Model No. 728

► **Josef Hoffmann**
Bar room of the
Cabaret Fledermaus,
Vienna, 1907

Josef Hoffmann

Variation of the
Cabaret Fledermaus
chair, 1905–1906

Stained, bent solid
beech frame with
moulded laminated
wood seat and turned
beech elements |
Rahmen aus geboge-
ner Buche, schwarz-
weiß lackiert, Sitz-
fläche und Rücken-
lehne gepolstert |
Châssis en hêtre
massif cintré, siège en
bois contre-plaqué
moulé et éléments en
hêtre tourné

GEBRÜDER THONET,
VIENNA

"It [the Cabaret Fledermaus] is wonderful – the proportions, the light atmos-
phere, cheerful flowing lines, elegant light fixtures, comfortable chairs of
new shape and, finally, the whole tasteful ensemble. Genuine Hoffmann."
Ludwig Hevesi, 1907 (L. Hevesi, "Kabarett Fledermaus" in: *Altkunst-
Neukunst, Vienna, 1894–1908*, p. 243)
»Es [das Kabarett Fledermaus] ist wunderbar – die Proportionen, die helle Atmo-
sphäre, die fröhlich fließenden Linien, die eleganten Leuchten, die bequemen
Stühle mit ihren neuen Formen und, schließlich, das ganze geschmackvolle
Ensemble. Echter Hoffmann.« Ludwig Hevesi, 1907
« Il [le modèle Cabaret Fledermaus] est superbe : les proportions, le senti-
ment de légèreté, les lignes allègrement fluides, les détails légers et élé-
gants, l'ensemble plein de goût. Du pur Hoffmann. » Ludwig Hevesi, 1907

Koloman Moser

Armchair, Model No. 719/F, 1901

Bent solid beech frame with upholstered seat and back and brass sabots | Rahmen aus gebogener Buche, Sitzfläche und Rückenlehne gepolstert, Fußmanschetten aus Messing | Châssis en hêtre massif cintré, siège rembourré et sabots en laiton

JACOB & JOSEF KOHN, VIENNA

▼ **Gustav Siegel**
Interior with applied bent-wood wall decoration and chair of bent solid wood, Jacob & Josef Kohn display at the 1900 Paris Exhibition

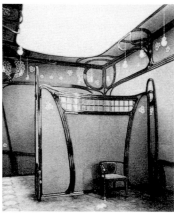

Gustav Siegel headed J. & J. Kohn's design studio while both Moser and Hoffmann also designed for the firm. This chair, which is very similar to Siegel's earlier No. 715/F, is generally attributed to Moser.

Gustav Siegel arbeitete zu der Zeit, als Moser und Hoffmann für das Unternehmen Entwürfe lieferten, als Leiter der Entwurfsabteilung von J. & J. Kohn. Dieser Stuhl, der dem früheren Siegel-Entwurf Nr. 715/F ähnelt, wird allgemein Moser zugeschrieben.

Gustav Siegel dirigeait l'atelier de dessin de J. & J. Kohn au moment où Moser et Hoffmann travaillaient pour la firme. Ce fauteuil, très similaire au n° 715/F antérieur de Siegel, est généralement attribué à Moser.

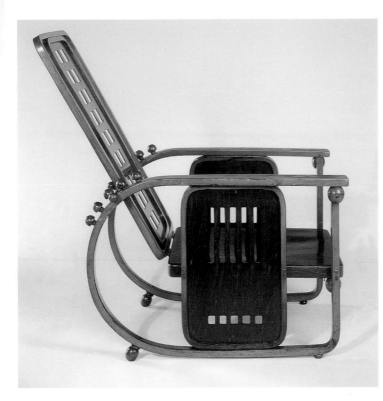

Josef Hoffmann

Sitzmaschine, Model
No. 670, c. 1908

Stained, laminated
wood, bent solid
beech and turned
wood frame with
brass fittings |
Rahmen aus Buche
und Schichtholz,
teilweise gedrechselt,
gebeizt, Messing-
beschläge | Châssis en
bois contre-plaqué
teinté, hêtre massif
cintré, éléments
tournés et garnitures
en laiton

JACOB & JOSEF
KOHN, VIENNA

▼ Josef Hoffmann
Hall interior of a
small country house,
Jacob & Josef Kohn
display at the
"Wiener Kunst-
schau", Vienna,
1908

Although originally sold with seat and back cushions, the "Sitzmaschine" can be regarded as having predicted later Rietveld designs because of its strict geometric vocabulary of form.

Die »Sitzmaschine« wurde ursprünglich mit Sitz- und Rückenkissen vertrieben, aber selbst gepolstert nimmt sie mit ihrer streng geometrischen Formensprache spätere Schöpfungen Rietvelds vorweg.

Vendue à l'origine avec des coussins pour le siège et le dossier, cette « Sitzmaschine » aux formes strictement géométriques peut être considérée comme l'anticipation de certaines réalisations de Rietveld.

Chair, 1903–1904

Oak frame inlaid with maple and cherry, leather upholstered seat | Rahmen aus Eiche, Intarsien aus Ahorn und Kirschholz, Sitzfläche mit Lederpolsterung| Châssis en chêne avec incrustations d'érable et de cerisier, siège en cuir rembourré

GUSTAV STICKLEY'S,
CRAFTSMAN
WORKSHOPS,
EASTWOOD AND NEW
YORK, NEW YORK

Harvey Ellis

Armchair, 1903–1904

Stained oak frame
inlaid with maple and
cherry, caned seat |
Rahmen aus Eiche,
gebeizt, Intarsien aus
Ahorn- und Kirsch-
holz, Sitzfläche aus
Rohrgeflecht | Châssis
en chêne teinté,
incrustations d'érable
et de cerisier, siège
canné

GUSTAV STICKLEY'S
CRAFTSMAN
WORKSHOPS,
EASTWOOD & NEW
YORK, NEW YORK,
1903–1904
(REISSUED BY
L. & J. G. STICKLEY)

▼ Detail of Harvey
Ellis' design

Influenced by Voysey and Baillie Scott, Ellis' inlaid chairs
were designed for Gustav Stickley's Craftsman Workshops. Designs such as this, however, were discontinued after 1904 as they were too costly to produce.
*Von Voysey und Baillie Scott beeinflußt, hat Ellis für
Gustav Stickleys Craftsman Workshops Stühle mit Intarsien
entworfen. Die Produktion derartiger Entwürfe wurde nach
1904 jedoch eingestellt, da sie zu kostspielig war.*
Influencés par Voysey et Baillie Scott, les sièges à incrustations d'Ellis furent dessinés pour les ateliers de
Gustav Stickley. Ce genre de modèle fut cependant
abandonné après 1904 car sa leur production était trop
coûteuse.

Frank Lloyd Wright

Armchair, c. 1906

Stained oak construction with leather-upholstered seat | Rahmen aus Eiche, gebeizt, Sitzfläche mit Lederpolsterung | Chêne teinté, siège rembourré

▼ **Frank Lloyd Wright**
Chair for the Larkin Company Administration Building, 1904

Wright designed several variants of this type of high-backed chair. Using either slab or spindle backs, this group has a clear affinity with Stickley's Mission furniture. Wright's chairs, however, have a stronger vertical and geometric emphasis. Chairs such as this influenced later Rietveld designs.

Wright hat mehrere Varianten dieses Sessels mit hoher Rückenlehne entworfen. Für die Gestaltung der Rückenlehne verwendete er entweder eine durchgehende Platte oder parallel laufende Stäbe, womit diese Art der Möbel eindeutig auf Stickleys »Missions«-Möbel Bezug nimmt. Allerdings werden bei Wrights Sitzmöbeln die Senkrechte

Frank Lloyd Wright

Chair for the Isabel Roberts House & chair for the Francis W. Little House, 1908 & 1902

Stained wood constructions (poplar and oak respectively) with leather upholstered seats | Rahmen aus Pappel bzw. Eiche, gebeizt, Sitzfläche mit Lederpolsterung | Bois teinté (respectivement peuplier et chêne), sièges rembourrés

▼ Frank Lloyd Wright
Dining room at the Frederick C. Robie House, Chicago, Illinois, 1906–1909

und überhaupt das Geometrische deutlicher betont. Von Stühlen wie diesen ist später Rietveld beeinflußt worden.

Wright dessina plusieurs variantes de ces sièges à dossier haut. Avec ses dossiers pleins ou ajourés, cette série présente une affinité certaine avec le mobilier de style Mission de Stickley. Les sièges de Wright, cependant, mettent davantage l'accent sur la verticalité et la géométrie. Ils allaient plus tard influencer Rietveld.

83

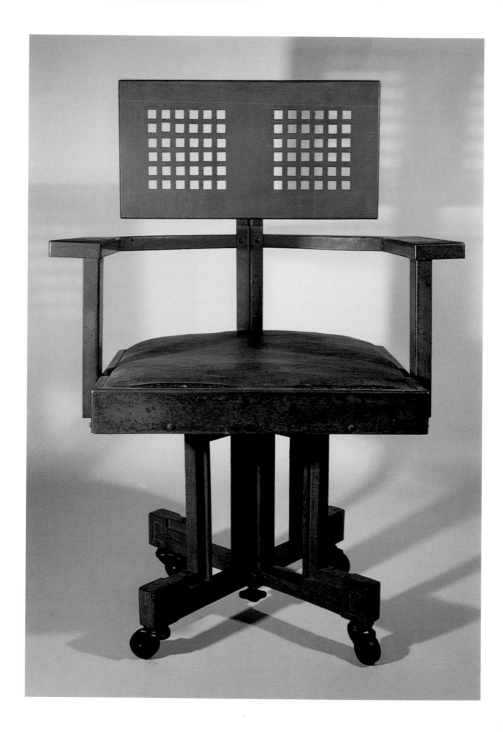

Frank Lloyd Wright

Swivel armchair for the offices of the Larkin Company Administration Building, 1904

Painted steel frame with leather-upholstered seat on swivelling steel base terminating on castors | Rahmen aus Stahl, lackiert, drehbar, Sitzfläche gepolstert, auf Rollen | Châssis en acier peint, siège en cuir rembourré sur piètement pivotant en acier, roulettes

VON DORN IRON WORKS COMPANY, CLEVELAND, OHIO

▼ Frank Lloyd Wright
Director's office, Larkin Company Administration Building, Buffalo, New York, c. 1905

Wright's integrated design for the Larkin Company Building revolutionised the concept of the workplace environment. Echoing the geometry of the building, the office chair was both visually and functionally unified with its surroundings.

Wright hat diesen Bürostuhl auf seinen Gesamtentwurf des Bürogebäudes für die Larkin Company abgestimmt und damit die Vorstellungen vom Arbeitsplatz revolutioniert. In Übereinstimmung mit der Geometrie des Gebäudes war der Bürostuhl sowohl optisch als auch funktionell in seine Umgebung eingebunden.

Le design intégré de Wright pour l'immeuble de la Larkin Compagny révolutionna la conception de l'environnement du lieu de travail. Faisant écho à la géométrie de l'immeuble, ce fauteuil de bureau était à la fois visuellement et fonctionnellement en harmonie avec son environnement.

Frank Lloyd Wright

Peacock chair for the Imperial Hotel, Tokyo, c. 1921–1922

Oak frame with seat and back upholstered in oil cloth | Rahmen aus Eiche, Sitzfläche und Rückenlehne gepolstert | Châssis en chêne, siège et dossier en toile cirée rembourrée

▶ **Frank Lloyd Wright**
Chair for Midway Gardens, Chicago, Illinois, 1914

(REISSUED BY CASSINA)

▶▶ **Frank Lloyd Wright**
Reclining armchair for the Francis W. Little House, Peoria, Illinois, 1903

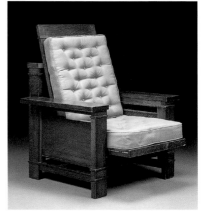

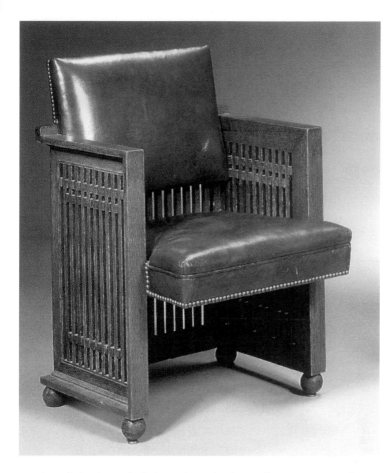

William Gray Purcell, George Feick & George Grant Elmslie

Armchair for the Merchants Bank of Winona, Minnesota, 1912–1913

Oak frame with leather-upholstered seat and back | Rahmen aus Eiche, Sitzfläche und Rückenlehne mit Lederpolsterung | Châssis en chêne, dos et siège rembourrés

W. G. PURCELL,
G. FEICK & G. GRANT
ELMSLIE WORKSHOP,
MINNEAPOLIS

Wright and Elmslie worked alongside each other in the architectural offices of Lyman Silsbee and Louis Sullivan. While both designed integrated Prairie School architectural schemes, Wright's designs were the more inventive.

Sowohl Wright als auch Elmslie arbeiteten in den Architekturbüros von Lyman Silsbee und Louis Sullivan. Beide schufen Gesamtkunstwerke im Stil der » Prairie School«, wobei Wrights Entwürfe die innovativeren waren.

Wright et Elmslie travaillèrent côte à côte dans l'agence d'architecture de Lyman Silsbee et Louis Sullivan. Tous deux élaborèrent des projets intégrés dans le style « Prairie School », les dessins de Wright étant plus inventifs.

Paul Iribe

Armchair, 1913

Carved mahogany frame with silk-covered, upholstered seat, back and arms | Rahmen aus Mahagoni, geschnitzt, Sitzfläche, Arm- und Rückenlehne gepolstert und mit Seidenbezug | Châssis en acajou sculpté, siège et côtés rembourrés et recouverts de soie

PAUL IRIBE, PARIS

A caricaturist, fashion illustrator and decorator, Iribe established his own studio, after collaborating with Pierre Legrain, to produce luxurious proto-Art Deco designs for wealthy and influential clients. Iribe later worked as a set designer in Hollywood for, among others, the director Cecil B. De Mille.
Der Karikaturist, Modezeichner und Dekorateur Iribe, gründete, nachdem er zunächst mit Pierre Legrain zusammengearbeitet hatte, sein eigenes Atelier, wo er für reiche und einflußreiche Kunden luxuriöse Entwürfe im Stil eines Proto-Art Deco schuf. Später arbeitete Iribe als Bühnenbildner in Hollywood, u. a. für den berühmten Produzenten Cecil B. De Mille.
Caricaturiste, illustrateur de mode et décorateur, Iribe créa son propre studio, après avoir collaboré avec Pierre Legrain à la réalisation de luxueux modèles annonçant l'Art déco, destinés à une clientèle aisée et influente. Il travailla par la suite comme décorateur à Hollywood, entre autres pour Cecil B. de Mille.

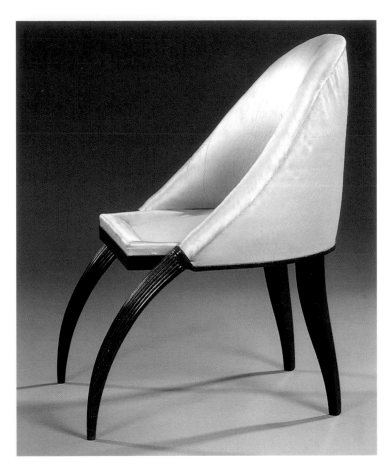

Jacques-Émile Ruhlmann

Défenses chair,
c. 1920

Carved mahogany frame with silk-covered, upholstered seat and back sections| Rahmen aus Mahagoni, geschnitzt, Sitzfläche und Rückenlehne gepolstert und mit Seidenbezug | Châssis en acajou sculpté, siège et côtés rembourrés et recouverts de soie

ÉTABLISSEMENTS RUHLMANN ET LAURENT, PARIS

▼ **Jacques-Émile Ruhlmann**
Elephant armchair,
c. 1920

ÉTABLISSEMENTS RUHLMANN ET LAURENT, PARIS

This elegant and luxurious chair was inspired by the Neo-classical revivalism of the Louis Philippe period. Exquisitely crafted, it represents the high point of Ruhlmann's career and presages the Art Deco style. *Dieser elegante und luxuriöse Stuhl wurde durch den Neoklassizismus der Louis Philippe-Zeit inspiriert. Der das Art Deco vorwegnehmende Entwurf ist wundervoll ver-arbeitet und stellt einen Höhepunkt im Werk von Ruhlmann dar.* Ce fauteuil élégant et luxueux est inspiré du style néo-classique Louis-Philippe. Remarquablement exécuté, il marque le sommet de la carrière de Ruhlmann et annonce le style Art déco.

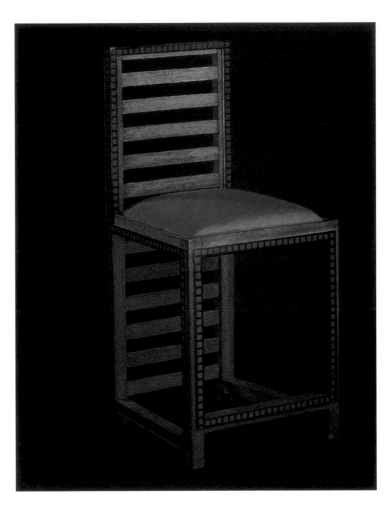

Charles Rennie Mackintosh

Chair for the guest bedroom at 78 Derngate, Northampton, 1919

Oak frame with stencilled motif and blue "Erinoid" (a plastic made from casein) inlay, silk-upholstered seat | Rahmen aus Eiche, Schablonenmalerei, Intarsien aus blauem »Erinoid« (einem Kunststoff auf Kasein-basis), Sitzfläche gepolstert und mit Seidenbezug | Châssis en chêne avec motif au pochoir et incrus-tations d'« Erinoid » (plastique à base de caséine), siège rembourré en soie

◄◄ **Charles Rennie Mackintosh**
Reconstruction of the guest bedroom, 78 Derngate, Northampton, Hunterian Art Gallery, Glasgow

This chair design by Mackintosh is remarkable for its unrelenting geometry, which predicts the Art Deco style, and for its early use of plastic inlay.

Auffallend an diesem Stuhlentwurf Mackintoshs ist die alles bestimmende Geometrie, die den Art Deco-Stil bereits vorwegnimmt. Bemerkenswert ist auch der frühe Gebrauch von Kunststoffintarsien.

Ce modèle de Mackintosh est remarquable par sa géométrie sans conces-sion qui annonce le style Art déco, et par l'utilisation du plastique en incrus-tation.

Walter Gropius

Bench for the entrance hall of the Faguswerk, 1911

Ebonised wood frame with fabric-upholstered seat and back | Rahmen aus Holz, schwarz gebeizt, Sitzfläche und Rückenlehne gepolstert mit Stoffbezug | Châssis en bois noirci, siège et dossier en tissu rembourré

(REISSUED BY TECTA)

From 1908 to 1910, Gropius worked in Peter Behrens' architectural office. In 1910 he established his own practice and became a member of the Deutscher Werkbund. These chairs, dating from the same year, were originally designed for his Fagus factory and encapsulate the Werkbund's debate about whether standardization and creative expression could be reconciled: the construction of this seat furniture is suitable for standardized production, yet its aesthetic is decidedly individualistic.

Von 1908 bis 1910 arbeitete Gropius im Architekturbüro von Peter Behrens. 1910 gründete er sein eigenes Büro und wurde Mitglied im Deutschen Werkbund. Aus diesem Jahr stammen auch diese ursprünglich für das Faguswerk angefertigten Stuhlentwürfe. Sie spiegeln die im Werkbund geführte Debatte wider, ob sich Standardisierung und Individualität versöhnen ließen: Die Konstruktion dieser Sitzmöbel erlaubt die Serienproduktion, zeigt zugleich aber eine entschieden persönliche Handschrift.

Armchair for the
entrance hall of the
Faguswerk, 1911

Ebonised wood frame
with fabric-
upholstered seat and
back | Rahmen aus
Holz, schwarz
gebeizt, Sitzfläche
und Rückenlehne
gepolstert mit
Stoffbezug | Châssis
en bois noirci, siège et
dossier en tissu
rembourré

(REISSUED BY TECTA)

▼ Walter Gropius
Faguswerk,
Alfeld/Leine, c. 1912

De 1908 à 1910, Gropius travailla dans le bureau d'architecture de Peter Behrens. En 1910, il ouvre sa propre agence et devient membre du Deutsche Werkbund. Ces modèles, qui datent de la même année, furent dessinés à l'origine pour l'usine Fagus et résument le débat du Werkbund sur la possibilité d'une réconciliation entre la standardisation et la créativité : la construction de ce fauteuil est étudiée pour une production en série, même si son esthétique est résolument originale.

▲ Gerrit Rietveld
White version of the
Red/Blue chair, 1921

GERRIT RIETVELD,
UTRECHT

▼ Gerrit Rietveld
(seated) with G. A.
van der Groenekan
(behind chair),
Utrecht, c. 1918

Originally designed in 1917–1918 with a natural wood finish, Rietveld painted this revolutionary chair in 1921 as a result of his association with the De Stijl movement. With its simplified construction, the design speculated on going into standardised production.

Ursprünglich zwischen 1917 und 1918 ohne Lackierung entworfen, bemalte Rietveld 1921 diesen revolutionären Stuhl, nachdem er in engen Kontakt zu der De Stijl-Bewegung gekommen war. Die einfache Bauweise des Stuhls zielte auf eine spätere Serienproduktion.

Conçu à l'origine avec une finition en bois naturel (1917–1918), ce siège révolutionnaire fut peint par Rietveld en 1921 au moment où il se rapprocha du groupe De Stijl. De conception simplifiée à l'extrême, ce modèle était prévu pour une production en série.

Red/Blue chair, 1918/1923

Painted solid beechwood and plywood construction | Rahmen aus Buche, Sitzfläche und Rückenlehne aus Schichtholz, lackiert | Hêtre massif et contre-plaqué peints

GERRIT RIETVELD, UTRECHT AND LATER BY GERARD VAN DE GROENEKAN UTRECHT, FROM 1918/1923 (REISSUED BY CASSINA)

Gerrit Rietveld

Kinderstoel,
c. 1915–1919

Deal construction with leather sling seat and back | Rahmen aus Kiefer, Sitzfläche und Rückenlehne aus Lederbespannung | Pin, dossier et siège en cuir tendu

GERRIT RIETVELD,
UTRECHT

▶ **Gerrit Rietveld**
Design for the Rietveld-Schröder House, Utrecht, 1924

▶▶ The son of the original owner (a Classics teacher) sitting in the Kinderstoel, 1922

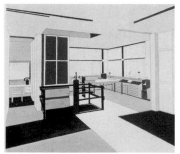

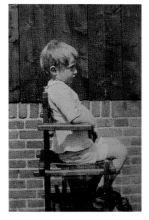

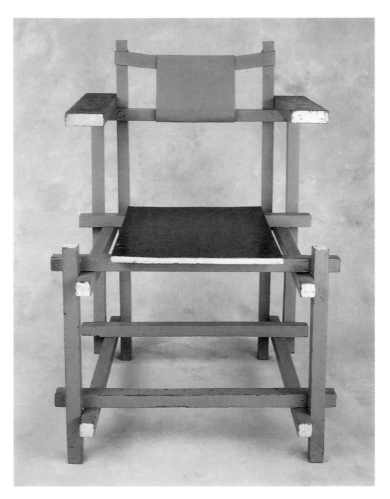

Gerrit Rietveld

Hogestoel, 1919

Painted oak
construction with
leather sling back |
Rahmen aus Eiche,
lackiert, Rückenlehne
aus Lederbespannung |
Chêne peint et cuir

GERRIT RIETVELD,
UTRECHT

Rietveld purged ornament to get aesthetic and functional purity and
stripped his chairs' structure to the barest and most utilitarian form. The
play of verticals and horizontals lends them remarkable spatial qualities.
*Rietveld vermied jedes Ornament, um ästhetischen und funktionalen Purismus
zu erzielen. Die konstruktiven Elemente sind auf schlichte und gebrauchsorien-
tierte Formen reduziert, das Spiel mit senkrechten und waagerechten Kompo-
nenten gibt den Stühlen dennoch ausdrucksvoll räumliche Qualitäten.*
Rietveld se débarrasse de l'ornement pour atteindre à la pureté esthétique et
fonctionnelle. Les éléments structurels de ces modèles sont réduits à leur
forme et à leur fonction les plus simples tandis que le jeu des verticales et
des horizontales assure à ce siège de remarquables qualités spatiales.

Gerrit Rietveld

Berlin chair, 1923

Painted solid deal construction | Massivholzbretter, lackiert | Bois massif et contre-plaqué peints

G. A. VAN DE
GROENEKAN,
UTRECHT

► **Gerrit Rietveld**
Piano stool, 1923,
commissioned
by the architect
J. J. Oud

GERRIT RIETVELD,
UTRECHT

►► **Gerrit Rietveld**
Militar chair, 1923

G. A. VAN DE
GROENEKAN,
UTRECHT

Marcel Breuer

Slatted chair,
1922–1924

Stained maple frame
with horsehair cloth
seat and back
sections | Rahmen
aus Ahorn, gebeizt,
Sitzfläche und
Rückenlehne aus
Roßhaargewebe |
Châssis en érable
teinté, siège et dossier
en crin de cheval

FURNITURE WORK-
SHOP, STAATLICHES
BAUHAUS, WEIMAR

▼ Ebert Wils
Cherry framed chair
with canvas sling
seat and back, 1928

STAATLICHES
BAUHAUS, DESSAU

Breuer's slatted chair demonstrates the influence of
Rietveld, who had exhibited furniture at the Bauhaus in
1921. His "Berlin" chair was designed for the "Juryfreie
Kunstschau", Berlin 1923.
Breuers Lattenstuhl zeigt Rietvelds Einfluß, dessen Möbel
1921 im Bauhaus gezeigt worden waren. Den »Berlin«-
Stuhl hatte Rietveld 1923 für die Juryfreie Kunstschau
Berlin entworfen.
Ce fauteuil en lattes de bois de Breuer montre l'in-
fluence de Rietveld qui avait exposé ses meubles au
Bauhaus en 1921. Son siège « Berlin » fut conçu pour le
« Juryfreie Kunstschau » de Berlin en 1923.

Walter Gropius

**Armchair for the
Bauhaus Weimar
director's office, 1923**

*Upholstered and
ebonised wood frame |
Rahmen aus Holz,
schwarz gebeizt,
gepolstert | Châssis en
bois noirci et
rembourré*

FURNITURE WORK-
SHOP, STAATLICHES
BAUHAUS, WEIMAR
(REISSUED BY TECTA)

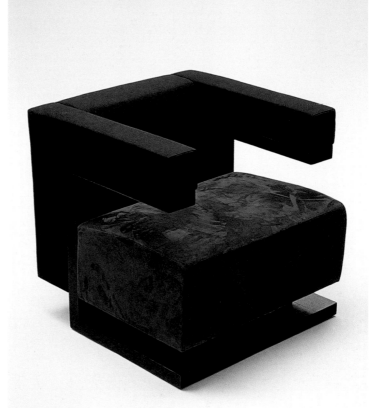

▼ Walter Gropius
Bauhaus director's
office, Weimar, 1923

Gropius' chair with its cantilevered construction was designed for the director's room at the Bauhaus in
Weimar. Its unusual form is the result of Gropius' research into state-of-the-art construction methods.
*Diesen Sessel mit seiner freitragenden Bauweise hat
Gropius für die Direktionsräume des Weimarer Bauhauses
entworfen. Die außergewöhnliche Formgebung ist das
Ergebnis von Gropius' Auseinandersetzung mit den avantgardistischen Konstruktionsmethoden seiner Zeit.*
Le fauteuil de Gropius avec sa structure en porte à faux
fut conçu pour le bureau du directeur du Bauhaus de
Weimar. Sa forme provient des recherches de Gropius
sur les méthodes avant-gardistes de fabrication.

Marcel Breuer

*Armchair for the
Sommerfeld House,
1921*

*Solid cherry frame
with red and black
leather-covered
upholstery | Rahmen
aus Kirschholz, rot-
schwarzes Leder-
polster | Châssis en
cerisier massif,
rembourrage en cuir
rouge et noir*

FURNITURE WORK-
SHOP, STAATLICHES
BAUHAUS, WEIMAR

▼ Marcel Breuer
Chair, 1921 (wool
seat and back de-
signed by Gunta
Stölzl)

FURNITURE WORK-
SHOP, STAATLICHES
BAUHAUS, WEIMAR

This interpretation of a club chair utilises traditional materials, while its "modern" cubic form, which recalls
Itten's appeal for elemental geometry, gives its design a
rather solid appearance.

*Diese Version eines Klubsessels verwendet traditionelle
Materialien; seine »moderne« kubische Form, die Ittens
Forderung nach einer elementaren Geometrie zu folgen
scheint, läßt diesen Entwurf äußerst wuchtig erscheinen.*

Cette conception de fauteuil club fait appel à des matériaux traditionnels tandis que sa forme cubique « moderne », qui rappelle le goût de Itten pour les formes
géométriques élémentaires, lui donne un aspect assez
massif.

Erich Dieckmann

**Chair and armchair,
c. 1926**

*Stained cherry frames
with woven cane
seats | Rahmen aus
Kirschholz, Sitzfläche
aus Rohrgeflecht |
Châssis en cerisier
teinté, sièges cannés*

FURNITURE WORK-
SHOP, STAATLICHE
BAUHOCHSCHULE,
WEIMAR

▲ **Erich Dieckmann**
Chair, c. 1926

FURNITURE WORKSHOP, STAATLICHE
BAUHOCHSCHULE, WEIMAR

▲ **Erich Dieckmann**
Chair profiles, various prototypes, 1930–1931

Erich Dieckmann

Armchair, c. 1926

Stained beech frame
with upholstered seat
and back | Rahmen
aus Buche, gebeizt,
Sitzfläche und
Rückenlehne
gepolstert | Châssis en
hêtre teinté, siège et
dossier rembourrés

FURNITURE WORK-
SHOP, STAATLICHE
BAUHOCHSCHULE,
WEIMAR

While training at the Bauhaus in Weimar, Dieckmann designed his cherry
and cane chair synthesising craft and functionalism. Later, he headed the
furniture and interior design department at the Staatliche Bauhochschule.
*Während seiner Ausbildung am Weimarer Bauhaus entwarf Dieckmann seinen
Armlehnstuhl aus Kirschholz und Rohrgeflecht, der Handwerk und Funktionalismus in Einklang bringt. Er wurde
später zum Leiter des Fachbereichs
Möbel und Innenarchitektur an der
Staatlichen Bauhochschule berufen.*
C'est pendant ses études au
Bauhaus de Weimar que Dieckmann conçoit ses sièges en cerisier
et cannage qui associent artisanat
et fonctionnalisme. Plus tard, il
dirigera le département de mobilier
et d'architecture intérieure de la
Staatliche Bauhochschule.

▼ **Erich Dieckmann**
Armchair, 1930–1931

FURNITURE WORK-
SHOP, KUNST-
GEWERBESCHULE
BURG GIEBICHEN-
STEIN, HALLE

Marcel Breuer

**Model No. B6,
1926–1927**

*Chromed tubular
steel frame with
painted wood seat |
Rahmen aus
gebogenem Stahlrohr,
verchromt, Sitzfläche
und Rückenlehne aus
Holz, lackiert |
Châssis en tube
d'acier chromé, siège
en bois peint*

STANDARD-MÖBEL,
BERLIN

▶ **Marcel Breuer**
Model No. B5,
1926–1927

STANDARD-MÖBEL,
BERLIN
(REISSUED BY TECTA)

▶▶ Dining room,
Moholy-Nagy House,
Bauhaus, Dessau,
1925–1926

Marcel Breuer

*Wassily, Model
No. B3, 1925–1927*

Bent, nickelled
tubular steel frame
(later chrome-plated)
with canvas, fabric or
leather seat and back
sections | Rahmen
aus gebogenem
Stahlrohr, vernickelt
(später verchromt),
Sitzfläche, Rücken-
und Armlehnen mit
Leinen-, Textil- oder
Lederbespannung |
Châssis en tube
d'acier cintré et
nickelé (ultérieure-
ment chromé), siège
et dossier en toile,
tissu ou cuir

STANDARD-MÖBEL,
BERLIN & GEBRÜDER
THONET, FRANKEN-
BERG, FROM C. 1928
(REISSUED BY KNOLL
INTERNATIONAL,
FROM 1968 TO
PRESENT)

Designed for Wassily Kandinsky's quarters at the Dessau Bauhaus, the No. B3 utterly transformed the language of chair design. It was particularly revolutionary in its use of tubular steel and its method of manufacture.

Nr. B3, ursprünglich ein Entwurf für die Wohnung von Wassily Kandinsky am Bauhaus in Dessau, stellt eine völlige Erneuerung des traditionellen Sitzmöbels dar. Revolutionär waren insbesondere die Verwendung von Stahlrohr und das Herstellungsverfahren.

Créé pour l'appartement de Kandinsky au Bauhaus de Dessau, le n° B3 modifia profondément la conception du siège moderne. Il était particulièrement révolutionnaire par son utilisation du tube d'acier et son processus de fabrication.

▲ Marcel Breuer
Model No. B4, 1926–1927

STANDARD-MÖBEL, BERLIN
(REISSUED BY TECTA FROM 1981 AS D4)

Mart Stam

Model No. S33, 1926

Lacquered, cast tubular steel frame, internally reinforced with metal rods, fabric seat and back | Rahmen aus Guß-stahlrohr, lackiert, im Innern durch Metall-stäbe verstärkt, Sitzfläche und Rückenlehne mit Stoffbespannung | Châssis en tube d'acier laqué renforcé par des tiges de métal internes, siège et dossier en tissu

L. & C. ARNOLD, SCHORNDORF (REISSUED BY GEBRÜDER THONET, FRANKENBERG)

▼ **Mart Stam**
Living room, Weißenhof-Siedlung, Stuttgart, 1927

In 1926 Stam constructed a prototype of his revolutionary cantilever chair from welded gas pipes. He showed drawings of the prototype to Mies van der Rohe who, inspired by the concept, designed his own versions. *1926 konstruierte Stam den ersten Prototyp eines Frei-schwingers aus verschweißten Gasrohren. Er zeigte Mies van der Rohe Zeichnungen des Prototyps, der nun seiner-seits, von Stams Konzept inspiriert, eigene Versionen schuf.* En 1926, Stam construisit un prototype de sa chaise en porte à faux révolutionnaire à partir de tuyaux de gaz soudés. Il montra des dessins de ce prototype à Mies van der Rohe qui s'inspira de ce concept pour créer ses propres versions.

Heinz & Bodo Rasch

Sitzgeiststuhl, 1927

Lacquered laminated
and solid wood
construction | Massiv-
und Schichtholz,
lackiert | Bois massif
et contre-plaqué
laqués

HEINZ & BODO
RASCH, BERLIN

▼ Sitzgeiststuhl de-
signed by Mies van
der Rohe for the
Weißenhof project

At the 1926 meeting of architects taking part in the
Weissenhof Exhibition, Heinz Rasch undoubtedly also
saw the drawings of Stam's cantilever chair. He, too,
developed his own interpretation of it.

*Auch Heinz Rasch wird während des Stuttgarter Archi-
tektentreffens aus Anlaß der Weißenhof-Ausstellung von
1926 die Zeichnungen von Stams Freischwinger gesehen
und daraufhin die eigene Interpretation dieses Typs entwickelt haben.*

Lors de la rencontre d'architectes qui se tint à l'occasion
de l'Exposition de Weissenhof de 1926, Heinz Rasch a
certainement dû voir les dessins de la chaise en porte à
faux de Stam, dont il tira sa propre version.

Marcel Breuer

Model No. B33,
1927–1928

Chrome-plated
tubular steel frame
with "Eisengarn" or
leather seat and
back | Rahmen aus
gebogenem Stahlrohr,
verchromt, Sitzfläche
und Rückenlehne mit
Bespannung aus
Eisengarngewebe oder
Leder | Châssis en
tube d'acier chromé,
siège et dossier en cuir
tendu ou en toile
« Eisengarn »

GEBRÜDER THONET,
FRANKENBERG,
FROM C. 1929 TO
PRESENT

▼ **Marcel Breuer**
Cantilever stool,
1927

►▼ **Walter Gropius**
Reading room of an
apartment house,
"Bauausstellung",
Berlin, 1931

Unlike Stam's S33, on which their designs were based, Breuer's B33 and slightly later B64 utilise non-reinforced tubular steel. This gives their constructions greater resilience and, thereby, more comfort. These designs, like other cantilevered chairs, eliminate the visual division between the base and seat sections through the use of a continuous supporting frame.

Für seinen Stuhl B33 und den wenig später entwickelten B64 nutzt Breuer, anders als Stam für den zuvor entworfenen S33, unverstärktes Stahlrohr. Das verleiht dem B33 größere Elastizität und damit mehr Sitzkomfort. Diese Entwürfe heben, wie andere Freischwinger-Typen auch, die optische Trennung zwischen Unterbau und Sitz auf, indem sie einen durchgängigen tragenden Rahmen verwenden.

À la différence du S33 de Stam, le B33 de Breuer et le B64 légèrement ultérieur font appel à des tubes non renforcés, ce qui donne au siège plus d'élasticité et donc plus de confort. Ces modèles, comme d'autres en porte à faux, suppriment la différenciation visuelle entre le piètement et le siège lui-même grâce à une structure de soutien continue.

Marcel Breuer

Model No. B32 and Model No. B64, 1928

Chrome-plated tubular steel frames with stained bentwood and woven cane seats and backs | Rahmen aus gebogenem Stahlrohr, Sitzfläche und Rückenlehne aus Rohrgeflecht in geformtem Holzrahmen, schwarz gebeizt | Châssis en tube d'acier chromé, sièges et dossiers en bois cintré teinté, cannage

GEBRÜDER THONET, FRANKENBERG, FROM C. 1929 TO PRESENT (REISSUED BY KNOLL INTERNATIONAL, FROM 1968 TO PRESENT)

Marcel Breuer

Model No. B25,
1928–1929

Chromed bent
tubular steel frame
with woven cane seat
and back, painted
solid wood armrests
and chromed metal
springs | Rahmen aus
gebogenem Stahlrohr,
verchromt, Sitzfläche
und Rückenlehne aus
Weidengeflecht,
Armlehnen aus Holz,
lackiert, Metallfedern,
verchromt | Châssis
en tube d'acier
chromé, siège et
dossier en jonc tressé,
accoudoirs en bois
massif peint, ressorts
en métal chromé

GEBRÜDER THONET,
FRANKENBERG,
FROM C. 1930

▼ Marcel Breuer
Armchair, Model
No. B55, 1928–1929

GEBRÜDER THONET,
FRANKENBERG,
1928–1929 (REIS-
SUED BY TECTA)

▲ Walter Gropius
Function room of a Residential Tower Block with ad-
joining sports room, at the 1930 "Deutscher
Werkbund" Exhibition in Paris

Marcel Breuer

Model No. B35,
1928–1929

Chromed bent
tubular steel frame,
fabric covering and
painted solid wood
armrests | Rahmen
aus gebogenem
Stahlrohr, verchromt,
Bespannung aus
Segeltuch, Armlehnen
aus Holz, lackiert |
Châssis en tube
d'acier chromé, siège
et dossier en tissu
tendu, accoudoirs en
bois massif peint

GEBRÜDER THONET,
FRANKENBERG,
FROM C. 1930

The adjustable B25, shown at the 1930 Deutscher Werkbund Exhibition in Paris, and the more unified B35, which gives the impression of having been executed from a single length of bent tubing, are both highly standardised designs.

Der Sessel B25 mit verstellbarer Rückenlehne, 1930 auf der Ausstellung des Deutschen Werkbunds in Paris gezeigt, und der Armlehnstuhl B35, der den Eindruck erweckt, als sei er aus einem einzigen Stück Stahlrohr geformt, sind hoch standardisierte Entwürfe.

Le modèle B25 réglable, présenté lors de l'exposition du Deutscher Werkbund à Paris en 1930, et le modèle plus sobre B35, qui donne l'impression d'avoir été réalisé avec un seul tube, sont tous deux hautement standardisés.

Ludwig Mies van der Rohe

Model No. MR20, 1927

Nıckel-plated bent tubular steel frame and steel stretcher with woven cane seat and back | Rahmen aus gebogenem Stahlrohr, vernickelt, Querstreben aus Stahl, Sitzfläche und Rückenlehne aus Rohrgeflecht | Châssis en tube d'acier nickelé et traverse d'acier, siège et dossier cannés

BERLINER METALL-GEWERBE JOSEF MÜLLER, BERLIN, 1927–1930 (REISSUED BY THONET & KNOLL INTERNATIONAL)

◄ Ludwig Mies van der Rohe
Model No. MR10, 1927

BERLINER METALLGEWERBE JOSEF MÜLLER, BERLIN (REISSUED BY THONET & KNOLL INTER-NATIONAL)

◄ Ludwig Mies van der Rohe
Interior, "Bau-ausstellung" Berlin, 1939

► Ludwig Mies van der Rohe
Model No. MR20, 1927

BERLINER METALL-GEWERBE JOSEF MÜLLER, BERLIN (REISSUED BY THONET & KNOLL INTERNATIONAL)

Ludwig Mies van der Rohe

Model No. MR10,
1927

Chrome-plated bent tubular steel frame and steel stretcher with "Eisengarn" textile seat and back | Rahmen aus gebogenem Stahlrohr, verchromt, Querstrebe aus Stahl, Sitzfläche und Rückenlehne mit Eisengarngewebe bespannt | Châssis en tube d'acier nickelé et traverse d'acier, siège et dossier en tissu « Eisengarn»

BERLINER METALL-
GEWERBE JOSEF
MÜLLER, BERLIN,
1927–1930
(REISSUED BY
THONET & KNOLL
INTERNATIONAL)

The MR10 and MR20 are more aesthetically refined but more awkward in use than most other cantilevered designs, because of their arced frames.

Die Freischwinger MR10 und MR20 sind ästhetisch raffinierter, doch wegen ihrer geschwungenen Rahmen nicht so sicher im Gebrauch wie die meisten anderen freischwingenden Konstruktionen.

Les modèles MR10 et MR20 sont esthétiquement plus raffinés, mais leurs courbes amples les rendent moins pratiques à utiliser que la plupart des sièges en porte à faux.

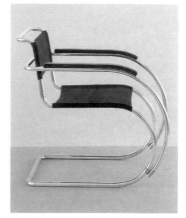

Ludwig Mies van der Rohe

Barcelona, Model No. MR90, 1929

Bent chromed flat steel frame with leather straps and buttoned leather-upholstered cushions | Rahmen aus gebogenem Flachstahl, verchromt, Lederriemen, darauf durchgeknöpfte lederbezogene Polsterkissen | Châssis en acier plat chromé, sangles de cuir et coussins de cuir capitonnés

BERLINER METALL-GEWERBE JOSEF MÜLLER, BERLIN, FROM C. 1929 (REISSUED BY KNOLL ASSOCIATES INTERNATIONAL, FROM 1948)

▼ Ludwig Mies van der Rohe
Barcelona Pavilion for the 1929 Barcelona International Exhibition

The MR90 was designed by Mies van der Rohe for use in the German Pavilion at the 1929 International Exhibition Barcelona. Opulent, yet imparting a Modern appearance, the chair's form was based on the *sella curulis*, a Roman magistrate's stool.

Der MR90 wurde von Mies van der Rohe für den Deutschen Pavillon auf der Weltausstellung 1929 in Barcelona entworfen. Luxuriös, aber dennoch von moderner Erscheinung, basiert die Formgebung dieses Sessels auf dem »sella curulis«, einem römischen Magistratsstuhl.

Le MR90 fut conçu par Mies van der Rohe pour le pavillon allemand de l'Exposition internationale de Barcelone (1929). Opulente, mais d'apparence résolument moderne, cette chauffeuse tire sa forme de la chaise curule pliante romaine.

Ludwig Mies van der Rohe

Brno, Model No. MR50, 1929–1930

Chromed bent flat steel frame with upholstered wood seating section | Gestell aus gebogenem Flachstahl, verchromt, Sitz und Rückenlehne aus gepolsterten Holzplatten | Châssis en acier plat chromé, siège et dossier en bois rembourré

BERLINER METALL-GEWERBE JOSEF MÜLLER, BERLIN, FROM C. 1930 (REISSUED BY KNOLL INTERNATIONAL, FROM 1960)

Designed for Fritz and Grete Tugendhat's home in Brno, Czechoslovakia, this chair utilises a flat steel frame. The steel used is of a very heavy gauge, making it expensive but also strong enough to support a cantilevered structure.

Dieser Stuhl, entworfen für das Haus von Fritz und Grete Tugendhat im tschechischen Brünn, ist wegen seines Flachstahlrahmens aufwendig in der Produktion. Der großzügig dimensionierte, schwere Flachstahl ist jedoch stark genug für eine freischwingende Konstruktion.

Conçu pour la maison de Fritz et Grete Tugendhat à Brno, République tchèque, ce fauteuil est réalisé à partir d'un châssis en acier plat très lourd, qui rend sa fabrication coûteuse, mais lui permet de supporter un poids important en porte à faux.

▲ **Ludwig Mies van der Rohe**
Pair of Brno chairs with tubular steel frames, 1929–1930

BERLINER METALLGEWERBE JOSEF MÜLLER, BERLIN (REISSUED BY KNOLL INTERNATIONAL)

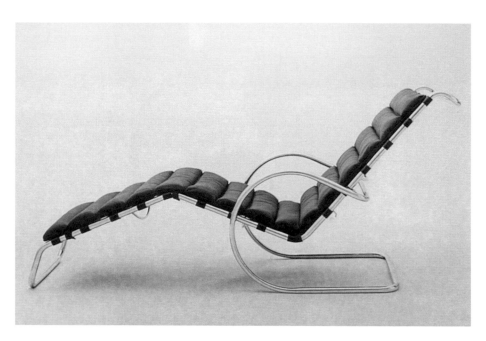

Ludwig Mies van der Rohe

Chaise longue, 1931

Chromed tubular
steel frame with
leather straps and
leather-upholstered
covering | Rahmen
aus gebogenem
Stahlrohr, verchromt,
Lederpolsterung mit
Lederriemen be-
festigt | Châssis en
tube d'acier chromé,
sangles de cuir et
coussin en cuir
rembourré

BAMBERG METALL-
WERKSTÄTTEN,
BERLIN, FROM 1932
(REISSUED BY KNOLL
INTERNATIONAL)

This adjustable chaise longue exploits the aesthetic qualities of tubular steel,
a supposedly utilitarian material while exuding luxury through the contrast
between padded leather and the minimalism of its chromed frame.

*Diese verstellbare Liege lebt von den ästhetischen Qualitäten des Stahlrohrs,
das angeblich nur wegen seiner Funktionalität Verwendung fand. Die Gegen-
sätzlichkeit von Lederpolstern und minimalistischem, verchromtem Rahmen
unterstreicht den luxuriösen Eindruck.*

Cette chaise longue réglable exploite les qualités esthétiques du
tube d'acier, matériau considéré
comme utilitaire, mais le contraste
entre le rembourrage de cuir et le
minimalisme de la structure chromée donne néanmoins une impression de luxe.

◀ Ludwig Mies van der Rohe
Model No. MR40, 1931

BAMBERG METALLWERKSTÄTTEN, BERLIN, FROM
1932 (REISSUED BY KNOLL INTERNATIONAL)

Ludwig Mies van der Rohe

Tugendhat, Model No. MR70, 1929–1930

Chromed flat steel frame, tubular steel connecting spring, buttoned leather-covered upholstered seat and back sections | Rahmen aus gebogenem Flachstahl, verchromt, Federspange aus Stahlrohr, Sitz und Rückenlehne mit durchgeknöpfter Lederpolsterung | Châssis en acier plat chromé, traverse tubulaire, siège et dossier en cuir capitonné

BERLINER METALL-GEWERBE JOSEF MÜLLER, BERLIN, FROM C. 1930 (REISSUED BY KNOLL INTERNATIONAL, FROM C. 1948)

Designed for the Tugendhat house in Brno, this chair incorporates an unusual cantilevered structure which gives greater flexibility to the frame – a feature which was patented by Mies van der Rohe in 1936.

Die ungewöhnliche Konstruktion des freischwingenden Fußes dieses Stuhls, der für das Haus Tugendhat in Brünn entworfen wurde, verleiht ihm eine größere Flexibilität. Mies van der Rohe hat sich das System 1936 patentieren lassen.

Réalisé pour la maison Tugendhat à Brno, ce fauteuil adopte une structure en porte à faux inhabituelle qui donne une plus grande flexibilité au cadre, système breveté par Mies van der Rohe en 1936.

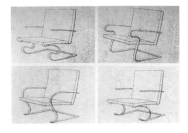

▲ Ludwig Mies van der Rohe
Sketches for four of twelve different versions of the Tugendhat chair which were patented in 1936

Marcel Breuer

Couch, 1930–1931

Chromed tubular and
flat steel frame with
leather-upholstered
seat and back
cushions | Rahmen
aus gebogenem Stahl-
rohr und Flachstahl,
verchromt, Sitzfläche
und Rückenlehne
gepolstert und mit
Lederbezug | Châssis
en tube d'acier et
acier plat chromé,
coussins de dossier et
de siège en cuir
rembourré

(REISSUED BY TECTA)

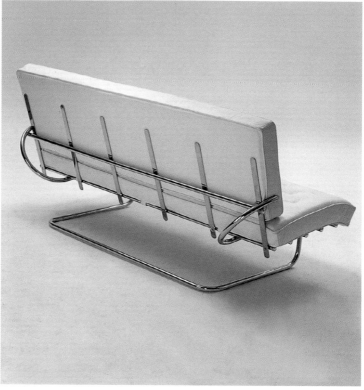

▼ Marcel Breuer
Model No. bt24,
1931–1932

METZ & CO.,
AMSTERDAM

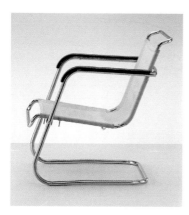

The prototype of this elegant design was exhibited at the
"Bauausstellung", Berlin, in 1931. Cantilevered sofas are
rare because a frame intended to support more than
one person requires immense strength.

*Der Prototyp dieses eleganten Entwurfs wurde 1931 auf der
Berliner Bauausstellung vorgestellt. Es gibt nur wenige
Sofas auf freischwingendem Rahmen, denn dieser muß
äußerst kräftig ausgelegt sein, damit er mehr als eine
Person trägt.*

Le prototype de cet élégant modèle fut exposé à la
« Bauausstellung » de Berlin en 1931. Les canapés en
porte à faux sont rares car la structure doit être particulièrement résistante pour supporter le poids de plusieurs personnes.

Anton Lorenz

Armchair, 1932

Chrome-plated
tubular steel and
woven cane frame
with leather-uphol-
stered cushions and
cane armrests |
Gestell aus ver-
chromtem Stahlrohr
und Rohrgeflecht,
Sitzkissen mit
Lederbezug | Châssis
en tube d'acier
chromé et jonc tressé,
coussins en cuir
rembourré, accoudoirs
en jonc

(REISSUED BY TECTA,
FROM 1987)

Lorenz designed for Standardmöbel Lengyel, before going on to found his
own manufacturing company, Deutsche Stahlmöbel (Desta). He subse-
quently spent much of his life in litigation with various designers and manufacturers in an attempt to protect his rights to the cantilever principle.
Lorenz arbeitete als Designer für die Firma Standardmöbel Lengyel, bevor er un-
ter dem Namen Deutsche Stahlmöbel (Desta) eine eigene Firma gründete.
Später, als er versuchte, seine Rechte auf die Freischwinger-Konstruktion schüt-
zen zu lassen, verwickelte er sich mit verschiedenen Designern und Herstellern in
endlose juristische Streitereien.
Lorenz dessina des modèles pour Standardmöbel Lengyel avant de créer
sa propre manufacture, Deutsche Stahlmöbel (Desta). Il passa une grande
partie de sa vie en procès avec divers designers et fabricants pour tenter de
protéger ses droits au principe du cantilever.

Hans & Wassili Luckhardt

Model No. ST14,
1929

Chromed bent tubular steel frame with painted moulded plywood seat and back | Rahmen aus Stahlrohr, verchromt, Sitzfläche und Rückenlehne aus geformtem Schichtholz, lackiert | Châssis en tube d'acier chromé cintré, siège et dossier en contreplaqué moulé et peint

DESTA BERLIN,
FROM C. 1930
(REISSUED BY
GEBRÜDER THONET,
FRANKENBERG,
FROM C. 1933 AS
S36P)

▼ Hans & Wassili
Luckhardt
Dining area,
Desta House,
"Bauausstellung",
Berlin, 1931

After having produced several Expressionist structures, the Luckhardts had adopted a more rational approach to design by 1925. The ST14's standardisation reflects this shift in attitude.

Nachdem die Luckhardts mehrere expressionistische Bauten entworfen hatten, schlugen sie 1925 in ihrer Formgebung eine rationalere Richtung ein. Die Standardisierung des Freischwingers, Modell Nr. ST14, reflektiert diese Veränderung.

Après avoir participé à plusieurs manifestations expressionnistes, les Luckhardt adoptèrent en 1925 une approche du design plus rationnelle. La standardisation du modèle ST14 reflète ce changement d'attitude.

◄ **Herbert Bayer**
Presentation of chairs (designed by Breuer, Luckhardt, Ankel, Schneck) at the Werkbund Exhibition, xxᵉ Salon des Artistes Décorateurs, Paris, 1930

121

Robert Mallet-Stevens

Pair of armchairs, c. 1929–1930

Chromed metal rod frames with ebonised wood armrests and side panels, leather-covered upholstered seating sections | Rahmen aus Metallstäben, verchromt, Armlehnen und Seitenteile aus Holz, schwarz gebeizt, Sitzschale mit Lederpolsterung | Châssis en tige de métal chromé, accoudoirs et côtés en bois noirci, siège en cuir rembourré

Influenced by Hoffmann's criticism of Art Nouveau's decorative excesses, Mallet-Stevens was the first designer to introduce the ideals of function and simplicity into France. Unable to shake off the French decorative tradition, however, his designs appear stylistically "moderne" rather than Modern.

Mallet-Stevens hat, beeinflußt durch Hoffmanns Kritik an den Dekor-Exzessen des Jugendstils, als erster Designer die Ideale von Funktion und Einfachheit nach Frankreich gebracht. Weil er sich aber doch nicht ganz von dem ornamentalen französischen Stil lösen konnte, haben seine Entwürfe stilistisch etwas gewollt »modernes«.

Influencé par Hoffmann qui critiquait les excès décoratifs de l'Art nouveau, Mallet-Stevens fut le premier designer à faire connaître en France les idéaux du fonctionnalisme et de la simplicité. Sa difficulté à s'affranchir de la tradition décorative française se manifeste toutefois dans un style se voulant plus moderne qu'il n'est.

attributed to
**Robert
Mallet-Stevens**

Chair, c. 1928

*Enamelled tubular
and sheet steel
construction |
Rahmen aus Stahl-
rohr und Stahlblech,
einbrennlackiert |
Châssis en tube
d'acier cintré laqué et
tôle d'acier, siège en
contre-plaqué*

(REISSUED BY ECART
INTERNATIONAL)

▼ Robert
Mallet-Stevens
Office interior,
Paris, c. 1928

This diminutive design is generally credited to Mallet-Stevens due to its similarity to other chairs he created for the 1935 "Salon des Arts Ménagers", Paris. It is likely that its form was inspired by a bentwood chair by Thonet.

Dieser puristische Entwurf wird allgemein Mallet-Stevens zugeschrieben, weil er den Stühlen ähnelt, die dieser 1935 für den Pariser »Salon des Arts Ménagers« geschaffen hat. Wahrscheinlich ist die Formgebung durch die Thonet-Bugholzstühle beeinflußt.

Ce modèle minimaliste est généralement attribué à Mallet-Stevens par simi-larité avec d'autres chaises qu'il créa en 1935 pour le Salon des arts ména-gers à Paris. Il est possible que cette forme lui ait été inspirée par une chaise en bois courbé de Thonet.

Pierre-Émile Legrain

Chaise longue, c. 1925

Lacquered beech frame inlaid with mother-of-pearl, with zebra-patterned velvet-covered upholstered seat and back section | Rahmen aus Buche, lackiert, Intarsien aus Perlmutt, Sitzfläche und Rückenlehne gepolstert mit Samtbezug in Zebradekor | Châssis en hêtre laqué, incrustations de nacre, rembourrage recouvert de velours zébré

PIERRE-ÉMILE LEGRAIN WORKSHOP, PARIS

Legrain collaborated on several projects with Paul Iribe, before being put in charge of decorations and furniture at the couturier Jacques Doucet's studio in Neuilly. In 1923 he set up his own workshop producing furniture inspired by Cubism and African art. Having had no formal training as a cabinetmaker, his innovative designs were not the result of preconceived notions about what a chair should look like. All his designs emphasize the textural qualities of their often unusual materials.

Legrain hatte bei mehreren Projekten mit Paul Iribe zusammen gearbeitet, bevor er die Abteilung für Innendekoration und Möbel im Atelier des Couturiers Jacques Doucet in Neuilly übernahm. 1923 eröffnete er eine eigene Werkstatt und stellte Möbel her, die vom Kubismus und von afrikanischer Kunst inspiriert waren. Er war kein ausgebildeter Kunsttischler, darum entsprangen seine innovativen Entwürfe auch nicht vorgeprägten Vorstellungen davon, wie ein Stuhl aussehen sollte. Seine Entwürfe betonen die strukturellen Qualitäten ihrer oft ungewöhnlichen Materialien.

Pierre-Émile Legrain

Armchair, c. 1925

Mahogany frame with leather-covered seating section and metal fittings | Rahmen aus Mahagoni, Sitzfläche mit Lederbezug, Metallbeschläge | Châssis en acajou, siège recouvert de cuir, garnitures en métal

PIERRE-ÉMILE
LEGRAIN
WORKSHOP, PARIS

Legrain collabora à plusieurs projets avec Paul Iribe avant d'être chargé de la décoration et de l'aménagement du « studio » du couturier Jacques Doucet à Neuilly. En 1923, il ouvrit son propre atelier, réalisant des meubles inspirés de l'art africain ou du cubisme. Son absence de formation théorique d'ébéniste explique l'originalité de ses projets novateurs. Tous mettent en valeur la qualité des différentes textures de surface des matériaux utilisés, souvent inhabituels.

Paul Theodore Frankl

Stool, c. 1925

Ebonised carved wood construction with upholstered seat | Rahmen aus Holz, geschnitzt, schwarz gebeizt, Sitzfläche gepolstert | Bois noirci sculpté, siège rembourré

PAUL FRANKL, NEW YORK

▲ **Pierre-Émile Legrain**
Tabouret Ashanti, c. 1922

PIERRE-ÉMILE LEGRAIN, PARIS

Born in Vienna, Frankl moved to the USA in 1914. His work, which bears a close affinity to that of his French contemporaries, exudes a sense of luxury. Inspired by African art, this stool reflects the spirit of 1920s New York and the age of Jazz.

Frankl stammte aus Wien und war 1914 in die USA ausgewandert. Seine Arbeiten zeigen eine große Affinität zu denen seiner französischen Zeitgenossen und haben etwas sehr Luxuriöses. Der afrikanischen Kunst nachempfunden, spiegelt dieser Hocker den Geist der 20er Jahre in New York und die Jazz-Ära wider.

Né à Vienne, Frankl s'installe aux États-Unis en 1914. Son travail, très proche de celui de ses contemporains français, dégage un sentiment de luxe. Inspiré de l'art africain, ce petit siège reflète l'esprit du New York des années 20 et de l'ère du jazz.

Jules-Émile
Leleu & André
Leleu

Stool, c. 1925

*Shagreen-faced wood
frame with ivory
inlay | Rahmen aus
Holz mit Rochen-
hautfurnier, Intarsien
aus Elfenbein |
Châssis en bois
recouvert de peau de
chagrin, incrustations
d'ivoire*

JULES-ÉMILE LELEU
WORKSHOPS,
BOULOGNE

With its luxurious materials, this highly refined stool exudes quality. Visually delicate in comparison to the bulkiness of much Art Deco design, it tentatively predicts the designers' more Modern approach in the 1930s.

Durch die luxuriösen Materialien strahlt dieser edle Hocker Qualität aus. Verglichen mit der Massivität vieler anderer Art Deco-Entwürfe wirkt er optisch eher leicht und weist in die 30er Jahre voraus, in denen sich der Designer intensiver der Moderne zuwendete.

Avec ses matériaux luxueux, ce tabouret très raffiné affiche sa qualité. D'une grande finesse visuelle par rapport à la massivité de beaucoup de modèles Art déco, il annonce à sa façon l'approche plus moderniste des créateurs des années 30.

▲ Unknown
Chair

ANDRÉ GROULT,
PARIS, C. 1925

Jacques-Émile Ruhlmann

Maharaja, c. 1929

Leather-covered upholstered seat section on metal base with height mechanism and part veneered in mahogany | Lederbezogener Sitz, höhenverstellbarer Metallfuß, teilweise mit Mahagoniholz furniert | Siège rembourré en cuir sur base en métal réglable en hauteur, placage partiel d'acajou.

ÉTABLISSEMENTS RUHLMANN ET LAURENT, PARIS

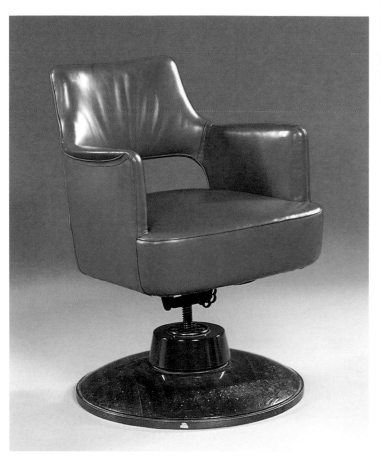

▼ Jacques-Émile Ruhlmann
Study bedroom for a crown prince, the Viceroy of India, "Salon des Artistes Décorateurs", 1929

The "Maharaja" chair was designed for the Maharaja of Indore's palace and curiously combines metal with mahogany veneer. The most avant-garde of Ruhlmann's designs, however, is the "Palette" chair which speculated on a systemised approach to production. Regrettably this design remained a prototype and its potential for mass manufacture was unexploited.
Der »Maharaja«-Schreibtischsessel, für den Palast des Maharadschas von Indore entworfen, verbindet kurioserweise Metall mit Mahagonifurnier. Der »Palette«-Stuhl ist in Ruhlmanns Werk sicher der avantgardistischste, mit

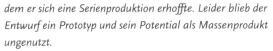

Jacques-Émile Ruhlmann

Palette, c. 1925

Enamelled metal frame with leather-upholstered seat | Rahmen aus emailliertem Metall, Sitzfläche mit Leder-polsterung | Châssis en métal émaillé, siège en cuir rembourré

(PROTOTYPE)
ÉTABLISSEMENTS
RUHLMANN ET
LAURENT, PARIS

▼ Jacques-Émile Ruhlmann
Armchair, c. 1925

ÉTABLISSEMENTS
RUHLMANN ET
LAURENT, PARIS

dem er sich eine Serienproduktion erhoffte. Leider blieb der Entwurf ein Prototyp und sein Potential als Massenprodukt ungenutzt.

Le fauteuil « Maharaja » fut créé pour le palais du maharajah d'Indore et associe de manière orginale le métal et le placage d'acajou. Le plus novateur des projets de Ruhlmann, cependant, est la chaise « Palette » qui prend en compte les contraintes de la production en série. Malheureusement, ce modèle en resta au stade du prototype et son potentiel commercial ne fut jamais exploité.

Le Corbusier, Pierre Jeanneret & Charlotte Perriand

Basculant, Model No. B301, c. 1928

Chromed bent tubular steel frame, calfskin seat and back with slung leather arms | Rahmen aus Stahlrohr, verchromt, Metallbeschläge, Sitzfläche und Rückenlehne mit Kalbfellbespannung, Armlehnen aus Ledergurten | Châssis en tube d'acier cintré chromé, siège et dossier en vachette, accoudoirs en cuir tendu

THONET FRÈRES, PARIS, FROM 1929 (REISSUED BY CASSINA)

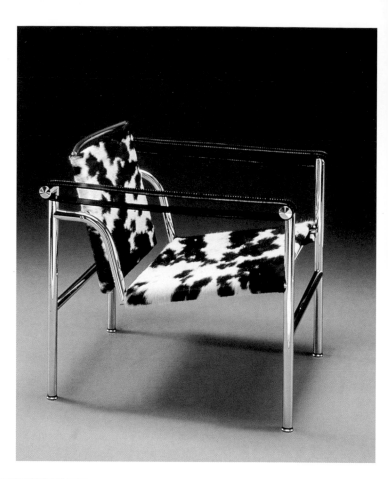

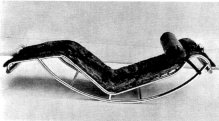

▲ Le Corbusier, Pierre Jeanneret & Charlotte Perriand
Model No. B306 (early version used as rocking chair)

▲ Le Corbusier, Pierre Jeanneret & Charlotte Perriand
Apartment interior, "Salon d'Automne", Paris, 1929

The first systemised tubular steel designs by Le Corbusier's studio appeared in 1928 and were described as "équipement de l'habitation". The best known of this furniture group is the B306 which has an ergonomically resolved form.

Das erste Programm von Stahlrohrmöbeln aus Le Corbusiers Atelier wurde 1928 als »équipement de l'habitation« vorgestellt. Das bekannteste Stück aus dieser Gruppe ist die Liege B306, ein betont ergonomischer Entwurf.

Les premiers modèles en tube d'acier du studio de Le Corbusier apparaissent en 1928. Ils sont alors décrits comme des « équipements de l'habitation ». Le modèle le plus connu de cette série est le B306, à la forme ergonomique.

Le Corbusier, Pierre Jeanneret & Charlotte Perriand

Model No. B306, 1928

Painted bent tubular metal frame with canvas covering painted sheet steel base | Rahmen aus gebogenem Stahlrohr, lackiert, Leinenbespannung, Gestell aus verschweißtem Stahlblech | Châssis en tube métallique peint, recouvrage de toile, base en tôle métallique peinte

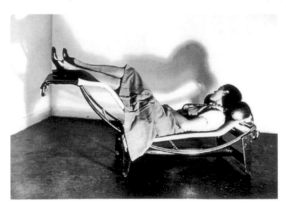

◄ Charlotte Perriand sitting in the chaise longue at the "Salon d'Automne", Paris, 1929

THONET FRÈRES, PARIS, FROM C. 1929 & EMBRU, RÜTI (REISSUED BY CASSINA)

Le Corbusier, Pierre Jeanneret & Charlotte Perriand

Model No. B302, 1928–1929

Chromed bent tubular steel frame with leather-uphol-stered seat and backrail | Rahmen aus Stahlrohr, verchromt, Sitzfläche und Rückenlehne mit Lederpolsterung | Tube d'acier chromé, siège et boudin de dossier en cuir rembourré

THONET FRÈRES, PARIS, FROM C. 1929 (REISSUED BY CASSINA)

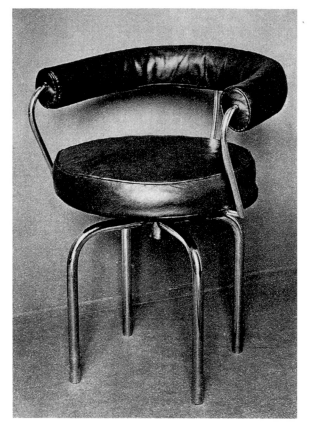

▶ **Charlotte Perriand**
Design for a dining room interior, c. 1929

▶ **Le Corbusier, Pierre Jeanneret & Charlotte Perriand**
Reissued version

Le Corbusier, Pierre Jeanneret & Charlotte Perriand

Grand Confort, Model No. LC2, 1928

Chromed bent tubular steel frame with leather-upholstered cushions | Rahmen aus verchromtem Stahlrohr, Polsterkissen mit Lederbezug | Châssis en tube d'acier cintré chromé, coussins en cuir

THONET FRÈRES, PARIS, FROM C. 1929 (REISSUED BY CASSINA)

▼ Le Corbusier, Pierre Jeanneret & Charlotte Perriand
Grand Confort, Model No. LC3, 1928

THONET FRÈRES, PARIS (REISSUED BY CASSINA)

With its external frame and sumptuous cushions, the "Grand Confort" projects luxury and epitomises the International Style. The B302 demonstrates the designers' interest in the structural possibilities of tubular steel.

Mit seinem nach außen sichtbaren Rahmen und den üppigen Polstern vermittelt der »Grand Confort« Luxus und verkörpert zugleich den Internationalen Stil. Der B302 zeigt, wie sehr sich die Designer für die konstruktiven Möglichkeiten des Stahlrohrs interessierten.

Avec son cadre apparent et ses somptueux coussins, le « Grand Confort » affiche son luxe et incarne le style international. Le B302 illustre l'intérêt de ses créateurs pour les possibilités structurelles du tube d'acier.

El Lissitzky

**Armchair for the
Hygiene Exhibition,
Dresden, 1930**

*Painted plywood con-
struction with solid
wood seat and metal
fittings | Rahmen aus
Schichtholz, lackiert,
Sitzplatte aus Massiv-
holz, Metall-
beschläge | Contre-
plaqué peint, siège en
bois massif et garni-
tures métalliques*

(REISSUED BY TECTA
AS D61)

▼ Reissued version
of D61 by Tecta,
1960

Armlehnstuhl, D 61, El Lissitzky 1930

El Lissitzky taught at the Vkhutemas Moscow design
institute and was a co-founder of Constructivism. He
associated with De Stijl members, Bauhaus designers
and Dada artists and their influence can be seen in his
designs. The D61 was originally designed for the Dresden Hygiene Exhibition, while the D62 was created for
the Pressa Exhibition, Cologne.

*El Lissitzky lehrte an der sowjetischen Kunstschule
VChUTEMAS und war Mitbegründer des Konstruktivismus.
Er stand in regem Austausch mit der Gruppe De Stijl, dem
Bauhaus und den Dadaisten; diese Einflüsse sind in seinen*

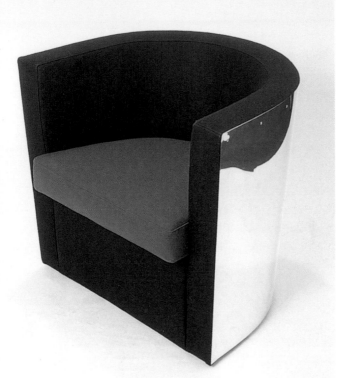

El Lissitzky

Armchair for the
Pressa Exhibition,
Cologne, 1928

Aluminium frame
with internal
upholstery and
upholstered cushion |
Gestell aus Alu-
minium, integrierte
Polsterung und
Polsterkissen | Châssis
en aluminium,
intérieur et coussin
rembourrés

(REISSUED BY TECTA
AS D62)

▼ El Lissitzky
Original drawing of
the armchair for the
Pressa Exhibition,
Cologne, 1928

Entwürfen zu erkennen. Der D61 entstand für die Hygiene-
Ausstellung in Dresden. Der D62 wurde für die Pressa-
Ausstellung in Köln geschaffen.
El Lissitzky enseignait à l'Institut soviétique de design
Vkhutemas et fut le cofondateur du constructivisme. Il
était en rapport avec les membres du groupe De Stijl,
les designers du Bauhaus et les artistes Dada. Leur influence se note dans ses projets. Le D61 fut conçu à
l'origine pour l'exposition Hygiène de Dresde et le D62
pour l'exposition Pressa à Cologne.

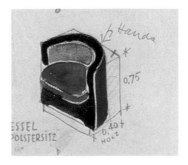

Gerrit Rietveld

Chair, 1925

Painted bent tubular
steel frame with
painted moulded
plywood seat and
back | Rahmen aus
gebogenem Stahlrohr,
lackiert, Sitzfläche
und Rückenlehne aus
formgebogenem
Schichtholz, lackiert |
Châssis en tube
d'acier cintré et peint,
siège et dossier en
contre-plaqué moulé
et peint

G. A. VAN DE
GROENEKAN,
UTRECHT, FROM
C. 1926

▼ **Gerrit Rietveld**
Beugelstoel, 1927

METZ & CO.,
AMSTERDAM,
FROM 1930

Used in the dining area of the Schröder House, this tubular steel chair shows the influence of Breuer's designs. Initially Rietveld had inspired the Bauhaus designers, but by 1925 it was vice versa.

Dieser Stuhl aus gebogenem Stahlrohr für das Eßzimmer des Hauses Schröder läßt eindeutig den Einfluß von Breuer erkennen. Hatte Rietveld anfänglich die Bauhaus-Designer beeinflußt, kehrten sich nach 1925 die Verhältnisse um.

Destinée à la salle à manger de la maison Schröder, cette chaise en tube d'acier cintré témoigne de l'influence de Breuer. Initialement, Rietveld avait inspiré les designers du Bauhaus, avant que le mouvement ne s'inverse en 1925.

Gerrit Rietveld

Beugelstoel 2, 1927

Painted bent tubular
steel frame with
painted moulded
plywood seat and
solid armrests |
Rahmen aus geboge-
nem Stahlrohr,
lackiert, Sitz- und
Rückenfläche aus
formgebogenem
Schichtholz, lackiert,
Armlehnen aus
Massivholz | Châssis
en tube d'acier cintré
peint, siège en contre-
plaqué moulé peint,
accoudoirs en bois
massif

METZ & CO.,
AMSTERDAM, FROM
C. 1928

▼ Gerrit Rietveld
Metz & Co. show-
room at the
"L'Union des
Artistes Modernes"
Exhibition,
Paris, 1930

The plywood seat section of this chair is screwed onto
the tubular steel frame. This chair and its several variants were the first Rietveld designs to be put into true
mass production.

*Die Sitzfläche dieses Sessels wird auf den Stahlrohrrahmen
geschraubt. Der Sessel und verschiedene Varianten waren
die ersten Rietveld-Entwürfe, die tatsächlich in Serienproduktion gingen.*

La section en contre-plaqué de ce fauteuil est vissée sur
le cadre tubulaire en acier. Le fauteuil et ses diverses
variantes furent les premiers modèles de Rietveld à être
produits en série.

137

Pierre Chareau

**Model No. MF158,
c. 1928**

*Sycamore-veneered
beech frame with
textile-covered
upholstery on silver-
plated copper feet* |
*Rahmen aus Buche
mit Sykomoren-
furnier, stoffbezogenes
Polster, Füße aus
Kupfer, versilbert* |
*Châssis en hêtre
plaqué de sycomore,
rembourrage
recouvert de tissu,
pieds en cuivre
argenté*

PIERRE CHAREAU,
PARIS, FROM C. 1928

▼ **Pierre Chareau**
Model No. MF15,
1920–1921

PIERRE CHAREAU,
PARIS

The MF158 armchair epitomises Chareau's partiality to
luxury woods such as sycamore, mahogany and rosewood, as well as to the heavily upholstered geometric
forms which gave his designs a massive appearance.
*Der Sessel MF158 zeigt Chareaus Vorliebe für edle Hölzer
wie z. B. Sykomore, Mahagoni und Rosenholz und auch für
kräftig gepolsterte geometrische Formen, die seine Entwürfe
recht massig wirken lassen.*
Le fauteuil MF158 incarne le goût de Chareau pour les
bois précieux comme le sycomore, l'acajou et le bois de
rose, et pour les formes géométriques très rembourrées
qui donnent à ses modèles une apparence de lourdeur.

Pierre Chareau

Model No. MC767, c. 1927

Painted metal frame with wicker seat and back | Rahmen aus Metall, lackiert, Sitzfläche und Rückenlehne aus Weidengeflecht | Châssis en métal peint, siège et dossier en osier

PIERRE CHAREAU, PARIS, FROM C. 1927

▼ Pierre Chareau
Bench, c. 1927

PIERRE CHAREAU, PARIS

This folding chair, a response to Le Corbusier's appeal for "équipement de l'habitation", was included in the interior of the golf Clubhouse at Beauvallon which had been designed by Chareau and Bernard Bijvoët in 1926. *Dieser Klappstuhl, eine Antwort auf Le Corbusiers Forderung nach Möbeln als »équipement de l'habitation«, wurde für die Innenräume des Golfklubs von Beauvallon geschaffen, die Chareau und Bernard Bijvoët 1926 entworfen hatten.* Cette chaise pliante – réponse à l'appel de Le Corbusier en faveur d'un « équipement de l'habitation » – faisait partie du décor du Clubhouse du golf de Beauvallon, qui avait été conçu par Chareau et Bernard Bijvoët en 1926.

Jean Prouvé

*Chaise inclinable
en tôle d'acier,
1924–1930*

*Nickel-plated steel
frame with uphol-
stered seat and back |
Rahmen aus Stahl,
vernickelt, Sitzfläche
und Rückenlehne
gepolstert | Châssis en
acier nickelé, siège et
dossier rembourrés*

JEAN PROUVÉ,
NANCY, FROM 1930
(REISSUED BY TECTA
IN 1981)

▼ **Jean Prouvé**
Design for the
chaise inclinable en
tôle d'acier, 1924

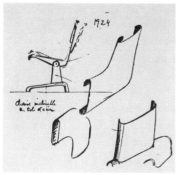

Incorporating Prouvé's novel process of "tube aplati",
which flattened out metal tubing where greater strength
was needed, this chair could be easily stacked for storage when the seat had been folded.

*Für diesen Stuhl nutzte Prouvé sein neues Verfahren des
»tube aplati«, mit dem das Rohr an den Stellen, an denen
es stabiler sein mußte, abgeflacht wurde. Der Stuhl läßt
sich mit hochgeklapptem Sitz platzsparend stapeln.*

Mettant en œuvre la nouvelle technique du « tube
aplati » mise au point par Prouvé, qui permettait d'accroître la résistance à certains endroits, cette chaise
pouvait être facilement empilée, une fois le siège replié.

This lounge chair, which was exhibited at the first UAM exhibition in 1930, has a series of springs in its adjustment mechanism, and a highly innovative structure, with the side sections and armrests forming the back legs.

Dieser Sessel wurde 1930 auf der ersten Ausstellung der UAM gezeigt. Durch einen komplizierten Federmechanismus läßt sich die Sitzposition verstellen. Die Bauweise ist äußerst innovativ. Seitenteile und Armlehne formen die hinteren Stuhlbeine.

Le mécanisme de réglage de ce fauteuil, présenté lors de la première exposition de l'UAM en 1930, fonctionne grâce à une série de ressorts. Sa structure est très novatrice : les côtés et les accoudoirs forment les pieds arrière.

Jean Prouvé

Fauteuil de grand repos, 1928–1930

Steel frame with leather-upholstered sprung seat, armrests and headrest on castors | Rahmen aus Stahl, vernickelt, Sitzfläche und Rückenlehne mit Federmechanismus und Lederpolsterung, Rollen | Châssis d'acier, siège, dossier et repose-tête en cuir rembourré, roulettes

JEAN PROUVÉ, NANCY, FROM C. 1930 (REISSUED BY TECTA)

◄ **Jean Prouvé**
Fauteuil métallique, 1927

JEAN PROUVÉ, NANCY (REISSUED BY TECTA)

Jean Prouvé

Chaise standard demontable, 1930

Painted bent tubular steel and steel frame with lacquered moulded plywood seat and back, rubber feet | Rahmen aus Stahlrohr und Stahlblech, lackiert, Sitzfläche und Rückenlehne aus geformtem Schichtholz, Gummifüße | Châssis en tube d'acier cintré et peint, tôle peinte, siège et dossier en bois contreplaqué moulé et peint, pieds en caoutchouc

JEAN PROUVÉ, NANCY (REISSUED BY TECTA, 1980)

▼ **Jean Prouvé**
Office swivelling chair, 1920s

JEAN PROUVÉ, NANCY

This standardised stacking chair and the earlier prototype office swivelling chair illustrate Prouvé's early interest in providing solutions for the institutional and contract markets.

Dieser standardisierte Stapelstuhl und der ältere Prototyp eines Bürodrehstuhls zeigen Prouvés frühes Interesse an Lösungen für Großkunden und Auftragsarbeiten.

Cette chaise empilable standardisée et le prototype plus ancien de chaise de bureau pivotante illustrent l'intérêt précoce de Prouvé pour le mobilier de bureau.

Unknown

Chair, c. 1930

Painted stamped steel frame with upholstered seat and backrail | Rahmen aus gestanzten Stahlblechteilen, lackiert, Sitzfläche und Rückenlehne gepolstert | Châssis en acier estampé peint, siège et galette de dossier rembourrés

EVERAUT, FRANCE

▼ **Xavier Pauchard**
A56, Fenêtre sur Cour, France, 1934

This is an example of a "generic" type of stacking chair which was and still is produced in large quantities in Continental Europe. It is a low-cost solution due to its ease of manufacture and economic use of materials.

Ein Beispiel für einen »typischen« Stapelstuhl, wie er in Europa noch immer in großen Mengen produziert wird. Er ist ohne große Probleme und materialsparend herzustellen, insofern also eine preiswerte Lösung.

Exemple d'un type de siège empilable « générique » que l'on continue à produire en grande quantité en Europe. Son coût de production très bas s'explique par sa facilité de fabrication et ses matériaux économiques.

Eileen Gray

Transat, 1925–1926

Lacquered wood frame, upholstered sling seat and chromed metal fittings | Rahmen aus Holz, eingehängtes Sitzpolster aus Leder, Metallbeschläge, verchromt| Châssis en bois laqué noir, siège suspendu rembourré, garnitures en metal chromé

JEAN DÉSERT, PARIS, FROM C. 1926 (REISSUED BY ECART, FROM 1978)

▼ **Eileen Gray**
Drawing for Transat, c. 1925

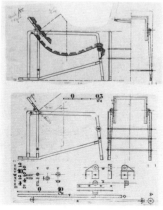

Gray's designs rejected historicism and conveyed a strong sense of modernity. They can be seen as concrete expressions of her belief that the challenges of the machine age necessitated new ways of thinking.
Grays Entwürfe stehen für Modernität. Historische Formen lehnte sie ab. Man kann diese Entwürfe als konkrete Umsetzung ihrer Überzeugung betrachten, daß den Herausforderungen des Maschinenzeitalters nur mit neuen Denkweisen zu begegnen war.
Les modèles de Gray rejettent l'historicisme au profit d'un sens appuyé de la modernité. Ils expriment sa conviction selon laquelle l'âge de la machine posait de nouveaux défis aux modes de pensée.

Eileen Gray

Non-Conformist, 1926

Chromed tubular metal frame with leather-covered upholstery | Rahmen aus Stahlrohr, Lederpolster | Châssis en tube métallique, cuir rembourré

JEAN DÉSERT, PARIS, 1926 (REISSUED BY CLASSICON UNDER LICENCE FROM ARAM DESIGNS)

▼ Eileen Gray
Bibendum armchair, 1929

JEAN DÉSERT, PARIS, 1929 (REISSUED BY CLASSICON UNDER LICENCE FROM ARAM DESIGNS)

▼◄ Eileen Gray
S chair, 1932–1934

JEAN DÉSERT, PARIS

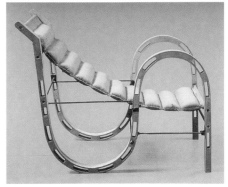

Eileen Gray

Roquebrune, 1932

Chromed tubular steel frame with laced leather seat and back | Rahmen aus Stahlrohr, Sitzfläche und Rückenlehne mit Lederbespannung | Châssis en tube d'acier chromé, siège et dossier en cuir tendu

JEAN DÉSERT, PARIS, FROM C. 1932 (REISSUED BY CLASSICON UNDER LICENCE FROM ARAM DESIGNS)

One of the most rational of Gray's designs, this chair was executed specifically for the E-1027 house built by Gray and Jean Badovici at Roquebrune, near Monte Carlo (1924–1929). Reputedly, it was Gray's favourite design.

Dieser Stuhl von Eileen Gray, einer ihrer rationellsten Entwürfe, wurde eigens für das Haus E-1027 kreiert, das sie von 1924 bis 1929 zusammen mit Jean Badovici in Roquebrune bei Monte Carlo baute. Dieser Stuhl soll Grays Lieblingsentwurf gewesen sein.

L'un des projets les plus rationalistes de Gray, cette chaise fut spécialement réalisée pour la maison E-1027 que l'artiste construisit avec Jean Badovici à Roquebrune, près de Monte-Carlo, de 1924 à 1929. C'était apparemment le modèle préféré d'Eileen Gray.

Only recently "rediscovered", the designs of Warren McArthur epitomise the optimistic spirit of America and the streamlined glamour of the 1930s Art Deco style.

Erst in letzter Zeit wurden die Entwürfe von Warren McArthur »wiederentdeckt«. Sie verkörpern den optimistischen Geist Amerikas und den Stromlinien-Zauber des Art Deco der 30er Jahre.

Récemment « redécouverts », les modèles de Warren McArthur incarnent l'esprit optimiste de l'Amérique et le glamour du style Art déco épuré des années 30.

Warren McArthur

Ambassador, 1932

Silver anodised tubular aluminium frame with leather-upholstered seat, back and arms | Rahmen aus Aluminiumrohr, silbereloxiert, Armlehnen, Sitzfläche und Rückenlehne gepolstert und mit Leder bezogen | Châssis en tube d'aluminium anodisé, siège, dossier et bras en cuir rembourré

WARREN MCARTHUR CORPORATION, LOS ANGELES, FROM C. 1932 (REISSUED BY CLASSICON)

▶ **Warren McArthur**
Biltmore chair, 1933

WARREN MCARTHUR CORPORATION, LOS ANGELES (REISSUED BY CLASSICON)

▲ René Herbst
Chromed tubular
metal chairs, c. 1930

▲ René Herbst
Dining room, c. 1930

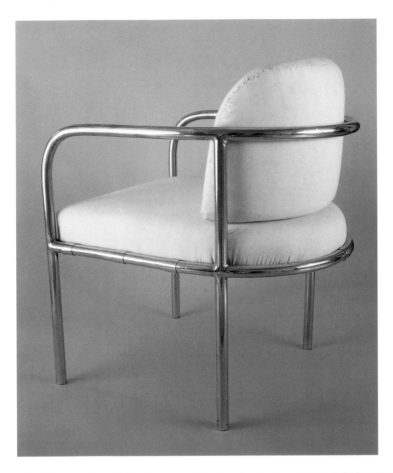

René Herbst

Armchair, c. 1928

Bent chromed tubular
steel and flat steel
frame with textile-
covered upholstered
seat and back |
Rahmen aus
Flachstahl und
gebogenem,
verchromtem Stahl-
rohr, Rücken- und
Sitzpolster mit Stoff
bezogen | Châssis en
tube d'acier chromé
cintré et acier plat,
siège et dossier en
tissu rembourré

PROBABLY LES ÉTAB-
LISSEMENTS SIEGEL
ET STOCKMAN
RÉUNIS, PARIS,
C. 1928

▼ René Herbst
Chaise longue,
C. 1935

PROBABLY LES ÉTAB-
LISSEMENTS SIEGEL
ET STOCKMAN
RÉUNIS, PARIS

This chair was first exhibited as part of an installation by
Herbst at the "Salon des Artistes Décorateurs" (1928).
The superlative finish of his chromed tubular steel de-
signs suggests labour-intensive production methods.
Dieser Stuhl wurde zuerst innerhalb einer Einrichtung ge-
zeigt, die Herbst für den »Salon des Artistes Décorateurs«
(1928) entworfen hatte. Der Hochglanz des verchromten
Stahlrohrs verrät arbeitsintensive Produktionsverfahren.
Ce fauteuil fut exposé pour la première fois lors d'une
installation réalisée par Herbst pour le Salon des
Artistes décorateurs (1928). La remarquable finition de
la structure tubulaire témoigne de méthodes de production avancées.

149

René Herbst

**Sandows chair,
1928–1929**

Chromed tubular
steel frame with
elasticated straps |
Rahmen aus
Stahlrohr, verchromt,
Gummi-Spanngurte |
Châssis en tube
d'acier chromé,
sandows

ÉTABLISSEMENTS
RENÉ HERBST, PARIS,
FROM C. 1930
(REISSUED BY
FORMES NOUVELLES)

▼ René Herbst
Chairs, c. 1930

ÉTABLISSEMENTS
RENÉ HERBST, PARIS

These designs form part of a series of chairs that were
executed between 1928 and 1929. Herbst's use of elasti-
cated straps, or "sandows", is a very early example of
incorporating "objets trouvés" into the design of chairs.
The structural simplicity and transparency of form give
these designs a skeletal minimalism.

*Diese Entwürfe gehören zu einer Serie von Sitzmöbeln,
die zwischen 1928 und 1929 entstanden sind. Herbst hat
Gummi-Spanngurte (»sandows«) benutzt – ein sehr frühes
Beispiel für den Einsatz von »objets trouvés« im
Stuhldesign. Die konstruktive Einfachheit und Transparenz
verleihen diesen Stühlen eine minimalistische Aura.*

René Herbst

Fauteuil de repos,
1928–1929

Enamelled tubular
steel frame with
elasticated straps |
Rahmen aus
Stahlrohr, schwarz
lackiert, Gummi-
Spanngurte | Châssis
en tube d'acier
émaillé, sandows

ÉTABLISSEMENTS
RENÉ HERBST, PARIS,
FROM C. 1930
(REISSUED BY
FORMES NOUVELLES)

▼ **René Herbst**
Interior, c. 1932

Ces modèles font partie d'une série de sièges exécutés entre 1928 et 1929. L'utilisation de sandows est un des premiers exemples d'incorporation d'objets trouvés dans la conception de sièges. La simplicité structurelle et la transparence de la forme confèrent à ces modèles un minimalisme extrême.

Gabriele Mucchi

Genni, 1935

Chromed tubular steel frame with steel springs and leather armrests, leather-upholstered seat cushion and headrest | Rahmen aus gebogenem Stahlrohr, verchromt, Stahlfeder, Sitzfläche, Rückenlehne und Nackenstütze mit Lederpolsterung | Châssis en tube d'acier chromé, ressorts en acier, accoudoirs en cuir, coussin de siège et repose-tête en cuir rembourré

CRESPI, EMILIO PINA, MILAN, FROM C. 1935 (REISSUED BY ZANOTTA, FROM 1982)

Active in the anti-Fascist group "Corrente", Mucchi was part of the Rationalist movement in design and architecture. Ironically, Rationalism is frequently identified with the Italian Fascist movement.

Mucchi, ein Aktivist in der antifaschistischen Gruppe »Corrente«, gehörte zur Bewegung der Rationalisten in Design und Architektur. Ironischerweise wird der Rationalismus häufig mit dem italienischen Faschismus in Verbindung gebracht.

Participant actif au groupe antifasciste « Corrente », Mucchi faisait partie du mouvement rationaliste de design et d'architecture. Ironiquement, le rationalisme est fréquemment identifié au fascisme italien.

◄ Prototype of the Genni lounge chair, c. 1935

Piero Bottoni

Lira, 1934

Chromed tubular steel frame with pre-stressed wire, leather-upholstered seat | Rahmen aus gebogenem Stahlrohr, verchromt, eingespannte Drahtseile, Sitzfläche gepolstert | Châssis en tube d'acier chromé, tiges de métal précontraint, siège en cuir rembourré

GEBRÜDER THONET,
FRANKENBERG OR
THONET FRÈRES,
PARIS, FROM C. 1934
(REISSUED BY
ZANOTTA)

▼ Piero Bottoni
Commedia, 1932

(REISSUED BY
ZANOTTA)

The "Lira" chair has a seat section that is solely supported by tension wires, which give the design a strong dynamism. It is a quintessential Rationalist design.
Die Sitzfläche des »Lira«-Stuhls wird ausschließlich von gespannten Drähten gehalten, was dem Entwurf eine starke Dynamik verleiht. Es handelt sich um ein durch und durch rationales Design.
Le fauteuil « Lira », qui connut un grand succès, possède un siège uniquement soutenu par des tiges en tension qui lui donnent son dynamisme. C'est un des modèles essentiels du design rationaliste.

Giuseppe Terragni

Sant'Elia, 1936

Chromed tubular steel frame with leather-upholstered seat, back and armrests | Rahmen aus gebogenem Stahlrohr, verchromt, Sitzfläche, Rückenlehne und Armlehnen mit Lederpolsterung | Châssis en tube d'acier chromé, siège, dossier et accoudoirs en cuir rembourré

(REISSUED BY ZANOTTA, FROM 1970)

▼ **Giuseppe Terragni**
Lariana, 1935–1936

(REISSUED BY ZANOTTA, FROM 1971)

◄ Casa del Fascio (later renamed Casa del Popolo), Como, c. 1936

Giuseppe Terragni

Follia, 1934–1936

Painted wood seating
frame and backrest
with sprung stainless
steel connectors |
Sitzgestell und
Rückenlehne aus
lackiertem Holz,
federnde Stahlverbin-
dungen | Châssis et
dosseret en bois peint,
lames d'acier chromé

(REISSUED BY
ZANOTTA, FROM
1971)

▼ Giuseppe Terragni
Casa del Fascio,
1932–1936

These chairs were used in Terragni's Casa del Fascio,
the Italian Fascist headquarters in Como. Rationalist
designs such as these were favoured by the Fascists
during the early 1930s.

*Diese Stühle standen in Terragnis Casa del Fascio, dem
Hauptquartier der italienischen Faschisten in Como.
Rationalistische Entwürfe wie diese wurden während der
frühen 30er Jahre von den Faschisten durchaus geschätzt.*

Ces sièges équipaient la Casa del Fascio de Terragni, le
siège du parti fasciste de Côme. De telles réalisations
rationalistes bénéficiaient de l'appui des fascistes au début des années 30.

Gerrit Rietveld

Moolenbeek Zig-Zag armchair, 1942

Oak construction with perforated back and metal fittings | Eiche, Rückenlehne perforiert, Metallbeschläge | Chêne, dos perforé et garnitures en métal

METZ & CO., AMSTERDAM, FROM C. 1942

▼ **Gerrit Rietveld**
White version of Zig-Zag chair, c. 1934

G. A. VAN DE GROENEKAN, UTRECHT

The 45° angle of the "Zig-Zag" chair's cantilever can be seen as a response to Theo van Doesburg's call in 1924 for the introduction of "oblique" lines to resolve the tension between vertical and horizontal elements.

Der 45°-Winkel im Sockelbereich des »Zig-Zag«-Stuhls könnte eine Reaktion auf Theo van Doesburg sein, der 1924 dafür plädierte, die Spannung zwischen senkrechten und horizontalen Elementen durch eine Diagonale aufzulösen.

L'angle de 45° du siège en porte à faux « Zig-Zag » peut être considéré comme une réponse à l'appel lancé par Theo van Doesburg en 1924 en faveur des lignes obliques, afin de résoudre le problème de la tension entre éléments verticaux et horizontaux.

Gerrit Rietveld

Zig-Zag chair,
c. 1932–1934

Oak construction with
brass fittings | Eiche,
Messingbeschläge |
Chêne, garnitures en
cuivre

METZ & CO.,
AMSTERDAM,
1935–C. 1955
(REISSUED BY
CASSINA)

◄ ▼ **Gerrit Rietveld**
Working drawing of
Zig-Zag chair,
1932–1934

▼ **Gerrit Rietveld**
Interior in Stoop
Family House, 1950

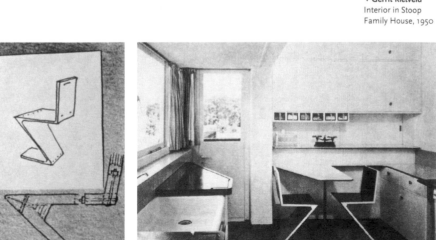

Gerrit Rietveld

Crate, 1934

Red spruce
construction |
Rottannenholz |
Epicéa rouge

METZ & CO.,
AMSTERDAM,
FROM C. 1935
(REISSUED BY
CASSINA)

The "Crate" chair was intended for use in weekend homes and, like the "Zig-Zag" chair, reveals Rietveld's return to elemental constructions. As a response to the economic slump of the 1930s, this system of seating can be seen as an early example of "Poor Art".

Der »Crate«-Stuhl war für die Benutzung in Wochenendhäusern konzipiert und belegt, wie der »Zig-Zag«-Stuhl, Rietvelds Rückkehr zu elementaren Formen. Zu Beginn der 30er Jahre als Reaktion auf den ökonomischen Zusammenbruch entstanden, kann dies Sitzmöbelprogramm als ein frühes Beispiel der Arte Povera betrachtet werden.

Le fauteuil « Crate » fut conçu pour les maisons de campagne et, comme la chaise « Zig-Zag », annonce le retour de Rietveld à une simplicité élémentaire de construction. Réponse à la crise économique des années 30, ce type de siège est l'un des premiers exemples d'Art pauvre.

Kit Nicholson

Standard, c. 1935

*Painted plywood
construction on
castors | Sperrholz,
lackiert, auf Rollen |
Contre-plaqué peint,
roulettes*

▼ **Frank Lloyd
Wright**
Chair for the
Clarence W.
Sondernhouse,
Kansas City,
Missouri, 1940

Created for the Pioneer Health Centre in Peckham,
London, by the brother of the sculptor Ben Nicholson,
this design was entitled the "Standard" because six
chairs could be made from a single sheet of plywood.
*Dieser Entwurf, vom Bruder des Bildhauers Ben Nicholson
für das Pioneer Health Centre entwickelt, wurde zu Recht
»Standard« genannt, weil aus einer Sperrholzplatte die
Teile für sechs Stühle geschnitten werden konnten.*
Créé pour le Pioneer Health Center de Peckham par le
frère du sculpteur Ben Nicholson, ce modèle fut appelé
« Standard » car on pouvait fabriquer six chaises à partir
d'une seule feuille de contre-plaqué.

Alvar Aalto

Model No. F35, 1930

Chromed tubular
steel frame with
moulded plywood
seat and back section |
Rahmen aus
Stahlrohr, verchromt,
Sitzschale aus
geformtem Schicht-
holz | Châssis en tube
d'acier chromé, siège
et dossier en contre-
plaqué moulé

HUONEKALU-JA
RAKENNU-
STYÖTEHDAS, ÅBO,
TURKU
(REISSUED BY ARTEK)

▼ **Alvar Aalto**
Dining room, on
display at
Bowman Bros.,
London, c. 1938

Although generally acclaimed to be Aalto's first
Modernist chair, the tubular metal and plywood F35 can
be seen as a rather awkward hybrid design lacking the
elegance of his later all-wood constructions.
*Obwohl allgemein als Aaltos erster moderner Stuhl gefeiert,
könnte man den aus Stahlrohr und Sperrholz konstruierten
F35 als eine ziemlich unbeholfene Zwischenlösung betrachten, die noch nichts von der Eleganz von Aaltos späteren
Ganzholz-Konstruktionen hat.*
Généralement salué comme le premier siège moderniste d'Aalto, le F35 est cependant un modèle hybride
plutôt maladroit qui n'a pas l'élégance des créations en
bois ultérieures de l'artiste.

Alvar Aalto

Model No. 31,
1931–1932

Bent laminated and
solid birch frame with
lacquered bent
plywood seat section |
Rahmen aus lami-
nierter und massiver
Birke, Sitzschale aus
geformtem Schicht-
holz, lackiert | Châssis
en bouleau contre-
plaqué cintré, siège en
contre-plaqué cintré
laqué

HUONEKALU-JA
RAKENNU-
STYÖTEHDAS, ÅBO,
TURKU, 1932–1935
(REISSUED BY ARTEK,
FROM 1935 TO
PRESENT)

▼ Alvar Aalto
Armchair, 1931–1932

HUONEKALU-JA
RAKENNU-
STYÖTEHDAS, ÅBO,
TURKU,
C. 1931–1932

The frame of the model No. 31 was revolutionary in that
it marked the first use of laminated wood in a cantilevered structure. Through this design, Aalto was also
able to achieve an unprecedented unity of materials.
Der Rahmen des Modells Nr. 31 war revolutionär, denn
zum ersten Mal wurde hier Schichtholz für einen
Freischwinger verwendet. Mit diesem Entwurf fand Aalto
zu einer bis dahin unerreichten Materialeinheit.
Le châssis du modèle n° 31 fut révolutionnaire car c'était
la première fois que l'on utilisait du contre-plaqué dans
une structure en porte à faux. Avec ce modèle, Aalto
atteignit à une unité de matériaux sans précédent.

▲ Alvar Aalto
Armchair, Model No. 37, 1935–1936

ARTEK, HELSINKI, FROM C. 1936 TO PRESENT

▲ Alvar Aalto
Armchair, Model No. 44,
1935–1936

ARTEK, HELSINKI, FROM C. 1935 TO PRESENT

Alvar Aalto

Paimio, Model
No. 41, 1930–1931

Bent laminated and
solid birch frame with
lacquered bent
plywood seat section |
Rahmen aus geboge-
ner, laminierter Birke,
Sitzschale aus
geformtem Schicht-
holz, lackiert | Châssis
en bouleau contre-
plaqué cintré, siège en
contre-plaqué cintré
laqué

HUONEKALU-JA
RAKENNU-
STYÖTEHDAS, ÅBO,
TURKU, 1932–1935
(REISSUED BY ARTEK,
FROM 1935 TO
PRESENT)

◄▲ Alvar Aalto
Bent laminated
wood sections for
Alvar Aalto's chair
designs, Model
Nos. 41 & 44

Although not part of the original furnishing scheme at
the Paimio Sanatorium, this revolutionary chair is often
associated with the project. Where there was a need for
great pliancy, such as in the scrolls of the plywood seat
and back, Aalto thinned the lamination by removing
several layers of veneer.

Auch wenn dieser revolutionäre Stuhl nicht zum ursprüng-
lichen Ausstattungsprogramm des Sanatoriums Paimio
gehörte, wird er häufig mit diesem Projekt in Verbindung
gebracht. Wo größere Elastizität zum Biegen benötigt
wurde, z. B. bei den eingerollten Enden der Sitzschale,
machte Aalto das Schichtholz durch Entfernen einiger
Furnierschichten dünner.

Bien qu'il ne fasse pas partie du mobilier d'origine du
sanatorium de Paimio, ce siège révolutionnaire est souvent associé à ce projet. Lorsqu'il avait besoin d'une
grande flexibilité, comme dans l'enroulement du siège
et du dossier, Aalto amincissait le contre-plaqué en éli-
minant quelques couches de placage.

Alvar Aalto

Model No. 60,
1932–1933

Bent laminated birch
construction |
Gebogene, laminierte
Birke | Contre-plaqué
cintré plaqué de
bouleau

HUONEKALU-JA
RAKENNU-
STYÖTEHDAS, ÅBO,
TURKU, 1933–1935
(REISSUED BY ARTEK,
FROM 1935 TO
PRESENT)

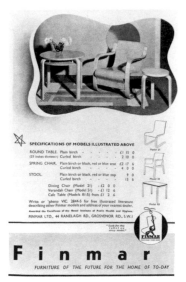

▲ Alvar Aalto
Model No. 69, c. 1933

HUONEKALU-JA RAKENNUSTYÖTEHDAS, ÅBO,
TURKU, 1933–1935 (REISSUED BY ARTEK,
FROM 1935 TO PRESENT)

▲ Finmar advertisement, c. 1935

Alvar Aalto

Model No. 43, 1936

Bent laminated wood and solid birch frame with textile webbing | Gestell aus laminiertem und gebogenem Holz und massivem Birkenholz, Liegefläche aus Textilgeflecht | Bouleau contre-plaqué cintré, bouleau massif, textile tressé

ARTEK, HELSINKI, FROM C. 1937 TO PRESENT

The model No. 60 stool and model No. 69 chair demonstrate Aalto's interest in basic functional forms. The later model No. 43 chaise longue and model No. 406 chair are less utilitarian and more suited to domestic settings.

Der Hocker Modell Nr. 60 und der Stuhl Modell Nr. 69 demonstrieren Aaltos Interesse an funktionalen Grundformen. Die spätere Liege Modell Nr. 43 und der Stuhl Modell Nr. 406 wirken weniger funktional, fügen sich aber besser in Wohnumgebungen ein.

Le tabouret modèle n° 60 et la chaise modèle n° 69 révèlent l'intérêt d'Aalto pour les formes fonctionnelles basiques. La chaise longue modèle n° 43 et le fauteuil modèle n° 406, tous deux ultérieurs, sont moins utilitaires et mieux adaptés à un usage domestique.

▲ **Alvar Aalto**
Armchair, Model No. 406, 1938–1939

ARTEK, HELSINKI, FROM C. 1939 TO PRESENT

Marcel Breuer

Model No. 301,
1932–1934

Bent aluminium
frame with painted
moulded and
laminated seat and
backrest | Rahmen
aus gebogenem
Aluminiumprofil,
Sitzfläche und
Rückenlehne aus
geformtem Schicht-
holz, lackiert | Châssis
en aluminium cintré,
siège et dosseret en
contre-plaqué moulé,
peints

EMBRU, RÜTI,
ZURICH, FROM 1934

▼ Marcel Breuer
Armchair, Model
No. 301 & armchair,
Model No. 336,
1932–1934

EMBRU, RÜTI,
ZURICH, FROM 1934

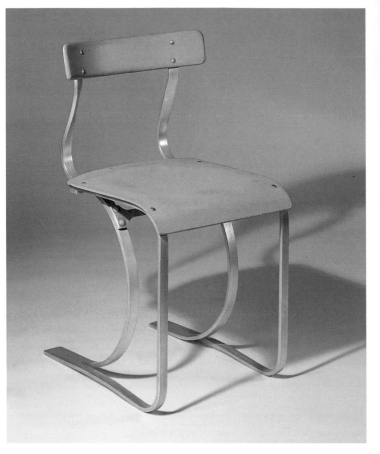

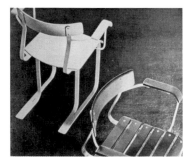

In the early 1930s, Breuer experimented with flat aluminium in his designs for seating. Although not as
resilient or strong as tubular metal, this medium was
considerably cheaper. Intended for the mass-market, his
flat steel designs were retailed through the Wohnbedarf
stores in Switzerland. The concave back legs are a
hybrid of the cantilever principle and were a structural
necessity.

*In den frühen 30er Jahren experimentierte Breuer in seinen
Entwürfen für Sitzmöbel mit Aluminiumprofilen. Auch
wenn dieses Material weniger elastisch und stark ist als
Stahlrohr, so ist es doch erheblich preiswerter. Für den
Massenmarkt konzipiert, wurden diese Aluminiummodelle*

durch die Läden der Schweizer Firma Wohnbedarf vertrieben. Die konkav geschwungenen, zusätzlichen hinteren Beine, eine unechte Freischwinger-Lösung,
waren aus statischen Gründen notwendig.

Au début des années 30, Breuer expérimente la réalisation de sièges en aluminium. Moins élastique ou résistant que le métal tubulaire, il était toutefois bien moins cher. Conçus pour le marché grand public, ces modèles en
acier plat furent commercialisés en Suisse par les magasins Wohnbedarf.
Les pieds arrière concaves sont une solution hybride de porte-à-faux et répondaient à une nécessité structurelle.

Marcel Breuer

Model No. 313,
1932–1934

Bent aluminium
frame with
aluminium slats and
beech armrests |
Rahmen aus geboge-
nem Aluminiumprofil
und Aluminium-
streben, Armlehnen
aus Buche | Châssis
en aluminium cintré,
traverses en alu-
minium et accoudoirs
en bois de hêtre

EMBRU, RÜTI,
ZURICH, FROM 1934

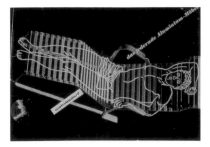

◄ **Herbert Bayer**
Cover of Wohn-
bedarf catalogue,
Das federnde
Aluminium-Möbel,
1934

Marcel Breuer

Chaise longue,
1935–1936

Bent laminated birch
frame with bent
plywood seat section |
Rahmen aus geboge-
ner und laminierter
Birke, Liegefläche aus
geformtem Schicht-
holz | Châssis en
bouleau contre-
plaqué cintré, siège en
contre-plaqué cintré

ISOKON FURNITURE
COMPANY, LONDON,
FROM 1936

Breuer's plywood and laminated wood chaise longue and lounge chair were part of a group of furniture designed for Jack Pritchard's Isokon Furniture Company. Reflecting the popularity of Aalto's designs, which had been exhibited in London in 1933, Breuer's designs are all-wood translations of his earlier metal designs. These later designs were structurally flawed, for the tenon joins which attached the seat section to the frame loosened over time. *Breuers Liege und Sessel aus Schicht- und Formholz gehören zu einer Möbelserie, die für Jack Pritchards Isokon Möbelwerke geschaffen wurde. Als Ganzholzversionen seiner früheren Entwürfe belegen sie den Einfluß Alvar Aaltos, dessen Möbel ab 1933 in London zu sehen waren. Breuers Konstruktion litt darunter, daß sich die Verzapfungen zwischen Sitz und Rahmen nach einiger Zeit lösten.*

▶ **Marcel Breuer**
Working drawing,
1936

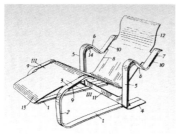

Marcel Breuer

Armchair, 1936

Bent laminated birch
frame with bent
plywood seat section |
Rahmen aus geboge-
ner und laminierter
Birke, Liegefläche aus
geformtem Schicht-
holz | Châssis en
bouleau contre-
plaqué cintré, siège en
contre-plaqué cintré

ISOKON FURNITURE
COMPANY, LONDON,
FROM 1936

Les fauteuils et les chaises longues en contre-plaqué faisaient partie d'un groupe de meubles dessinés pour la firme de meubles Isokon de Jack Pritchard. Rappelant les modèles d'Aalto, qui avaient été exposés à Londres en 1933, les créations de Breuer sont des adaptations tout en bois de ses œuvres antérieures en métal. Avec le temps, apparaît une faiblesse structu-relle au niveau du tenon qui joint la partie du siège au cadre.

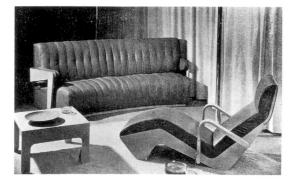

◄ Marcel Breuer
Group of furniture
designed for Heal's,
c. 1936

Marcel Breuer

Chair, 1936–1937

Cut-out and moulded plywood construction | Geformtes Schichtholz | Contre-plaqué moulé et découpé

ISOKON FURNITURE COMPANY, LONDON, FROM C. 1937 (REISSUED BY WINDMILL FURNITURE)

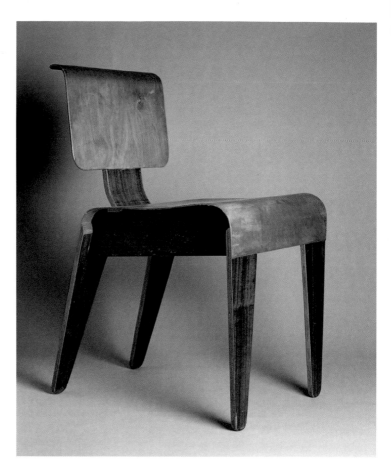

▼ Marcel Breuer
Chair (Prototype), 1936

The most structurally resolved of all Breuer's plywood chairs, this design presages the Eameses' moulded plywood chairs of 1945–1946. An early version of the chair incorporated only two moulded elements.

Der konstruktiv reifste von Breuers Schichtholzentwürfen nimmt die Formholzstühle von Ray und Charles Eames aus den Jahren 1945–1946 vorweg. Eine frühe Version dieses Stuhls bestand aus nur zwei Formholzteilen.

Modèle de siège en contre-plaqué de Breuer, le plus réussi structurellement et visuellement, cette chaise annonce les créations des Eames des années 1945–1946. Une version précédente ne comportait que deux éléments moulés.

Kem Weber

Airline, c. 1934–1935

Birch and ash frame with fabric-covered upholstered seat section | Rahmen aus Birke und Esche, Sitzfläche und Rückenlehne gepolstert und mit Stoff bezogen | Châssis en bouleau et en frêne, siège en tissu rembourré

AIRLINE CHAIR CO., LOS ANGELES, FROM 1935

▼ The unpacking and assembling of an Airline chair

The reductivist streamlined form of the "Airline" chair is a thoroughly American expression of Modernism. Intended to be hygienic as well as comfortable, it was also easy to distribute due to its flat-pack design.

Die reduzierte Stromlinienform des »Airline«-Stuhls ist äußerst typisch für die amerikanische Formgebung der Moderne. Der Stuhl sollte sowohl hygienisch wie auch bequem sein. Die zerlegbare Konstruktion erlaubte eine flache Verpackung und erleichterte so den Vertrieb.

La forme épurée de ce fauteuil « Airline » est une expression tout à fait américaine du modernisme. Se voulant aussi hygiénique que confortable, ce siège était livré à plat, ce qui facilitait sa distribution.

► **Bruno Mathsson**
Pernilla, chaise
longue, c. 1934

KARL MATHSSON,
VÄRNAMO, FROM
C. 1935

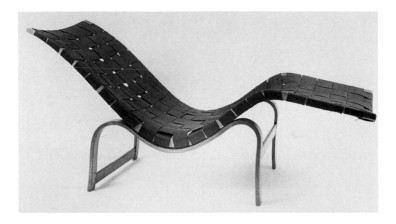

► **Bruno Mathsson**
Pernilla lounge chair
with bookrest,
C. 1934

KARL MATHSSON,
VÄRNAMO, FROM
C. 1935

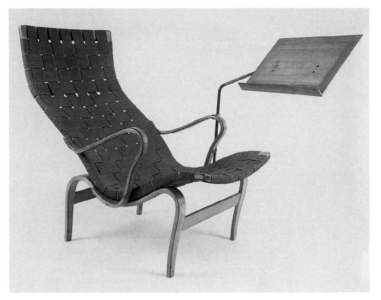

Although bearing a strong similarity to designs by Aalto, Mathsson's "Eva" chair and "Pernilla" chaise longue, lounge chair and ottoman exude a greater sense of luxury. The seat frames of these designs, to which the hemp webbing was attached, were not actually made of laminated wood like the supporting frames, but were executed from solid wood that had been carved into curved sections and then jointed.

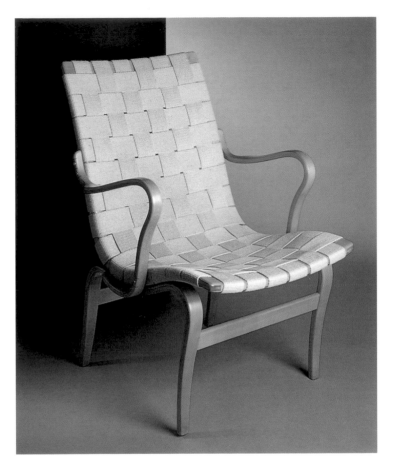

Bruno Mathsson

Eva, 1934

Bent plywood and
solid birch frame with
hemp webbing | Rahmen aus geboge-
ner, laminierter und
massiver Birke,
Bespannung aus
Hanfgeflecht | Châssis
en contre-plaqué
cintré et bouleau
massif, sangles de
chanvre

KARL MATHSSON,
VÄRNAMO, FROM
1935
(REISSUED BY DUX)

Mathssons Stuhl »Eva«, die Liege »Pernilla«, der Sessel und die Ottomane
haben eine starke Ähnlichkeit mit Aaltos Entwürfen, dennoch zeigen sie ein
etwas luxuriöseres Flair. Die Rahmen, an denen das Hanfgewebe befestigt ist,
bestehen nicht wie die tragenden Teile aus laminiertem Formholz, sondern aus
massivem Holz, das in Einzelteilen in geschwungene Formen geschnitten und
dann verbunden wurde.

Bien que très similaires aux modèles d'Aalto, le fauteuil « Eva », la chaise
longue « Pernilla », la chaise de salon et l'ottomane de Mathsson, sont
beaucoup plus luxueux. Le cadre de la partie siège de ces modèles n'était
pas en contre-plaqué mais en bois massif sculpté et assemblé.

Gerald Summers

Armchair, 1933–1934

Bent plywood construction | Formgebogenes Schichtholz | Contreplaqué cintré

MAKERS OF SIMPLE FURNITURE, LONDON, 1935–1940

This lounge chair was designed for use in tropical conditions. Because traditional wood joinery is adversely affected by increased humidity, this chair was innovatively constructed from a single piece of bent plywood. Its lack of upholstery meant that it was less prone to insect infestation and rot, both common problems in the tropics. The side chairs' "cut-out" legs are also a highly innovative use of plywood.

Dieser Stuhl wurde für den Gebrauch in den Tropen entworfen. Weil herkömmliche Holzverbindungen unter erhöhter Luftfeuchtigkeit leiden, entstand diese innovative Konstruktion aus einer einzigen Schichtholzplatte. Dadurch, daß auf Polsterung verzichtet wurde, widerstand der Sessel Insekten- und

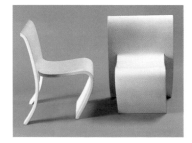

◀ **Gerald Summers**
Pair of chairs, c. 1938

MAKERS OF SIMPLE FURNITURE, LONDON, c. 1938–1940

Gerald Summers

Pair of chairs, c. 1938

Birch-faced cut-out and moulded plywood constructions finished with white polish, textile-covered upholstered seats | Gestell aus zugeschnittenem und formgebogenem Schichtholz, weißer Schleiflack, mit Stoff bezogene Sitzpolster | Contre-plaqué moulé et découpé, placage de bouleau, vernis blanc, sièges rembourrés et recouverts de tissu

MAKERS OF SIMPLE FURNITURE, LONDON, C. 1938–1940

▼ Gerald Summers
Dressing table and chair, c. 1938

MAKERS OF SIMPLE FURNITURE, LONDON, C. 1938

Schimmelbefall, zwei bekannte Plagen tropischer Zonen. Auch die beiden Stühle oben mit ihren ausgeschnittenen Formholzbeinen wirken äußerst innovativ.

Ce fauteuil fut conçu pour les conditions de vie en pays tropical. Les assemblages étant sensibles à l'humidité, Summers eut le premier l'idée de proposer un siège découpé dans une seule feuille de contre-plaqué cintré. L'absence de rembourrage le mettait à l'abri des insectes et de la moisissure. Les pieds en contre-plaqué découpé de ces chaises sont également très originaux.

175

Kaare Klint

Chair and armchair,
1927

Teak frames with
leather-upholstered
seat and backs |
Rahmen aus Teak-
holz, Sitzflächen und
Rückenlehnen mit
Lederpolsterung |
Châssis en teck, siège
et dossier en cuir
rembourré

RUD RASMUSSENS
SNEDKERIER,
COPENHAGEN,
TO PRESENT

▼ **Kaare Klint**
Fåborg chair, 1914

RUD RASMUSSENS
SNEDKERIER,
COPENHAGEN,
TO PRESENT

Klint believed that design should be evolutionary,
resulting from a contemplation of what has gone before.
His designs are restatements of classical solutions
which combine comfort with simplicity.
Klint war überzeugt davon, daß Design etwas Evolutionäres
und deshalb aus der Besinnung auf Vergangenes zu ent-
wickeln sei. Seine Entwürfe sind Überarbeitungen klassi-
scher Lösungen, in denen sich Bequemlichkeit mit schlich-
ter Formgebung verbindet.
Klint pensait que le design devait suivre une évolution
et s'inspirer de ce qui avait été fait jusque-là. Ses modèles sont des interprétations de solutions classiques
alliant le confort et la simplicité.

Eliel Saarinen

Chair for the dining room of the Saarinen House, 1929

Ebonised pine and natural maple construction with textile-covered horsehair-upholstered seat | Rahmen aus Pinie, schwarz gebeizt, und Ahorn, Sitzfläche mit Roßhaarpolsterung und Stoffbezug | Pin et érable naturel noircis, siège rembourré en crin de cheval et recouvert de textile

THE COMPANY OF
MASTER CRAFTSMEN,
W. & J. SLOANE,
NEW YORK, 1929
(REISSUED BY
ADELTA)

▼ Eliel Saarinen
Dining room,
Saarinen House,
c. 1930

This dining chair, designed for the Saarinen House at Cranbrook, shows the influence of the French Art Deco ébénistes, whose work Saarinen had seen at the 1925 International Exhibition in Paris.

Dieser Eßzimmerstuhl, für das Haus Saarinen in Cranbrook entworfen, belegt den Einfluß der französischen Art Deco-Möbeltischler, deren Arbeiten Saarinen 1925 auf der Internationalen Ausstellung in Paris gesehen hatte.

Cette chaise de salle à manger, dessinée pour la maison de Saarinen à Cranbrook, montre l'influence des ébénistes Art déco français, dont l'artiste avait pu voir les œuvres à l'Exposition internationale de Paris, en 1925.

Gordon Russell

Armchair, 1929

Oak frame with
leather-upholstered
seat cushion |
Rahmen aus Eiche,
Sitzkissen mit Leder-
bezug | Châssis en
chêne, coussin de
siège en cuir
rembourré

GORDON RUSSELL,
BROADWAY,
WORCESTERSHIRE

▼ **Gordon Russell**
Workshops' show-
room, Broadway,
c. 1928

Russell continued the Arts & Crafts tradition of truth to
materials, revealed construction and fitness for purpose
– principles upon which the earlier utilitarian "Indian"
chair was also based.

Russell steht in der Tradition der Arts & Crafts-Bewegung,
was die Materialgerechtigkeit, die nach außen hin sichtbare
Konstruktion und die Gebrauchstüchtigkeit seiner Entwürfe
belegen. Vergleichbare Qualitäten birgt auch der zeitlich
frühere »Indian«-Stuhl.

Russell perpétua la tradition Arts & Crafts qui prône
l'authenticité des matériaux, dévoilant la construction et
l'adaption à un usage précis, principes auxquels se rat-
tachait également le modèle « Indian ».

Unknown

Indian chair, Model No. 1761N, c. 1904

Collapsible teak frame with rot-proof canvas seat and back, leather strap arm-rests | Rahmen aus Teakholz, zerlegbar, Sitzfläche und Rückenlehne aus witterungsfestem Segeltuch, Armlehnen und Verspannung aus Lederriemen | Châssis en teck, siège et dossier en toile imputrescible, accoudoirs en sangles de cuir

MAPLE & CO.,
LONDON, 1904–1956

▲ Maple & Co. sales catalogue, c. 1925

Kaare Klint

Deck, 1933

Solid teak
construction with
retractable footrest |
Rahmen aus
massivem Teakholz,
mit ausziehbarer
Fußstütze | Teck
massif, repose-pied
rétractable

RUD RASMUSSENS
SNEDKERIER,
COPENHAGEN, FROM
C. 1933 TO PRESENT

Both the "Deck" chair and "Safari" chair are reinterpretations of existing types. Klint's belief in the "rightness" of forms that have evolved over a period of time was in complete opposition to the Modern Movement's distaste of historicism. The idea of evolution rather than revolution in design is a more humanist approach and is often demonstrated in Scandinavian design.

Sowohl der »Deck«- als auch der »Safari«-Stuhl stellen Neuinterpretationen bereits existenter Stuhltypen dar. Klint war überzeugt von der »Angemessenheit« solcher Formen, die sich über längere Zeit entwickelt haben, und stand damit in direkter Opposition zur Bewegung der Moderne und ihrer Abneigung gegen jeglichen Historismus. Daß evolutionäre Entwicklungen in der Formgebung humaner sind als revolutionäre Brüche, wird vom skandinavischen Design immer wieder vorgeführt.

► **Knud Friis &
Elmar Moltke
Nielsen**
Interior of a house in
Denmark, 1958

Kaare Klint

Safari, 1933

Collapsible ash frame
with leather straps,
canvas seat and back
coverings | Rahmen
aus Esche, zerlegbar,
Sitzfläche und
Rückenlehne aus
Segeltuch, Armlehnen
und Verspannung aus
Lederriemen | Châssis
démontable en frêne,
sangles de cuir, siège
et dossier en toile

RUD RASMUSSENS
SNEDKERIER,
COPENHAGEN, FROM
C. 1933 TO PRESENT

Cette chaise longue « Deck » et le modèle « Safari » sont des réinterpréta-
tions de modèles existants. Klint croyait beaucoup en la « justesse » des
formes qui ont évolué avec le temps, ce qui était en complète opposition
avec le mépris des modernistes à égard de l'historicisme. L'idée d'une évolution des formes plutôt que d'une révolution est une approche plus huma-
niste, souvent illustrée par le design scandinave.

Mogens Koch

MK, 1932

Beech frame with canvas seat and back, leather arm straps | Rahmen aus Buche, Sitzfläche und Rückenlehne aus Segeltuch, Armlehnen aus Lederriemen | Châssis en hêtre, siège et dossier en toile, accoudoirs en sangles de cuir

INTERNA, RUD RASMUSSENS SNEDKERIER, COPENHAGEN, FROM 1960 TO PRESENT

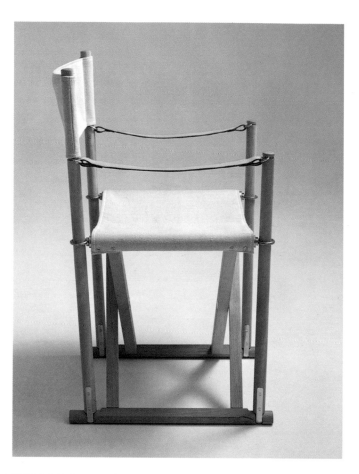

The "MK" chair has a timelessness derived from its traditional folding form. Practical and unpretentious Scandinavian designs like this became popular in the USA and Britain during the post-war years.
Die Zeitlosigkeit des »MK«-Stuhls entspringt der traditionellen Form des Klappstuhls. Derart praktische und unprätentiöse skandinavische Designs waren in den Nachkriegsjahren in den USA und in Großbritannien sehr beliebt.
Le fauteuil pliant « MK » semble hors du temps. Pratique et sans prétention, le design scandinave fut très populaire aux États-Unis et en Grande-Bretagne pendant l'après-guerre.

Carlo Scarpa

Model No. 765, 1934

Walnut frame with leather-covered seat cushion | Rahmen aus Walnußholz, Sitzkissen mit Lederbezug | Châssis en noyer, coussin en cuir

BERNINI, MILAN, FROM 1977 TO PRESENT

Scarpa's love of natural materials is eloquently communicated through this chair. The organic form of the back, which expresses the very nature of the wood it is carved from, contrasts strongly with the geometry of the base. Aesthetically ahead of its time, the No. 765 was not produced until 1977.

Deutlich läßt dieser Stuhl Scarpas Vorliebe für natürliche Materialien erkennen. Die organische Formgebung des Rückens, die dem Werkstoff Holz sehr entgegenkommt, steht in Kontrast zur Geometrie der Basis. Der Stuhl Nr. 765 war seiner Zeit ästhetisch weit voraus und ging erst 1977 in Produktion.

La passion de Scarpa pour les matériaux naturels s'exprime de manière éloqente avec ce siège. La forme organique du dossier restitue la nature même du bois dont il est sculpté et contraste fortement avec la géométrie rigide du piètement. Esthétiquement trop en avance sur son temps, le modèle n° 765 ne fut mis en production qu'en 1977.

Wharton Esherick

Pair of armchairs, c. 1939

Oak frames with woven leather seating sections | Rahmen aus Eiche, Sitzfläche und Rückenlehne aus Ledergeflecht | Châssis en chêne, siège en cuir tressé

WHARTON ESHERICK, USA, C. 1939

Wharton Esherick, a sculptor as well as a furniture designer, was a central figure in the Crafts Revival in America. His carved wood forms were often highly expressive.

Der Bildhauer und Möbeldesigner Wharton Esherick war eine zentrale Figur für das »Crafts Revival« in den USA. Seine aus Holz geschnitzten Formen sind oft sehr expressiv.

Wharton Esherick, sculpteur et designer, joua un rôle central dans le « Crafts Revival » aux États-Unis. Ses créations en bois sculpté étaient souvent très expressives.

Russel Wright

Armchair, 1934

Carved wood frame
with canvas sling back
and calf-skin-covered
upholstered seat | *Rahmen aus Holz,
geschnitzt, gepolstert
mit Kalbslederbezug,
Rückenlehne mit
Bespannung aus
Segeltuch* | *Châssis en
bois sculpté dossier
inclinable et coussin
en vachette rem-
bourré*

PROBABLY
HEYWOOD-
WAKEFIELD,
GARDNER,
MASSACHUSETTS,
C. 1934

▼ **Hammond Kroll**
Chair, c. 1930

In the mid-1930s, Russel Wright shifted his attention to natural materials. This was a rejection not only of the machine aesthetic but also of the increasing European influence on American design.

Mitte der 30er Jahre richtete Russel Wright seine Aufmerksamkeit auf natürliche Werkstoffe. Dies bedeutete nicht nur eine Ablehnung der Maschinenästhetik, sondern auch der zunehmenden europäischen Einflüsse auf das amerikanische Design.

Au milieu des années 30, Russel Wright s'intéressa aux matériaux naturels, non seulement par rejet de l'esthétique industrielle mais également à cause de l'influence européenne grandissante sur le design américain.

Jean-Michel Frank

Chair, 1935

Solid wood frame
covered in woven
rattan | Rahmen aus
Massivholz, mit
Rattangeflecht über-
zogen | Châssis en
bois massif recouvert
de rotin tressé

(REISSUED BY ECART)

▼ Jean-Michel Frank
Pickled oak arm-
chair, c. 1932

Initially working as a cabinetmaker for Ruhlmann, Frank
was also influenced by the Modernism of Le Corbusier
and Mallet-Stevens. His designs reveal his profound interest in the textural qualities of materials.

*Frank arbeitete zunächst als Kunsttischler für Ruhlmann,
ließ sich aber auch vom Modernismus Le Corbusiers oder
Mallet-Stevens' beeinflussen. Seine Entwürfe geben sein
tiefes Interesse an den Oberflächenbeschaffenheiten von
Werkstoffen zu erkennen.*

Au départ ébéniste pour l'atelier de Ruhlmann, Frank fut
également influencé par le modernisme de Le Corbusier
et de Mallet-Stevens. Ses modèles reflètent l'intérêt pro-
fond qu'il portait aux textures des matériaux.

Jorge Ferrari-
Hardoy,
Juan Kurchan &
Antonio Bonet

**Butterfly, Model
No. 198, 1938**

*Enamelled tubular
steel frame with
leather sling seat |
Gestell aus Stahlrohr,
lackiert, Sitzbespan-
nung aus Leder |
Châssis en tube
d'acier peint, siège en
cuir*

KNOLL ASSOCIATES,
NEW YORK,
C. 1947–C. 1975
(REISSUED BY STÖHR
IMPORT-EXPORT)

▼ Unlicensed copy
of the Butterfly chair,
1950s

Originally manufactured by Artek-Pascoe, production
was taken over by Knoll after 1945. Later, Knoll lost a
copyright infringement lawsuit which allowed the
Butterfly to be copied by a plethora of firms.
*Dieser Stuhl wurde zunächst von Artek-Pascoe, nach 1945
dann von Knoll produziert. Später verlor Knoll einen
Rechtsstreit um das Urheberrecht, so daß der Butterfly
schließlich von sehr vielen Firmen hergestellt und vertrieben
werden konnte.*
Réalisée à l'origine par Artek-Pascoe, la production de ce
siège fut reprise par Knoll après 1945. Plus tard, Knoll
perdit un procès sur ses droits de reproduction, ce qui
permit à d'innombrables fabricants de copier ce modèle.

The working drawing for this design was made by Edward James according to a suggestion made by Salvador Dalí in 1936. The chair was produced specifically for James' residence, West Dean.

Die Entwurfszeichnung für diesen Stuhl hat Edward James nach einer Idee angefertigt, die Salvador Dalí 1936 geäußert hat. Den Stuhl hat James für sein eigenes Haus in West Dean anfertigen lassen.

Les dessins d'exécution de ce modèle furent réalisés par Edward James, sur une suggestion de Salvador Dalí en 1936. Cette chaise fut spécifique-ment fabriquée pour la maison de James, à West Dean.

Salvador Dalí

Hands chair, c. 1936

Carved walnut frame with purple leather-covered seat | Rah-men aus Walnußholz, geschnitzt, Sitzfläche mit Bezug aus purpurfarbenem Leder | Châssis en noyer sculpté, siège recouvert de cuir pourpre

ARTHUR ENGLISH, WEST DEAN, C. 1936

The concept for this Surrealist sofa came from a 1934 gouache entitled *Mae West*. The sofas were executed by Green & Abbot, London, and Jean-Michel Frank in Paris. A variation was designed for a proposed Marx Brothers film.

Die Idee für dieses surrealistische Sofa stammt von einer 1934 entstandenen Gouache mit dem Titel »Mae West«. Die Sofas wurden von Green & Abbot,

London, und von Jean-Michel Frank, Paris, produziert. Eine Variante entstand für einen Film der Marx Brothers.

Le concept de ce sofa surréaliste provient d'une gouache de 1934 intitulée *Mae West*. Les sofas furent fabriqués par Green & Abbot, à Londres, et par Jean-Michel Frank, à Paris. Une variante en fut proposée pour un film des Marx Brothers.

Salvador Dalí
Mae West sofa,
c. 1936

Felt-covered upholstered wood frame | Holzgestell, gepolstert und mit Fell bezogen | Châssis en bois rembourré recouvert de feutre

GREEN & ABBOTT,
LONDON, C. 1936

◄ **Salvador Dalí**
Mae West, c. 1934
(gouache on paper)

▲ **Frank Lloyd Wright**
Office space and
workroom, S. C.
Johnson & Son
Administration
Building, Racine,
Wisconsin, c. 1939

Like the Larkin Building, the Johnson Wax Administration Building was a completely integrated project. The workstations and office chairs were site-specific in their design and predicted the advent of office systems furniture.
Wie das Larkin Gebäude entstand auch das Johnson Wax-Verwaltungsgebäude nach einem Gesamtentwurf. Die Schreibtische und Bürostühle waren auf den Gesamtentwurf abgestimmt und nehmen die Erfindung der Büromöbelsysteme späterer Jahre vorweg.
Comme le Larkin Building, le siège administratif de la Johnson Wax était un projet totalement intégré. Les postes de travail et les sièges de bureau furent spécialement conçus pour cette occasion et annoncent l'arrivée du concept de « système » dans le mobilier de bureau.

Frank Lloyd Wright

Chair for the S. C. Johnson & Son Administration Building, c. 1936

Painted tubular metal frame with upholstered seat and back | Rahmen aus Stahlrohr, lackiert, Sitzfläche und Rückenlehne gepolstert | Châssis en tube d'acier peint, siège et dossier rembourrés

STEELCASE, GRAND RAPIDS, MICHIGAN, FROM 1937 TO PRESENT

▼ Frank Lloyd Wright
Armchair for the S. C. Johnson & Son Administration Building, c. 1936

STEELCASE, GRAND RAPIDS, MICHIGAN, FROM 1937 TO PRESENT

▲ Frank Lloyd Wright
Workstation for the S. C. Johnson & Son Administration Building, c. 1936

Hans Coray

Landi, 1938

*Bent and pressed
aluminium
construction |
Konstruktion aus
gestanztem und
geformtem
Aluminium |
Aluminium cintré et
estampé*

P. & W. BLATTMANN
METALLWAREN-
FABRIK, WÄDENSWIL,
FROM C. 1939
(REISSUED BY
ZANOTTA, FROM 1971
AS 2070 SPARTANA)

▼ Attributed to Josef
Hoffmann & Oswald
Haerdtl
Armchair, 1929

PROBABLY THONET-
MUNDUS, VIENNA

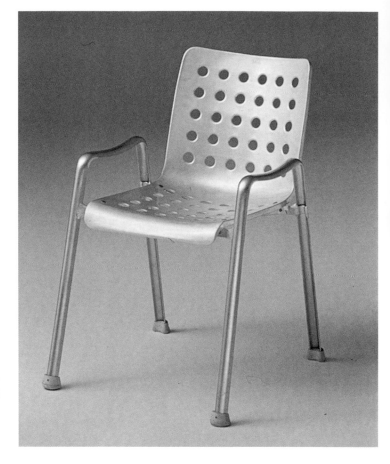

The "Landi" chair was designed for the grounds of the
1939 "Landesausstellung" exhibition, Zurich. Its perforations reduced weight and allowed water drainage for
outdoor use.
*Der »Landi«-Stuhl wurde für die Züricher Landesausstel-
lung von 1939 entworfen. Die Perforation der Sitzschale hat
zwei Vorteile: Sie reduziert das Gewicht, und das
Regenwasser kann ablaufen, wenn der Stuhl im Freien benutzt wird.*
Le fauteuil « Landi » avait été conçu pour les installations de la « Landesausstellung » de Zurich (1939). Ses
perforations l'allégeaient et permettaient l'écoulement
de l'eau en utilisation extérieure.

Gerrit Rietveld

Aluminium chair,
1942

Pressed and stamped
aluminium
construction |
Konstruktion aus
gestanztem und
geformtem Alu-
minium | Aluminium
moulé et estampé

GERARD VAN DE
GROENEKAN & WIM
RIETVELD, UTRECHT,
FROM 1942

▼ Gabriele Mucchi
Aluminium chairs
shown at the VII
Milan Triennale,
1940

This chair was probably inspired by military aircraft
seats. Constructed from a bent, single sheet of stamped
aluminium, the design pushed the material's technical
and aesthetic limits further than ever before.

Dieser Sessel hat sein Vorbild vermutlich in den Sitzen von
Militärflugzeugen. Aus einem einzigen gestanzten und ge-
formten Stück Aluminiumblech hergestellt, hat dieser
Entwurf technische und ästhetische Maßstäbe für die
Verwendung von Aluminium gesetzt.

Ce fauteuil a probablement été inspiré par les sièges
des avions militaires. Réalisé à partir d'une seule feuille
d'aluminium estampée et cintrée, il a repoussé les
limites techniques et esthétiques de son matériau.

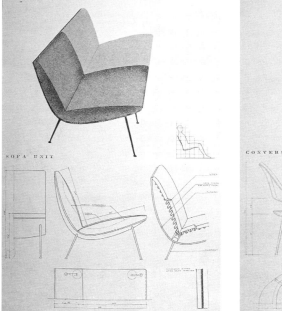

▲ **Charles Eames & Eero Saarinen**
Submitted drawing of sectional sofa unit. Utilising plywood shells again, this system allowed the units to be separated for use as individual chairs

Eames and Saarinen's entries for the Museum of Modern Art's "Organic Design in Home Furnishings" competition were among the most important furniture designs of the 20th century. Their chair designs, comprising single-piece compound-moulded plywood seat shells, were exceptionally innovative and heralded a totally new direction in Modern furniture.

Eames' und Saarinens Beiträge zum Wettbewerb »Organic Design in Home Furnishings«, vom New Yorker Museum of Modern Art ausgeschrieben, gehören zu den bedeutendsten Möbelentwürfen des 20. Jahrhunderts.

▲▶ **Charles Eames & Eero Saarinen**
Submitted drawing of A3501 moulded plywood shell armchair. This original design shows aluminium legs that were to be connected with novel rubber-weld joints. However, the prototypes made from this design had to incorporate wooden legs due to the wartime restrictions

▶ **Charles Eames & Eero Saarinen**
Interior showing armchair and side chair prototypes with competition proposal for standardised case furniture system

Ihre Stühle mit Sitzschalen aus Schichtholz, die aus einem Stück geformt waren, stellten etwas völlig Neues dar und wiesen dem zeitgenössischen Möbeldesign eine gänzlich andere Richtung.

Les œuvres realisées par Eames et Saarinen pour le concours «Organic Design in Home Furnishings», organisé par le Museum of Modern Art de New York, représentent quelques-uns des plus importants projets de mobilier design du XXe siècle. Leurs sièges, qui faisaient appel à des coquilles en une seule pièce de contre-plaqué moulé, étaient remarquablement novateurs et ouvraient une nouvelle voie au mobilier moderne.

▲ Charles Eames & Eero Saarinen
Furniture designed for the "Organic Design in Home Furnishings" competition at the Museum of Modern Art, New York, 1940, prototypes

◄ The cover for the "Organic Design in Home Furnishings" catalogue

Charles & Ray Eames

LCW (Lounge Chair Wood), 1945

Bent birch-faced plywood frame attached to moulded birch-faced plywood seat and back with rubber shock-mounts | Rahmen, Sitzfläche und Rückenlehne aus geformtem Schichtholz mit Birkenfurnier, Gummipuffer zwischen Rahmen und Sitzfläche| Châssis en contre-plaqué cintré, placage de bouleau, siège et dossier plaqués bouleau, amortisseurs de suspension en caoutchouc

EVANS PRODUCTS
COMPANY, VENICE,
CALIFORNIA,
1946–1949 AND
HERMAN MILLER
FURNITURE CO.,
ZEELAND,
MICHIGAN,
1949–1958

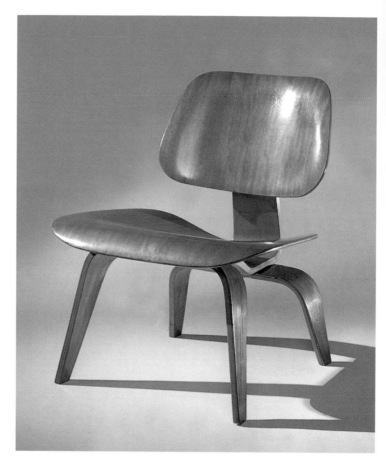

◄◄ Charles &
Ray Eames
Child's chair, 1945

EVANS PRODUCTS
COMPANY, VENICE,
CALIFORNIA

◄ Charles &
Ray Eames
Prototype lounge
chair, 1946

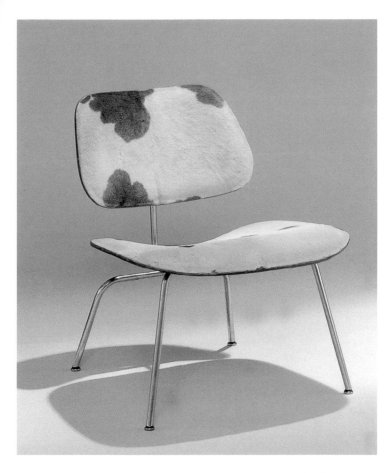

Charles & Ray Eames

LCM (Lounge Chair Metal), 1945–1946

Chrome-plated tubular steel frame attached to "Slunk-skin" (animal hide) – covered moulded plywood seat and back with rubber shock-mounts | Rahmen aus gebogenem Stahlrohr, verchromt, Sitzfläche und Rückenlehne aus geformtem Schichtholz mit Pelzbespannung, Gummipuffer zwischen Rahmen und Sitzfläche | Châssis en tube d'acier chromé, siège et dossier en contre-plaqué moulé recouvert de peau, amortisseurs en caoutchouc

EVANS PRODUCTS COMPANY, VENICE, CALIFORNIA 1946–1949 AND HERMAN MILLER FURNITURE CO., ZEELAND, MICHIGAN, FROM 1949 (THIS VERSION PRODUCED TO 1953)

The Eameses' landmark plywood chairs were mainly the result of their wartime research into the development of an inexpensive and efficient method of moulding plywood into compound forms.

Die Schichtholzstühle von Ray und Charles Eames, Meilensteine im modernen Möbelbau, sind das Ergebnis eines Forschungsprogramms, an dem die beiden während des Krieges arbeiteten. Es ging darum, eine preiswerte und effektive Methode zu entwickeln, mit der sich Schichtholz in dreidimensionale Formen pressen ließ.

Cette célèbre chaise en contre-plaqué réalisée par les Eames est principalement issue des recherches qu'ils menèrent pendant la guerre pour mettre au point une méthode efficace et économique de moulage du contre-plaqué.

Jean Prouvé

Visiteur, 1942

Bent tubular steel, lacquered oak and sheet-zinc construction | Konstruktion aus gebogenem Stahlrohr, Eiche, lackiert und Zinkblech | Tube d'acier cintré, chêne laqué, tôle de zinc

LES ATELIERS JEAN PROUVÉ, NANCY, FROM C. 1942

▼ **Jean Prouvé**
Working drawing, 1942

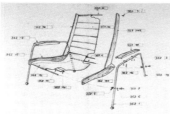

Although originally retailed with an upholstered seat and back, this chair's use of sheet-zinc is most unusual. The ball foot motif became increasingly popular throughout the 1950s.

Ursprünglich wurde dieser Sessel mit gepolsterter Sitzfläche und Rückenlehne vertrieben. Äußerst ungewöhnlich ist die Verwendung von Zinkblech. Runde Möbelfüße wurden in den 50er Jahren zunehmend beliebter.

Commercialisé à l'origine avec un dossier et un siège rembourrés, ce fauteuil utilise de façon très inhabituelle la tôle de zinc. L'extrémité du pied en forme de boule allait devenir très à la mode au cours des années 50.

Jean Prouvé

Chair, 1945

Oak frame with birch-veneered moulded plywood seat and back | Rahmen aus Eiche, Sitzfläche und Rückenlehne aus geformtem Schichtholz mit Birkenfurnier | Châssis en chêne, siège et dossier en contre-plaqué moulé, placage de bouleau

LES ATELIERS JEAN PROUVÉ, NANCY, FROM C. 1945

▼ Cover of Steph Simon catalogue, c. 1950

This wooden chair is one of a series of collapsible designs by Prouvé. A similar chair dating from c. 1930 utilised a metal frame – a less attractive variation because of its compromised visual unity.

Dieser Holzstuhl gehört zu einer Serie von Klappstühlen von Prouvé. Ein ähnlicher Entwurf, der um 1930 entstanden war, besaß noch einen Metallrahmen und war damit weniger attraktiv, denn ihm fehlte die optische Einheit.

Cette chaise de bois appartient à une série de modèles pliants conçus par Prouvé. Une chaise similaire, datant de 1930 environ, faisait appel à un châssis de métal, solution moins satisfaisante car elle nuisait à l'unité visuelle.

Jens Risom

Model No. 666 WSP,
1942

Birch frame with plastic-webbed seat and back | Rahmen aus Birke, Sitzfläche und Rückenlehne aus Plastikgurtgeflecht | Châssis en bouleau, siège et dossier en plastique tressé

(REDESIGNED
C. 1946) HANS G.
KNOLL FURNITURE
CO. (LATER KNOLL
ASSOCIATES,
NEW YORK),
C. 1943– C. 1954

▼ Jens Risom
The first chair to be manufactured by Knoll, 1941–1942

The model 666 WSP was one of 15 designs produced by Risom for Knoll's company. Constrained by wartime materials restrictions, the chairs were constructed of only "regulated" woods and army surplus webbing.
Das Modell Nr. 666 WSP war einer der 15 Entwürfe, die Risom für Knoll entwickelte. Wegen der kriegsbedingten Materialknappheit bestanden die Stühle nur aus Hölzern und überschüssigem Gurtband aus Armeebeständen.
Le modèle 666 WSP fait partie des 15 projets réalisés par Risom pour Knoll. Soumises aux restrictions des années de guerre, ces chaises étaient construites en bois et en déchets récupérés dans les surplus militaires.

Y-leg stool,
1946–1947

*Bent birch-faced
laminated wood
frame with woven
seat | Rahmen aus
gebogenem, laminier-
tem Holz mit Birken-
furnier, Sitzfläche
geflochten | Châssis
en contre-plaqué
cintré, placage de
bouleau, siège en
textile tressé*

ARTEK, HELSINKI,
FROM C. 1947
TO PRESENT

▼ Alvar Aalto
Armchair, Model
No. 45, 1946–1947

ARTEK, HELSINKI,
FROM C. 1947
TO PRESENT

Aalto's innovative Y-leg construction is created by setting two L-leg half-sections at right angles to each other
– a solution which provides both physical and visual
lightness.

*Aaltos innovative Y-Konstruktion der Hockerbeine wurde
aus zwei im rechten Winkel zueinander montierten
L-Beinen entwickelt – eine Lösung, durch die der Hocker
wenig Gewicht hat und die auch optisch leicht wirkt.*

L'idée novatrice de ce tabouret aux pieds en Y vient du
rapprochement de deux sections en L à angle droit, solution qui apporte une légèreté aussi bien physique que
visuelle.

Lloyd Loom Studio

Model No. U64, 1945

Wood frame-covered in woven spun paper fibre with central core in every upright strand | Holzrahmen, bespannt mit einem Geflecht aus gesponnenen Papierfasern und einem Kern in jeder senkrechten Litze | Châssis en bois recouvert de papier câblé sur fil de fer

W. LUSTY & SONS,
CHIPPING CAMPDEN,
FROM 1945 TO
PRESENT

▼ **Lloyd Loom Studio**
Model No. 85, 1922

W. LUSTY & SONS,
CHIPPING CAMPDEN,
FROM 1922 TO
PRESENT

In 1917, the American Marshall Burns Lloyd patented a new process for producing wicker out of twisted paper. By 1940 over ten million of his Lloyd Loom furniture items had been sold.

1917 hat sich der Amerikaner Marshall Burns Lloyd ein neues Verfahren zur Herstellung von Korbgeflecht aus gesponnenen Papierfasern patentieren lassen. Bis 1940 wurden über zehn Millionen seiner Lloyd Loom-Möbel verkauft.

En 1917, l'Américain Marshall Burns Lloyd dépose le brevet d'un nouveau procédé de fabrication du papier tressé. Ce siège avait déjà été vendu à plus de dix millions d'exemplaires en 1940.

Joseph-André Motte

Tripode, 1949

Beech and steel frame with woven rattan seating section | Rahmen aus Buche und Stahl, Sitzschale aus Rattangeflecht | Châssis en hêtre et en acier, siège en rotin

ROUGIER, FRANCE, FROM 1950

▼ French interior, c. 1950

Influenced by other designers also studying at the École des Arts Appliqués, Motte designed installations for Orly airport and took part in the renovation of the Louvre's Grande Galerie.

Während seines Studiums an der École des Arts Appliqués entwarf Motte, von anderen Designern dort inspiriert, Einbauten für den Flughafen Orly und war auch an der Renovierung der Grande Galerie des Pariser Louvre beteiligt.

Influencé par autres designers au cours de ses études à l'École des arts appliqués, Motte dessina les installations de l'aéroport d'Orly et participa à la rénovation de la Grande galerie du Louvre.

Ernest Race

BA armchair, 1945

Cast aluminium
frame with
upholstered plywood
seat and back |
Rahmen aus Guß-
aluminium, Sitzfläche
und Rückenlehne aus
geformtem Schicht-
holz, gepolstert |
Châssis en fonte
d'aluminium, siège et
dossier en contre-
plaqué moulé et
rembourré

ERNEST RACE,
LONDON (LATER
RACE FURNITURE),
FROM 1945 TO
PRESENT

From 1945 to 1964 over 250,000 "BA" chairs were produced from 850 tons of resmelted aluminium wartime scrap. First exhibited at the "Britain Can Make It" exhibition of 1946, the design was awarded a gold medal at the Milan IX Triennale in 1951.

Von 1945 bis 1964 wurden 850 Tonnen Kriegsschrott zu über 250 000 Alumi-niumgestellen für den »BA«-Stuhl umgeschmolzen. Er wurde 1946 auf der Ausstellung »Britain Can Make It« zum ersten Mal gezeigt und 1951 auf der IX. Mailänder Triennale mit einer Goldmedaille ausgezeichnet.

Entre 1945 et 1964, plus de 250 000 fauteuils « BA » furent produits à partir de 850 tonnes de déchets d'aluminium militaire refondus. Exposé pour la première fois lors de l'exposition « Britain Can Make It », en 1946, ce modèle reçut une médaille d'or à la IXe Triennale de Milan, en 1951.

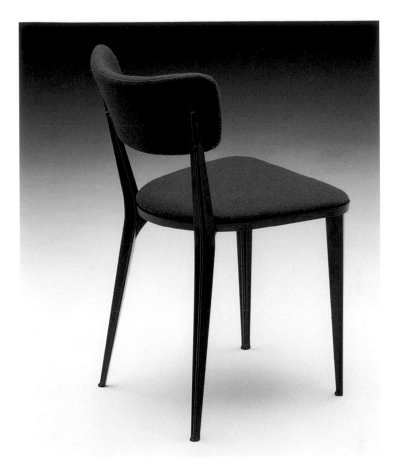

Ernest Race

BA chair, 1945

Cast aluminium
frame with
upholstered plywood
seat and back |
Rahmen aus Guß-
aluminium, Sitzfläche
und Rückenlehne aus
Schichtholz, gepol-
stert | Châssis en
fonte d'aluminium,
siège et dossier en
contre-plaqué
rembourré

ERNEST RACE,
LONDON (LATER
RACE FURNITURE),
FROM 1945 TO
PRESENT

▼ Ernest Race
advertisement, 1947

◄ Restaurant interior showing BA chairs, c. 1950

Andrew J. Milne

Armchair, 1947

Solid rosewood frame
with upholstered seat
and back | Rahmen
aus Palisander, Sitz-
fläche und Rücken-
lehne gepolstert |
Châssis en bois de
rose massif, siège et
dossier rembourrés

MINES & WEST UK,
HIGH WYCOMBE,
FROM C. 1947

This design was influenced by the contemporary
"Turinese Baroque" style. Until 1952, the chair was heavily taxed and, therefore, extremely expensive because of
its use of a luxury wood.

*Dieser Entwurf wurde vom zeitgenössischen »Turiner
Barock« beeinflußt. Bis 1952 wurde der Stuhl wegen der
Verwendung von Edelhölzern mit einer hohen Steuer belegt
und war entsprechend teuer.*

Le design de ce modèle doit beaucoup au style « Baroque turinois » de l'époque. Jusqu'en 1952, il était
fabriqué dans un bois de luxe lourdement taxé et donc
très coûteux.

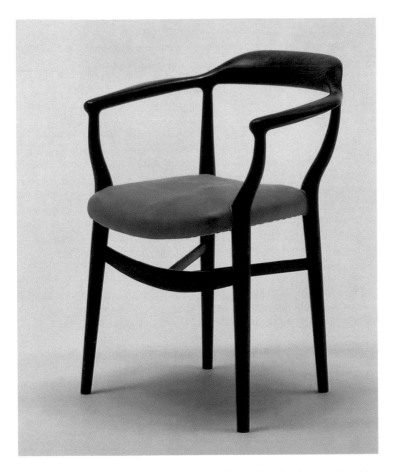

Finn Juhl

Model No. NV-44,
1944

Carved rosewood
frame with leather-
covered upholstered
seat | Rahmen aus
Palisander, Sitzfläche
mit Lederpolsterung |
Châssis en bois de
rose sculpté, siège en
cuir rembourré

NIELS VODDER,
COPENHAGEN, 1944
(REISSUED BY NIELS
ROTH ANDERSEN)

While only twelve NV-44 chairs were originally produced, Juhl considered it his favourite design. The chair's sculptural organic form exudes superior craftsmanship and Juhl's virtuosity as a designer.

Obwohl ursprünglich nur zwölf Exemplare des Armlehnstuhls NV-44 hergestellt wurden, betrachtete Juhl diesen Sessel als seinen gelungensten Entwurf. Die plastisch-organische Formgebung des Stuhls zeigt hohe handwerkliche Kunst und belegt Juhls Können als Designer.

Ce modèle NV-44 ne fut réalisé à l'origine qu'en douze exemplaires, et devint le favori de Finn Juhl. Sa forme organique reflète l'exceptionnelle qualité de sa fabrication artisanale et la virtuosité du designer.

Finn Juhl

Chieftain, 1949

Rosewood frame with leather-covered upholstered seat and back | Rahmen aus Palisander, Sitzfläche und Rückenlehne mit Lederpolsterung | Châssis en bois de rose massif, siège et dossier en cuir rembourré

NIELS VODDER,
COPENHAGEN,
FROM 1949
(REISSUED BY NIELS
ROTH ANDERSEN)

Most of the 78 "Chieftain" chairs originally produced by the master crafts-man Niels Vodder were purchased for Danish embassies. A very masculine chair, its title, which alludes to King Frederik, was coined by Juhl at a Furni-ture Guild exhibition which was opened by the monarch. The NV-45 is, per-haps, his most representative design with its graceful curves and crisp lines. *Die meisten der 78 »Chieftain«-Sessel, ursprünglich vom Schreinermeister Niels Vodder produziert, wurden für dänische Botschaften aufgekauft. Der Name des sehr maskulin wirkenden Stuhls spielt auf den dänischen König Frederik IX. an, der die Ausstellung der Möbelinnung eröffnete, auf der der Stuhl präsentiert wurde. Mit dem NV-45 schuf Juhl seinen vielleicht repräsentativsten Entwurf, der durch seine eleganten Schwünge und klare Linienführung überzeugt.*

Finn Juhl

Model No. NV-45,
1945

Mahogany frame
with textile-covered
upholstered seating
section | Rahmen aus
Mahagoni, Sitzfläche
und Rückenlehne
gepolstert und mit
Stoffbezug | Châssis
en bois d'acajou, siège
en tissu rembourré

NIELS VODDER,
COPENHAGEN,
FROM 1945
(REISSUED BY NIELS
ROTH ANDERSEN)

▼ Finn Juhl
Model No. NV-48,
1948

NIELS VODDER,
COPENHAGEN
(REISSUED BY NIELS
ROTH ANDERSEN)

La plupart de ces fauteuils « Chieftain », réalisés à l'origine par le maître-artisan Niels Vodder, furent acquis pour des ambassades danoises. Le nom de ce fauteuil très masculin, qui fait allusion au roi Frédéric IX, fut trouvé par Juhl lors d'une exposition de la Guilde du meuble inaugurée par le monarque. Le modèle NV-45, avec ses courbes gracieuses et ses lignes tendues, est l'œuvre la plus caractéristique du style de ce designer.

Hans J. Wegner

Y chair, Model
No. 24, 1950

Oak frame with
woven paper cord
seat | Rahmen aus
Eiche, Sitzfläche aus
Papierkordelgeflecht |
Châssis en chêne,
siège en corde de
papier tressée

CARL HANSEN &
SØN, ODENSE, FROM
1950 TO PRESENT

Wegner has been described as the "chair-maker of chair-makers" and certainly few other designers have consistently produced such high-quality designs. The "Y" chair, sometimes known as the "Wishbone", is Wegner's most commercially successful design. The timeless quality of the "Round" chair led it to be known by its admirers as the "Classic Chair" or simply, "The Chair".

Wegner ist als »Stuhlhersteller par excellence« bezeichnet worden, und ganz sicher haben nur wenige andere Designer immer wieder Entwürfe von so hoher Qualität geliefert. Der »Y«-Stuhl, manchmal auch als »Wishbone« (Brustbein)-Stuhl bezeichnet, war der Verkaufsschlager unter seinen Entwürfen. Die Zeitlosigkeit des »runden« Stuhls führte dazu, daß seine Bewunderer ihn den »Klassischen Stuhl« oder einfach nur »Den Stuhl« nannten.

Hans J. Wegner

Round chair, Model No. JH 501, 1949

Teak frame with woven cane seat | Gestell aus Teak, Sitzfläche aus Rohrgeflecht | Châssis en teck, siège en jonc tressé

JOHANNES HANSEN, SOEBORG, 1949–1992 (REISSUED BY P.P. MØBLER, ALLERØD, FROM 1992)

▼ CBS bought twelve JH 501 chairs for the famous televised presidential debate between John F. Kennedy and Richard M. Nixon in 1961

Wegner a pu être qualifié de « fabricants de sièges par excellence » tant il est certain que peu de designers ont produit avec une telle constance des modèles d'une aussi grande qualité. Le fauteuil « Y », parfois appelé « Wishbone », est celle de ses créations qui a remporté le plus grand succès commercial. La qualité intemporelle du « Fauteuil rond » l'a fait baptiser par ses admirateurs le « Fauteuil classique », ou plus simplement encore « Le Fauteuil ».

Hans J. Wegner

Chinese, 1943

Solid cherry construction with seat cushion | Rahmen aus Kirschholz, Sitzkissen | Cerisier massif, galette de siège

FRITZ HANSEN, ALLERØD, FROM C. 1943 TO PRESENT

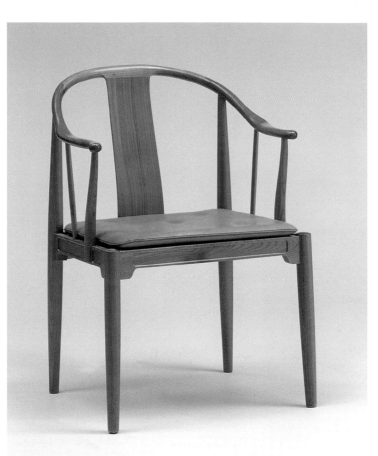

Like Klint, Wegner was influenced by traditional forms. He saw an illustration of an archetypal Chinese chair in Ole Wanscher's *Types of Furniture* (1932) and was inspired by the single-piece back rail which curves round to form the arms.

Wie Klint wurde Wegner von traditionellen Formen beeinflußt. Als er die Abbildung eines archetypischen chinesischen Sessels in Ole Wanschers »Types of Furniture« (1932) fand, ließ er sich zu der aus einem einzigen Stück geformten Rückenlehne inspirieren, die in die Armlehnen ausschwingt.

Comme Klint, Wegner était influencé par les formes traditionnelles. Il avait repéré une illustration d'un fauteuil chinois classique dans l'ouvrage *Types of Furniture* d'Ole Wanscher (1932) et s'en était inspiré pour la pièce de bois qui forme à la fois le haut du dossier et les accoudoirs.

Hans J. Wegner

*Peacock, Model
No. JH 550, 1947*

Ash frame with teak
armrests, woven
paper cord seat |
Rahmen aus Esche,
Sitzfläche aus
Papierkordelgeflecht,
Armlehnen aus Teak |
Châssis en frêne,
accoudoirs en teck,
siège en corde de
papier tressée

JOHANNES HANSEN,
SOEBORG,
C. 1947–1992
(REISSUED BY
P. P. MØBLER,
ALLERØD, FROM
1992)

This design is one of a score of reinterpretations of the traditional "Windsor" chair by Wegner. Its title was derived from the chair's slatted fan-back which brings to mind the tail feathers of a peacock.

Dieser Entwurf gehört zu einer ganzen Reihe von Neuinterpretationen des traditionellen »Windsor«-Stuhls, die Wegner präsentierte. Seinen Namen hat dieser Stuhl wegen der fächerförmig aufgespreizten Sprossen der Rückenlehne, die an das Rad eines Pfaus erinnern.

Ce modèle n'est que l'une des multiples interprétations du fauteuil « Windsor » de Wegner. Son nom s'explique par la forme de son dossier en éventail.

Hans J. Wegner

Model No. PP-512, 1949

Teak frame with woven cane seat and back | Rahmen aus Teak, Sitzfläche und Rückenlehne aus Rohrgeflecht | Châssis en teck, siège et dossier en jonc tressé

JOHANNES HANSEN, SOEBORG, C. 1949–1992 (REISSUED BY P. P. MØBLER, ALLERØD, FROM 1992)

▼ **Hans J. Wegner** Stacking chairs, Model No. FH-4103, 1952

FRITZ HANSEN, ALLERØD

The PP-512 was designed to fold up and be hung on a wall for easy storage. Every element of the chair, from the handles to the indentation on the stretcher, was informed by these functional requirements.

Der PP-512 sollte, damit er leichter zu verstauen war, faltbar und an der Wand aufhängbar sein. Jedes Element des Stuhls – von den Griffen bis zur Ausbuchtung des Spanners – war gemäß dieser funktionalen Anforderung gestaltet.

Le PP-512 a été conçu pour être accroché à un mur, une fois replié. Chaque élément de cette chauffeuse, des poignées jusqu'au découpage du châssis, répondait à cet objectif.

Børge Mogensen

Model No. 1789,
1945

*Beech frame with
upholstered cushions
and leather ties |
Rahmen aus Buche,
gepolsterte Kissen,
Lederriemen | Châssis
en hêtre, coussins
rembourrés, attaches
en cuir*

FRITZ HANSEN,
ALLERØD,
FROM C. 1945
TO PRESENT

▼ Børge Mogensen
Øresund, Model
No. 538, 1955

KARL ANDERSSON
& SÖNER,
HUSKVARNA,
1955–1973

The No. 1789 sofa was one of a number of designs by
Mogensen, who had worked with both Wegner and
Klint, that were successful reinterpretations of tradi-
tional seating types.

*Die Sitzbank Nr. 1789 war eine der vielen erfolgreichen
Neuinterpretationen klassischer Möbelformen, die
Mogensen ersann. Er hatte zuvor mit Wegner und auch mit
Klint zusammengearbeitet.*

Le canapé n° 1789 de Mogensen, qui avait travaillé avec
Wegner et Klint, est l'une de ses nombreuses réinterpré-
tations de sièges traditionnels.

conversation, rest & play

Gondola,Comfortable,Duchesse,Psyche,Kangaroo: are some names of the past for a type of seating that fills a difficult-to-define need of the time.

THE FORM OF THIS CHAIR DOES NOT PRETEND
TO CLEARLY ANTICIPATE THE VARIETY OF NE
IT IS TO FILL. THESE NEEDS ARE AS YET
INDEFINITE AND THE SOLUTION OF THE FORM
IS TO A LARGE DEGREE INTUITIVE. THE FO
CAN ONLY SUGGEST A FREER ADAPTION OF MA
TO NEED AND STIMULATE INQUIRY INTO WHAT
NEEDS MAY BE.

plan & elevation of base 1/8 scale

side elevation 1/8 scale

front elevation 1/4 scale

These shells can be made of low pressure
glass mat laminates with the inner surface
an integral finish in any designated color.

The tooling cost is low, and in production
the cost of the shell would be around.......$15.00
With a base of wood and stainless rod
        at approximately.......$12.00
The factory price of such a chair should be.$27.00

back elevation 1/4 scale

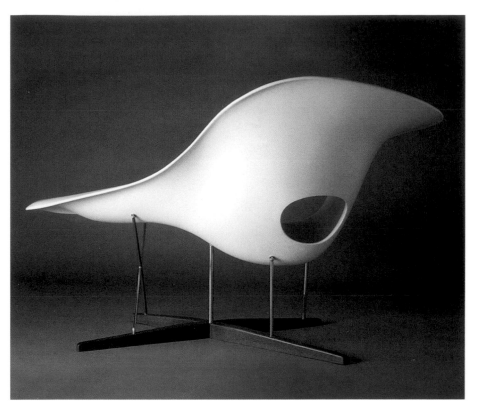

Submitted by the Eameses for the Museum of Modern Art's "International Competition for Low-Cost Furniture Design" in 1948, this highly abstract organic design proved too expensive to manufacture.

Dieser auf das notwendigste reduzierte organische Stuhlentwurf wurde 1948 von den Eames zu dem »International Competition for Low-Cost Furniture Design« des Museum of Modern Art eingereicht. Als »La Chaise« dann in Produktion gehen sollte, erwies sich diese zunächst als zu teuer.

Proposé par les Eames au concours « International Competition for Low-Cost Furniture Design », organisé par le Museum of Modern Art en 1948, ce modèle organique abstrait se révéla trop coûteux à fabriquer.

Charles & Ray Eames

La Chaise, 1948

Fibreglass seat shell on a wood and steel rod base | Sitzschale aus Fiberglas, Untergestell aus Stahlstäben auf Holzsockel | Coquille de siège en fibre de verre, piètement en acier et en bois

VITRA, BASLE, FROM 1990 TO PRESENT

◀ **Charles & Ray Eames**
Proposal panel submitted for the Museum of Modern Art's "International Competition for Low-Cost Furniture Design", 1948

Charles & Ray Eames

RAR (Rocking Armchair Rod), 1948–1950

Moulded fibreglass-reinforced polyester seat shell connected to a metal rod and birch sled base with rubber shock mounts | Sitzschale aus geformtem, fiberglasverstärktem Polyester, Untergestell aus Stahlstäben auf Kufen aus Birke, Gummipuffer | Coquille en polyester moulé renforcé de fibre de verre, piètement en tiges de métal et patins en bouleau, montage sur amortisseurs en caoutchouc

ZENITH PLASTICS, GARDENA, CALIFORNIA, 1950 – C. 1953 AND HERMAN MILLER FURNITURE CO., ZEELAND, MICHIGAN, C. 1953– C. 1972

◄ Page from Herman Miller catalogue, 1952

► Charles & Ray Eames Stacking chairs, 1955

HERMAN MILLER FURNITURE CO., ZEELAND, MICHIGAN, FROM 1955 TO PRESENT

◄ Charles & Ray Eames
LAR-1 (Lounge Armchair Rod) with "cat's cradle" base, c. 1953

HERMAN MILLER FURNITURE CO., ZEELAND, MICHIGAN, C. 1953–C. 1972

Charles & Ray Eames

DAR (Dining Armchair Rod), 1948–1950

Moulded fibreglass-reinforced polyester seat shell connected to an "Eiffel Tower" metal rod base with rubber shock mounts | Sitzschale aus geformtem, fiberglasverstärktem Polyester, Untergestell »Eiffel Turm« aus Stahlstäben, Gummipuffer | Coquille en poly-ester moulé renforcé de fibre de verre, piètement en tiges de métal « Tour Eiffel », montage sur amortisseurs en caoutchouc

ZENITH PLASTICS, GARDENA, CALIFOR-NIA, 1950–C. 1953 AND HERMAN MILLER FURNITURE CO., ZEELAND, MICHIGAN C. 1953–C. 1972

The culmination of earlier experiments in moulded plywood, the revolutionary Plastic Shell Group of chairs was amongst the very first unlined plastic seat furniture to be truly mass-produced.

Der Höhepunkt früherer Experimente mit geformtem Schichtholz waren die Schalensitze der revolutionären »Plastic Shell Group«, die zu den allerersten ungepolsterten Sitzmöbeln gehörten, die tatsächlich in Serienproduktion gingen.

Aboutissement d'expériences antérieures dans le moulage du contre-plaqué, cette série révolutionnaire de fauteuils à coque plastique figure parmi les premiers sièges en plastique non armé réellement fabriqués en série.

H. V. Thaden

Chair, 1947

Birch-faced moulded plywood construction with metal rivets and solid wood feet elements | Geformtes Schichtholz mit Birkenfurnier, Steckverbindungen aus Metall, Fußleisten aus Massivholz | Contreplaqué moulé, placage de bouleau, rivets métalliques, pieds en bois massif

THADEN JORDAN FURNITURE CORPORATION, ROANOKE, VIRGINIA, FROM C. 1947

▼ **Isaac Cole**
Patent model for moulded plywood chair, 1873

This chair bears a striking resemblance to a design registered by Isaac Cole in 1873. An innovative system of pins allowed the height of the single-piece plywood seat and back to be adjusted.

Dieser Stuhl hat starke Ähnlichkeit mit einem Stuhlentwurf, den sich Isaac Cole 1873 patentieren ließ. Durch das innovative Stecksystem konnten die aus einem Stück Schichtholz gefertigte Sitzfläche und Rückenlehne höhenverstellt werden.

Cette chauffeuse ressemble étonnamment à un modèle déposé par Isaac Cole en 1873. Un nouveau système d'agrafes permettait de régler la hauteur du siège et du dossier, fabriqués en un seul morceau de contre-plaqué.

Han Pieck

Armchair, 1946–1947

Teak-faced moulded single-form plywood construction with brass stabilising fixtures | Aus einem Stück geformtes Schichtholz, mit Teakfurnier, stabilisierende Messingbeschläge | Contreplaqué moulé d'une pièce, placage de teck, stabilisateurs en laiton

LAWO,
NETHERLANDS,
FROM C. 1948

▼ **Gerrit Rietveld**
Danish chair, 1950

This single-form moulded plywood chair, unlike Summer's earlier lounge chair, had a resilient back which was achieved by the addition of a brass stabilising bar. It could also be stacked in sets of three.
Dieser aus einem Stück geformte Schichtholzstuhl hat, anders als Summers frühere Entwürfe, eine elastische Rückenlehne, was durch eine Messingstrebe ermöglicht wird. Drei dieser Sessel lassen sich übereinander stapeln.
À la différence du précédent fauteuil de Summer, cette chaise en contre-plaqué moulé d'une pièce possède un dossier souple grâce à l'ajout d'une barre stabilisatrice en métal. Ce siège était également empilable par trois.

Donald Knorr

Model No. 132U,
c. 1949

Bent zinc-plated steel
seating section on
painted tubular steel
legs | Sitzfläche aus
geformtem Stahl-
blech, verzinkt, Stuhl-
beine aus Stahlrohr,
lackiert | Section de
siège en acier zingué,
piètement en tube
d'acier peint

KNOLL ASSOCIATES,
NEW YORK,
C. 1950–1952

▼ Donald Knorr
Prototype chairs
submitted to the
"International
Competition for
Low-Cost Furniture
Design", Museum of
Modern Art

The innovative model No. 132U shared first prize at the
"International Competition for Low-Cost Furniture
Design" in New York. The prototype seat shells were
made from sheets of thermoset plastic.

Das innovative Modell Nr. 132U war einer der mit dem
ersten Preis des »International Competition for Low-Cost
Furniture Design« in New York ausgezeichneten Entwürfe.
Die Sitzschalen der Prototypen sind noch aus wärmegehär-
tetem Kunststoff hergestellt worden.

Ce modèle très novateur n° 132U remporta le premier
prix ex-aequo du « International Competition for Low-Cost
Furniture Design». Les coquilles du prototype étaient en
plastique thermoformé.

Ray Komai

Model No. 939, 1949

Walnut-faced
moulded single-form
plywood seat
attached to a nickel-
plated bent tubular
steel frame | Sitz-
schale aus einem
Stück geformtem
Schichtholz, Walnuß-
furnier, Untergestell
aus gebogenem Stahl-
rohr, vernickelt | Siège
en contre-plaqué
moulé d'une pièce,
placage de noyer,
piètement en tube
d'acier cintré nickelé

J. G. FURNITURE
SYSTEMS,
QUAKERTOWN,
PENNSYLVANIA,
1950–1955 &
1987–1988

The walnut veneer used to face the No. 939's compound-moulded plywood seat shell and the nickel-
plated connecting brace provide this chair with a sense
of luxury that belies the utility of its design.
*Das Walnußfurnier der Sitzschale aus geformtem Schicht-
holz sowie deren vernickelte Verbindungsspange verleihen
dem Modell Nr. 939 einen Hauch von Luxus, der im Gegensatz zu seiner strengen Funktionalität steht.*
Le placage de noyer de ce modèle n° 939 en contre-plaqué moulé et l'agrafe nickelée donnent à ce siège un caractère luxueux qui fait oublier son aspect utilitaire.

Carlo Mollino

**Armchair for the
Minola House, 1944**

*Ebonised wood frame
with velvet-covered
upholstery | Rahmen
aus Holz, schwarz
gebeizt, Polsterung
mit Samtbezug |
Châssis en bois noirci,
velours rembourré*

PROBABLY APELLI
& VARESIO, TURIN,
1944

▼ **Carlo Mollino**
Living room of the
Minola House,
Turin, 1944

This chair and the other furnishings designed for the
Minola House in Turin were produced at the height of
the war. Skilled craftsmanship compensated for the
dearth of quality materials.
*Dieser Sessel und andere Möbel, speziell für die Casa
Minola in Turin entworfen, wurden im 2. Weltkrieg produziert. Erfahrene Handwerker glichen den Mangel an
hochwertigen Materialien aus.*
Ce fauteuil, ainsi que d'autres meubles conçus pour la
maison Minola à Turin, furent fabriqués en pleine
guerre. L'habileté du travail artisanal compensait la
pénurie des matériaux de qualité.

Carlo Mollino

Chair designed for Lisa & Gio Ponti, 1940

Polished brass frame with Resin-flex-upholstered seat and back | Rahmen aus poliertem Messing, Sitzfläche und Rückenlehne gepolstert, mit Resinflexbezug, gepolsterte Sitze | Châssis en laiton poli, siège et dossier rembourrés en Resin-flex

PROBABLY APELLI & VARESIO, TURIN, 1940

▼ Carlo Mollino
Chair design for Lisa & Gio Ponti, 1940

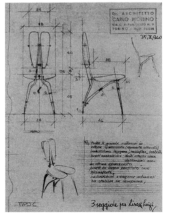

This chair was designed for Lisa and Gio Ponti. Its bifurcated form is clearly based on a cloven hoof and reflects Mollino's life-long interest in the occult.

Dieser Stuhl wurde für Lisa und Gio Ponti entworfen. Seine zweigeteilte Form ist eindeutig von einem gespaltenen Huf abgeleitet – und belegt Mollinos lebenslanges Interesse am Okkulten.

Cette chaise fut dessinée pour Lisa et Gio Ponti. Sa forme bifide s'inspire nettement d'un sabot fourchu, et rappelle l'intérêt prononcé de Molino pour l'occultisme.

Marco Zanuso

Antropus, 1949

Moulded plywood frame fully upholstered in fabric-covered latex foam | Rahmen aus geformtem Schichtholz, Latexschaumstoffpolsterung mit Stoffbezug | Châssis en contre-plaqué moulé entièrement rembourré en mousse de latex tendue de tissu

ARFLEX, MILAN, GIUSSANO, FROM 1950 TO PRESENT

▼ **Marco Zanuso**
Maggiolina, 1947

ZANOTTA, MILAN

The "Antropus" was the first chair manufactured by Arflex, a division of the Pirelli Company which had commissioned Zanuso in 1948 to investigate the potential of latex foam as an upholstering material.

»Antropus« war der erste Stuhl, der von Arflex, einem Unternehmenszweig von Pirelli, hergestellt wurde. 1948 war Zanuso beauftragt worden, die Möglichkeiten von Latexschaumstoff als Polstermaterial zu erproben.

« Antropus » est le premier siège fabriqué par Arflex, un département de la société Pirelli qui avait chargé Zanuso, en 1948, d'étudier les possibilités d'utilisation de la mousse de latex dans le rembourrage des fauteuils.

226

Finn Juhl

Pelican, 1940

*Fully upholstered
seating section with
maple legs |
Sitzschale gepolstert,
Beine aus Ahorn |
Siège entièrement
rembourré, pieds en
érable*

NIELS VODDER,
COPENHAGEN, 1940

Juhl's admiration of the sculptor, Jean Arp, is revealed in the expressive organic form of this design. Very different from his other models, the "Pelican" is remarkable for its date.

Die Bewunderung Juhls für den Bildhauer Hans Arp läßt sich an der extrem organischen Formgebung dieses Stuhls ablesen. Der »Pelican«-Sessel hat keinerlei Ähnlichkeit mit Juhls anderen Entwürfen, aber aufgrund der frühen Verwendung organischer Formen ist er erwähnenswert.

L'admiration de Juhl pour le sculpteur Jean Arp se révèle dans cette forme organique expressive. Très différent des autres créations du designer, le fauteuil « Pelican » est remarquablement précoce pour l'époque.

Eero Saarinen

Grasshopper, Model No. 61, 1946–1947

Bent laminated wood frame with fully upholstered moulded plywood seat shell | Rahmen aus geformtem Schichtholz, Sitzschale aus geformtem Sperrholz, gepolstert | Châssis en contreplaqué cintré, coquille de siège en contreplaqué moulé rembourré

KNOLL ASSOCIATES, NEW YORK, FROM C. 1948

▼ **Eero Saarinen**
Grasshopper chair with ottoman, 1946–1947

KNOLL ASSOCIATES, NEW YORK, C. 1948

The "Grasshopper" armchair was Saarinen's first design to be introduced by Knoll. According to Florence Knoll, "It was a perfectly nice chair but it wasn't one of the great successes".

Der »Grasshopper«-Sessel war der erste Saarinen-Entwurf, den Knoll auf dem Markt brachte. Florence Knoll zufolge »ein äußerst hübscher Stuhl, aber kein großer Erfolg«.

Le fauteuil « Grasshopper » est le premier modèle de Saarinen présenté par Knoll. Selon Florence Knoll, « C'était un siège tout à fait réussi mais qui ne connut pas un grand succès. »

Eero Saarinen

Womb chair, Model No. 70, 1947–1948

Bent tubular steel frame with fabric-covered upholstered moulded fibreglass seat shell and latex foam cushions, nylon glides | Rahmen aus glasfaserverstärktem Polyester, Latex-schaumstoffpolste-rung mit Stoffbezug, Gleitfüße aus Nylon | Châssis en tube d'acier cintré, coquille de siège en fibre de verre moulée et tissu rembourré, coussins en mousse de latex, patins en nylon

KNOLL ASSOCIATES,
NEW YORK,
1948–1993

▼ Eero Saarinen
The Womb collection, 1947–1948

KNOLL ASSOCIATES,
NEW YORK,
1948–1993

The No. 70 incorporated a moulded fibreglass seat shell. With its generous proportions and organic form, it invited the user to curl up in it. Because of this it eventually became known as the "Womb" chair.

Die Sitzschale des Nr. 70 besteht aus glasfaserverstärktem Polyester. Großzügig bemessen und organisch in der Form lädt der Sessel zum Zusammenrollen ein. Er wurde darum auch »Womb chair« (Mutterschoß) genannt.

Ce n° 70 faisait appel à une coquille de siège en fibre de verre moulée. De proportions généreuses, il incitait à se blottir dans sa forme organique. C'est une des raisons pour lesquelles il fut appelé le « Womb chair » (la matrice).

Isamu Noguchi

**Model No. IN22,
1949**

*Painted birch seat
and parabolic leg with
chromed tubular
metal legs | Sitzfläche
und hinteres Hocker-
bein aus Birke,
lackiert, vordere
Hockerbeine aus
Stahlrohr | Siège
et pied profilé en
bouleau peint, pieds
en tube de métal
chromé*

HERMAN MILLER
FURNITURE CO.,
ZEELAND,
MICHIGAN, FROM
1949

◄ Herman Miller ad-
vertising photograph
showing Isamu
Noguchi's parabolic
leg dining table with
matching stools,
1949

Through his work as a sculptor and designer, Noguchi considered himself "an interpreter of the East to the West". Informed by nature, his highly abstract and sculptural furniture designs were often intended to express the essence of natural landscape.

Der Designer und Bildhauer Noguchi betrachtete sich als »Dolmetscher des Ostens für den Westen«. Von der Natur inspiriert, sollten seine sehr reduzierten und skulpturalen Möbelentwürfe das Wesen natürlicher Landschaften widerspiegeln.

Par son œuvre de sculpteur et de designer, Noguchi se considérait comme « un interprète de l'Orient en Occident ». Inspirés de l'observation de la nature, ses modèles de meubles abstraits et sculpturaux se proposaient souvent d'exprimer l'essence d'un paysage.

Isamu Noguchi

Sofa, Model No. IN 70 & ottoman, Model No. IN 71, 1946

Fabric-covered upholstered seat and back section on tapering birch legs | Sitzfläche und Rückenlehne gepolstert und mit Stoffbezug, Füße aus Birke | Siège et dossier rembourrés, recouverts de tissu, pieds fuselés en bouleau

HERMAN MILLER FURNITURE CO., ZEELAND, MICHIGAN, FROM 1946

Davis Pratt

Airchair, 1948

Steel rod frame with
inflatable rubber tube
and cotton covering |
Rahmen aus gebogenen Stahlstäben,
aufblasbarer
Gummischlauch,
Baumwollbezug |
Châssis en tiges
d'acier, chambre à air
en caoutchouc
recouverte de tissu en
coton

One of the first examples of inflatable furniture, the "Airchair" did not
have an underlying radical design agenda like many of its successors. It was
an entry to the MoMA's "International Competition for Low-Cost Furniture
Design".

Dem »Airchair«, einem der ersten Beispiele für aufblasbare Möbel, lag kein radikales Designprogramm zugrunde, wie dies bei vielen seiner Nachfolger der Fall
war. Dieser Stuhl wurde zum »International Competition for Low-Cost
Furniture Design« eingereicht, den das MoMA ausgeschrieben hatte.

Un des premiers exemples de mobilier gonflable, cet « Airchair » n'était cependant pas d'un design aussi radical que la plupart de ses successeurs. Il
participa au « International Competition for Low-Cost Furniture Design ».

▶ Structural components of the Airchair

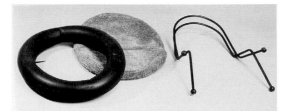

Eva Zeisel

Chair, 1948–1949

*Chromed tubular
steel frame with
cotton cover | Rah-
men aus gebogenem
Stahlrohr, verchromt,
Baumwollbespan-
nung | Châssis en
tube d'acier chromé
recouvert de coton*

HUDSON FIXTURES,
NEW YORK, FROM
C. 1949

▼ Tubular steel
frame of the Eva
Zeisel chair

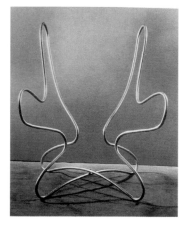

This easily collapsible chair was designed for both indoor domestic use and for outdoor use such as picnic-
king or camping. The frame is essentially a large spring
which provides a great deal of flexibility and comfort.
*Dieser Stuhl, der sich leicht auseinandernehmen läßt,
wurde zur Benutzung sowohl im Haus wie im Freien, z. B.
bei Picknicks oder beim Zelten, entworfen. Der Rahmen ist
wie eine große Feder aufgebaut, die für hohe Elastizität und
entsprechenden Sitzkomfort sorgt.*
Cette chaise facilement démontable fut conçue aussi
bien pour la maison que pour le camping. Son châssis
consiste essentiellement en un gros ressort qui offre
beaucoup de souplesse et de confort.

Edward J. Wormley

Listen to Me, 1947

White maple, cherry, brass and copper frame with wool-covered upholstery | Rahmen aus Ahorn, Kirschbaum, Messing und Kupfer, Liegefläche gepolstert und mit Wollstoff-bezug | Châssis en érable blanc, cerisier, cuivre et laiton, rembourrage recouvert de tissu de laine

DUNBAR FURNITURE CORPORATION OF INDIANA, BERNE, INDIANA, FROM C. 1947

Wormley translated the latest design trends into a more acceptable mainstream style for the American luxury market. His refined and beautifully executed furniture was influenced by Scandinavian and Italian design.

Wormley übersetzte avantgardistische Designtrends in einen Stil, der vom Publikumsgeschmack des amerikanischen Luxusmarkts leichter akzeptiert wurde. Für seine raffinierten und wunderschön ausgeführten Möbelstücke ließ er sich vom skandinavischen und italienischen Design inspirieren.

Wormley adapta les nouvelles tendances du design à un style plus facilement acceptable par le marché haut de gamme américain. Ses meubles raffinés et superbement réalisés étaient influencés par le design italien et scandinave.

◄ Edward J. Wormley
Riemerschmid chair, Model No. 4797, c. 1946

DUNBAR FURNITURE CORPORATION OF INDIANA, BERNE, INDIANA, 1947–1981

Terence Harold
Robsjohn-
Gibbings

Armchair, c. 1950

Solid beech frame
with upholstered seat
and back cushions |
Rahmen aus Buche,
Sitz- und Rücken-
kissen gepolstert |
Châssis en hêtre
massif, coussins de
siège et de dossier

WIDDICOMB
FURNITURE CO.,
GRAND RAPIDS,
MICHIGAN, FROM
C. 1950

Robsjohn-Gibbings' conservative and well-crafted chairs epitomise the style
of furniture produced by numerous Grand Rapids manufacturers during the
post-war period.

*Robsjohn-Gibbings entwarf konservative und solide gebaute Stühle, die genau
den Stil repräsentieren, in dem die zahlreichen Hersteller aus Grand Rapids in
der Nachkriegszeit ihre Möbel produzierten.*

Les fauteuils classiques et bien exécutés de Robsjohn-Gibbings incarnent un
style adopté par de nombreux fabricants de Grand Rapids pendant l'après-
guerre.

Robin Day

Hillestak, 1950

Beech frame with walnut-faced moulded plywood seat and back | Rahmen aus Buche, Sitzfläche und Rückenlehne aus geformtem Schichtholz mit Walnußfurnier | Châssis en hêtre, siège et dossier en contre-plaqué moulé, placage de noyer

HILLE INTER-
NATIONAL & CO.,
LONDON,
FROM 1950

▼ **Robin Day**
Armchair designed
for the Royal Festival
Hall, London, 1951

HILLE INTER-
NATIONAL & CO.,
LONDON

Without the technology for compound moulding, Day was limited to bending plywood in one direction only. The "Hillestak" chair was intended to bring high-quality, low-cost Modern design to the British public.

Day verfügte nicht über die Technik, mit der sich Schichtholz in unterschiedliche Richtungen formen ließ, und mußte sich damit begnügen, seine Schichtholzplatten in nur eine Richtung zu biegen. Der »Hillestak«-Stuhl sollte modernes Design von hoher Qualität preiswert auf den britischen Markt bringen.

Avant l'apparition de la nouvelle technologie du moulage, Day ne pouvait cintrer le contre-plaqué que dans un sens seulement. Le modèle « Hillestak » répondait à une volonté d'introduire des créations économiques et de haute qualité sur le marché public britannique.

The "Neptune" chair was commissioned by the shipping company, P & O. Because these deck chairs had to withstand extremes of temperature and the effects of salt water, the plywood was bonded with a waterproof adhesive. The face veneer was later changed to a harder wearing gaboon mahogany.

Der »Neptune«-Stuhl wurde von der Schiffahrtsgesellschaft P & O in Auftrag gegeben. Weil diese Liegestühle extremen Temperaturen und dem Salzwasser standhalten mußten, wurde das Schichtholz mit wasserfestem Klebstoff verleimt. Später wurde Gabun-Mahagoni als Furnier verwendet, weil dieses Holz weniger rasch verwittert.

Le modèle « Neptune » avait été commandé par la Compagnie de navigation P & O. Ces chaises longues devant résister à de fortes différences de température et à l'eau de mer, le contre-plaqué était collé avec un produit adhésif résistant à l'eau. Le placage de surface fut ultérieurement abandonné au profit d'un acajou du Gabon plus dur.

Ernest Race

Neptune, 1953

Folding, laminated beech frame with padded covering | Klappbarer Rahmen aus laminierter Buche, gefütterter Bezug | Châssis en hêtre laminé, rembourrage matelassé

ERNEST RACE,
LONDON,
1953– c. 1960

Poul Kjaerholm

Model No. PK25,
1951

Chromed flat steel frame with flag halyard seat and back | Rahmen aus geschnittenem Flachstahl, verchromt, Sitzfläche und Rückenlehne mit Seilbespannung | Châssis en acier plat chromé, siège et dossier en corde

FRITZ HANSEN,
ALLERØD, FROM
C. 1955 TO PRESENT

The flag halyard wound around the frame of the PK25 for seat and back support gives the design remarkable optical qualities akin to Op sculpture. With its two-piece moulded plywood construction, Kjaerholm's PK0 also has a powerful sculptural form.

Sitzfläche und Rückenlehne des PK25 bestehen aus Seil, das um das Gestell gewickelt und gespannt wurde. Dies gibt dem Stuhlentwurf das optische Erscheinen einer Op Art-Skulptur. Auch Kjaerholms PK0 mit seiner zweiteiligen Konstruktion aus geformtem Schichtholz hat eine expressiv plastische Qualität.

La corde tendue sur le cadre métallique du PK25 pour constituer le siège et le dossier confère à cette chauffeuse de remarquables qualités optiques qui évoquent une sculpture Op art. Construit en deux parties de contre-plaqué moulé, le PK0 de Kjaerholm présente une forme nettement sculpturale.

Poul Kjaerholm

Chair, Model No. PK0, 1952

Lacquered moulded plywood construction | Aus formgebogenem und lackiertem Schichtholz | Contreplaqué moulé laqué.

FRITZ HANSEN, ALLERØD, DENMARK, FROM 1997 TO PRESENT

Hans J. Wegner

**Valet, Model
No. PP 250, 1953**

*Solid pine frame with
solid teak seat and
brass fittings |
Rahmen aus Kiefer,
Sitzfläche aus Teak,
Messingbeschläge |
Châssis en pin massif,
siège en teck massif,
garnitures en laiton*

JOHANNES HANSEN,
COPENHAGEN,
1953–1992
(REISSUED BY
P. P. MØBLER,
ALLERØD, FROM
1992 TO PRESENT)

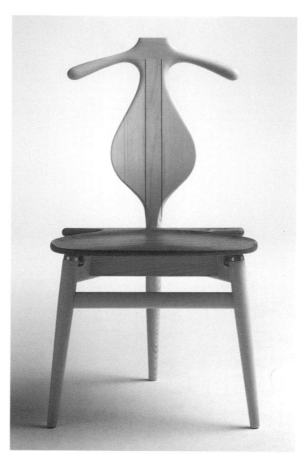

Through its novel form, this design directly addresses
one of the age-old functions of the chair. The seat can
be lifted to provide a rail to hang trousers over and underneath it there is a small storage space.

*In neuer Form geht dieser Entwurf auf eine alte Funktion
des Stuhls ein. Den Sitz kann man nach vorne klappen, um
eine Hose über die dafür vorgesehene Schiene zu hängen;
unter der Sitzplatte befindet sich ein kleiner Stauraum.*

Par sa forme radicalement nouvelle, ce modèle donne
une interprétation intéressante d'une très ancienne
fonction de la chaise. Le siège se soulève pour permettre d'accrocher des pantalons et dégage en dessous
un petit volume de rangement.

Hans J. Wegner

Cowhorn, Model No. PP 505, 1952

Solid mahogany frame with woven cane seat | Rahmen aus Mahagoni, Sitzfläche aus Rohrgeflecht | Châssis en acajou massif, siège en jonc tressé

JOHANNES HANSEN, COPENHAGEN, 1952–1992 (REISSUED BY P. P. MØBLER, ALLERØD, FROM 1992)

▼ Finn Juhl
Model No. 96, 1957

SØREN WILLADSENS MOBELFABRIK, COPENHAGEN, 1957

The "Cowhorn" chair is one of Wegner's most abstract and organic designs. The swelling and tapering form of its backrail is reminiscent of Juhl's work. Wegner designed a very similar chair in 1961, the "Bull chair".

Der »Cowhorn«-Stuhl ist einer der reduziertesten und zugleich organischsten Entwürfe Wegners. Die anschwellende und sich verjüngende Form der Rückenlehne erinnert an Juhls Kreationen. 1961 hat Wegner einen Stuhl geschaffen, der dem »Cowhorn« sehr ähnlich ist: den »Bull«-Stuhl.

Le siège « Cowhorn » est l'un des projets les plus abstraits et les plus organiques de Wegner. Le renflement et le mouvement du dosseret rappellent Juhl. Wegner dessina un siège très similaire en 1961, le « Bull chair ».

Jean Prouvé

Antony, 1950

Painted bent tubular and flat steel frame with moulded plywood seat section | Rahmen aus gebogenem Stahlrohr und Flachstahl, lackiert, Sitzfläche aus geformtem Schichtholz | Châssis en acier plat et tubes d'acier cintrés, siège en contre-plaqué moulé

LES ATELIERS JEAN PROUVÉ, MAXÉVILLE, 1950–1954

▼ Detail of Antony chair

Designed for the University of Strasbourg, the "Antony" chair displays Prouvé's love of industrial roughness or "Art Brut". No attempt is made to hide the frame's welded joins or unfinished surface.

Der »Antony«-Stuhl, ein Entwurf für die Universität von Straßburg, zeigt Prouvés Vorliebe für das Industriell-Grobe, für »Art Brut«. Er unternimmt keinen Versuch, die Schweißnähte oder die unbehandelte Oberfläche zu verbergen.

Conçu pour l'université de Strasbourg, le siège « Antony » illustre le goût de Prouvé pour la rudesse industrielle de l'Art brut. Les soudures de la structure ou les surfaces laissées sans finition particulière ne sont pas dissimulées.

Peter Hvidt & Orla Mølgaard-Nielsen

AX, Model No. 6020, 1950

Teak-faced laminated wood frame with beech-faced moulded plywood seat and back | Rahmen aus Teakholz, Sitzfläche, Armlehnen und Rückenlehne aus formgebogenem Schichtholz mit Birkenfurnier | Châssis en contre-plaqué, placage de teck, siège et dossier en contre-plaqué moulé, placage de hêtre

FRITZ HANSEN, ALLERØD, FROM 1950

▼ Peter Hvidt & Orla Mølgaard-Nielsen AX with reversible leather seat, 1950

FRITZ HANSEN, ALLERØD, 1950

Mølgaard-Nielsen introduced plywood to the Danish furniture industry. Although influenced by the Eameses, the knockdown "AX" was largely the result of Fritz Hansen's ground-breaking lamella-gluing process.

Mølgaard-Nielsen führte das Schichtholz in die dänische Möbelindustrie ein. Der »AX« ist von den Entwürfen der Eames beeinflußt, doch war das zerlegbare Modell weitgehend das Ergebnis von Fritz Hansens bahnbrechendem »Lamellenklebeverfahren«.

Mølgaard introduisit l'usage du contre-plaqué dans l'industrie danoise du meuble. Influencé par les Eames, le « AX » démontable faisait toutefois surtout appel au procédé révolutionnaire de collage de Fritz Hansen.

Friso Kramer

Chair, 1954

Painted metal frame with moulded plywood seat and back | Rahmen aus Metall, lackiert, Sitzfläche und Rückenlehne aus formgebogenem Schichtholz | Châssis en métal peint, siège et dossier en contre-plaqué moulé

DE CIRKEL, ZWANENBURG, FROM C. 1954

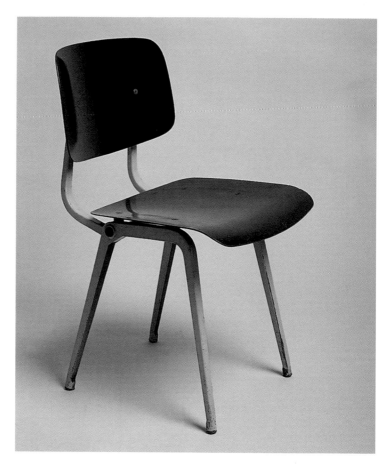

Kramer designed a series of moulded plywood chairs for the Dutch manufacturer, De Cirkel. This chair, with its shallow compound curved seat, reveals the international influence of the Eameses' earlier plywood chairs. *Kramer entwarf eine Reihe von Stühlen aus formgebogenem Schichtholz für den holländischen Hersteller De Cirkel. Dieser Stuhl mit seiner flachen, mehrfach geformten Sitzschale zeigt den internationalen Einfluß der früheren Schichtholzstühle von Charles und Ray Eames.* Kramer dessina une série de sièges en contre-plaqué moulé pour le fabricant néerlandais De Cirkel. Cette chaise au siège en creux révèle l'influence internationale des Eames sur les premiers sièges en contre-plaqué.

Egon Eiermann

Model No. SE18,
1952

Beech frame with
beech-faced moulded
plywood seat and
back with metal
fittings | Rahmen aus
Buche, Sitzfläche und
Rückenlehne aus
formgebogenem
Schichtholz, mit
Birkenfurnier, Metall-
beschläge | Châssis en
hêtre, siège et dossier
en contre-plaqué
moulé, placage de
hêtre, garnitures en
métal

WILDE & SPIETH,
ESSLINGEN, FROM
C. 1952

▼ Egon Eiermann
Model No. SE42,
1949

WILDE & SPIETH,
ESSLINGEN,
1950–1955

Known primarily as an architect, Eiermann was also a
skilled furniture designer. The SE18 is an inexpensive
and highly functional folding design which was exhibited at the Milan X Triennale in 1954.
*Eiermann hat sich vor allem als Architekt einen Namen ge-
macht, doch er war ein ebenso erfahrener Möbeldesigner.
Der SE18 ist ein preiswerter und sehr funktionaler Klappstuhl, der 1954 auf der X. Mailänder Triennale gezeigt wurde.*
Essentiellement connu pour ses réalisations en architecture, Eiermann était également un bon designer de mobilier. Le SE18 est un modèle pliant bon marché et très
fonctionnel qui fut exposé à la Xᵉ Triennale de Milan en
1954.

Frank Lloyd Wright

Chairs for the Donald Lovness House, Stillwater, c. 1956

Solid oak construction with seat and back cushions attached with tassels | Rahmen aus Eiche geschnitzt, Sitz- und Rückenkissen mit Schnüren am Rahmen befestigt | Chêne massif, coussins de siège et de dossier avec glands

These extraordinary chairs echo the architectural detailing of the Donald Lovness House in Stillwater, Minnesota. Their deeply carved surfaces and vibrant textile coverings, which were made by Virginia Lovness, allude to Native American art.

Diese außergewöhnlichen Stühle spiegeln die architektonischen Details von Donald Lovness' Haus in Stillwater, Minnesota, wider. Die stark profilierten Oberflächen und farbintensiven Stoffbezüge nach einem Entwurf von Virginia Lovness sind Anspielungen auf die Kunst der Ureinwohner Amerikas.

Ces extraordinaires fauteuils rappellent l'intérieur de la Résidence Donald Lovness à Stillwater, Minnesota. Leurs surfaces aux sculptures profondes et aux textiles de couleurs vibrantes, tissés par Virginia Lovness, évoque l'art des Indiens d'Amérique.

The Smithsons were part of the "Independent Group" which rejected Modernism and drew inspiration from popular culture. The "Trundling Turk", originally in primary colours, was a proto-Pop design with its low seat position and foam block construction.

Die Smithsons gehörten zur »Independent Group«, die die klassische Moderne ablehnte und sich stattdessen von der Volkskunst inspirieren ließ. Der »Trundling Turk«-Sessel war ursprünglich in Primärfarben gehalten. Aufgrund seiner tiefen Sitzposition und der aus Schaumstoff bestehenden Polsterung nimmt dieser Entwurf bereits Formen der 6oer Jahre vorweg.

Les Smithson appartenaient à l'« Independent Group » qui rejetait le modernisme et tirait son inspiration de la culture populaire. Ce modèle « Trundling Turk » au siège bas et aux coussins en blocs de mousse était à l'origine recouvert de tissus aux couleurs primaires et annonçait le Pop design.

Alison & Peter Smithson

Trundling Turk, Model No. NF 3400, 1954

Chromed metal frame with upholstered cushions on castors | Gestell aus verchromtem Metall auf Rollen, gepolsterte Kissen | Châssis en métal chromé, coussins, roulettes

TECTA, LAUENFÖRDE, FROM 1976 TO PRESENT (REDESIGNED IN 1994)

Hans J. Wegner

Flag Halyard, Model No. GE-225, 1950

Painted and chromed tubular steel pipe frame wound with flag halyard | Rahmen aus Stahlrohr, verchromt und lackiert, Seilbespannung | Châssis en tube d'acier chromé, siège et dossier en tressage de corde

GETAMA, GEDSTED, FROM C. 1950 TO PRESENT

▼ Flag Halyard chair with optional sheep-skin cover and cushions

With its flag halyard woven seat section and its long-haired sheep-skin covering, the "Flag Halyard" chair is unlike most other Wegner designs in that it has no historical precedent.

Mit seiner Seilbespannung und Auflage aus Schaffell ist der »Flag Halyard«-Stuhl anders als alle anderen Wegner-Entwürfe, die sich immer auf irgendein historisches Vorbild beziehen.

Avec son siège en cordage ou son revêtement en laine de brebis à poils longs, le modèle « Flag Halyard » est très différent de toutes les autres créations de Wegner car il ne possède pas de précédent historique.

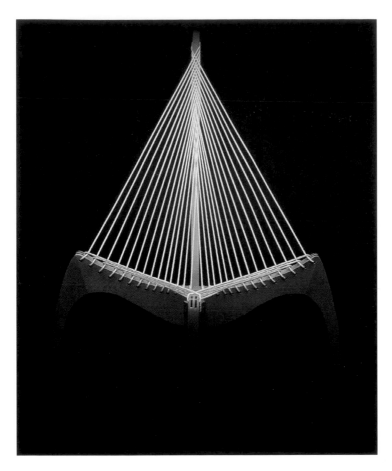

Jørgen
Høvelskov

Harp, 1968

*Solid ash frame with
flag line | Rahmen
aus Esche, Sitzfläche
und Rückenlehne aus
Seilbespannung |
Châssis en frêne
massif, cordage*

CHRISTENSEN &
LARSEN
MØBELHADVAERK,
COPENHAGEN, FROM
C. 1968

▼ French designer
Hoffer: Plan-O-
Spider chairs, c. 1958

PLAN, FRANCE

The "Harp" chair's form was based on a Viking ship's
bow section. The configuration of the flag halyard gives
the design a powerful optical quality – an effect shared
by the "Spider" chair with its elastic web.
*Die Form des »Harp«-Stuhls basiert auf dem Bug eines
Wikingerschiffs. Die Anordnung der Seilbespannung gibt
dem Entwurf eine starke optische Wirkung, wie sie auch der
»Spider«-Stuhl mit seinem elastischen Netz zeigt.*
La forme de ce fauteuil « Harp » s'inspire de la proue
des drakkars vikings. La corde crée un puissant effet op-
tique que l'on retrouve dans la chaise « Spider » avec sa
toile élastique.

Erwine & Estelle Laverne

Champagne, 1957

Moulded perspex seat shell on aluminium base with loose fabric-covered foam-filled cushion | Sitzschale aus formgebogenem Plexiglas, Untergestell aus Aluminium, lose Sitzkissen mit Schaumstoffüllung und mit Stoff bezogen | Coquille en Perspex moulé, piètement en aluminium, coussin amovible en tissu rembourré de mousse

LAVERNE
INTERNATIONAL,
NEW YORK,
1957–C. 1972

▼ **Erwine & Estelle Laverne**
Daffodil & Jonquil chairs from the Invisible Group, 1957

LAVERNE INTERNA-
TIONAL, NEW YORK,
1957–C. 1972

Inspired by Saarinen's earlier "Tulip" chair, the "Champagne" chair forms part of the Lavernes' "Invisible Group". The slender pedestal base and transparent shell give the design a visual lightness and timeless sophistication. The more expressive "Lotus" chair is particularly notable for the contrasting surface treatment of its seat shell.

Von Saarinens früherem »Tulip«-Stuhl inspiriert, gehört der »Champagne«-Stuhl zu den »Invisible Group«-

Erwine &
Estelle Laverne

Lotus, 1958

*Moulded fibreglass
seat shell on
aluminium base |
Sitzschale aus
Glasfaser geformt,
Untergestell aus
Aluminium | Coquille
en fibre de verre
moulée, piètement
d'aluminium*

LAVERNE
INTERNATIONAL,
NEW YORK,
1958–c. 1972

Stühlen, die von den Lavernes entworfen wurden. Die schlanke Fußsäule und die durchsichtige Sitzschale geben dem Entwurf optische Leichtigkeit und zeitlose Raffinesse. Auffallend am ausdrucksvolleren »Lotos«-Stuhl ist die plastischere Gestaltung der Sitzschale.

Inspiré de la chaise tulipe de Saarinen, le fauteuil « Champagne » appartient à l' « Invisible Group » des Laverne. Le mince piètement et la coquille transparente confèrent à ce modèle une légèreté visuelle et une sophistication intemporelle. Plus expressive, la chaise « Lotus » est remarquable par le traitement contrasté des surfaces de son siège coquille.

William Katavolos, Ross Littell & Douglas Kelley

New York, 1952

Chromed tubular steel and enamelled steel frame with buttoned leather-upholstered seat and back | Rahmen aus Stahlrohr, verchromt, und Flachstahl, einbrennlackiert, Sitzfläche und Rückenlehne mit durchgeknöpftem Lederpolster | Châssis en tube d'acier et acier plat émaillé, siège et dossier en cuir rembourré et capitonné

LAVERNE INTERNATIONAL, NEW YORK, FROM 1952 (REISSUED BY ICF)

Like Florence Knoll, Katavolos, Littell & Kelley continued the Modern Movement's tradition of geometric formalism. Their "New Furniture Group" comprised chairs, sofas and tables and included the "New York" sofa and the 3LC or "T" chair. The 3LC's system of concealed screws which secure the sling seat to the frame predates the Eameses' use of this device on their "Aluminium Group" chairs by six years.

Wie Florence Knoll setzten Katavolos, Littell & Kelley den geometrischen Formalismus der klassischen Moderne fort. Ihre »New Furniture Group« umfaßte Stühle, Sofas und Tische, darunter auch das Sofa »New York« und das Modell 3LC oder »T«-Stuhl. Mit seinem System verborgener Schrauben, das die Sitzbespannung sicher am Rahmen festhält, nimmt der 3LC das Konstruktionsprinzip der »Aluminium Group« von Charles und Ray Eames um sechs Jahre vorweg

◄ **Florence Knoll**
Model No. 1205 S3, 1954

KNOLL INTERNATIONAL, NEW YORK, FROM 1954 TO PRESENT

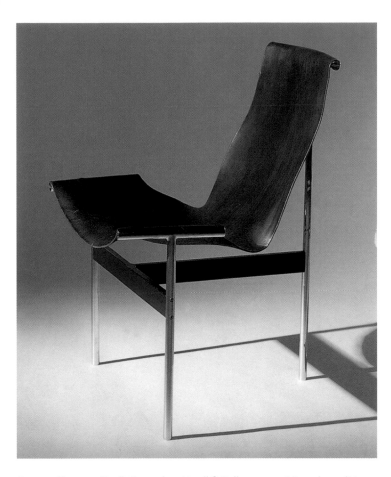

William Katavolos, Ross Littell & Douglas Kelley

T chair, Model No. 3LC, 1952

Chromed tubular steel and enamelled steel frame with leather sling seat | Rahmen aus Stahlrohr, verchromt und Flachstahl, einbrennlackiert, Lederbespannung | Châssis en tube d'acier et acier plat émaillé, siège en cuir tendu

LAVERNE INTERNATIONAL, NEW YORK, FROM 1952 (REISSUED BY CADSANA FROM c. 1988)

Comme Florence Knoll, Katavolos, Littell & Kelley poursuivirent la tradition moderniste du formalisme géométrique. Leur « New Furniture Group » comprenait des fauteuils, des canapés, des tables, le sofa « New York » et le fauteuil 3LC, appelé également « T chair ». Le système d'écrous dissimulés du 3LC, qui fixe le siège suspendu à la structure, annonce une technique identique que les Eames allaient utiliser six ans plus tard dans leur « Aluminium Group ».

Harry Bertoia

Model No. 420C,
1950–1952

Vinyl-coated bent and
welded steel rod
construction with
loose seat cushion |
Konstruktion aus
geformtem und ver-
schweißtem Stahl-
draht, vinylbeschich-
tet, loses Sitzkissen |
Fil d'acier gainé de
vinyle cintré et soudé,
galette de siège
amovible

KNOLL ASSOCIATES,
NEW YORK, FROM
C. 1953 TO PRESENT

▼► **Harry Bertoia**
Bird chair, Model
No. 423LU,
1950–1952

KNOLL ASSOCIATES,
NEW YORK, FROM
C. 1953 TO PRESENT

Harry Bertoia

Diamond, Model No. 421LU, 1950–1952

Vinyl-coated or chrome-plated, bent and welded steel rod construction | Konstruktion aus geformtem und ver-schweißtem Stahl-draht, verchromt bzw. vinylbeschichtet | Fil d'acier gainé de vinyle cintré et soudé

KNOLL ASSOCIATES, NEW YORK, FROM C. 1953 TO PRESENT

▼ Herbert Matter
Knoll Associates ad-vertisement showing Diamond chair, Model No. 422LU, c. 1955

Bertoia's designs not only addressed functional require-ments but were also studies in form and space. Mecha-nised production was attempted but it was found that the chairs were easier to produce by hand.

Bertoias Entwürfe sind nicht nur funktional, sondern erkun-den auch Form und Raum. Die Sitzmöbel sollten maschi-nell hergestellt werden, aber es zeigte sich, daß sie leichter von Hand zu produzieren sind.

Non seulement les créations de Bertoia répondaient à des contraintes pratiques mais elles constituaient de re-marquables études de forme et de volume. Après quelques essais de production à la machine, on réalisa que ces sièges étaient plus faciles à fabriquer à la main.

Norman Cherner

Cherner, 1958

Walnut-faced moulded plywood construction | Formgebogenes Schichtholz, Walnußfurnier | Contre-plaqué moulé, placage de noyer

PLYCRAFT,
LAWRENCE,
MASSACHUSETTS,
FROM 1957 TO
PRESENT

Having abandoned the manufacture of George Nelson's "Pretzel" chair for Herman Miller, Plycraft hired Norman Cherner in 1958 to design a chair that utilized similar production techniques.

Nachdem Plycraft die Produktion von George Nelson's »Pretzel«-Stuhl für Herman Miller einstellte, wurde 1958 Norman Cherner beauftragt, einen Stuhl mit ähnlichen Produktionstechniken zu entwerfen.

Après avoir abandonné la fabrication de la chaise «Pretzel» de George Nelson, Plycraft engagea Norman Cherner en 1958 et lui confia la conception d'une chaise aux procédés techniques identiques.

George Nelson

Pretzel, 1957

Bent, birch-faced laminated wood frame with upholstered seat | Rahmen aus form-gebogenem, laminier-tem Holz mit Birken-furnier, Sitzfläche gepolstert | Châssis en contre-plaqué cintré, placage de bouleau, siège rembourré

HERMAN MILLER FURNITURE CO., ZEELAND, MICHIGAN, 1958–1959 (REISSUED BY ICF FROM 1986)

▼ George Nelson Associates
Pretzel side chair, 1957

HERMAN MILLER FURNITURE CO., ZEE-LAND, MICHIGAN, FROM 1958

Nelson's objective was to create a chair so light in weight it could be lifted with two fingers. He achieved this with the "Pretzel" armchair, but the production was discontinued after one year.

Nelsons Ziel war es, einen Stuhl zu schaffen, der so leicht war, daß man ihn mit zwei Fingern heben konnte. Mit dem »Pretzel«-Stuhl hat er dieses Ziel erreicht, aber die Produktion wurde bereits nach einem Jahr eingestellt.

L'objectif de Nelson était de créer une chaise si légère qu'on puisse la soulever à l'aide de deux doigts seulement. Il atteignit son but avec ce modèle « Pretzel » qui fut abandonné au bout d'un an.

Eero Saarinen designed the Pedestal Chair for Knoll Associates. See it at the Museum of Modern Art in New York or Knoll Showrooms in 28 countries.

Knoll Associates, Inc., Furniture and Textiles, 320 Park Avenue, New York, New York 10022

▲ Knoll advertisement for Tulip, c. 1960

▲ **Eero Saarinen**
Sketches for a pedestal chair, c. 1955

▲▲ **Eero Saarinen**
Tulip Pedestal Group, 1955–1956

KNOLL ASSOCIATES, NEW YORK, FROM 1956 TO PRESENT

Eero Saarinen

**Tulip, Model
No. 150, 1955–1956**

*Plastic-coated cast
aluminium base
supporting moulded
fibreglass seat shell
with loose upholstered
latex foam cushion |
Fuß aus Gußalumi-
nium, lackiert, Sitz-
schale aus geform-
tem, fiberglasverstärk-
tem Polyester,
lackiert, loses Sitz-
kissen mit Schaum-
stoffüllung |
Piètement en fonte
d'aluminium gainée
de plastique soutenant
une coquille en fibre
de verre moulée,
coussin amovible en
mousse de latex*

KNOLL ASSOCIATES,
NEW YORK, FROM
1956 TO PRESENT

▼ Eero Saarinen
Tulip, Model
No. 151, 1955–1956

KNOLL ASSOCIATES,
NEW YORK, FROM
1956 TO PRESENT

Plastics technology precluded Saarinen from achieving a
single-material, single-form chair. The "Pedestal Group"
did, however, fulfil his objective of cleaning up the
"slum of legs" in domestic interiors.

*Die damalige Kunststofftechnologie machte es Saarinen
unmöglich, einen Stuhl aus einem Material und einem
Guß zu schaffen. Mit der »Pedestal Group« konnte er aber
eines seiner Ziele erreichen: mit dem »elenden Wirrwarr
aus Beinen« in Häusern und Wohnungen aufzuräumen.*

Saarinen aurait voulu fabriquer des sièges en un seul
matériau et un seul élément. Avec le « Pedestal Group »,
il atteignit un de ses objectifs : débarrasser la maison de
tout ce « misérable fouillis de pieds ».

Eero Saarinen

Model No. 71 series, Saarinen Collection, 1951

Textile-covered upholstered fibreglass reinforced polyester shell with moulded plywood seat on range of bases | Rückenschale aus glasfaserverstärktem Polyester mit Stoffpolsterung, Sitzfläche aus geformtem Schichtholz, verschiedene Untergestelle | Coquille en polyester renforcé de fibre de verre gainée de tissu, siège en contre-plaqué moulé, divers piètements

KNOLL INTERNATIONAL, NEW YORK, FROM 1951 TO PRESENT

Saarinen and Eames' entries to the Museum of Modern Art's "Organic Design in Home Furnishings" competition of 1940 can be seen as harbingers of the No. 71 series – one of the first office seating programmes.

Die Stuhlserie Nr. 71 basiert auf den Entwürfen von Saarinen und Charles Eames für den 1940 vom Museum of Modern Art ausgeschriebenen Wettbewerb »Organic Design in Home Furnishings«. Es handelt sich um eine der ersten Büromöbelserien.

Les envois de Saarinen et des Eames pour le concours « Organic Design in Home Furnishings » du Museum of Modern Art (1940) annoncent la série n° 71, l'un des tout premiers programmes spécialisés de sièges de bureau.

◄ **George Nelson**
DAF chair, 1956–1958

HERMAN MILLER FURNITURE CO., ZEELAND, MICHIGAN, 1958–1964

George Nelson

MAA, 1958

Moulded fibreglass seat and back with stainless steel fittings on bent tubular steel base | Sitzfläche und Rückenlehne aus geformtem, fiberglas-verstärktem Kunststoff, Verbindungen aus rostfreiem Stahl, Untergestell aus gebogenem Stahlrohr | Siège et dossier en fibre de verre moulée, garnitures en acier inoxydable, piètement en tube cintré

HERMAN MILLER
FURNITURE CO.,
ZEELAND,
MICHIGAN,
1958–1959

The "Swagged-Leg Group" comprising tables, desks and chairs, included the "DAF" and "MAA" chairs. The most innovative design was the MAA which used a metal ball and rubber socket connection to allow articulation of the back.

Der »DAF«- und »MAA«-Stuhl gehörten beide zur »Swagged-Leg Group«, die auch Tische, Schreibtische und Stühle umfaßte. Durch seine neuartigen Verbindungselemente aus Stahlkugeln in Gummifassungen, die die Rückenlehne beweglich halten, war der »MAA«-Stuhl sicherlich der innovativste.

Le groupe « Swagged-Leg » comprenait des tables, des bureaux et des fauteuils, dont les modèles « DAF » et « MAA ». Le projet le plus novateur était le « MAA » qui faisait appel à une articulation en caoutchouc et à bille de métal pour permettre l'inclinaison du dossier.

▲ Herman Miller advertising photograph displaying the 90 degree flexibility of the MAA chair's articulated back

George Nelson

Modular, 1956

Steel frames with textile-covered upholstered seat, back and armrests | Stahlrahmen, gepolsterte und mit Stoff bezogene Sitzflächen, Rücken- und Armlehnen | Châssis en acier, siège, dossier et accoudoirs recouverts de tissu

HERMAN MILLER FURNITURE CO., ZEELAND, MICHIGAN, C. 1957–C. 1975

Nelson's "Modular" system is an early example of this type of seating which later came to dominate the contract market. Though less geometrically severe, Nelson's designs for domestic seating, such as the "Kangaroo" chair, which alludes to traditional club chairs with its buttoned upholstery, and the 5490 chaise longue were still very Modern in spirit.

Nelsons System »Modular« ist ein frühes Beispiel für einen Typus von Sitzmöbeln, der später den öffentlichen Raum dominieren sollte. Seine Entwürfe für den Wohnbereich – wie z. B. der »Kangaroo«-Sessel, der mit seiner durchgeknöpften Polsterung auf traditionelle Klubsessel anspielt, oder auch die Liege 5490 – waren geometrisch weniger streng, blieben den Entwürfen der Moderne aber weiterhin verpflichtet.

Le système « Modular » de Nelson est l'un des premiers exemples d'un type de siège qui allait bientôt dominer le marché du mobilier de bureau. D'une sévérité géométrique plutôt modérée, les modèles de Nelson conçus pour la maison – comme le fauteuil « Kangaroo » avec son rembourrage capitonné rappelant les fauteuils club traditionnels ou la chaise longue 5490 – étaient néanmoins d'esprit très moderne.

George Nelson

Kangaroo, Model No. 5672, 1956

Chromed tubular and flat steel frame with upholstered plywood seat shell and latex-foam seat and back cushions | Rahmen aus Stahlrohr und Flachstahl, verchromt, Sitzschale aus Schichtholz, gepolstert, latexgefülltes Sitz- und Rückenkissen | Châssis en tube d'acier cintré et acier plat, coquille en contre-plaqué rembourré, coussins de siège et de dossier en mousse de latex

HERMAN MILLER FURNITURE CO., ZEELAND, MICHIGAN, 1956–1964

▼ Herman Miller advertising photograph of the Kangaroo chair in contemporary interior, c. 1956

▲ **George Nelson**
Model No. 5490, c. 1954

HERMAN MILLER FURNITURE CO., ZEELAND, MICHIGAN, FROM 1956

George Nelson

Coconut, 1955

Fabric-covered, foam-upholstered steel shell on chromed tubular metal and metal rod legs | Sitzschale aus Stahl, Schaumstoffpolsterung mit Stoffbezug, Beine aus Aluminiumröhren und -stäben | Coquille en acier rembourrée de mousse et recouverte de tissu, piètement en tube d'acier chromé et cintré

HERMAN MILLER
FURNITURE CO.,
ZEELAND,
MICHIGAN,
1955–1978
(REISSUED BY VITRA,
BASLE, FROM 1988)

▼ Herman Miller advertising photograph of Coconut chairs

Although visually light, the "Coconut" chair is in fact extremely heavy owing to its steel seat shell. As its name suggests, the chair's form was inspired by a cracked section of coconut.

Obwohl der »Coconut«-Sessel optisch sehr leicht wirkt, weist er durch seine Sitzschale aus Stahl ein sehr hohes Gewicht auf. Wie der Name andeutet, wurde die Stuhlform von einem Fragment einer aufgeschlagenen Kokosnußschale inspiriert.

Malgré son apparence légère, le siège «Coconut» est en fait extrêmement lourd à cause de sa coquille en métal. Comme son nom le suggère, sa forme était inspirée d'un morceau de noix de coco.

George Nelson

Marshmallow, 1956

Painted tubular steel
frame with vinyl-
covered latex foam-
filled circular pads
backed with steel
discs | Rahmen aus
Stahlrohr, lackiert,
Polsterung aus run-
den Latexkissen mit
Schaumstoffpolste-
rung und Vinylbezug
auf Stahlscheiben |
Châssis en tube
d'acier peint,
« pastilles » réalisées
à partir d'un disque
d'acier rembourré de
mousse de latex et
recouvert de vinyle

HERMAN MILLER
FURNITURE CO.,
ZEELAND,
MICHIGAN,
1956–1965

▼ George Nelson
Sketch for the
Marshmallow sofa,
c. 1956

Like his clock designs, the form of Nelson's "Marshmallow" sofa has been exploded into separate parts.
The bold colour scheme, which emphasised this sepa-
rateness, and the geometry of the sofa predicted Pop
design.

*Wie bei Nelsons Uhrenentwürfen ist auch die Form des
»Marshmallow«-Sofas in ihre Einzelteile zerlegt. Die kühne
Farbkombination, mit der die Wirkung der Einzelformen
noch unterstrichen wird, und die Geometrie des Sofas nehmen die Formensprache späterer Entwürfe des Pop-Designs
vorweg.*

La forme du canapé « Marshmallow » de Nelson est ex-
plosée en multiples pastilles. Ses couleurs vives, qui
renforçaient l'autonomie de chaque élément et la géométrie de l'ensemble, annonçaient le Pop design.

Alvar Aalto

Fan-leg stools, Model Nos. X601 & X600, 1954

Painted wood seat, laminated wood legs | Sitzflächen aus farbigem Holz, Beine aus laminiertem Holz | Siège en bois peint, pieds en bois lamellé- collé

ARTEK, HELSINKI, FROM C. 1954 TO PRESENT

One of Aalto's most sophisticated solutions, the Fan-leg evolved from his earlier Y-leg construction. The concave knee of the Fan-leg is ribbed and resembles a Gothic fan vault through its fluid transition from the vertical to the horizontal.

Eine von Aaltos raffiniertesten Konstruktionslösungen: das Fächer-Bein, eine Weiterentwicklung des früheren Y-Beins. Das konkave Knie des Fächer-Beins mit seinem fließenden Übergang aus der Vertikalen in die Horizontale ist einem gotischen Fächergewölbe entlehnt.

Cette forme sophistiquée en éventail Fan-leg est une évolution de l'articulation en Y-leg antérieure. La partie concave est rainée et évoque les nervures d'une voûte gothique dans sa fluidité de transition entre la verticale et l'horizontale.

Sori Yanagi

Butterfly, 1956

*Moulded plywood
with brass stretcher |
Geformtes Schicht-
holz, Spannvorrich-
tung aus Messing |
Contre-plaqué moulé,
tendeur en laiton*

TENDO MOKKO CO.,
TOYKO, FROM
C. 1956

The "Butterfly" stool can be seen as an elegant and harmonic synthesis of Eastern and Western cultures. Highly favoured in America during the 1950s, it was easy to dismantle and transport.

Der »Butterfly«-Hocker stellt eine elegante und harmonische Synthese der östlichen und westlichen Kultur dar. Der leicht zu zerlegende und zu transportierende Hocker war während der 50er Jahre in den Vereinigten Staaten sehr beliebt.

Le tabouret « Butterfly » est une élégante et harmonieuse synthèse entre les cultures de l'Orient et de l'Occident. Très apprécié aux États-Unis dans les années 50, il était facile à démonter et à transporter.

Max Bill

Ulmer Hocker, 1954

Ebonised wood construction | Holz, schwarz gebeizt | Bois noirci

HOCHSCHULE FÜR GESTALTUNG, ULM, FROM 1954 (REISSUED BY ZANOTTA, MILAN)

Trained at the Dessau Bauhaus, Max Bill was the first director of the Hochschule für Gestaltung at Ulm. This design is indicative of Bill's commitment to functionalism and extreme geometric formalism.

Max Bill war, am Bauhaus Dessau ausgebildet, der erste Direktor der Hochschule für Gestaltung in Ulm. Dieser Entwurf zeigt, wie sehr er dem Funktionalismus und einem extremen geometrischen Formalismus verpflichtet war.

Formé au Bauhaus de Dessau, Max Bill fut le premier directeur de la Hochschule für Gestaltung de Ulm. Ce tabouret illustre son intérêt pour le fonctionnalisme et le formalisme géométrique extrême.

Isamu Noguchi

Rocking stool, 1954

Painted wood seat
and base-connected
with chromed steel
rod structure |
*Sitzfläche und Sockel-
platte aus farbigem
Holz, Verbindungs-
gestell aus verchrom-
ten Stahlstäben* |
*Siège et base en bois
peint, réunis par une
structure en tige de
métal chromé*

KNOLL ASSOCIATES,
NEW YORK, FROM
1954

▼ Isamu Noguchi
Prototype woven
bamboo lounge
chair, 1951

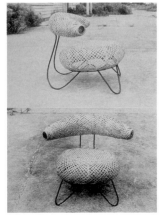

Noguchi's rocking stool and prototype bamboo chair
reveal his fascination with the formal qualities of structure. The stool in particular is imbued with a balanced
tension.

*Noguchis Schaukelhocker und sein Prototyp eines Bambus-
stuhls zeigen, wie sehr ihn die formalen Qualitäten einer
Konstruktion faszinierten. Insbesondere der Hocker ist von
ausgewogener Spannung.*

Ce tabouret de Noguchi et son prototype de fauteuil en
bambou révèlent la fascination de l'artiste pour les qualités formelles des structures. Le tabouret en particulier
fait preuve d'une tension pleine d'équilibre.

Carl Jacobs

Jason, 1950

Solid beech frame
with bent beech-faced
plywood seat |
Rahmen aus Buche,
Sitzschale aus
geformtem Schicht-
holz, Buchenfurnier |
Châssis en hêtre
massif, siège en
contre-plaqué,
placage de hêtre

KANDYA,
MIDDLESEX,
1950–C. 1970

Designed as an inexpensive stacking chair, the "Jason's" extraordinarily resilient seat section was made from a single piece of bent and interlocking
plywood. Metal-legged versions of the chair were later produced.

Als preiswerter Stapelstuhl konstruiert, hat »Jason« eine sehr elastische
Sitzschale, die aus einem Stück Schichtholz geformt ist. Durch die Aussparungen
der Sitzschalen sind die Stühle stapelbar. Später wurde auch eine Version mit
Metallbeinen produziert.

L'extraordinaire souplesse du modèle « Jason », une chaise empilable bon
marché, est obtenue à partir d'une seule pièce de contre-plaqué cintré. Des
versions à pieds métalliques furent réalisées ultérieurement.

This simple yet elegant design by the Bauhaus-trained Swiss architect, Hans Bellmann, is notable for its high-quality construction. Robin Day's similar, though more utilitarian chair could be stacked.

Dieser einfache, aber elegante Stuhl von Hans Bellmann, einem Schweizer Architekten und Bauhausschüler, fällt durch die hohe Entwurfsqualität auf. Der ganz ähnliche, wenn auch funktionellere Stuhl von Robin Day war stapelbar.

Le modèle simple mais élégant de cet architecte suisse formé au Bauhaus, Hans Bellmann, est remarquable par sa grande qualité de construction. La chaise similaire, plus utilitaire, de Robin Day était empilable.

Hans Bellmann

Chair, 1952

Birch-faced moulded plywood seating section on painted tubular steel frame |
Sitzschale aus geformtem Schichtholz mit Birkenfurnier, Untergestell aus lackiertem Stahlrohr |
Coquille en contreplaqué moulé, placage de bouleau, piètement en tube d'acier peint

AG MÖBELFABRIK
HORGEN-GLARUS,
ZURICH,
C. 1952–C. 1965

▶ **Robin Day**
Q Stak chair, 1953

HILLE INTERNA-
TIONAL & CO.,
LONDON, 1953–1960

Ernest Race

Antelope chair, 1950

Painted bent steel rod frame with moulded plywood seat | Rahmen aus gebogenen Stahlstäben, Sitzfläche aus geformtem Schichtholz | Châssis en tige d'acier cintré peint, siège en contre-plaqué moulé

ERNEST RACE, LONDON (LATER TO BECOME RACE FURNITURE), FROM 1951 TO PRESENT

Constrained by national rationing, Race designed the "Antelope" and "Springbok" chairs for use on the Royal Festival Hall's outdoor terraces during the 1951 Festival of Britain. The chairs' spindly legs terminating on ball feet echoed popular interest in the imagery of molecular chemistry and nuclear physics.

Beschränkt durch die kriegsbedingte Materialrationierung in England, hat Race den »Antelope«- und den »Springbok«-Stuhl 1951 aus Anlaß des Festival of Britain für die Außenterrassen der Royal Festival Hall entworfen. Die dünnen Stuhlbeine, die auf Kugelfüßen stehen, spiegeln das damals weit verbreitete Interesse an der Metaphorik von Molekularchemie und Kernphysik wider.

Soumis au rationnement de l'après-guerre, Race conçoit les fauteuils « Antelope » et « Springbok » pour les terrasses extérieures du Royal Festival Hall, à l'occasion du Festival of Britain de 1951. Les pieds maigrelets se terminant par de petites boules rappelaient l'intérêt de l'époque pour la chimie moléculaire et la physique nucléaire.

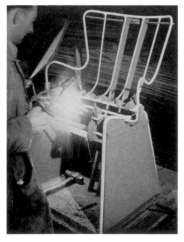

▲ Welding of the Antelope chair's "cold-bent" steel rod frame

▲ **Ernest Race**
Springbok stacking chairs, c. 1951

ERNEST RACE, LONDON

Ernest Race

Antelope bench, 1950

Painted bent steel rod frame with moulded plywood seat | Rahmen aus ge- bogenen Stahlstäben, Sitzfläche aus geform- tem Schichtholz | Châssis en tige d'acier cintré peint, siège en contre-plaqué moulé

ERNEST RACE,
LONDON (LATER TO
BECOME RACE
FURNITURE), 1951

Charles & Ray Eames

DKW-2 (Dining Bikini Wood), 1951

Bent and welded steel rod seat shell with leather "Harlequin" upholstery on birch and metal rod base | *Sitzschale aus verschweißtem Drahtgeflecht, Lederpolsterung »Harlekin«, Stuhlbeine aus Birke mit Verstrebungen aus Stahlstäben |* Coquille en tige de métal cintrée et soudée, rembourrage «Harlequin» en cuir, piètement en bouleau et tiges de métal

BANNER METALS, COMPTON, FOR HERMAN MILLER FURNITURE CO., ZEELAND, MICHIGAN, 1951–1967

▼ PKW, DKW, DKR, LKX, RKR & LKR versions, Herman Miller catalogue, 1952

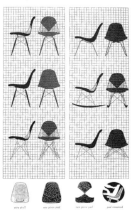

The Eameses first considered a series of wire-mesh chairs when they were working on their "Plastic Shell Group". Utilising the same bases, the wire-mesh seat sections echoed the form of the plastic shells. The rim of the metal seats was made from a heavier gauge of wire which was doubled for additional strength. The chairs were available with either full or two-piece upholstery.

Während ihrer Arbeit an der »Plastic Shell Group« kam den Eames die Idee, die Sitzschalen dieser Stuhlserie aus Drahtgeflecht herzustellen. Die Formgebung der Sitzschalen blieb dabei gleich. Ihr Rand besteht aus einem

*DKR-2 (Dining Bikini
Rod), 1951*

*Bent and welded steel
rod seat shell with
fabric "Harlequin"
upholstery on "Eiffel
Tower" metal rod
base | Sitzschale aus
verschweißtem Draht-
geflecht, Stoffbezug
»Harlekin«, Unter-
gestell »Eiffelturm«
aus verschweißten
Stahlstäben | Coquille
en tige de métal
cintrée et soudée,
rembourrage « Harle-
quin » en tissu, piète-
ment en tiges de
métal « Tour Eiffel »*

BANNER METALS,
COMPTON, FOR HER-
MAN MILLER FURNI-
TURE CO., ZEELAND,
MICHIGAN,
1951–1967
(REISSUED BY VITRA,
BASLE, FROM 1958 TO
PRESENT)

▼ Herman Miller ad-
vertising photograph
showing wire chairs,
1952

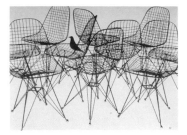

*stärkeren Draht, dessen Verdoppelung für zusätzliche
Stabilität sorgt. Die Stühle waren mit ein- oder zweiteiliger
Polsterung lieferbar.*

Les Eames commencèrent à s'intéresser à une série
de sièges en fil de fer alors qu'ils travaillaient sur
leur projet « Plastic Shell Group ». Sur les mêmes bases,
leurs sièges en fil de fer rappelaient la forme des coquilles de plastique. La bordure était réalisée dans un fil
de diamètre supérieur, doublé pour lui donner plus de
force. Ces sièges était entièrement ou partiellement
recouverts .

Charles & Ray Eames at home, 1958

Based on a prototype exhibited at the Museum of Modern Art's "Organic Design in Home Furnishings" competition in 1940, the No. 670 was the Eameses' most constructionally complex chair and their first design for the luxury end of the market.

Der Sessel Nr. 670 basiert auf einem Prototyp, der 1940 für den vom Museum of Modern Art ausgeschriebenen Wettbewerb »Organic Design in Home Furnishings« entworfen wurde. Konstruktionstechnisch ist dieser Sessel der aufwendigste Entwurf der Eames' und außerdem ihr erster für das obere Marktsegment.

Issu d'un prototype présenté au concours «Organic Design in Home Furnishings» au Museum of Modern Art en 1940, le n° 670 est le siège le plus complexe jamais réalisé par les Eames et leur premier projet pour le marché haut de gamme.

Charles & Ray Eames

Model No. 670 &
Model No. 671, 1956

Rosewood-faced moulded plywood seat shells with leather-covered cushions, cast aluminium base | Sitzschalen aus geformtem Schichtholz, Palisanderfurnier, lederbezogene Kissen, Fuß aus Aluminiumformguß | Coquilles en contre-plaqué moulé, placage de bois de rose, coussins en cuir, piètement en aluminium

HERMAN MILLER FURNITURE CO., ZEELAND, MICHIGAN, FROM 1956 TO PRESENT

Charles & Ray Eames

Aluminium Group, Model No. EA 105, 1958

Aluminium frame with leather- or vinyl-upholstered sling seat | Rahmen und Untergestell aus Aluminium, gepolsterte Sitzbespannung mit Leder- bzw. Vinyl-bezug | Châssis en aluminium, siège tendu de cuir ou de vinyle rembourré

HERMAN MILLER FURNITURE CO., ZEELAND, MICHIGAN & VITRA AG, BASLE, FROM 1958 TO PRESENT

▼ **Charles & Ray Eames**
Aluminium Group lounge chair with ottoman, 1958

HERMAN MILLER FURNITURE CO., ZEE-LAND, MICHIGAN, FROM 1958 TO PRESENT

The "Aluminium Group" was originally designed for indoor and outdoor domestic use, and during its development was often referred to as the "Leisure Group". Ironically, it is now used almost exclusively in offices.

Die Sitzmöbel der »Aluminium Group« wurden ursprünglich für die private Nutzung im Innen- und Außenbereich entworfen und daher auch »Leisure Group« (Freizeit) genannt. Heute werden diese Möbel meist in Büros verwendet.

L' « Aluminium Group » fut conçu à l'origine aussi bien pour l'intérieur que pour l'extérieur de la maison. Au cours de sa mise au point, il portait le nom de « Leisure Group » (série Loisirs). Il est aujourd'hui surtout utilisé dans les bureaux.

Charles & Ray Eames

Aluminium Group, Model No. EA 117, 1958

Enamelled aluminium frame and base with textile-upholstered sling seat | Rahmen und Untergestell aus Aluminium, einbrennlackiert, gepolsterte Sitz-bespannung | Châssis et piètement en aluminium émaillé, siège tendu en tissu rembourré

HERMAN MILLER
FURNITURE CO.,
ZEELAND, MICHIGAN
& VITRA AG, BASLE,
FROM 1958 TO
PRESENT

▲ Herman Miller photograph of Aluminium Group chairs showing outdoor use

◀ Herman Miller interior with Aluminium Group, Model No. EA 115

279

Charles & Ray Eames

Sofa Compact, 1954

Chromed and black-enamelled flat steel folding frame with wire sprung uphol-stered seat and back pads | Rahmen mit verstellbarer Rücken-lehne aus verchrom-tem und einbrenn-lackiertem Stahl, Drahtfederung, Sitz- und Rückenauflage gepolstert | Châssis articulé en acier plat chromé et émaillé noir, coussins de siège et de dossier rembourrés

HERMAN MILLER FURNITURE CO., ZEELAND, MICHIGAN, FROM 1954 TO PRESENT

Like the Eameses' prototype wire-mesh sofa of 1951, the Sofa "Compact" has a folding back for easier transportation. It was the Eameses' last low-cost furniture design.

Wie bei dem Prototyp eines Drahtgeflechtsofas aus dem Jahr 1951 nach Entwurf von Charles und Ray Eames, läßt sich die Rückenlehne des Sofas »Compact« umklappen, was den Transport erleichtert. Dies war der letzte Entwurf eines Niedrigpreis-Möbels, den Ray und Charles Eames vorstellten.

Comme le prototype de sofa en fil de fer des Eames, datant de 1951, le sofa «Compact» possédait un dossier pliable pour faciliter son transport. Ce fut le dernier projet de meuble économique des Eames.

◄ The Eameses' friend, Dorothy Jeakins, sitting on the sofa Compact, c. 1954

Poul Kjaerholm

Model No. PK22,
1955–1956

Chromed flat steel
frame with leather
seat and back |
Rahmen aus Flach-
stahl, verchromt,
Sitzfläche und
Rückenlehne mit
Lederbespannung |
Châssis en acier plat
chromé, siège et
dossier en cuir

E. KOLD
CHRISTENSEN,
HELLERUP,
C. 1956–C. 1970
(REISSUED BY FRITZ
HANSEN, ALLERØD,
FROM C. 1970 TO
PRESENT)

▼ Poul Kjaerholm
Models No. PK11,
1957

E. KOLD CHRIS-
TENSEN, HELLERUP,
C. 1957–C. 1970 &
FRITZ HANSEN,
ALLERØD, FROM
C. 1970
TO PRESENT

Kjaerholm's elegant designs owe much to the designers
of the Modern Movement. His PK22 is reminiscent of
Mies van der Rohe's "Barcelona" chair of 1929. The
PK22 was also available with a woven cane seat.
Kjaerholms elegante Entwürfe sind der klassischen Moderne
verpflichtet. Der PK22 erinnert an Mies van der Rohes
»Barcelona«-Stuhl von 1929. Der Stuhl war auch mit
einem Sitz aus Rohrgeflecht lieferbar.
Les élégants modèles de Kjaerholm doivent beaucoup
aux designers modernistes. Le PK22 rappelle le siège
« Barcelona » de Mies van der Rohe (1929). Il était éga-
lement proposé en version cannée.

Børge Mogensen

Spanish chair, Model No. 2226, 1959

Solid birch frame with leather seat and back, metal buckles | Rahmen aus Birke, Sitzfläche und Rückenlehne mit Lederbespannung, Metallschnallen | Châssis en bouleau massif, siège et dossier en cuir, boucles de métal

FREDERICIA
STOLEFABRIK,
FREDERICIA, FROM
C. 1958 TO PRESENT

▼ **Børge Mogensen**
Model No. 2337,
1962

FREDERICIA STOLE-
FABRIK, FREDERICIA,
FROM C. 1962 TO
PRESENT

This robust chair delights in the natural and humanising qualities of its materials. Based on a vernacular Spanish chair, Mogensen's design achieves a certain timelessness.

Dieser robuste Sessel überzeugt durch seine natürlichen und den menschlichen Bedürfnissen angepaßten Werkstoffen. Seine Formgebung basiert auf einem traditionellen spanischen Stuhltypus und wirkt daher zeitlos.

Ce robuste fauteuil ravit par la qualité naturelle et conviviale de ses matériaux. Inspiré d'un fauteuil traditionnel espagnol, il reste néanmoins relativement intemporel.

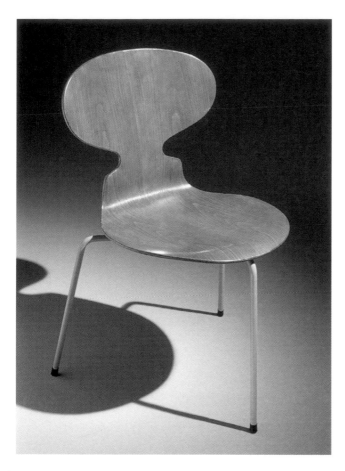

Arne Jacobsen

Ant, Model No. 3100,
1951–1952

*Teak-faced plywood
seat connected to
tubular steel base,
rubber cap feet |
Sitzschale aus
geformtem Schicht-
holz mit Teakfurnier,
Stuhlbeine aus Stahl-
rohr, Gummikappen |
Siège en contre-
plaqué, placage de
teck, piètement en
tube d'acier, patins en
caoutchouc*

FRITZ HANSEN,
ALLERØD, FROM 1952
TO PRESENT

▼ Fritz Hansen
photograph of Ant
chairs

None of his earlier moulded plywood chairs were as
visually resolved nor as strong in character as
Jacobsen's highly successful "Ant" chair.

*Keiner seiner schon früher produzierten Stühle aus geform-
tem Schichtholz wirkt optisch so gelungen wie Jacobsens
äußerst erfolgreicher »Ant« (Ameisen)-Stuhl.*

Bien que d'autres chaises aient déjà été réalisées au-
paravant en contre-plaqué, aucune n'était aussi réussie
et de caractère aussi affirmé que le modèle « Ant »
(Fourmi) de Jacobsen qui allait connaître un très grand
succès.

Arne Jacobsen

Series 7, Model No. 3107, 1955

Teak-faced moulded plywood seat connected to chromed bent tubular steel base with rubber cap feet | Sitzschale aus geformtem Schichtholz mit Teakholzfurnier, Stuhlbeine aus Stahlrohr, verchromt, mit Gummikappen | Siège en contre-plaqué moulé, placage de teck, piètement en tube cintré chromé, patins en caoutchouc

FRITZ HANSEN, ALLERØD, FROM C. 1955 TO PRESENT

▶ Fritz Hansen promotional photograph of series 7 chairs

Arne Jacobsen

Series 7, Model No. 3217, 1955

Lacquered moulded plywood seat on a height adjustable chromed tubular steel frame with double-wheel castors | Sitz-schale aus geformtem Schichtholz, lackiert, höhenverstellbarer Rahmen aus Stahl-rohr, verchromt, auf Doppelradrollen | Siège en contre-plaqué moulé laqué, piètement en tube d'acier réglable en hauteur, doubles roulettes

FRITZ HANSEN,
ALLERØD, FROM
C. 1955 TO PRESENT

The series 7 is one of the most commercially successful chair programmes ever produced. Jacobsen's approach to the complex moulding of the continuous plywood seat and back was influenced by the Eameses' earlier designs.

Die Serie 7 ist eines der kommerziell erfolgreichsten Stuhlprogramme, das je pro-duziert wurde. Jacobsens Verwendung von geformtem Schichtholz für die Konstruktion der Sitzschale ist von den früheren Entwürfen von Charles und Ray Eames beeinflußt worden.

La série 7 est l'une des séries de sièges les plus vendues jamais produites. L'approche par Jacobsen des problèmes complexes de moulage du siège et du dossier en continu fut influencée par certains modèles antérieurs de Charles et Ray Eames.

Arne Jacobsen

Egg, Model No. 3316,
1957–1958

Fabric-covered, foam-
upholstered moulded
fibreglass seat shell on
a swivelling cast
aluminium base with
loose seat cushion |
Sitzschale aus ge-
formtem, fiberglasver-
stärktem Kunststoff
mit Schaumstoff-
polsterung und Stoff-
bezug, loses Sitz-
kissen, drehbares
Untergestell aus
Aluminiumguß |
Coquille en fibre de
verre moulée rem-
bourrée de mousse et
recouverte de tissu,
piètement pivotant,
en fonte d'alu-
minium, coussin de
siège amovible

FRITZ HANSEN,
ALLERØD, FROM 1958
TO PRESENT

▼ Egg chairs in Fritz
Hansen showroom,
c. 1960

Designed originally for the Royal SAS Hotel in Copen-
hagen, these highly sculptural chairs were the result of
Jacobsen's search for lightweight, fluid seating forms
which required a minimum of padding for comfort.
Diese betont skulpturalen Sessel, ursprünglich für das
Royal SAS Hotel in Kopenhagen entworfen, sind das
Resultat von Jacobsens Suche nach leichten, fließenden
Formen für Sitzmöbel, die auch mit einem Minimum
an Polsterung Bequemlichkeit bieten.
Conçus à l'origine pour le Royal SAS Hotel de Copenhague, ces fauteuils
sculpturaux résultaient des recherches de Jacobsen dans le domaine des
formes fluides et légères qui ne nécessitaient qu'un minimum de rembour-
rage pour être très confortables.

Arne Jacobsen

Swan, Model No. 3320, 1957–1958

Fabric-covered, foam-upholstered moulded fibreglass seat shell on a swivelling cast aluminium base | Sitzschale aus geformtem, fiberglasverstärktem Kunststoff mit Schaumstoffpolsterung und Stoffbezug, loses Sitzkissen, drehbares Untergestell aus Aluminiumguß, mit Kippvorrichtung | Coquille en fibre de verre moulée rembourrée de mousse et recouverte de tissu, piètement pivotant en fonte d'aluminium, coussin de siège amovible

FRITZ HANSEN, ALLERØD, FROM 1958 TO PRESENT

▲ Fritz Hansen photograph showing interior with Swan chairs, c. 1960

▲ **Arne Jacobsen**
Swan sofa, 1957–1958

Arne Jacobsen

Grand Prix, Model No. 4130, 1955

Partially upholstered beech-faced moulded plywood seat shell connected to profiled laminated wood legs | Sitzschale aus geformtem Schichtholz, Buchenfurnier, teilweise gepolstert, profilierte Stuhlbeine aus gebogener, laminierter Buche | Coquille en bois moulé, placage de hêtre, rembourrage partiel, piètement en bois lamellé-collé profilé

FRITZ HANSEN, ALLERØD, FROM C. 1955 TO PRESENT

The No. 4130 chair was awarded a Grand Prix at the Milan XI Triennale in 1957. The use of a wooden base, rather than a metal base as used on the 3107 chair, provides the design with a greater visual coherence.

Der Stuhl Nr. 4130 wurde 1957 auf der XI. Mailänder Triennale mit einem Grand Prix ausgezeichnet. Im Unterschied zum Modell Nr. 3107, das Metallbeine hatte, sind hier die Beine aus Holz, was dem Entwurf größere optische Geschlossenheit gibt.

Le fauteuil n° 4130 reçut le Grand Prix à la XIᵉ Triennale de Milan, en 1957. Le recours à un piètement en bois plutôt qu'en acier, comme sur le modèle n° 3107, lui donne une plus grande cohérence visuelle.

Superleggera, Model No. 699, 1951–1957

Ash frame with woven rush seat | Rahmen aus Esche, Sitzfläche aus Binsengeflecht | Châssis en frêne, siège en jonc tressé

CASSINA, MEDA, MILAN, FROM 1957 TO PRESENT

▼ Cassina photograph demonstrating the lightness of the Superleggera of 1957

The remarkably light "Superleggera" was based on a traditional Italian chair design. Ponti created interiors and objects of a timeless classicism and this chair has been described as "the consummate chair".

Der bemerkenswert leichte »Superleggera«-Stuhl basiert auf einem traditionellen italienischen Stuhltyp. Ponti schuf zeitlos klassische Interieurs und Objekte, und dieser Stuhl wurde als »Stuhl an sich« bezeichnet.

Cette remarquable « Superleggera » s'inspire d'une chaise traditionnelle italienne. Ponti créa des intérieurs et des objets d'un classicisme sans âge et sa chaise fut qualifiée de « chaise par excellence ».

Osvaldo Borsani

Model No. P40, 1954

Pressed and tubular steel frame with latex-foam upholstery and rubber-covered steel spring arms | Rahmen aus Stahlrohr und Stahlblech, Latex-schaumstoffpolsterung, Armlehnen aus gummiüberzogenen Stahlfedern | Châssis en tube d'acier et acier estampé, rembourrage en mousse de latex, accoudoirs souples recouverts de caoutchouc

TECNO, MILAN, FROM 1954 TO PRESENT

▲ Osvaldo Borsani
Lounge chair, Model No. P40 & sofa, Model No. D70, 1954

TECNO, MILAN, FROM 1954 TO PRESENT

Based on Borsani's belief that design should be born out of technical research, the P40 and D70 are highly innovative in the flexibility they offer. With all the main elements of its design being adjustable, the remarkably versatile P40 can be manipulated into 486 positions. The D70 functions as a divan-bed with a back that can be adjusted through various angles to 90 degrees. Its seat and back can also fold together vertically for ease of storage.

Borsanis Überzeugung entsprechend, daß Design aus dem Erforschen technischer Möglichkeiten entsteht, sind P40 und D70 mit der Flexibilität, die sie bieten, hoch innovativ. Alle Bestandteile des P40 sind verstellbar, womit dieser bemerkenswert vielseitige Liegesessel in 486 Positionen

Osvaldo Borsani

Model No. D70, 1954

Pressed and tubular steel frame with latex-foam upholstery | Rahmen aus Stahlrohr und Stahlblech, Latexschaumstoffpolsterung | Châssis en tube d'acier et acier estampé, rembourrage en mousse de latex

TECNO, MILAN, FROM 1954 TO PRESENT

gebracht werden kann. Das Sofa D70 kann durch seine Rückenlehne, die in verschiedenen Winkeln bis zu 90° herablaßbar ist, auch als Schlafgelegenheit benutzt werden. Um das Sofa platzsparend zu verstauen, können Sitzfläche und Rückenlehne vertikal gegeneinander geklappt werden.

Fruits de la conviction de Borsani selon laquelle le design doit s'appuyer sur une recherche technique, le P40 et le D70 innovent radicalement par leur souplesse d'utilisation. Ses principaux éléments étant tous réglables, la P40, remarquablement polyvalente, peut prendre jusqu'à 486 positions. La D70 servait de divan-lit avec un dossier pouvant s'abaisser à 90°. Le siège et le dossier peuvent également se replier verticalement pour faciliter son rangement.

Marco Zanuso

Martingala, 1954

Latex foam
upholstered seat shell
with removable covers
on tapering chromed
metal legs termina-
ting on ball feet | Mit
Latexschaum gepol-
sterte Sitzschale,
abnehmbare Bezüge,
konische Metallbeine,
verchromt, mit Kugel-
füßen | Coquille de
siège rembourrée en
mousse de latex,
housse amovible,
pieds fuselés en métal
chromé

ARFLEX, MEDA,
MILAN, FROM 1954
TO PRESENT

▼ **Osvaldo Borsani**
Armchair, Model
No. P32, 1956

TECNO, MILAN,
FROM C. 1956 TO
PRESENT

Zanuso wrote of latex-foam: "One could revolutionise not only the system of upholstery but also the structural manufacturing and formal potential. When our proto-types acquired visually exciting and new contours, a company (Arflex) was founded to put models like the 'Lady' into production with industrial standards that were previously unimaginable." (Albrecht Bangert, *Italian Furniture Design: Ideas Styles Movements*, Bangert Verlag, Munich 1988, p. 33)

Zum Latex-Schaum hat Zanuso geschrieben: »Man konnte nicht nur Polstersysteme, sondern auch strukturelle, herstel-lungstechnische und formale Möglichkeiten revolunieren. Als unsere Prototypen aufsehenerregende neue formale Konturen gewannen, wurde eine Firma (Arflex) gegründet, um solche Modelle, wie den ›Lady‹-Sessel in Produktion gehen zu lassen. In einem industriellen Maßstab, den man sich bisher nicht vorstellen konnte.«

Marco Zanuso

Lady, 1951

Wood frame with elastic straps and fabric-covered latex-foam upholstery on chromed tubular metal legs | Rahmen aus Holz, Schaum-stoffpolsterung mit Stoffbezug, elastische Spanngurte, Sessel-beine aus Stahlrohr, verchromt | Châssis en bois, rembourrage en mousse de caout-chouc recouverte de tissu, suspension par sangles de caout-chouc, pieds en tube de métal chromé

ARFLEX, MEDA,
MILAN, FROM 1951
TO PRESENT

▼ Arflex photograph
of Lady armchairs,
c. 1951

Zanuso écrivit au sujet de la mousse de latex : « On pourrait révolutionner non seulement le système de rembourrage, mais également la fabrication de la structure et le potentiel de formes. Lorsque nos prototypes eurent acquis leurs contours, visuellement réussis et novateurs, une société fut fondée (Arflex) pour fabriquer des modèles comme le ‹ Lady ›, selon des standards industriels jusque-là inimaginables. »

Marco Zanuso

Triennale, 1951

Wood frame with elastic straps and fabric-covered latex-foam upholstery on painted aluminium legs | *Rahmen aus Holz, Schaum-stoffpolsterung und Stoffbezug, elastische Spanngurte, Alumi-niumfüße, lackiert* | *Châssis en bois, rembourrage en mousse de caout-chouc recouverte de tissu, suspension par sangles de caout-chouc, pieds en tube d'aluminium peint*

ARFLEX, MEDA, MILAN, FROM C. 1951 TO PRESENT

The "Triennale" sofa was exhibited at the Milan IX Triennale of 1951 where Zanuso won a Grand Prix and two gold medals. In 1954, he designed a sofa-bed version of the "Triennale" known as the "Sleep-o-matic".

Das Sofa »Triennale« wurde 1951 auf der IX. Mailänder Triennale präsentiert, wo Zanuso einen Grand Prix und zwei Goldmedaillen gewann. 1954 entwarf er eine Bettsofa-Version von »Triennale«, die als »Sleep-o-matic« bekannt wurde.

Le sofa « Triennale » fut exposé à la IXe Triennale de Milan, en 1951, où Zanuso remporta un Grand Prix et deux médailles d'or. En 1954, il conçut une version canapé-lit de ce même sofa, appelée « Sleep-o-matic ».

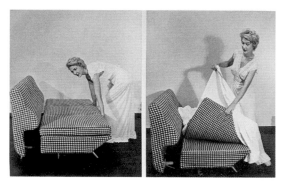

◄ Arflex photographs showing Sleep-o-matic sofa being transformed into a divan bed, c. 1954

Lodovico Barbiano di Belgiojoso & Enrico Peresutti

Elettra, 1953

Tubular steel frame with fabric-covered latex-foam upholstered seat and back | Rahmen aus Stahlrohr, Sitzfläche und Rückenlehne mit Latex-Schaumstoff-polsterung und Stoffbezug | Châssis en tube d'acier, siège et dossier rembourrés en mousse de latex recouverte de tissu

ARFLEX, MEDA, MILAN, FROM 1953 TO PRESENT

▼ Erberto Carboni
Delfino, 1954

ARFLEX, MEDA, MILAN, FROM 1954 TO PRESENT

Both the "Elettra" and "Delfino" were manufactured by Arflex – one of the first Italian companies to propose that design and industry should be integrated and that new ways of living required new design solutions.
Sowohl der »Elettra«- als auch der »Delfino«-Sessel werden von Arflex produziert – einem der ersten italie-nischen Möbelhersteller, der sich von der Vorstellung leiten ließ, daß Design und Industrie zu integrieren seien und daß neue Lebensformen auch neue Designlösungen erfordern.
Les fauteuils « Elettra » et « Delfino » étaient fabriqués par Arflex, l'une des premières sociétés italiennes à pro-poser l'intégration du design et de l'industrie, et à dé-fendre l'idée que de nouveaux modes de vie exigeaient de nouvelles solutions de design.

Franco Albini

Fiorenza, 1952

Wood frame with latex-foam upholstered seat, back and armrests | Rahmen aus Holz, Sitzfläche, Rückenlehne und Armlehnen mit Latex-schaumstoff-polsterung | Châssis en bois, siège, dossier et accoudoirs rembourrés en mousse de latex

ARFLEX, MEDA,
MILAN, FROM 1952
TO PRESENT

▼ Franco Albini
Rocking chaise,
Model No. PS16,
1956

CARLO POGGI, PAVIA,
1956

Albini was the foremost Neo-Rationalist designer. His "Fiorenza" chair, a pared-down reworking of the traditional wing chair, did away with the need for bulky springing through its use of latex-foam upholstery.

Albini war der führende Designer unter den Neo-Rationalisten. Sein Sessel »Fiorenza«, eine aufs notwendigste reduzierte Version des traditionellen Ohrensessels, machte Schluß mit voluminöser Federung durch den Einsatz einer Polsterung aus Latex-Schaumstoff.

Albini est le principal designer néorationaliste. Son fauteuil « Fiorenza », une interprétation épurée du traditionnel fauteuil à oreilles, éliminait le problème des encombrants ressorts par un rembourrage en mousse de latex.

Franco Albini

Gala, 1950

*Rattan and Indian
cane construction |
Konstruktion aus
Rattan und indischem
Bambusrohr | Rotin
et bambou indien*

VITTORIO
BONACINA & C.,
LURAGO D'ERBA,
FROM 1951 TO
PRESENT

▼ Franco Albini
Margherita, 1950

VITTORIO BONACINA
& C., LURAGO
D'ERBA, FROM 1951
TO PRESENT

Using readily available, inexpensive craft materials, Albini produced thoroughly modern compositions such as the "Gala" and "Margherita". This innovative use of traditional materials was central to Italy's reconstruction.

Aus vorhandenen, preiswerten Werkstoffen schuf Albini so moderne Stuhlkreationen wie »Gala« und »Margherita«. Diese innovative Materialverwendung hatte für Italiens Wiederaufbau nach dem Krieg große Bedeutung.

À partir de matériaux classiques accessibles et bon marché, Albini produisit des créations très modernes comme le « Gala » et le « Margherita ». Cette utilisation novatrice de matériaux traditionnels joua un grand rôle lors de la reconstruction de l'Italie, après la guerre.

Carlo Mollino

Chair for the restaurant Pavia, Cervinia, c. 1954

Solid oak construction with brass fittings |
Aus massiver Eiche, Messingbeschläge |
Chêne massif, garnitures en laiton

ETTORE CANALI,
PRESCIA

▼ **Carlo Mollino**
Chair for the Faculty of Architecture, Turin, 1962

PROBABLY APELLI &
VARESIO, TURIN
(REISSUED BY ZAN-
OTTA AS 211 FENIS,
FROM 1985)

The bipartite chair is typical of Mollino's many chair de-
signs. Here, in the 1954 chair for the Pavia restaurant in
Cervinia, the back is held together with brass screws.
*Typisch für viele Stuhlentwürfe Mollinos, wie auch für den
um 1954 entworfenen Stuhl für das Restaurant Pavia in
Cervinia, sind die zweigeteilten Rückenlehnen, die hier mit
Messingschrauben zusammengehalten werden.*
La plupart des sièges conçus par Mollino, comme par
exemple la chaise qu'il créa en 1954 pour le restaurant
Pavia à Cervinia, se caractérisent par des dossiers com-
posés de deux parties, assemblées ici avec des vis de
laiton.

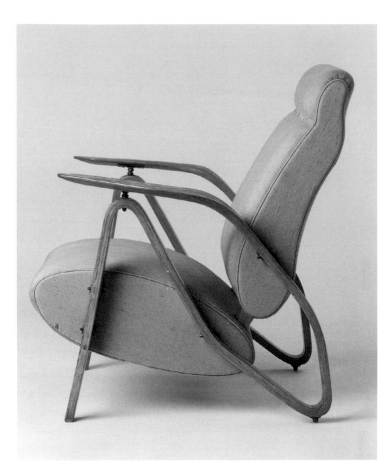

Carlo Mollino

Armchair, 1952

Bent laminated wood frame with uphol-stered seat and back section with brass fittings | Rahmen aus gebogenem, laminier-tem Holz, Sitzfläche und Rückenlehne gepolstert, Messing-beschläge | Châssis en bois lamellé-collé, siège et dossier rembourrés, garniture en laiton

PROBABLY APELLI & VARESIO, TURIN

▼ Carlo Mollino
Chair for the Casa Catlaneo, Agra, 1953

APELLI & VARESIO, TURIN

Unlike his American counterparts, who progressed the utilitarian potential of plywood, Mollino exploited its ex-pressive qualities. This chair relates to an earlier reclin-ing chair designed for the Casa del Sole in Cervinia.
Die Amerikaner entwickelten das funktionelle Potential des Schichtholzes weiter, Mollino hingegen dessen expressive Qualitäten. Mit diesem Modell bezieht er sich auf seinen frühen Ruhesessel für die Casa del Sole in Cervinia.
À la différence de ses pairs américains, qui s'intéres-sèrent surtout aux possibilités techniques du contre-plaqué, Mollino sut exploiter ses qualités expressives. Ce fauteuil se rapproche d'une chaise longue antérieure conçue pour la Casa del Sole à Cervinia.

Carlo Mollino & Aldo Morbelli

Armchair for the RAI Auditorium, Turin, 1951

Velvet-covered upholstered plywood and metal frame with brass number plate on tubular brass base | Rahmen aus Metall und Sperrholz, Polsterung mit Samtbezug, Untergestell aus Messingrohr, Platznummernschild aus Messing | Châssis en métal et contreplaqué, recouvert de velours rembourré, indication du numéro de siège sur plaque de laiton, piètement en laiton

▼ Carlo Mollino & Aldo Morbelli
Hall of the RAI Auditorium, Turin, 1951

Designed for the RAI Auditorium in Turin, this chair is a particularly sumptuous example of an often-ignored type of seating. The hall's interior scheme is considered one of Mollino's most successful.

Dieser Sessel, ein Entwurf für das RAI-Auditorium in Turin, ist ein besonders schönes Beispiel für einen Sitzmöbeltyp, der nicht immer die gebührende Beachtung findet. Die Innenausstattung des Auditoriums wird als einer der gelungensten Entwürfe Mollinos betrachtet.

Créé pour l'auditorium de la RAI à Turin, ce fauteuil est un exemple particulièrement somptueux d'un type de siège souvent ignoré. La décoration intérieure de cette salle est l'une des plus grandes réussites de Mollino.

Carlo Mollino

Chair for the Lattes Publishing House, 1951

Walnut frame with moulded plywood back, upholstered seat, brass stretchers and screws | Rahmen aus Walnußholz, Rückenlehne aus geformtem Schichtholz, gepolsterte Sitzfläche, Messingstreben und -schrauben | Châssis en noyer, dossier en contre-plaqué moulé, siège rembourré, tendeurs et visserie en laiton

PROBABLY APELLI & VARESIO, TURIN

▼ Carlo Mollino
Room setting for the "Italy at Work" exhibition, 1950–1951

The superlative quality of Mollino's designs is revealed even in the smallest of details. Here, the specially cast, twisted brass fittings give this comparatively simple chair a sense of luxury.

Die überragende Qualität von Mollinos Entwürfen zeigt sich auch in den kleinsten Details. Bei diesem Entwurf verleihen die speziell angefertigten, gedrehten Beschläge aus Messingguß dem vergleichsweise schlichten Stuhl einen Hauch von Luxus.

La superbe qualité des œuvres de Mollino se révèle dans les plus petits détails. Ici, les garnitures en laiton spécialement dessinées et fondues pour l'occasion donnent à cette chaise assez simple un aspect luxueux.

Carlo Graffi

Armchair, c. 1950

*Birch-faced plywood
and laminated wood
frame with brass
fittings and
upholstered seat
cushions | Rahmen
aus gebogenem
Schichtholz mit
Birkenfurnier,
Messingbeschläge,
gepolsterte Sitzkissen |
Châssis en contre-
plaqué, placage de
bouleau, garnitures
en laiton, coussins de
siège et de dossier
rembourrés*

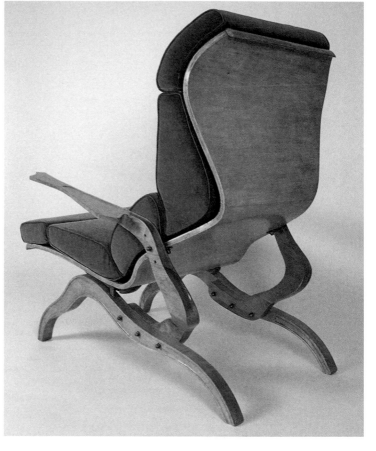

▼ **Vittorio Gregotti,
Lodovico Meneghetti,
Giotto Stoppino**
Birch-faced plywood
chair, 1954

SIM, NOVARA, MILAN

Like many Italian designers, Graffi exploited the expressive potential of plywood. He worked closely on several
architectural projects with Mollino and his exuberant
designs exemplify the "Turinese Baroque" style.

*Wie viele italienische Designer nutzte Graffi das gestalte-
rische Potential von Schichtholz. Bei mehreren Projekten
arbeitete er eng mit Mollino zusammen. Seine extra-
vaganten Entwürfe sind typisch für das »Turiner Barock«.*

Comme de nombreux designers italiens, Graffi exploita
le potentiel expressif du contre-plaqué. Il travailla sur
plusieurs projets d'architecture en collaboration étroite
avec Mollino, et ses projets exubérants illustrent bien le
style « Baroque turinois ».

Gregotti, Meneghetti and Stoppino designed several items of furniture using cut-out plywood which slotted together. This chaise longue bears a remarkable similarity to Friedrich Kiesler's chair sculptures of 1942.

Gregotti, Meneghetti und Stoppino haben mehrere Möbelstücke entworfen, für die sie zugesägte Teile aus Sperrholz verwendeten, die zusammengesteckt wurden. Diese Liege hat eine bemerkenswerte Ähnlichkeit mit Friedrich Kieslers Stuhl-Skulpturen von 1942.

Gregotti, Meneghetti et Stoppino conçurent plusieurs éléments de mobilier composés de découpes en contre-plaqué à encoches qui s'imbriquaient les unes dans les autres. Cette chaise longue est remarquablement similaire aux sculptures-sièges de Frederick Kiesler, de 1942.

Studio Architetti Associati
Chaise longue, 1953

Rosewood-veneered plywood side panels and stretched fabric sling seating section |
Sperrholzseitenteile mit Palisanderfurnier, Liegebespannung aus Stretchstoff |
Panneaux latéraux en bois, placage de bois de rose, structure interne en deux blocs, partie siège recouverte de tissu extensible

SIM, NOVARA, MILAN, FROM C. 1953

▲ SIM advertising photograph of Studio Architetti Associati chaise longue

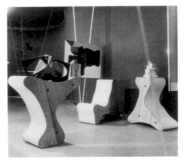

◄ Friedrich Kiesler Chair sculptures for Peggy Guggenheim's gallery, New York, 1942

Achille & Pier Giacomo Castiglioni

Sanluca, 1959

Leather-covered polyurethane foam upholstered frame, rosewood legs | Mit Polyurethanschaumstoff gepolsterter und mit Leder bezogener Rahmen, Beine aus Palisander | Châssis rembourré en mousse de polyuréthane et recouvert de cuir, pieds en bois de rose

GAVINA, BOLOGNA, FROM C. 1960 (REISSUED BY BERNINI, FROM 1990 TO PRESENT)

▼ **Achille & Pier Giacomo Castiglioni**
Sketch for Sanluca chair, c. 1959

◄ Dino Gavina, Achille & Pier Giacomo Castiglioni photographed with the Sanluca in the San Luca portico, Bologna, 1960

Gunnar
Aagaard
Andersen

Chair, 1952–1953

*Prototype, initially
made of chicken-wire
and newspaper, with
proposal to be
executed in either
stamped aluminium
or fibreglass | Prototyp
aus Maschendraht
und Zeitungspapier,
sollte aus gepreßtem
Aluminium oder aus
fiberglasverstärktem
Kunststoff gefertigt
werden | Prototype,
initialement réalisé en
fil de fer et papier
journal, pouvant être
fabriqué en alu-
minium estampé ou
en fibre de verre*

Sacrificing stylistic convention in the pursuit of experimentation, the "Sanluca" was nonetheless designed within a rationalist framework. Similarly, Andersen's prototype, which predates Panton's stacking chair by seven years, disregards traditional forms while speculating on an efficient seating solution for mass-production.

Für den »Sanluca«-Sessel wurde die traditionelle Sesselform zugunsten neuer Formexperimente geopfert, dennoch steht dieser Sessel im Kontext des Rationalismus. Dies gilt auch für den Prototyp eines Stapelstuhls, der die Entwürfe von Panton um sieben Jahre vorwegnimmt; hier verabschiedet sich auch Andersen von traditionellen Formen, weil er nach einer effizienten Lösung für die Massenproduktion sucht.

Sacrifiant les conventions stylistiques à l'exploration formelle, le « Sanluca » n'en fut pas moins conçu dans un esprit rationaliste. De même, le prototype d'Andersen qui précède de sept années la chaise empilable de Panton, écarte les formes traditionnelles au profit d'une recherche d'efficacité répondant aux contraintes de la production en grande série.

Piero Fornasetti

Lyre and Sun,
1951 & 1955

Lacquered and screen-
printed moulded
plywood seats on
painted tapering
tubular metal legs
(originally wooden
legs) | Sitzschalen aus
geformtem Schicht-
holz, lackiert und
siebbedruckt, konische
Stuhlbeine aus
Metallrohr (ursprüng-
lich Holzbeine) |
Sièges en contre-
plaqué moulé, peint
et laqué, pieds fuselés
en tube de métal
peint (initialement
pieds en bois)

FORNASETTI, MILAN,
FROM C. 1951 &
FROM C. 1955 TO
PRESENT

▼ **Piero Fornasetti**
Early version of Lyre,
1951

FORNASETTI, MILAN

The eccentric spirit of Fornasetti's designs, with their
surreal and exuberant "trompe-l'œil" decoration, influenced the Italian Anti-Design movement of subsequent
decades.

Die Exzentrik von Fornasettis Entwürfen mit ihren
surrealen und üppigen »trompe-l'œil«-Dekors beeinflußte
die italienische Anti-Design-Bewegung der folgenden
Jahrzehnte.

L'excentricité des créations de Fornasetti, avec leur
décor en trompe-l'œil surréaliste et exubérant, allait
influencer le mouvement italien de l'anti-design au
cours des décennies suivantes.

▶ Detail of Sun chair

Piero Fornasetti

Moor, c. 1955

*Lacquered and screen-printed moulded plywood seats on painted tapering tubular metal legs |
Sitzschale aus geformtem Schichtholz, lackiert und siebbedruckt, Stuhlbeine aus Stahlrohr |
Siège en contre-plaqué moulé sérigraphié et laqué, pieds fuselés en tube de métal*

FORNASETTI, MILAN,
FROM C. 1955 TO
PRESENT

Fornasetti rejected the fundamental principles of the Modern Movement
through his use of applied decoration. By juxtaposing classical and art-
historical motifs onto quirky modern forms, he made humorous jibes at
the elevation and what he saw as the pretensions of both academic art and
Modernism.

*Fornasettis gedruckte Dekore mißachteten die Prinzipien der Moderne. Durch
die Kombination klassischer kunsthistorischer Motive mit eigenwilligen modernen Formen verhöhnte er das Etablierte und die Anmaßungen des Akademismus
und der Moderne.*

Piero Fornasetti

Corinthian Capitello,
c. 1955

*Lacquered and screen-printed moulded plywood seat on painted tapering tubular metal legs |
Sitzschale aus geformtem Schichtholz, lackiert und siebbedruckt, Stuhlbeine aus Stahlrohr |
Siège en contre-plaqué moulé sérigraphié et laqué, pieds fuselés en tube de métal*

FORNASETTI, MILAN,
FROM C. 1955 TO
PRESENT

▼ Piero Fornasetti
Ionic Capitello chair,
c. 1955

FORNASETTI, MILAN,
C. 1955 TO PRESENT

À travers ses décors appliqués, Fornasetti rejette les principes fondamentaux du modernisme. En appliquant des motifs antiques et historiques sur des formes modernes bizarres, il se moque avec humour de ce qu'il considérait comme les prétentions de l'art académique et du modernisme.

309

Achille & Pier Giacomo Castiglioni

Mezzadro, 1957

Lacquered tractor seat on chromed flat steel stem with wing-nut and solid beech footrest | Traktorsitz, lackiert, verchromte Stahlfeder mit Flügelmutter, Fußstütze aus Buche | Siège de tracteur laqué, pied en acier plat chromé, repose-pied en hêtre massif, fixation par vis à papillon

ZANOTTA, MILAN, FROM 1983 TO PRESENT

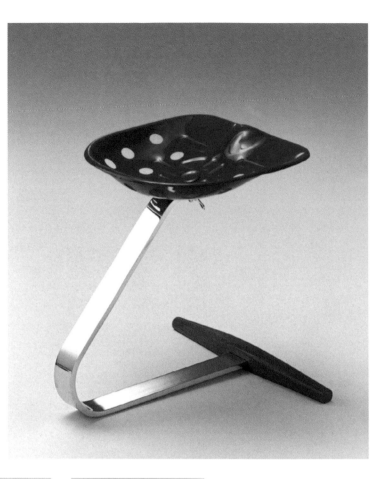

▼ **Benjamin Baldwin**
Tractor seat chair, c. 1953

BALDWIN-MACHADO, NEW YORK

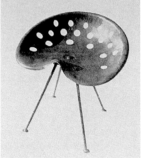

▲ Canadian tractor seat, 19th century

▲ **Mies van der Rohe**
Sketch of tractor seat, c. 1940

Exploiting Duchamp's concept of the ready-made in furniture design, the "Mezzadro" and "Sella" stools were deemed too radical to be put into production until 1983. Interestingly, earlier precedents for tractor-seat stools exist including Benjamin Baldwin's design of c. 1953.

Der »Mezzadro«- und der »Sella«-Hocker, die von Duchamps Konzept des Ready-made im Möbeldesign Gebrauch machen, galten als zu radikal und gingen erst 1983 in Produktion. Interessanterweise gibt es für den Traktorsitz-Hocker Vorläufer, so etwa den um 1953 entstandenen Entwurf von Benjamin Baldwin.

Exploitant le concept des ready-made de Marcel Duchamp dans la création de mobilier, les modèles « Mezzadro » et le « Sella » furent jugés trop radicaux pour êtres mis en production avant 1983. D'autres exemples d'utilisation détournée de sièges de tracteurs avaient été publiés par le passé, dont celui de Benjamin Baldwin, vers 1953.

**Achille &
Pier Giacomo
Castiglioni**

Sella, **1957**

Racing bicycle saddle on lacquered tubular steel column with cast-iron base | Fahrrad-Rennsattel auf einer lackierten Stahlstange, Fuß aus Gußeisen | Selle de vélo de course, pied-colonne en tube d'acier peint, base en fonte de fer

ZANOTTA, MILAN, FROM 1983 TO PRESENT

Unknown

Model No. LSt 21B,
c. 1958

Tubular steel frame
with vinyl-covered
upholstered seat and
back | Rahmen aus
Stahlrohr, Sitzfläche
und Rückenlehne
gepolstert und mit
Vinylbezug | Châssis
en tube d'acier, siège
et dossier en vinyle
rembourré

MAUSER-WERKE,
WALDECK,
FROM 1958

The strong geometry and striking textile pattern of this
unusual, reverse cantilevered chair predicts Pop design.
A version of the chair with arms was also produced.
Die betonte Geometrie und das auffällige Muster des
Bezugs dieses ungewöhnlich konstruierten (umgekehrten)
Freischwingers nimmt die Entwürfe des Pop-Designs vor-
weg. Von diesem Stuhl existiert auch eine Version mit
Armlehnen.
La forte présence géométrique et le tissu de cette
chauffeuse curieuse en porte à faux inversé annonce le
Pop design. Une version avec accoudoirs fut également
fabriquée.

▶ Verner Panton
sitting in Heart
chair, 1959

The futuristic "Cone" chair and slightly later "Heart" chair were the result of a conscious decision by Panton to divorce himself from any preconceived notions of what a chair should look like.

Der futuristische »Cone«-Stuhl und der etwas später entstandene »Heart«-Stuhl waren das Resultat von Pantons entschiedenem Bestreben, sich von allen vorgefaßten Vorstellungen, was ein Stuhl sein soll, zu lösen.

Ce fauteuil « Cone » futuriste, ainsi que la chauffeuse légèrement ultérieure « Heart », résultant de la volonté de Panton de se débarrasser de tous les préjugés existants sur la forme d'un fauteuil.

Verner Panton

Cone, 1958

Fabric-covered foam-upholstered bent sheet metal construction, metal base | Gebogenes Stahlblech, Schaumstoffpolsterung mit Stoffbezug, Kreuzfuß | Structure en tôle cintrée, rembourrage de mousse recouverte de tissu, piètement métallique

PLUS-LINJE, COPENHAGEN (REDESIGNED AND REISSUED IN 1994 BY POLYTHEMA)

Verner Panton

Wire Cone, 1960

Chromed bent steel rod frame on swivelling four-point metal base and later on circular base with loose foam-uphol-stered seat and back cushions | Gebogener Stahldraht, ver-chromt, Sitz- und Rückenkissen mit Schaumstoffpolste-rung und Stoffbezug kreuzförmiger (später runder) drehbarer Metallfuß | Châssis en fil de métal cintré chromé, base métallique pivotante, coussins de siège et de dossier rembourrés de mousse

PLUS-LINJE, COPEN-HAGEN, FROM C.1960 (REISSUED BY FRITZ HANSEN UNTIL C. 1990)

▼ Verner Panton
Wire chair, 1959

PLUS-LINJE, COPEN-HAGEN

Panton has always concerned himself primarily with the inherent potential of new materials and their application. In doing so, he has consistently generated highly innovative forms.

Panton hat sich immer mit den Möglichkeiten neuer Werkstoffe und ihrer Verwendung beschäftigt. Auf diese Weise hat er äußerst innovative Formen geschaffen.

Tout au long de sa carrière, Panton s'est essentielle-ment intéressé au potentiel des ma-tériaux nouveaux et à leurs applica-tions. Ce faisant, il a réussi à créer des formes extrêmement nova-trices.

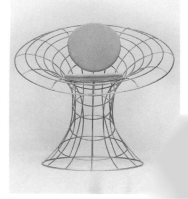

◄ Verner Panton
Adjustable Peacock chair, 1960

PLUS-LINJE, COPEN-HAGEN

Mathieu Matégot

Nagasaki, 1951

Painted tubular steel frame with perforated metal seat and back | Rahmen aus Stahlrohr, lackiert, Sitzfläche und Rückenlehne aus perforiertem Stahlblech | Châssis en tube d'acier peint, siège et dossier en métal perforé

Preferring metal to any another material, Matégot utilised tubular steel, steel rods and perforated metal in his furniture designs. The form of this chair was dictated by a minimum use of materials.

Matégot, der Metall allen anderen Materialien vorzog, verwendete Stahlrohr, Stahlstäbe und perforiertes Blech für seine Möbelentwürfe. Sparsamster Materialeinsatz führte zur Form dieses Stuhls.

Préférant le métal à tout autre matériau, Matégot fit largement appel au tube d'acier, aux tiges d'acier et à la tôle perforée dans ses créations. La forme de ce siège était dictée par la volonté d'utiliser le moins de matériau possible.

Charlotte Perriand

Synthese des Arts,
1953

Painted bent plywood
construction |
Konstruktion aus
gebogenem Schicht-
holz, lackiert | Contre-
plaqué cintré peint

PROBABLY GALERIE
STEPH SIMON,
PARIS, FROM 1955

Perriand lived in Japan (1940–1946) at the invitation of the Japanese
government and was responsible for a cultural exchange between East and
West. This diminutive chair can be seen as a "synthesis of the arts" of
Oriental and Western culture.

Perriand hat auf Einladung der japanischen Regierung von 1940 bis 1946 in
Japan gelebt und war hier verantwortlich für den kulturellen Austausch zwischen
Ost und West. Dieser kleine Stuhl kann als eine »Synthese der Kunst« fernöstli-
cher und abendländischer Kultur betrachtet werden.

Charlotte Perriand vécut au Japon de 1940 à 1946, à l'invitation du
Gouvernement japonais, et fut responsable des échanges culturels entre
l'Orient et l'Occident. Cette petite chaise est une sorte de « synthèse des
arts » des deux cultures.

Achille &
Pier Giacomo
Castiglioni

Spulga, 1960

*Painted bent tubular
steel frame with
upholstered seat |
Rahmen aus geboge-
nem und lackiertem
Stahlrohr, gepolsterte
Sitzfläche | Châssis en
tube d'acier cintré
peint, siège rembourré*

ZANOTTA, MILAN,
FROM 1980 TO
PRESENT

In 1996, Ingo Maurer wrote to
Achille Castiglioni: "One of the
qualities I most appreciate and
greatly admire is the absolute absence of bourgeoisie in your work.
Never have I detected even the
slightest trace of pretentiousness
. . . And this, I'm certain, is the
fruit of your way of thinking 'pure-
naturalfrankspontanousgenuine-
transparent' which stems from the
beauty of your heart."
*1996 schrieb Ingo Maurer an Achille
Castiglioni: »Was ich an den
Qualitäten Ihrer Arbeit am meisten
schätze und bewundere, ist das absolute Fehlen alles Bourgeoisen.
Nirgends habe ich auch nur einen
    ouch von Prätentiösität ent-
        n können . . . Und das,
        ich mir sicher, ist die
            r >purnatürlichfrei-
                nsparenten<
                'er Schönheit
                ingt.«*

En 1996, Ingo Maurer écrivit à Achille Castiglioni
« L'une des qualités que j'apprécie et admire le plus
dans votre œuvre est l'absence totale d'esprit bour-
geois. Jamais je n'y ai détecté la plus infime trace de
prétention . . . Et ceci vient, j'en suis certain, de votre
mode de pensée, ‹ purnaturelfrancspontanéauthentique-
lumineux › qui sort tout droit de votre cœur. »

Achille &
Pier Giacomo
Castiglioni

Allunaggio, 1966

*Enamelled tubular
steel frame with
aluminium seat |
Gestell aus geboge-
nem Stahlrohr,
einbrennlackiert,
Sitzfläche aus
Aluminium |
Structure en tube
d'acier émaillé, siège
en aluminium*

ZANOTTA, MILAN,
FROM 1980 TO
PRESENT

◀ Achille Castiglioni
on the Allunaggio
(Moon Landing)
chair, 1981

Grete Jalk

Chair, 1963

Teak-faced moulded plywood construction with steel bolts | Konstruktion aus geformtem Schichtholz, Teakfurnier, Verbindungsbolzen aus Stahl | Contreplaqué cintré, plaqué teck, boulons en acier

POUL JEPPESEN,
STOR HEDDINGE,
1963–c. 1964

▼ **Grete Jalk**
Prototype of side chair, c. 1963

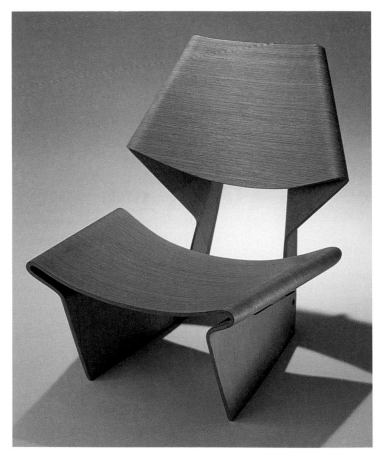

Jalk continued the tradition of exploring the structural and aesthetic potential of plywood. For the two-piece construction, the plywood has been bent to an unprecedented degree across a single plane.

Jalk steht in der Auseinandersetzung mit den technischen und ästhetischen Möglichkeiten von Schichtholz. Für die zweiteilige Konstruktion ist das Schichtholz in einem nicht für möglich gehaltenen Maß gebogen worden.

Avec ce modèle, Jalk poursuit la tradition d'exploration des qualités potentielles structurelles et esthétiques du contre-plaqué. Pour cette construction en deux éléments, la feuille de contre-plaqué a été pliée selon des angles encore jamais atteints.

Ray Eames was mostly responsible for the design of these stools for the Time & Life Building lobby. Conceived for use as either seats or low tables, each design shared identical upper and lower sections with only the central element of each differing. The designs were undoubtedly inspired by African stools.

Diese Hocker für das Foyer des Time & Life-Gebäudes sind hauptsächlich das Werk von Ray Eames. Ihre Entwürfe, gedacht als Hocker oder als kleine Tische, haben identische Kopf- und Fußteile, der Mittelteil dagegen variiert von Hocker zu Hocker. Anregung für diese Arbeit lieferten sicherlich die afrikanischen Hocker, von denen es im Haus der Eames' mehrere gab.

Ces tabourets du hall d'accueil du Time & Life Building sont essentiellement dus à Ray Eames. Conçu pour servir aussi bien de siège que de table basse, chaque modèle possède une partie supérieure et une base identiques; seul l'élément central diffère. Ces créations sont certainement inspirées de tabourets africains dont les Eames possédaient plusieurs exemplaires dans leur maison.

Charles & Ray Eames

Time-Life stools, 1960

Turned solid walnut constructions | Massives Walnuß-holz, gedrechselt | Noyer massif tourné

HERMAN MILLER FURNITURE CO., ZEELAND, MICHIGAN FROM 1960 TO PRESENT

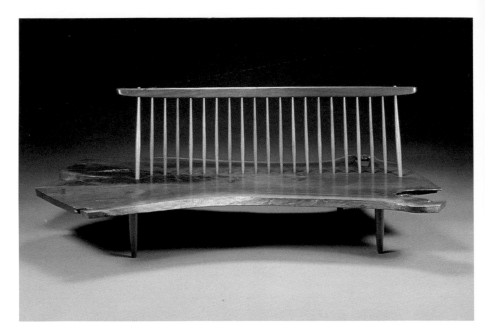

George Nakashima

Conoid, c. 1961

Solid walnut construction | Konstruktion aus massivem Walnußholz | Noyer massif

A proponent of the Craft Revival, Nakashima preferred the title "woodworker" to craftsman. His workshop was part-mechanised in order to be competitive, but quality and creative expression were never compromised.

Nakashima, eine führende Figur des »Crafts Revival«, ließ sich lieber »Holzarbeiter« als »Kunsthandwerker« nennen. Obwohl seine Werkstatt nur teilweise mechanisiert war, um sie wettbewerbsfähig zu halten, kannte er in Fragen der Qualität und des kreativen Ausdrucks keine Kompromisse.

Défenseur du « Craft Revival », Nakashima préférait le titre d'ébéniste à celui d'artisan. Son atelier était partiellement mécanisé pour conserver des prix concurrentiels, mais ce ne fut jamais aux dépens de la qualité et de l'expression créatrice.

◄**George Nakashima**
Armchair, c. 1946

RETAILED BY KNOLL ASSOCIATES

Gerrit Rietveld

Steltman, 1963

*White painted oak
construction |
Konstruktion aus
Eiche, weiß lackiert |
Chêne peint en blanc*

GERARD A. VAN DE
GROENEKAN,
UTRECHT

▼ Contemporary
copy of Steltman
chair

Originally designed for the Steltman jewellery shop in
the Hague, Rietveld also created an upholstered version
of this chair. These were his last and most elemental
designs.

*Der ursprüngliche Entwurf entstand für den Laden des
Juweliers Steltman in Den Haag; Rietveld hat auch eine
gepolsterte Version dieses Stuhles geschaffen. Es handelt
sich um Rietvelds letzte und reduzierteste Entwürfe.*

Conçu à l'origine pour la bijouterie Steltman à La Haye,
ce modèle fut également proposé en version rembourrée par Rietveld. Ce furent là ses dernières et ses plus
pures créations.

David Rowland

Model No. GF 40/4,
1964

Fabric-covered
upholstered moulded
plywood seat and
back with chromed
steel rod frame and
laminate-faced ply-
wood tablet |
Rahmen aus Stahl-
stäben, verchromt,
Sitzschale und
Rückenlehne aus ge-
formtem Schichtholz,
Polsterung mit Stoff-
bezug, Klapptisch aus
Sperrholz mit Kunst-
stoffoberfläche | Siège
et dossier en contre-
plaqué moulé
rembourrés et
recouverts de tissu,
châssis en fil d'acier
chromé, tablette en
contre-plaqué
recouvert de stratifié

GENERAL
FIREPROOFING CO.,
YOUNGSTOWN,
OHIO, FROM 1964
TO PRESENT & HOWE
EUROPE, MIDDLE-
FART, FROM 1976 TO
PRESENT

▲ David Rowland
GF 40/4 series, 1964

GENERAL FIREPROOFING CO., YOUNGSTOWN,
OHIO, FROM 1964 TO PRESENT & HOWE
EUROPE, MIDDLEFART, FROM 1976 TO PRESENT

The GF 40/4 chair is one of the most successful contract chairs ever designed. Forty can be stacked on a
specially designed trolley to a height of only four feet –
hence its title. Rowland, who studied under László
Moholy-Nagy and later trained at the Cranbrook
Academy, was awarded a gold medal for this design
at the Milan XIII Triennale in 1964.

Der Stuhl GF 40/4 ist einer der erfolgreichsten Stuhl-
entwürfe für den öffentlichen Raum. Vierzig Stühle lassen
sich auf einem dafür entwickelten Transportkarren überein-
anderstapeln, wobei der Stapel nicht höher ist als

David Rowland

Model No. GF 40/4,
1964

Beech-faced moulded
plywood seat and
back with chromed
steel rod frame |
Rahmen aus Stahl-
stäben, verchromt,
Sitzfläche und
Rückenlehne aus
geformtem Schicht-
holz mit Buchen-
furnier | Siège et
dossier en contre-
plaqué moulé,
placage de hêtre,
châssis en fil d'acier
chromé

GENERAL
FIREPROOFING CO.,
YOUNGSTOWN,
OHIO, FROM 1964
TO PRESENT & HOWE
EUROPE, MIDDLE-
FART, FROM 1976 TO
PRESENT

ca. 1,30 m (4 Fuß); daher stammt auch seine Modellbezeichnung. Rowland, der
bei László Moholy-Nagy und später an der Cranbrook Academy studierte, wurde
für seinen Entwurf 1964 auf der XIII. Mailänder Triennale mit einer
Goldmedaille ausgezeichnet.

Le GF 40/4 est l'une des chaises de bureau les plus célèbres jamais fabriquées. Quarante d'entre elles peuvent être empilées sur un chariot spécialement conçu, sur une hauteur de 1,30 m seulement (40 sur 4 pieds, d'où son
nom). Rowland, qui étudia auprès de László Moholy-Nagy puis à la
Cranbrook Academy, reçut une médaille d'or pour ce modèle, lors de la
XIIIᵉ Triennale de Milan, en 1964.

▲ **Robin Day**
Polyprop,
c. 1962–1963

S. HILLE & CO.,
LONDON, (LATER TO
BECOME HILLE
INTERNATIONAL),
FROM 1963 TO
PRESENT

▲ **Robin Day**
Upholstered
Polyprop, c. 1963

S. HILLE & CO.,
LONDON, (LATER TO
BECOME HILLE
INTERNATIONAL),
FROM 1963 TO
PRESENT

▲ **Robin Day**
Polo chair,
1975

S. HILLE & CO.,
LONDON, (LATER TO
BECOME HILLE
INTERNATIONAL),
FROM 1975 TO
PRESENT

Inspired by the Eameses' "Plastic Shell" chairs, Day developed the "Polyprop" chair as an even lower cost seating solution. Its single-form seat shell was the first to be injection-moulded in polypropylene – a recently developed inexpensive, durable and lightweight thermoplastic. A single injection moulding tool can produce 4,000 seat shells a week. From 1963 to the present, over 14 million chairs from the "Polyprop" programme have been sold.

Angeregt durch die »Plastic Shell«-Stühle von Charles und Ray Eames, entwickelte Day mit dem »Polyprop«-Stuhl ein noch preiswerteres Sitzmöbel. Die einteilige Sitzschale war die erste aus Polypropylen – einem kurz zuvor entwickelten preiswerten, dauerhaften und leichten Thermoplast – im Spritzgußverfahren hergestellt wurde. Mit einer einzigen Spritzgußmaschine können pro Woche 4000 Sitzschalen gefertigt werden. Seit 1963 wurden mehr als 14 Millionen Stühle dieser Serie verkauft.

Robin Day

Polyprop,
1962–1963

Injection-moulded
polypropylene seat
shell on enamelled
bent tubular steel
base | Im Spritzguß-
verfahren hergestellte
Sitzschale aus Poly-
propylen, Stuhlbeine
aus gebogenem Stahl-
rohr, einbrenn-
lackiert | Coquille en
polypropylène moulé
par injection,
piètement en tube
d'acier émaillé cintré

S. HILLE & CO.,
LONDON (LATER TO
BECOME HILLE
INTERNATIONAL),
FROM 1963 TO
PRESENT

◄ **Robin Day**
Series E educational
seating, 1972

S. HILLE & CO.,
LONDON (LATER TO
BECOME HILLE
INTERNATIONAL),
FROM 1972 TO
PRESENT

Inspiré par les sièges à coquille plastique des Eames, Day mit au point ce modèle « Polyprop » encore meilleur marché. La coquille d'une pièce est la première à avoir été réalisée en polypropylène moulé par injection, un plastique bon marché, résistant, léger et récemment découvert. Un seul moule pouvait produire 4 000 coquilles de siège par semaine. Depuis 1963, plus de 14 millions de ces chaises ont été vendues.

Charles & Ray Eames

La Fonda, 1961

Moulded reinforced fibreglass seat shell on cast aluminium base | Sitzschale aus geformtem, fiberglasverstärktem Kunststoff, Untergestell aus Gußaluminium | Coquille de siège en fibre de verre moulée renforcée, piètement en fonte d'aluminium

HERMAN MILLER FURNITURE CO., ZEELAND, MICHIGAN, FROM 1961 TO PRESENT

Designed by the Eames Office in collaboration with Alexander Girard for the La Fonda del Sol restaurant in New York's Time & Life Building, these chairs are low-backed versions of the earlier "Plastic Shell" chairs. The "La Fonda" seat shells were also used in tandem seating systems for airports.

Für diese Stühle, die das Designbüro Eames in Zusammenarbeit mit Alexander Girard für das Restaurant La Fonda del Sol im Times & Life Gebäude, New York, entworfen hat, wurden verkürzte Versionen der Sitzschalen der älteren »Plastic Shell«-Stühle verwendet. Mit den »La Fonda«-Sitzschalen wurde auch das »Tandem Shell Seating«-System für Flughafenwartezonen bestückt.

Conçus par les Eames en collaboration avec Alexander Girard pour le restaurant La Fonda del Sol du New York Times & Life Building, ces sièges sont des versions à dossiers bas de modèles antérieurs à coquille plastique. Ils furent également utilisés dans les aéroports, en système de sièges disposés l'un à côté de l'autre.

Marc Held

Culbuto, 1967

*Fibreglass shells with
internal textile-
covered foam
upholstery | Sitz-
schalen aus fiberglas-
verstärktem Kunst-
stoff, Schaumstoff-
polsterung mit Stoff-
bezug | Coquilles en
fibre de verre,
intérieurement
rembourrées et
recouvertes de tissu*

KNOLL
INTERNATIONAL,
NEW YORK, FROM
1970

The rocking "Culbuto" series, which included a high-back chair, a low-back
chair and an ottoman was designed by Held for Knoll International in 1967.
Although not put into production until 1970, it was the first French-designed
seating to be manufactured by the company.

*Die Schaukelstuhlserie »Culbuto«, zu der ein hochlehniger und ein tieflehniger
Sessel sowie ein Fußhocker gehören, entwarf Held 1967 für Knoll International.
Mit der Produktion begann Knoll erst 1970, dennoch ist dieser Entwurf der erste
französische, den dieser Hersteller produziert hat.*

La série à bascule «Culbuto», qui comprenait un fauteuil à dossier haut, un
à dossier bas et une ottomane, fut dessinée par Marc Held en 1967 pour
Knoll International. Mis en production en 1970 seulement, ce fut le premier
siège conçu par un Français, à être fabriqué par cette firme.

Charles & Ray Eames

Tandem Shell Seating, 1962–1963

Moulded reinforced fibreglass seat shells with internal vinyl or fabric-covered upholstery on cast aluminium and steel beam base | Sitzschalen aus formgepreßtem, verstärktem Fiberglas, Polster mit Vinyl oder Stoff bezogen, Tragkonstruktion aus Aluminium und Stahl | Coquille de siège en fibre de verre moulée renforcée, rembourrage recouvert de vinyle ou de tissu, base en fonte d'aluminium et poutrelle d'acier

HERMAN MILLER
FURNITURE CO.,
ZEELAND,
MICHIGAN, FROM
1962 TO PRESENT

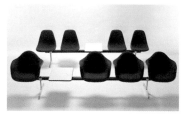

▲ **Charles & Ray Eames**
Tandem Shell Seating, 1962

HERMAN MILLER FURNITURE CO., ZEELAND,
MICHIGAN, FROM 1962 TO PRESENT

This system combines the Eameses' earlier plastic seat shells with the steel T-beam developed for their "Tandem Sling Seating", the most successful airport seating.

Für dieses Sitzmöbelsystem haben die Eames Sitzschalen aus Kunststoff von früheren Modellen mit einem T-förmigen Träger aus Stahl verbunden, den sie für das »Tandem Sling Seating« entwickelt hatten. Dieses System ist das erfolgreichste, das je für Flughäfen produziert wurde.

Ce système combine les premiers sièges à coquilles en plastique des Eames et le modèle à poutrelle d'acier en T développé pour le « Tandem Sling Seating ». C'est la formule de sièges pour aéroports la plus réussie.

The "Tandem Sling Seating" was developed initially to provide attractive, comfortable and durable seating for Dulles Airport in Washington and O'Hare Airport in Chicago. The heat-sealed Naugahyde sling seats were designed to withstand severe stress, while the continuous T-beams accommodated from two to ten seats in either single or back-to-back double rows.

Das »Tandem Sling Seating« wurde ursprünglich als attraktives, bequemes und strapazierfähiges Sitzsystem für den Washingtoner Dulles Airport und für den O'Hare Airport in Chicago entwickelt. Die Sitzbespannungen aus hitzeverschweißtem Naugahyde-Vinyl sollten großen Belastungen standhalten. Die durchlaufenden T-Träger können zwei bis zehn Sitze aufnehmen, entweder in einer Einzelreihe oder Rücken an Rücken in einer Doppelreihe.

Le « Tandem Sling Seating » fut mis au point à l'origine pour les aéroports Dulles de Washington et O'Hare à Chicago. Le modèle en Naugahyde scellé à chaud fut conçu pour des utilisations intensives. Les poutrelles en T pouvaient recevoir jusqu'à dix sièges en rangée simple ou double, dos à dos.

Charles & Ray Eames

Tandem Sling Seating, 1962

Cast aluminium and steel frame with vinyl foam, nylon sling seats, urethane armrests | Rahmen aus Gußaluminium und Stahl, Sitzfläche aus Vinylschaumstoff und Kunstleder, Armlehnen aus geformtem Urethan | Châssis en fonte d'aluminium et acier, mousse de vinyle, accoudoirs en uréthane

HERMAN MILLER FURNITURE CO., ZEELAND, MICHIGAN, FROM 1962 TO PRESENT

**Charles &
Ray Eames**

*Model No. ES106,
1968*

Nylon-coated cast
aluminium frame and
base with leather-
covered polyurethane
foam upholstered
seating section | Ge-
stell aus nylonbe-
schichtetem Gußalu-
minium, Polsterung
aus Polyurethan-
schaumstoff, mit
Lederbezug | Châssis
en fonte d'aluminium
gainé de nylon, rem-
bourrage en mousse
de polyuréthane
recouverte de cuir

HERMAN MILLER
FURNITURE CO.,
ZEELAND,
MICHIGAN, FROM
1968 TO PRESENT

Designed for Billy Wilder, who enjoyed brief naps, the narrowness of this
chaise required his arms to be folded across his chest when reclining. After
a short time, his arms would eventually fall to the side, waking him up.
*Diese Liege wurde für Billy Wilder entworfen, der gern ein kurzes Nickerchen
machte. Die Liege war so schmal, daß Wilder die Arme über der Brust verschrän-
ken mußte. Schlief er wirklich fest ein, fielen die Arme herab, und er erwachte.*
Conçu pour Billy Wilder, qui appréciait les courtes siestes, cette chaise-
longue est si étroite qu'elle suppose, en position allongée, que les bras restent croisés sur la poitrine. Après quelques minutes, ils retombent sur les
côtés, réveillant le dormeur.

▶ **Charles & Ray
Eames**
Time-Life executive
desk chair, 1960

HERMAN MILLER
FURNITURE CO.,
ZEELAND,
MICHIGAN, FROM
C. 1960 TO PRESENT

Charles & Ray Eames

Soft Pad Series,
Model No. EA435,
1969

Cast aluminium
frame on castors with
height adjustment
mechanism and sling
seat of urethane foam
upholstery wrapped in
polyester fibre batting
and covered in
leather | Höhenver-
stellbarer Rahmen
aus Gußaluminium
auf Rollen, einge-
hängte Polsterung aus
Urethanschaumstoff
und Polyesterwatte
mit Lederbezug |
Châssis en fonte
d'aluminium sur
roulettes, mécanisme
de réglage en
hauteur, siège en cuir
à rembourrage en
mousse d'uréthane
enveloppée d'une
ouate de fibre
polyester

HERMAN MILLER
FURNITURE CO.,
ZEELAND,
MICHIGAN, FROM
1969 TO PRESENT

◄ Charles & Ray
Eames
Soft Pad Series,
Model Nos. HEA
438 & 423, 1969

HERMAN MILLER
FURNITURE CO.,
ZEELAND,
MICHIGAN, FROM
1969 TO PRESENT

The "Soft Pad Series" utilises the same system of frames as the "Aluminium Group". With its leather cushions, this "executive" system complemented the Eameses' ES106 chaise and No. 670 lounge chair.

Für die »Soft Pad Series« verwendete man dasselbe Gestellsystem wie für die »Aluminium Group«. Diese leder-gepolsterten Sitzmöbel ergänzen die Sessel ES106 und Nr. 670 zu einem Programm für die Vorstandsetage.

La série « Soft Pad » fait appel au même système de châssis que de l' « Aluminium Group ». Avec ses coussins en cuir, ce siège de direction est un hommage aux fauteuils des Eames ES106 et n° 670.

George Nelson

Sling Sofa, 1964

Chromed tubular
steel frame, leather
sling and upholstered
cushions with rubber
supporting straps |
Rahmen aus Stahl-
rohr, verchromt,
Bespannung und
gepolsterte Sitzkissen
aus Leder, Gummi-
gurte | Châssis en
tube d'acier chromé,
cuir rembourré,
sangles de caoutchouc

HERMAN MILLER
FURNITURE CO.,
ZEELAND, MICHI-
GAN, FROM 1964

▶ **George Nelson**
Catenary, 1959

HERMAN MILLER
FURNITURF CO.,
ZEELAND, MICHI-
GAN, 1963–1968

The idea of a sling seat supported by rubber webbing was inspired by
Citroën's 2CV latex-supported car seat. The "cat's cradle" frame of the
"Catenary" chair reveals the influence of Buckminster Fuller.

*Die Idee zu einer von Gummigewebe getragenen Sitzbespannung wurde durch
die Latex-Autositze im Citroën 2CV angeregt. Das an ein Fadenspiel erinnernde
Untergestell des »Catenary«-Stuhls zeigt den Einfluß von Buckminster Fuller.*

L'idée d'un siège suspendu soutenu par des sangles de caoutchouc vint à
Nelson en regardant le siège de la 2CV Citroën. Le châssis en « panier de
chat » de la chauffeuse « Catenary » révèle l'influence de Buckminster Fuller.

Charles Pollock

Model No. 12E1, 1965

Fibreglass shell with chromed, extruded aluminium rim holding leather-covered upholstery, on swivelling aluminium base with castors | Sitzschale aus fiberglasverstärktem Kunststoff, integrierte Lederpolsterung, Einfassung aus Aluminium, drehbares Unterstell aus Aluminium, auf Rollen | Coquille de fibre de verre, cerclage en aluminium extrudé, cuir rembourré, piètement en fonte d'aluminium, roulettes

KNOLL INTER-
NATIONAL, NEW
YORK, FROM 1965
TO PRESENT

Pollock's executive 12E1 series has an extruded aluminium rim which holds the seat components of the chair together. This device also functions as one of the main supporting elements of the design.

Ein umlaufender Aluminiumwulst hält die einzelnen Elemente von Pollocks Vorstandssessel 12E1 zusammen, zugleich ist dieser Rahmen der eigentlich tragende Teil der Konstruktion.

La série de fauteuils de direction 12E1 de Pollock possède une armature en aluminium extrudé qui maintient ensemble les différents éléments. Ce système assure la principale fonction de soutien de ce siège.

◄ George Nelson
Catenary chairs with
matching table, 1959

HERMAN MILLER
FURNITURE CO.,
ZEELAND, MICHI-
GAN, 1963–1968

335

Gae Aulenti

April, Model No. 210, 1964

Chromed tubular steel frame with folding mechanism and leather sling seat and back | Rahmen aus Stahlrohr, verchromt, klappbar, Sitzfläche und Rückenlehne mit Lederbespannung | Châssis en tube d'acier chromé, système de repliement, siège et dossier en cuir tendu

ZANOTTA, MILAN, FROM C. 1964 TO PRESENT

▼ **Gionatan De Pas, Donato D'Urbino & Paolo Lomazzi**
Cassina 2290 chair, 1973

ZANOTTA, MILAN, FROM C. 1973 TO PRESENT

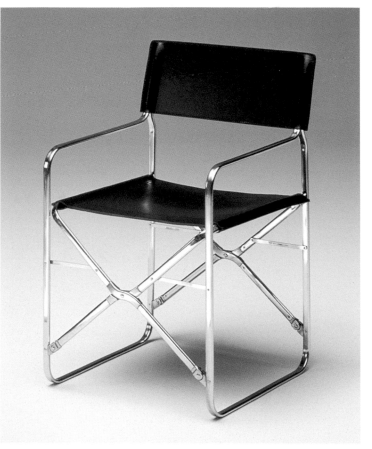

With this design, Aulenti continued the Modern Movement's preference for chromed steel and sling upholstery. Using these materials, she produced a highly efficient Modern reworking of a traditional folding chair.

Mit diesem Entwurf hält Aulenti an der Vorliebe fest, die die Moderne für verchromten Stahl und Spannsitze hegte. Mit diesen Materialien hat sie einen modernen, sehr funktionalen Neuentwurf eines traditionellen Klappstuhls geschaffen.

Avec ce modèle, Aulenti se maintient dans la ligne de la préférence moderniste pour l'acier chromé et les revêtements tendus. Elle réinterprète ici, dans un esprit moderne efficace, le traditionnel fauteuil pliant.

The upholstered sling of the "Duecavalli" chair affords great comfort to the user while the visual and structural simplicity of its frame provides the design with a strong and uncluttered profile.

Die gepolsterte Sitzbespannung des »Duecavalli«-Stuhls bietet dem Sitzenden Bequemlichkeit, während die optische und konstruktionstechnische Schlichtheit des Rahmens dem Stuhl einen starken und klaren Ausdruck verleiht.

La chauffeuse rembourrée « Duecavalli » offre un grand confort d'utilisation. La simplicité visuelle et structurelle de son ossature lui donne un profil puissant et épuré.

Gionatan De Pas, Donato D'Urbino & Paolo Lomazzi

Duecavalli, 1969

Chromed tubular steel frame with textile-covered quilted foam sling seat | Rahmen aus Stahlrohr, verchromt, gefaltete Schaumstoffbespannung mit Stoffbezug | Châssis en tube d'acier chromé, siège en mousse piquée recouverte de tissu

DRIADE, PIACENZA, FROM 1969

Don Albinson

Albinson, Model No. 1601, 1965

Cast aluminium frame with moulded polypropylene seat and back | Rahmen aus Gußaluminium, Sitzfläche und Rückenlehne aus geformtem Polypropylen | Châssis en fonte d'aluminium, siège et dossier en polypropylène moulé

KNOLL INTERNATIONAL, NEW YORK, FROM 1965

▼ Don Albinson
Albinson stacking chairs, 1965

KNOLL INTERNATIONAL, NEW YORK, 1965

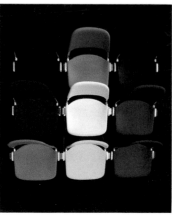

Albinson became Knoll's Design & Development director in 1964. While his stacking chair bears a similarity to Day's "Polyprop", it was intended for a higher end of the contract market.

1964 wurde Albinson Leiter der Design & Development Abteilung von Knoll. Sein Stapelstuhl, der Ähnlichkeiten mit Days »Polyprop«-Stuhl zeigt, wurde für den gehobeneren Büromöbelmarkt entwickelt.

Albinson devint directeur du département Design & Développement de Knoll en 1964. Bien que légèrement similaire au « Polyprop » de Day, ce siège était destiné à un secteur plus exigeant du marché du siège de bureau.

George Nelson

*Perch, Model
No. 64940, 1964*

Polished aluminium
frame with height
adjustment
mechanism and
footrest on castors
with upholstered seat
and backrest |
Höhenverstellbarer
Rahmen mit Fuß-
stütze aus poliertem
Aluminium auf
Rollen, Sitzfläche
und Rückenlehne
gepolstert | Structure
en aluminium poli,
mécanisme de réglage
de la hauteur, repose-
pied, dosseret et
roulettes

HERMAN MILLER
FURNITURE CO.,
ZEELAND,
MICHIGAN, FROM
1964 TO PRESENT

The "Perch" drafting seat allowed the user a great deal of freedom of movement. The desire for flexibility in furniture for the work environment gave
rise to Nelson's "Action Office I" system of 1964.
*Der Rollhocker »Perch« für den Zeichentisch läßt dem Benutzer große
Bewegungsfreiheit. Der Bedarf an flexiblen Möbeln für den Arbeitsbereich verhalf
Nelsons Büromöbelsystem »Action Office I« von 1964 zum Durchbruch.*
Le siège de dessinateur « Perch » permettait une grande liberté de mouvement. La recherche d'une souplesse toujours plus grande dans le mobilier
de bureau allait donner naissance au système « Action Office I » de Nelson,
en 1964.

Warren Platner

Model No. 1725 A, 1966

Nickel-plated steel construction with fabric-covered, foam-rubber upholstery | Rahmen aus Stahl, vernickelt, Schaumstoffpolsterung mit Stoffbezug | Construction en acier nickelé, rembourrage en mousse de caoutchouc recouverte de tissu

KNOLL INTERNATIONAL, NEW YORK, FROM 1966 TO PRESENT

Warren Platner said, "As a designer, I felt there was room for the kind of decorative, gentle, graceful kind of design that appeared in a period style like Louis XV. But it could have a more rational base instead of being applied decoration ... A classic is something that every time you look at it, you accept it as it is and you see no way of improving it."

Warren Platner: »Als Designer war mir klar, daß es Raum gab für ein dekoratives, liebenswürdiges, anmutiges Design, so wie zur Zeit des Louis Quinze. Aber es sollte auf rationalerer Basis stehen, es geht nicht um appliziertes Dekor ... Ein Klassiker ist etwas, das dir jedesmal, wenn du es anschaust, gefällt und von dem du nicht weißt, wie man es verbessern könnte.«

Warren Platner: « En tant que designer, je sentais qu'il y avait une place pour le type de meubles décoratifs, agréables et pleins de grâce apparus dans une période comme celle du style Louis XV. Mais ce mobilier pourrait s'appuyer sur une base beaucoup plus rationnelle, au lieu de se contenter d'un décor appliqué ... Un classique est quelque chose qui plaît chaque fois qu'on le regarde, et que l'on ne saurait améliorer. »

Poul Kjaerholm

Model No. PK20,
1967

Stainless steel frame,
leather-covered
upholstery | Rahmen
aus rostfreiem Stahl,
mit Lederpolsterung |
Châssis en acier
inoxydable, recouvert
de cuir rembourré

E. KOLD
CHRISTENSEN,
HELLERUP,
C. 1967–C. 1970
(REISSUED BY FRITZ
HANSEN, ALLERØD,
FROM 1970)

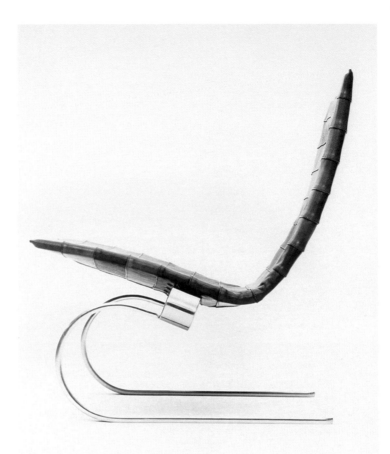

Kjaerholm tempered Modern Movement functionalism with a humanising, Scandinavian approach to design. He considered steel to be a natural material with the same artistic fineness as wood. His comprehensive PK series exploited the material's strength and springing ability. Each design from the series, and the PK24 in particular, is distinguished by its strong lines and high-quality construction.

Kjaerholm mäßigte den Funktionalismus der Moderne durch einen skandinavischen Ansatz im Möbeldesign. Er betrachtete Stahl als ein natürliches Material von der gleichen künstlerischen Schönheit wie Holz. Und mit seiner vielfältigen Serie PK nutzte er Kraft und Elastizität dieses Materials. Jedes Stück der Serie, und ganz besonders der Freischwinger PK24, ist geprägt von ausdrucksvoller Linienführung und der qualitativ hochwertigen Konstruktion.

Kjaerholm tempère le fonctionnalisme moderniste par une approche plus humaine, caractéristique du design scandinave. Pour lui, le tube d'acier est un matériau naturel qui offre les mêmes possibilités esthétiques que le bois. La série PK exploite la résistance et la souplesse de ce matériau. Chacun de ses modèles, et en particulier le PK24, se distingue par la puissance de ses lignes et une remarquable qualité d'exécution.

◄ **Poul Kjaerholm**
Hammock chaise, Model No. PK24, 1965 & Easy chair, Model No. PK22, 1955

E. KOLD CHRISTEN-SEN, HELLERUP, C. 1965–C. 1970, (REISSUED BY FRITZ HANSEN, ALLERØD, FROM C. 1970 TO PRESENT)

Poul Kjaerholm

Hammock, Model No. PK24, 1965

Stainless steel frame with woven cane seating section and leather-covered upholstered headrest | Rahmen aus rost-freiem Stahl, Sitz-fläche aus Rohr-geflecht, gepolsterte Kopfstütze mit Leder-bezug | Châssis en acier inoxydable, siège en jonc tressé, repose-tête en cuir rembourré

E. KOLD CHRISTENSEN, HELLERUP, FROM C. 1965–C. 1970, (REISSUED BY FRITZ HANSEN, ALLERØD, FROM C. 1970, TO PRESENT)

343

Richard Schultz

**Leisure Collection,
1966**

*Cast aluminium
frame with weather-
resistant finish and
woven dacron mesh
seat sections stitched
to vinyl straps |
Rahmen aus Guß-
aluminium mit
wetterfester Beschich-
tung, Sitz- bzw.
Liegeflächen aus auf
Vinylgurten befestig-
tem Dacrongewebe |
Châssis en fonte
d'aluminium,
revêtement résistant
aux intempéries, siège
en maille dacron et
sangles de vinyle*

KNOLL
INTERNATIONAL,
NEW YORK, FROM
C. 1966

The "Leisure Collection" was designed for the hotel contract market and incorporated water-resistant, nylon mesh seats and weather-resistant frames. Having evolved from an earlier steel-wire sun lounger by Schultz (1960–1964), the "Leisure Collection" was awarded an A.I.D. International Design Award in 1967.

Die »Leisure Collection« ist ursprünglich für Hotels bestimmt gewesen, ausge-stattet mit wasserabweisenden Sitz- bzw. Liegeflächen aus Nylongeflecht und wetterfestem Rahmen. Die Entwürfe basieren auf einem früheren Liegestuhl von Schultz, einem Modell mit Drahtgeflecht (1960–1964). 1967 wurde die »Leisure Collection« mit dem internationalen A.I.D.-Designpreis ausgezeichnet.

La « Leisure Collection » fut conçue pour le marché de l'hôtellerie, ce qui explique ses toiles de nylon à maille fine et ses châssis résistant aux intem-péries. Élaboré à partir d'une chaise longue antérieure de Schultz (1960–1964), cet ensemble reçut l'International Design Award de l'A.I.D. en 1967.

The "Amanta's" L-shaped fibreglass-reinforced polyester frame has a slit running down its back to provide a high degree of structural elasticity. It also has turned-up edges to hold the upholstered cushions in place. Variations of the "Amanta" with textile-covered frames were also offered as a means of broadening its appeal.

Die vertikalen Schlitze in den Rückenlehnen des L-förmigen, fiberglasverstärkten Polyesterrahmen des »Amanta«-Sofaprogramms verleihen diesen Sitzgelegenheiten eine hohe Elastizität. Die Kanten sind umgebogen, um den Sitzpolstern Halt zu geben. Variationen des »Amanta« mit stoffbezogenen Gestellen erweitern die Angebotspalette.

La fente du dossier du châssis en L réalisé en polyester renforcé de fibre de verre, de l' « Amanta » améliore l'élasticité de se siège. Ses rebords relevés maintiennent en place les épais coussins. Des variantes de ce siège, avec des châssis habillés de tissu furent également proposées pour séduire une clientèle encore plus large.

Mario Bellini

Amanta, 1966

Moulded fibreglass-reinforced polyester frame with textile-covered foam upholstery | Rahmen aus geformtem, fiberglasverstärktem Polyester, Schaum-stoffpolsterung mit Stoffbezug | Châssis en polyester renforcé de fibre de verre, rembourrage en mousse recouverte de tissu

B & B ITALIA,
NOVEDRATE, COMO,
FROM C. 1996
(REISSUED BY
HERMAN MILLER
FURNITURE CO.,
ZEELAND,
MICHIGAN, FROM
1995)

Dieter Rams

Model No. RZ 62,
1962

Fibreglass frame with
metal fittings and
internal leather-
covered latex foam
upholstery | Rahmen
aus fiberglasverstärk-
tem Kunststoff,
Metallbeschläge, inte-
grierte Latexschaum-
stoffpolsterung mit
Lederbezug | Châssis
en fibre de verre,
garnitures métalliques
et cuir rembourré de
mousse de latex

VITSOE & ZAPF,
ESCHBORN, FROM
C. 1962 TO PRESENT

▼ **Dieter Rams**
Lounge chairs,
Model Nos. 601 &
602, 1960

VITSOE & ZAPF,
ESCHBORN

Rams' designs are characterized by an economical geometric vocabulary of form. His chairs for Vitsoe are demonstrations of his desire "to make things that recede into the background".

Die Entwürfe von Rams zeichnen sich durch ein reduziertes geometrisches Formenvokabular aus. Seine Sitzmöbel für Vitsoe demonstrieren sein Verlangen, »Dinge zu schaffen, die mit dem Hintergrund verschmelzen«.

Les modèles de Rams se distinguent par un vocabulaire géométrique et restreint des formes. Ses sièges pour Vitsoe illustrent son désir « de créer des objets qui se fondent dans l'arrière-plan ».

Arne Jacobsen

*Oxford, Model
No. 3291, 1965*

Upholstered moulded
plywood seat shell on
swivelling cast
aluminium base with
castors | Gepolsterte
Sitzschale aus ge-
formtem Schichtholz,
drehbares Unter-
gestell aus Gußalu-
minium mit Rollen |
Coquille en contre-
plaqué moulé
rembourré, piètement
pivotant en alu-
minium, roulettes

FRITZ HANSEN,
ALLERØD, FROM 1965
TO PRESENT

Originally designed for Jacobsen's St. Catherine's College, Oxford architectural project (1960–1964), the "Oxford" series comprises high-backed and
armless variants on a range of bases including a floor-fixed model.

*Die »Oxford«-Serie entwarf der Architekt und Designer Jacobsen für
St. Catherine's College, das er von 1960 bis 1964 erbaute. Zu dieser Serie von
Stühlen gehören Varianten mit hohen Rückenlehnen bzw. ohne Armlehnen auf
unterschiedlichen Untergestellen, darunter auch eines, das am Boden zu
befestigen ist.*

Conçus à l'origine pour le St. Catherine's College d'Oxford, dont Jacobsen
fut l'architecte (1960–1964), la série « Oxford » comprend diverses versions
à dossier haut ou sans accoudoirs sur une série de piètements incluant un
modèle à sceller au sol.

Tobia Scarpa

Bonanza, 1969

Leather-covered polyurethane foam-upholstered tubular steel frame | Rahmen aus Stahlrohr, Polyurethanschaumstoffpolsterung mit Lederbezug | Châssis tubulaire en acier, rembourrage en mousse de polyuréthane recouverte de cuir

C & B ITALIA,
NOVEDRATE, COMO
(LATER TO BECOME
B & B ITALIA),
1969–1975

▲ Tobia Scarpa
Model No. 917, 1967

CASSINA, MEDA,
MILAN, 1967

Tobia Scarpa states, "Design does not define a precise activity or thing. In practical terms, it is a profession without a rule book . . . That which remains (and is worth talking about) is that final and concrete result: the object". His "Bonanza" was innovative in its use of a single-piece slipcover that did not need to be cut and then pieced back together. The Scarpas' No. 925 chair was influenced by Carlo Scarpa's No. 765 chair of 1934.

Tobia Scarpa hat einmal gesagt: »Das Wort Design definiert keine präzis zu umreißende Tätigkeit oder Sache. Praktisch ausgedrückt ist es ein Beruf ohne festgelegte Regeln . . . Was bleibt (und der Rede wert ist), ist das konkrete Endergebnis: das Objekt.« Der Sessel »Bonanza« von Scarpa war insofern neuartig, als sein Bezug aus einem Stück gefertigt war, das Leder mußte nicht zugeschnitten und dann vernäht werden. Der Stuhl Modell Nr. 925 wurde von Carlo Scarpas Stuhl Modell Nr. 765 (1934) beeinflußt.

Tobia & Afra Scarpa

Model No. 925, 1965

Walnut frame with leather-covered moulded plywood seat and back | Rahmen aus Walnuß-holz, Sitzschale und Rückenlehne aus Lederbezug | Châssis en noyer, siège et dossier en contre-plaqué moulé recouvert de cuir

CASSINA, MEDA, MILAN, FROM 1965 TO PRESENT

▼ Tobia Scarpa
Bastiano, 1960

GAVINA, BOLOGNA (LATER TO BECOME SIMON INTER-NATIONAL) (REISSUED BY KNOLL INTERNATIONAL, NEW YORK)

Tobia Scarpa : « Le mot *design* ne définit pas une activité ou une chose précise. En termes pratiques, c'est une profession sans règlement. Ce qui en reste (et qui vaut la peine que l'on en parle) est le résultat final et concret : l'objet. » Le fauteuil « Bonanza » de Scarpa in-nove avec sa housse d'une seule pièce, sans coupe ni couture. Le fauteuil n° 925 fut influencé par le modèle n° 765 de Carlo Scarpa (1934).

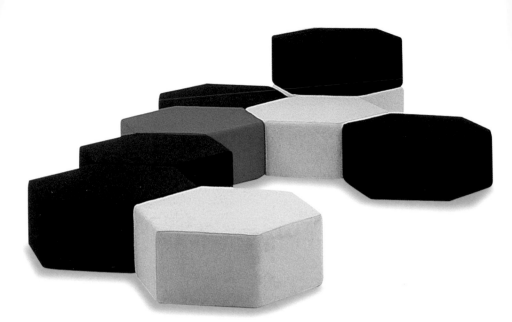

**Kazuhide
Takahama**

ESA, 1968

Textile-covered
polyurethane block
foam | Blöcke aus
Polyurethanschaum-
stoff mit Stoffbezug |
Blocs en mousse de
polyuréthane
recouverts de tissu

SIMON
INTERNATIONAL FOR
GAVINA, BOLOGNA,
FROM 1968

As a result of their meeting at the Milan X Triennale of 1954, the progressive Italian furniture manufacturer, Dino Gavina, invited Takahama, a Japanese architect, to work with him in Italy. Their first collaboration was Gavina's highly successful "Naeko" sofa of 1957. This was followed in 1965 by the "Marcel", "Raymond" and "Suzanne" – each a series of chairs and sofas that were the first to use polyurethane foam cut into large, elemental blocks. Takahama's slightly later "ESA" modular system also uses this construction. Like his other designs, it has strong sculptural qualities and possesses an internationalism which is born out of an aesthetic purity and an intrinsic rationalism.

Als Ergebnis ihres Treffens auf der X. Mailänder Triennale im Jahr 1954 lud der progressive italienische Möbelhersteller Dino Gavina den japanischen Architekten Takahama ein, in Italien mit ihm zusammenzuarbeiten. Ihr erstes gemeinsames Projekt war Gavinas höchst erfolgreiches Sofa »Naeko« aus dem Jahr 1957. 1965 folgten »Marcel«, »Raymond« und »Suzanne« – drei Stuhl- und Sofa-serien, die zum ersten Mal Polyurethanschaumstoff verwendeten, der in große Blöcke geschnitten war. Takahamas kurz darauf entworfenes Modulsystem »ESA« basiert auf dem gleichen Prinzip. Wie Takahamas andere Entwürfe zeich-net sich auch dieses System durch eine auffällige Formgebung und einen Internationalismus aus, der ästhetischer Reinheit und einem immanenten Rationalismus verpflichtet ist.

À la suite de leur rencontre à la Xe Triennale de Milan en 1954, le fabricant avant-gardiste italien Dino Gavina invita Takahama, architecte japonais, à venir travailler pour lui en Italie. Leur première collaboration fut le très réussi sofa « Naeko » (1957). Il fut suivi en 1965 par « Marcel », « Raymond » et « Suzanne », noms désignant chacun une série de fauteuils et de canapés qui représentaient la première application du principe de blocs structuraux en mousse de polyuréthane. Légèrement ultérieur, le système modulaire « ESA » utilise la même idée. Il possède d'évidentes qualités sculpturales, dans un esprit internationaliste issu de la recherche d'une pureté esthétique et de principes rationalistes.

Kazuhide Takahama

Suzanne, 1965

Textile-covered, polyurethane foam-upholstered, tubular steel frame with chromed steel fittings | Rahmen aus Stahlrohr, Polyurethanschaumstoffpolsterung mit Stoffbezug, Stahlbeschläge, verchromt | Châssis en tube d'acier, garnitures en acier chromé, rembourrage en mousse de polyuréthane recouverte de tissu

GAVINA, BOLOGNA, 1965–1968 & KNOLL INTERNATIONAL, NEW YORK, 1968–1989

Joe Colombo

LEM, 1964

Painted metal frame with leather-covered upholstered seat, back and armrests | Rahmen aus Preßstahl, lackiert, Sitzfläche, Rücken- und Armlehnen gepolstert und mit Lederbezug | Châssis en métal peint, siège, dossier et accoudoirs en cuir rembourré

BIEFFEPLAST,
CASELLE DI
SELVAZZANO,
FROM 1972

Originally, this design had a moulded plywood frame and was titled the "Supercomfort". A pressed steel frame was later adopted, however, and the design was renamed "LEM" (Lunar Excursion Module) because of its resemblance to the vehicle used for moon landings.

Ursprünglich hatte dieser Entwurf einen Rahmen aus geformtem Schichtholz und hieß »Supercomfort«. Später verwendete man dann einen Rahmen aus Preßstahl und taufte das Design wegen seiner Ähnlichkeit mit einer Mondlandefähre in »LEM« (Lunar Excursion Module) um.

Au départ, ce modèle alors appelé « Supercomfort », possédait un châssis en contre-plaqué qui fut remplacé par une ossature en acier. Il reçut le nom de « LEM » (Lunar Excursion Modules) à cause de sa ressemblance avec le véhicule utilisé lors de la première exploration de la lune.

Joe Colombo

Model No. 4801,
1963–1964

Lacquered moulded plywood three-part construction with rubber stoppers | Dreiteilige Konstruktion aus geformtem Schichtholz, lackiert, Gummipuffer | Construction en trois éléments, contreplaqué moulé laqué, pièces de blocage en caoutchouc

KARTELL, NOVIGLIO, MILAN, 1964–1975 (LIMITED EDITION)

▼ Joe Colombo
Model No. 4801, 1963–1964, with natural finish

KARTELL, NOVIGLIO, MILAN

Colombo strived for material and structural unity in his work. The armchair No. 4801 is constructed of only three interlocking moulded plywood elements that curve and flow into one another. The fluidity of this chair's form anticipates Colombo's later designs in plastic.

Colombo strebte in seinen Arbeiten stets nach der Einheit von Material und Konstruktion. Der Sessel Nr. 4801 besteht lediglich aus drei ineinandergreifenden Schichtholzteilen, die gebogen sind und einander durchdringen. Das Fließende dieser Sesselform findet sich in Colombos späteren Kunststoffentwürfen erneut.

Colombo était très attaché à l'unité de structure et de matériaux. Le fauteuil n° 4801 est constitué de trois éléments entrelacés en contre-plaqué moulé. La fluidité de la forme de ce siège annonce les futures créations en plastique du designer.

Joe Colombo

Additional Living System, 1967–1968

Textile-covered
moulded poly-
urethane foam on
tubular iron frame
with metal clamps |
Geformter und mit
Stoff bezogener
Polyurethanschaum
auf einem Rahmen
aus Eisenrohren mit
Metallklammern |
Châssis en tube de fer,
rembourrage en
mousse de poly-
uréthane recouverte
de tissu, agrafes en
métal

SORMANI, AROSIO,
COMO, 1968–1971

▶ Joe Colombo
Working drawing for
Additional Living
System, 1967

Colombo's highly functional "Additional Living System" is made up of a series of cushions in six different sizes that can be linked in a number of combinations with die-cast aluminium pins.

Colombos hoch funktionales »Additional Living System« setzt sich aus einer Reihe von Kissen in sechs verschiedenen Größen zusammen, die mit Hilfe von Klammern aus Gußaluminium auf verschiedene Weise verbunden und kombiniert werden können.

Le très fonctionnel «Additional Living System» de Colombo se compose d'une série de coussins de six tailles différentes, liés entre eux selon diverses combinaisons grâce à des agrafes en fonte d'aluminium.

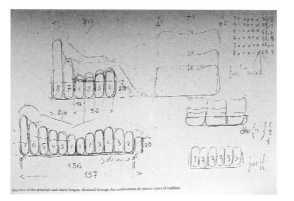

Sketches of the armchair and chaise-longue, obtained through the combination of various types of cushion.

Joe Colombo

Birillo, 1969–1970

Chromed steel and tubular steel frame with leather-covered upholstered seat and backrest on fibreglass base | Rahmen aus Stahlrohr und Stahl-blech, verchromt, Sitzfläche und Rückenlehne gepol-stert und mit Leder-bezug, Bodenplatte aus fiberglasverstärk-tem Kunststoff | Châssis en tube d'acier et acier chromé, siège et dosseret en cuir rembourré, base en fibre de verre

ZANOTTA, MILAN, FROM C. 1970 TO PRESENT

▼ Joe Colombo
Sella 1001,
1962–1963

COMFORT, MILAN, FROM C. 1963

This series, which also includes a stool and a table, takes its name from the Italian word for "bar stool". Designed for offices and bars, the "Birillo's" base conceals castors and the seat has an automatic return. *Diese Serie, zu der auch ein Hocker und ein Tisch gehören, wurde nach dem italienischen Wort für » Barhocker« be-nannt. »Birillo«, für Büros und Bars, verfügt über Lauf-rollen und kehrt automatisch in die Grundposition zurück.* Cette série, qui comprend également un tabouret et une table, tire son nom du terme italien « Birillo » désignant un tabouret de bar. Conçu pour les bureaux et les bars, sa base dissimule des roulettes et le siège revient auto-matiquement en position normale.

Hans J. Wegner

Ox chair, Model No. EJ 100, 1960

Leather-covered upholstered moulded plywood seat shell on chromed tubular steel base | Sitzschale aus geformtem Schichtholz, gepolstert und mit Lederbezug, Untergestell aus Stahlrohr, verchromt | Coquille en contreplaqué moulé, cuir rembourré

JOHANNES HANSEN, COPENHAGEN, C. 1960 – C. 1992 (REISSUED BY ERIK JØRGENSEN, COPENHAGEN, FROM C. 1992 TO PRESENT)

The "Ox" chair's form gives the design a distinctive and powerful character. Designed to allow much freedom of movement, it is extremely comfortable in use. The chair is reputably Wegner's personal favourite at home.

Die Form ist es, die dem »Ox«-Sessel seinen unverwechselbaren und kraftvollen Charakter verleiht. Er läßt viel Bewegungsfreiheit und ist extrem komfortabel. Man sagt, es sei der Sessel, in dem Wegner zu Hause am liebsten sitzt.

La forme de ce fauteuil « Ox » lui donne un caractère affirmé. Conçu pour offrir la plus grande liberté de mouvement possible, il est extrêmement confortable. Il s'agirait là du siège préféré de son concepteur.

Hans J. Wegner

*Three-legged
plywood chair, 1963*

Lacquered moulded
plywood construction |
Geformtes Schicht-
holz, lackiert | Contre-
plaqué moulé et
laqué

VITRA, WEIL AM
RHEIN, FROM 1997
TO PRESENT

Wegner has explored the use of plywood in chair design on only a few occasions, most notably with this design. While his three-legged chair displays a masterful handling of the medium, Wegner prefers to concentrate his efforts on solid-wood constructions.

Wegner hat die Verwendung von Schichtholz für Stuhldesigns nur bei wenigen Gelegenheiten erprobt, wobei diese Entwürfe besondere Beachtung verdienen. Obgleich dieser dreibeinige Sessel zeigt, wie meisterhaft Wegner mit diesem Werkstoff umzugehen weiß, hat er sich bei seinen Arbeiten vorzugsweise auf Konstruktionen aus Massivholz konzentriert.

Wegner n'a que rarement exploré les possibilités du contre-plaqué. Si ce fauteuil à trois pieds témoigne d'une réelle maîtrise de ce matériau, le designer n'en a pas moins préféré travailler le bois massif.

Walter Pichler

Galaxy 1, 1966

Enamelled pierced,
aluminium frame
with leather-covered
cushions | Gestell aus
emailliertem Alumi-
nium, lederbezogene
Kissen | Châssis en
aluminium percé et
émaillé, coussins en
cuir rembourré

SVOBODA & CO.,
VIENNA, FROM
C. 1966

Both Walter Pichler's "Galaxy 1" chair and Yrjö Kukkapuro's "Karuselli" chair
are forward-looking designs which make reference to the space age. The
ergonomic form of the "Karuselli's" seat shell was inspired, according to
Terence Conran, by the imprint of the designer's body in snow.
Sowohl bei Walter Pichlers »Galaxy 1«-Sessel als auch bei Yrjö Kukkapuros
»Karuselli«-Sessel handelt es sich um zukunftweisende Designansätze die dem
Raumfahrtzeitalter Tribut zollen. Die ergonomische Form der »Karuselli«-
Sitzschale wurde, wenn man Terence Conran glauben darf, vom Abdruck des
Designers im Schnee inspiriert.

Yrjö Kukkapuro

Karuselli, 1964–1965

Foam-upholstered reinforced fibreglass seat shell with chromed steel cradle on steel-reinforced moulded fibreglass base | Sitzschale und Fuß aus geformtem Fiberglas mit Schaumstoffpolsterung, Aufhängung aus Stahl, verchromt | Coquille en fibre de verre, rembourrage mousse, berceau en acier chromé, base en fibre de verre renforcée d'acier

HAIMI, HELSINKI, FROM 1965 (REISSUED BY AVARTE, HELSINKI)

Le fauteuil « Galaxy 1 » de Walter Pichler et le « Karuselli » de Yrjö Kukkapuro sont des sièges d'avant-garde qui se réfèrent explicitement à l'ère spatiale. La forme ergonomique de la coquille du « Karuselli » aurait été inspirée, si l'on en croit Terence Conran, par l'empreinte du corps du designer dans la neige.

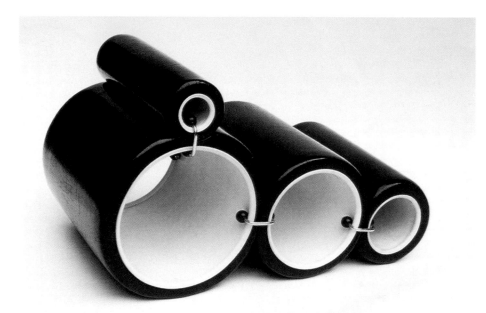

Joe Colombo

Tube, 1969–1970

Textile-covered,
polyurethane-foam
upholstered, semi-
rigid, lacquered
"Arcipiuma" cylinders
with tubular steel and
rubber connecting
joints | Halbstarre
Zylinder aus lackier-
tem »Arcipiuma«,
Verbindungsklam-
mern aus Stahl und
Gummi, Polsterung
aus Polyurethan-
schaumstoff mit Stoff-
bezug | Cylindres
semi-rigides en « Arci-
piuma » laqué, rem-
bourrés de mousse de
polyuréthane recou-
verte de tissu, joints
de connexion en acier
et caoutchouc

FLEXFORM, MILAN,
FROM C. 1970

The upholstered tubes of this chair could be joined in a number of combinations. Retailed in a drawstring bag, the "Tube" chair was an early example of
furniture that could literally be bought "off-the-shelf".

*Die gepolsterten Rohre dieses Sitzmöbels können auf verschiedene Weise zusam-
mengesetzt werden. In einem verschnürbaren Beutel verpackt und vertrieben,
war der »Tube«-Stuhl ein frühes Beispiel für Möbel, die man buchstäblich »von
der Stange« kaufen konnte.*

Les tubes rembourrés de ce fauteuil peuvent s'assembler selon plusieurs
combinaisons. Vendu dans sac, le fauteuil « Tube » fut l'un des premiers
exemples de meuble qui pouvait pratiquement se vendre en linéaire.

▶ Flexform
brochure, c. 1970

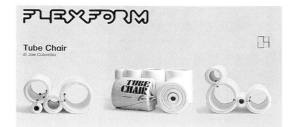

Joe Colombo

Elda, 1963–1965

Moulded fibreglass frame on metal swivelling mechanism with internal fabric or leather-covered foam upholstery and cushions attached with metal hooks | Sitzschale aus geformtem fiberglasverstärktem Kunststoff, auf einer Drehvorrichtung aus Metall, Innenpolsterung aus Schaumstoff mit Leder- bzw. Stoffbezug, Kissen mit Metallhaken befestigt | Châssis en fibre de verre moulée, système pivotant, rembourrage en mousse recouverte de cuir, coussins fixés par des crochets métalliques

COMFORT, MILAN, FROM C. 1965 TO PRESENT

The "Elda" was the first large armchair to utilise a self-supporting fibreglass frame. Its seven sausage-like cushions, rotating base and generous proportions provide a great deal of comfort.

»Elda« war der erste große Sessel mit einem freitragenden Rahmen aus fiberglasverstärktem Kunststoff. Seine sieben wurstähnlichen Polsterkissen, sein Drehfuß und seine großzügigen Proportionen bieten hohen Komfort.

Le modèle « Elda » est le premier grand fauteuil à faire appel à un châssis autoporteur en fibre de verre. Ses sept coussins en forme de boudins, sa base pivotante et ses proportions généreuses assurent un très grand confort.

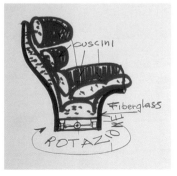

▲ Joe Colombo
Working drawing of Elda armchair, c. 1963

Marco Zanuso & Richard Sapper

Stacking child's chair, Model No. 4999/5, 1961–1964

Injection-moulded polyethylene ribbed seat section with separate injection-moulded polyethylene legs on rubber feet | Gerippte Sitzschale mit separaten Stuhlbeinen aus spritzguß-geformtem Polyethylen, Stuhlbeine mit Gummikappen | Siège à côtes en polyéthylène moulé par injection, pieds en polyéthylène moulés séparément, patins en caoutchouc

KARTELL, NOVIGLIO, MILAN, FROM 1964 TO PRESENT

The patents expired for polyethylene in the mid-1960s, thereby lowering the material's cost. Zanuso and Sapper were the first to explore the potential of this thermoplastic in seat furniture with their injection-moulded stacking child's chair.

Der patentrechtliche Schutz für Polyethylen erlosch Mitte der 6oer Jahre, und die Kosten für dieses Material sanken. Zanuso und Sapper waren mit dem Entwurf ihres spritzgußgeformten stapelbaren Kinderstuhls die ersten, die die Möglich-keiten dieses Thermokunststoffs für Sitzmöbel nutzten.

Les brevets d'exploitation du polyéthylène étant tombés dans le domaine public au milieu des années 60, le prix de ce matériau baissa. Zanuso et Sapper furent les premiers à mettre à profit le potentiel de ce thermo-plastique dans la création de sièges, en produisant cette chaise pour en-fants, empilable et moulée par injection.

Motomi
Kawakami

Fiorenza, 1968

Thermo-formed ABS
construction with
chromed metal
fittings | Wärme-
geformter ABS-
Kunststoff, Metall-
beschläge, verchromt |
Plastique ABS
thermoformé,
garnitures en métal

ALBERTO BAZZANI,
MILAN, FROM
c. 1968

The "Fiorenza" demonstrates how moulded thermoplastics took over from moulded plywood in the 1960s as the materials of preference for designers wishing to create expressive forms.

Der »Fiorenza«-Stuhl zeigt, wie geformter Thermokunststoff in den 60er Jahren das Schichtholz als bevorzugtes Material ablöste, wenn es den Designern darauf ankam, ausdrucksvolle Formen zu schaffen.

Le siège « Fiorenza » montre comment les thermoplastiques moulés prirent la place du contre-plaqué moulé dans les années 60 et devinrent le matériau préféré des designers à la recherche de formes expressives.

Joe Colombo

Universale, Model No. 4860, 1965–1967

Injection-moulded "Cycolac" ABS plastic (1974 to 1975 PA6 nylon & from 1975 to present polypropylene) | Spritzgußgeformter »Cycolac« ABS-Kunststoff, 1974–1975 aus PAG-Nylon, seit 1975 aus Polypropylen | Plastique ABS « Cycolac » moulé par injection (de 1974 à 1975 nylon PAG, depuis, polypropylène)

KARTELL, NOVIGLIO, MILAN, FROM 1967 TO PRESENT (RENAMED AS MODEL NO. 4867 IN 1974)

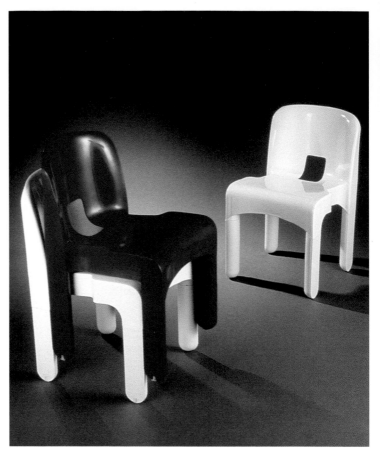

▼ Joe Colombo
Working drawing for Universale chair, c. 1965

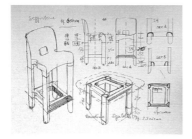

Intended originally for manufacture in aluminium, the "Universale" stacking chair was produced in ABS from 1967 as the first adult-sized injection-moulded chair. Its detachable legs were available in two heights.

Der ab 1967 in ABS-Kunststoff produzierte stapelbare Stuhl »Universale«, der ursprünglich aus Aluminium hergestellt werden sollte, war der erste spritzgußgeformte Stuhl für Erwachsene. Die Beine ließen sich abmontieren und waren in zwei Höhen lieferbar.

Conçu au départ pour être fabriqué en aluminium, le modèle empilable « Universale » fut réalisé en ABS à partir de 1967. C'est la première chaise pour adultes à avoir été moulée par injection. Ses pieds démontables existaient en deux tailles.

Verner Panton

Panton, 1959–1960

1968–1970: Moulded "Baydur" (PU-hard-foam) construction, 1970 onwards: Injection-moulded "Luran-S" (thermoplastic) construction | Konstruktion aus Spritzguß, 1968–1970: Polyurethan-Hartschaum »Baydur«, ab 1970: Thermoplast-Spritzguß »Luran-S« | 1968–1970 : « Baydur» moulé (mousse solide PU). Depuis 1970 : « Luran S » (thermoplastique) moulé par injection

VITRA, BASLE, FOR
HERMAN MILLER
FURNITURE CO.,
ZEELAND, MICHI-
GAN, FROM 1968
(REISSUED BY VITRA,
BASLE, FROM 1990
TO PRESENT)

Unlike Colombo's No. 4860 and Zanuso and Sapper's child's chair, Panton's stacking chair was wholly unified. It was the first single-material, single-form injection-moulded chair.

Anders als Colombos Nr. 4860 und Zanusos und Sappers Kinderstuhl bestand Pantons Stapelstuhl aus einem Stück. Damit war er der erste spritzgußgeformte Stuhl, der mit nur einem Werkstoff und einer Form hergestellt wurde.

À la différence du modèle n° 4860 de Colombo et de la chaise pour enfants de Zanuso et Sapper, la chaise de Panton était réalisée en un seul bloc. C'est le premier siège moulé par injection en un seul matériau et une pièce.

Peter Ghyczy

Garden Egg, 1968

*Fibreglass-reinforced
polyester shell with
fabric-covered internal
upholstery | Schale
aus fiberglasver-
stärktem Polyester,
Innenpolster mit
Stoffbezug | Coquille
en polyester renforcé
de fibre de verre,
rembourrage intérieur
recouvert de tissu*

REUTER PRODUCTS,
GERMANY, FROM
C. 1968

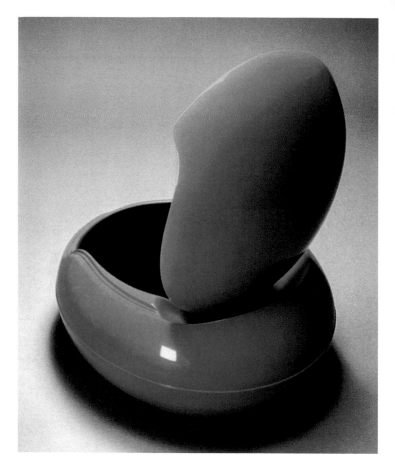

The back of this innovative indoor/outdoor chair could be folded down
when not in use to protect its internal upholstery from the elements.
*Die Rückenlehne dieses innovativen Stuhls für außen und innen konnte, wenn er
nicht in Gebrauch war, heruntergeklappt werden, um die Polsterung
vor der Witterung schützen.*
Le dossier de ce siège novateur, conçu aussi bien pour l'intérieur que pour
l'extérieur, se replie pour protéger son rembourrage interne.

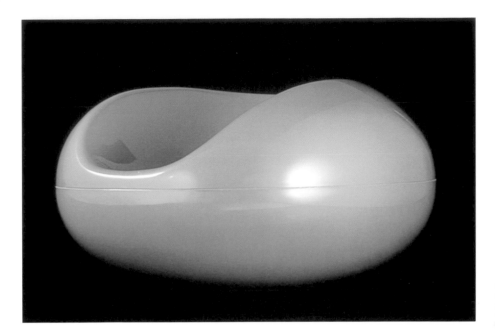

The "Pastille", sometimes referred to as the "Gyro", is a novel interpretation of a rocking chair. With its bold organic form, the chair exemplifies the sophisticated approach of many Scandinavian designers to synthetic materials. Designed for interior or exterior use, it won an A.I.D. award in 1968.

»Pastille«, manchmal auch »Gyro« genannt, ist die Neuinterpretation eines Schaukelstuhls. Mit seiner kühnen organischen Form steht der Stuhl stellvertretend für den raffinierten Umgang vieler skandinavischer Designer mit synthetischen Materialien. Für den Innen- und Außenbereich entworfen, erhielt er 1968 den internationalen Designpreis A.I.D.

Le « Pastille », parfois appelé « Gyro », est une interprétation entièrement

nouvelle du siège à bascule. De forme organique, il illustre bien l'approche raffinée des matériaux synthétiques de nombreux designers scandinaves. Conçu aussi bien pour la maison que pour l'extérieur, il remporta en 1968 un prix international de l' A.I.D.

Eero Aarnio

Pastille, 1967–1968

Moulded fibreglass-reinforced polyester structure | Schale aus geformtem fiberglasverstärktem Polyester | Polyester moulé renforcé de fibre de verre

ASKO LAHTI, FINLAND, 1968–c. 1980 (REISSUED BY ADELTA C/O FINLAND-CONTACT, DINSLAKEN, FROM 1991 TO PRESENT)

◄ Eero Aarnio's sitting room in Helsinki, c. 1970

Eero Aarnio

Armchair, c. 1967

Fibreglass-reinforced polyester seat shell on painted aluminium base with internal textile-covered foam upholstery and seat cushion | Sitzschale aus geformtem fiberglasverstärktem Polyester, Fuß aus lackiertem Aluminium, Innenpolster und Sitzkissen aus Schaumstoff mit Stoffbezug | Coquille en polyester renforcé de fibre de verre, piètement en aluminium peint, rembourrage interne recouvert de tissu, coussin en mousse

ASKO, LAHTI, FROM c. 1967

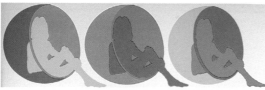

▲ Graphic portrayal of Eero Aarnio's Bubble chair from *Design from Scandinavia*, No. 3

Aarnio's belief that, "Design means constant renewal, realignment and growth", is declared in his iconoclastic furniture. Although he embodied the spirit of the 1960s in the novel forms of his visually exciting designs, he did not embrace Pop culture's ethos of ephemerality and disposability. His furniture is of a high quality and intended for durability. *Aarnios Auffassung, Design sei »ständige Erneuerung, Neuorientierung und Wachstum«, zeigt sich in seinen innovativen Möbeln. Obwohl die avantgardistischen Formen seiner visuell stimulierenden Entwürfe den Geist der 60er Jahre verkörperten, übernahm er nicht den Kurzlebigkeits- und Wegwerfethos der Popkultur. Seine Möbel sind von hoher Qualität und haltbar.*

Eero Aarnio

Ball (or Globe),
1963–1965

Moulded fibreglass-reinforced polyester seating section on painted aluminium base with internal fabric-covered foam upholstery | Sitzschale aus geformtem fiberglasverstärktem Polyester, Fuß aus lackiertem Aluminium, Innenpolster und Sitzkissen aus Schaumstoff mit Stoffbezug | Coquille en polyester renforcé dev fibre de verre, base en aluminium peint, rembourrage intérieur en mousse recouverte de tissu

ASKO, LAHTI
1966–C. 1980
(REISSUED BY ADEL-
TA, FROM 1992 TO
PRESENT)

▼ **Eero Aarnio**
Bubble chair, 1968

ASKO, LAHTI, FROM
C. 1968 (REISSUED BY
ADELTA, FROM 1996)

La conviction de Aarnio, pour qui « design signifie renouvellement, réalignement et évolution constants », s'affirme dans ses créations iconoclastes. Si le designer illustra bien l'esprit des années 60 à travers une nouveauté formelle séduisante, il ne se rallia pas pour autant à l'éthique de la culture pop de l'éphémère et du jetable. Son mobilier est de haute qualité et construit pour durer.

Sergio Mazza

Toga, 1968

Compression-
moulded fibreglass-
reinforced polyester |
Druckgeformtes,
fiberglasverstärktes
Polyester | Polyester
moulé renforcé de
fibre de verre

ARTEMIDE, MILAN,
FROM 1969

The stackable, single-material single-form "Toga" chair was first shown at the 1969 Milan International Furniture Exhibition to wide acclaim. It was manufactured in compression-moulded fibreglass-reinforced polyester. No longer in production, the chair was initially produced in only orange and white and later in red and black.

Der stapelbare, aus nur einer Form und nur einem Material bestehende Stuhl »Toga« wurde 1969 auf der Internationalen Mailänder Möbelmesse zum ersten Mal präsentiert – und fand großen Beifall. Gefertigt ist der Stuhl aus druck-geformtem, fiberglasverstärktem Polyester. Der heute nicht mehr produzierte Stuhl wurde zunächst nur in Orange und Weiß, später auch in Rot und Schwarz angeboten.

Le fauteuil empilable « Toga », moulé d'une pièce, fut présenté pour la pre-mière fois à l'Exposition internationale du meuble de Milan en 1969 où il remporta un énorme succès. Il était fabriqué en polyester renforcé de fibre de verre et moulé sous pression. Il fut d'abord proposé en orange et en blanc, puis en noir et en rouge. Sa fabrication a été interrompue.

Alberto Rosselli

Jumbo, 1969

Moulded fibreglass-
reinforced polyester |
Geformtes
fiberglasverstärktes
Polyester | Polyester
moulé renforcé de
fibre de verre

SAPORITI, BESNATE,
VERONA, FROM 1969
TO PRESENT

In 1950, Rosselli established with Gio Ponti and Antonio Fornaroli, Studio
PFR which was responsible for the Pirelli Tower, Milan (1956). His "Jumbo"
chair and "Moby Dick" chaise longue typify his interest in utilising new technology in the development of unprecedented yet functional forms.

*Rosselli gründete 1950 zusammen mit Gio Ponti und Antonio Fornaroli das
Studio PFR, das auch den 1956 gebauten Pirelli-Turm in Mailand entworfen hat.
Sein Stuhl »Jumbo« und das Sofa »Moby Dick« illustrieren Rossellis Interesse
an neuen Techniken für die Entwicklung innovativer und doch funktionaler
Formen.*

Rosselli fonda en 1950 avec Gio Ponti et Antonio Fornaroli le Studio PFR,
qui fut chargé du projet de la Tour Pirelli à Milan (1956). Son fauteuil

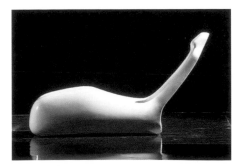

« Jumbo » et la chaise
longue « Moby Dick »
sont caractéristiques de
son intérêt pour l'application des technologies
nouvelles dans la mise au
point de formes origi-
nales et néanmoins
fonctionnelles.

◄ **Alberto Rosselli**
Moby Dick, 1974

SAPORITI, BESNATE,
VERONA, FROM 1974

Wendell Castle

Molar chair, 1969

Moulded fibreglass-reinforced polyester | Geformtes, fiberglasverstärktes Polyester | Polyester moulé renforcé de fibre de verre

BEYLERIAN, NEW YORK, 1970–C. 1975

▼ **Wendell Castle**
Castle armchair, 1969

BEYLERIAN, NEW YORK, 1970–C. 1975

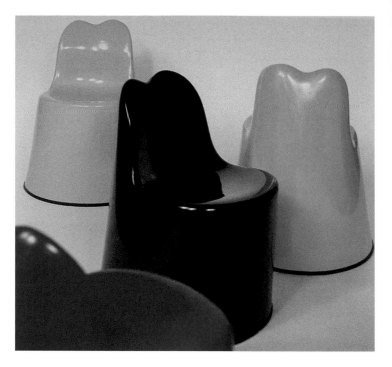

Best known for his superbly crafted wooden furniture, Castle translated his highly organic forms into plastic. The surrealistic "Molar" love-seat and matching "Molar" chairs were based on the shape of back teeth. Not intended for high-volume production, the "Molar" group and similar "Castle" series of chairs were exclusively distributed by Stendig, New York.

Castle, der sich vor allem mit seinen qualitativ hochwertigen Holzmöbeln einen Namen machte, übertrug deren extrem organische Formen auf das Medium Kunststoff. Das surrealistische Sofa »Molar« und die dazu passenden Stühle basieren auf der Form von Backenzähnen. Die Sitzgruppe »Molar« war nicht für die Serienproduktion gedacht und wurde, wie die Sitzgruppe »Castle«, ausschließlich durch Stendig, New York, vertrieben.

Surtout connu pour ses meubles en bois superbement réalisés, Castle adapta ses formes extrêmement organiques à la production en plastique. Le siège surréaliste « Molar» et les fauteuils assortis « Molar » sont inspirés de la forme d'une molaire. Conçue pour une production limitée, la série « Molar » et les autres créations de Castle étaient distribuées en exclusivité par Stendig, New York.

Wendell Castle

Molar sofa, 1969

Moulded fibreglass-reinforced polyester | Geformtes, fiberglasverstärktes Polyester | Polyester moulé renforcé de fibre de verre

BEYLERIAN, NEW YORK, 1970–C. 1975

373

Helmut Bätzner

Bofinger, Model No. BA 1171, 1964–1966

Compression-moulded fibreglass-reinforced polyester resin | Formgepreßtes, fiberglasverstärktes Polyester | Résine de polyester renforcée de fibre de verre et moulée sous pression

MENZOLIT-WERKE, ALBERT SCHMIDT, KRAICHTAL-MENZINGEN FOR WILHELM BOFINGER, ILSFIELD, 1966–1984

Launched at the 1966 Cologne Furniture Fair, the chair No. BA 1171 was the first single-piece plastic chair suitable for mass-production. It was compression-moulded using the "prepreg-process" and a ten ton double-shell heated press. The production cycle lasted five minutes and only a small degree of finishing was required. The anthropomorphic "Floris" chair, on the

other hand, exploits the expressive potential of fibreglass. Its two-part construction was too complicated for efficient industrial manufacture and had to be produced by hand.

Der Stuhl Modell Nr. BA 1171, auf der Kölner Möbelmesse 1966 zum ersten Mal präsentiert, war der erste Plastikstuhl, der, aus einem Stück geformt, für die Massenproduktion geeignet war. Für das »Prepreg«-Druckpreßverfahren wurde eine zehn Tonnen schwere Doppelmantel-Heißpresse eingesetzt. Ein Produktions-

Floris, 1967

Moulded fibreglass-
reinforced polyester
construction |
Geformtes, fiberglas-
verstärktes Polyester |
Polyester moulé
renforcé de fibre de
verre

GEBRÜDER BELTZIG
DESIGN, WUPPERTAL,
FROM 1968
(REISSUED BY
GALERIE OBJEKTE,
MUNICH, FROM
1992)

zyklus dauerte fünf Minuten, und es war so gut wie keine Nachbearbeitung notwendig. Der »Floris«-Stuhl hingegen, mit seiner anthropomorphen Form, lebt
von den gestalterischen Möglichkeiten des Werkstoffs Fiberglas. Seine zweiteilige
Konstruktion war zu kompliziert für eine effiziente industrielle Fertigung, der
Stuhl wurde darum von Hand hergestellt.

Lancée à la Foire du meuble de Cologne en 1966, la chaise n° BA 1171 est le
premier siège en plastique d'une seule pièce adapté à la production en
grande série. Il était moulé sous pression selon le procédé « prepreg » et
sur une presse de dix tonnes à double moule. Le cycle de production durait
cinq minutes et la finition était réduite au minimum. Le modèle anthropomorphe « Floris » exploite quant à lui le potentiel expressif de la fibre de
verre. Sa construction en deux parties était trop complexe pour une fabrication industrielle rentable et dut finalement être réalisé manuellement.

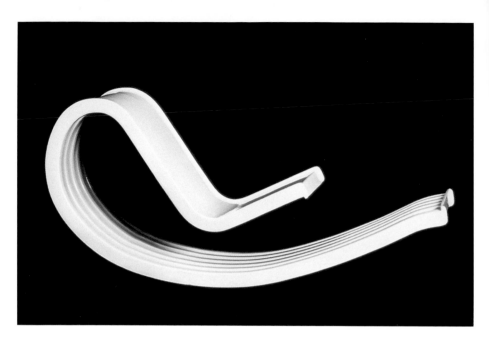

**Cesare Leonardi
& Franca Stagi**

Dondolo, 1967

Moulded fibreglass-reinforced polyester construction | Geformtes, fiberglas-verstärktes Polyester | Polyester moulé renforcé de fibre de verre

ELCO, VENICE, FROM C. 1967

The "Dondolo's" fibreglass construction was strengthened by incorporating ribbing. Its functionally conceived form shares a similar aesthetic with another Italian design, Gruppo G14's "Fiocco" chair of 1970.

Die Fiberglaskonstruktion des »Dondolo«-Schaukelstuhls wurde durch eingearbeitete Rippen verstärkt. Die funktionell ausgerichtete Form zeigt die gleiche Ästhetik wie ein anderer Entwurf aus Italien, der »Fiocco«-Stuhl der Gruppo G14 von 1970.

La structure en fibre de verre du « Dondolo » était renforcée par des nervures incorporées. Sa forme fonctionnelle présente la même esthétique qu'un autre fauteuil italien, le « Fiocco » du Gruppo G14, datant de 1970.

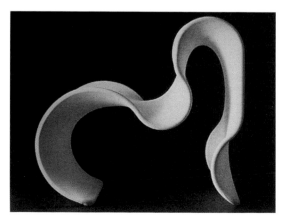

▶ **Gruppo G 14**
Fiocco, 1970

BUSNELLI, MILAN

Cesare Leonardi
& Franca Stagi

*Ribbon, Model
No. CL9, 1961*

Moulded fibreglass
seating section on a
chromed tubular steel
base | Sitzschale aus
geformtem, fiberglas-
verstärktem Polyester,
Untergestell aus
Stahlrohr, verchromt |
Siège en fibre de verre
moulée, piètement en
tube d'acier chromé

BERNINI, CARATE
BRIANZA, MILAN,
1961–1969
& ELCO, VENICE,
FROM 1969

The continuous band of moulded fibreglass forming the sculptural seat section of this remarkable design is attached to the tubular steel base by means of rubber shock-mounts. This connection and the cantilevered construction provide an inherent degree of springiness.

Die skulpturale Sitzschale dieses außergewöhnlichen Entwurfs in Form eines eingedrückten Rings besteht aus geformtem, fiberglasverstärktem Polyester. Durch die freitragende Stahlrohrkonstruktion, auf der die Sitzschale mit Gummimuffen befestigt ist, wird für ein gewisses Maß an Elastizität gesorgt.

Le bandeau continu en fibre de verre moulée qui forme la structure de ce remarquable modèle est fixé au piètement tubulaire par des blocs de caoutchouc. Ce type de montage et la construction en cantilever permettent un certain degré d'élasticité.

Roger Tallon

Module 400, 1964

Polished aluminium frame with latex-foam seating section | Rahmen aus poliertem Gußaluminium, Sitzschale mit Polsterung aus Latexschaumstoff | Châssis en aluminium poli, siège en mousse de latex

ÉDITIONS LACLOCHE, PARIS, 1966–1975

The "Module 400" series of 17 designs by Tallon included chairs, tables and stools. Each design used a standard pedestal base which occupied a floor area of 40 × 40 cm. The foam packing material provided an inexpensive, yet comfortable form of upholstery.

Die Möbelserie »Module 400« von Tallon bestand aus 17 unterschiedlichen Stuhl-, Tisch- und Hockermodellen. Jeder Entwurf hat als Basis den gleichen Standardsockel mit einer Grundplatte von 40 × 40 cm. Das Polstermaterial ist Schaumstoff aus der Verpackungsindustrie, eine preiswerte Möglichkeit der Polsterung, die dennoch für Sitzkomfort sorgt.

La série « Module 400 » de 17 modèles, créée par Tallon, comprenait des sièges, des tables et des tabourets. Chacun fait appel au même piètement modulaire, qui occupe une surface au sol de 40 x 40 cm. Le recouvrage en mousse est une solution économique et confortable de rembourrage.

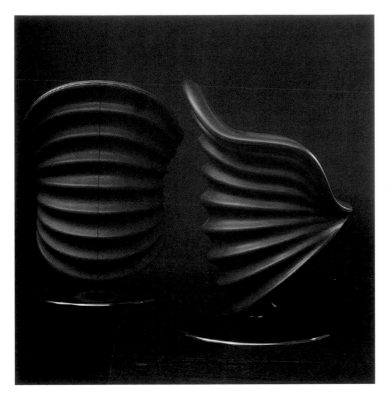

Mario Bellini

Teneride, 1968

Self-skinning polyurethane foam seating section on rotating fibreglass base | Sitzschale aus Polyurethan-Integralschaumstoff, Drehfuß aus Fiberglas | Siège en mousse de polyuréthane, piètement pivotant en fibre de verre

(PROTOTYPE)
CASSINA, MEDA, MILAN

This prototype design was intended as an office chair and was one of the first designs to utilise self-skinning polyurethane foam. The "Teneride's" self-supporting ribbed form was probably not strong enough to render the design viable.

Dieser Prototyp, einer der ersten Entwürfe, für den Integralschaumstoff aus Polyurethan verwendet wurde, war als Bürostuhl gedacht. Die sich selbst tragende, mit verstärkenden Rippen versehene Form des »Teneride« war offensichtlich jedoch nicht stark genug, um das Design produktionsreif zu machen.

Ce prototype de siège de bureau fut l'un des premiers projets à utiliser une mousse de polyuréthane qui évitait finition de surface et recouvrement. La forme autoporteuse à côtes n'était sans doute pas assez robuste pour que l'on se lance dans la fabrication industrielle de ce fauteuil.

Verner Panton

S chair, 1966

*Painted, bent
plywood construc-
tion | Konstruktion
aus geformtem
Schichtholz, lackiert |
Bois laminé cintré
peint*

GEBRÜDER THONET,
FRANKENBERG,
FROM 1966

Initially designed for a competition in 1956, the "S" chair was the first single-piece cantilevered chair executed in moulded plywood. This version was produced by Thonet in the 1960s. Panton continued to return to the plywood cantilevered theme over a number of years.

Der »S«-Stuhl, 1956 für einen Wettbewerb entworfen, war der erste aus einem Stück gefertigte Freischwinger aus geformtem Schichtholz. Diese Version wurde in den frühen 6oer Jahren von Thonet produziert. Panton beschäftigte sich einige Jahre lang immer wieder mit dem Thema Schichtholz-Freischwinger.

Conçu à l'origine comme projet de concours en 1956, le modèle « S » est le premier siège en porte à faux en contre-plaqué moulé d'une seule pièce. Cette version fut fabriquée par Thonet en Italie au début des années 60. Panton revint à plusieurs reprises sur le thème du contre-plaqué traité en cantilever.

**Erwine &
Estelle Laverne**

Tulip, c. 1960

Moulded fibreglass
seat shell on
aluminium base |
Sitzschale aus
geformtem, fiberglas-
verstärktem Kunst-
stoff, Untergestell aus
Aluminium | Coquille
en fibre de verre
moulée, piètement en
aluminium

LAVERNE
INTERNATIONAL,
NEW YORK ,
C. 1960–C. 1972

The "Tulip" chair is perhaps the Lavernes' most poetic design. The seat
shell appears almost to hover, giving the design a remarkable visual lightness. Its expressive organic form anticipates the optimism and exuberance
of the 1960s.

*Der »Tulip«-Sessel ist vielleicht der poetischste Entwurf der Lavernes. Die
Sitzschale scheint zu schweben, was dem Entwurf optisch eine bemerkenswerte
Leichtigkeit gibt. Seine ausdrucksvolle organische Form nimmt den Optimismus
und Überschwang der 6oer Jahre vorweg.*

Le fauteuil « Tulip » est sans doute la création la plus poétique des Laverne.
La coquille semble presque flotter, conférant à ce modèle une étonnante
légèreté. Sa forme expressive organique anticipe l'optimisme et l'exubérance
des années 60.

David Colwell

Contour, 1968

Moulded acrylic seat
shell on nylon-coated
steel rod frame |
Rahmen aus Stahl-
stäben, nylon-
beschichtet, Sitz-
schale aus geformtem
Acryl | Coquille en
acrylique moulé,
châssis en tige
métallique gainée de
nylon

4'S COMPANY,
LONDON, FROM
1968

David Colwell studied at the Royal College of Art, London, before becoming
a consultant to ICI Plastics. His "Contour" chair's seat section was heat-
formed from a single sheet of acrylic. Colourless versions were also produced.

*David Colwell hat am Royal College of Art in London studiert, bevor er Berater
der Firma ICI Plastics wurde. Die Sitzschale des Sessels »Contour« wird aus
einer einzigen Acrylplatte geformt. Versionen aus ungefärbtem Acryl wurden
auch produziert.*

David Colwell fit ses études au Royal College of Art de Londres, avant de devenir consultant auprès d'ICI Plastics. Le siège de ce fauteuil « Contour» est
mis en forme par procédé thermique à partir d'une seule feuille d'acrylique.
Des versions non colorées furent également réalisées.

Giancarlo
Piretti

Plia, 1969

Chromed steel frame
with moulded perspex
seat and back |
Rahmen aus Stahl-
rohr, verchromt, Sitz-
fläche und Rücken-
lehne aus geformtem
Plexiglas | Châssis en
acier chromé, siège et
dosseret en Perspex
moulé

CASTELLI, OZZANO
DELL'EMILIA,
BOLOGNA, FROM
1969 TO PRESENT

The "Plia" is an efficient modern reworking of the traditional wooden folding
chair. When collapsed, it is only an inch in depth, excluding the central hub.
The chair won several awards, including the federal German award "Gute
Form" in 1973.

Der Klappstuhl »Plia« ist eine strapazierfähige und moderne Weiterentwicklung
der älteren Modelle aus Holz. Zusammengeklappt ist der Stuhl nur 2,5 cm tief,
nur die Klappnabe in der Mitte ist etwas breiter. Der Stuhl gewann mehrere
Preise, darunter auch den Bundespreis »Gute Form« von 1973.

La chaise «Plia» est une adaptation moderne de la traditionnelle chaise
pliante en bois. Repliée, elle ne mesure que 2,5 cm d'épaisseur environ, en
dehors du moyeu central. Elle a remporté plusieurs récompenses, dont le
prix fédéral allemand «Gute Form» en 1973.

Vico Magistretti

Selene, 1969

Compression-
moulded "Reglar"
fibreglass reinforced
polyester structure |
Konstruktion aus
formgepreßtem,
fiberglasverstärktem
»Reglar«-Polyester |
Polyester « Reglar »
renforcé de fibre de
verre, moulé sous
pression

ARTEMIDE, MILAN,
FROM 1969 TO
PRESENT

Aiming to create a single-piece chair in compression-moulded plastic with a
traditional four-legged form, Magistretti resolved the technical difficulties
associated with the strength of the legs by configuring them in an S shape.
*Magistretti wollte einen aus einem Stück geformten Kunststoffstuhl in traditio-
nell vierbeiniger Form schaffen und löste die technischen Probleme, die sich dabei ergaben, indem er den Stuhlbeinen eine stabilisierende S-Form gab.*
Pour cette chaise traditionnelle d'une seule pièce en plastique moulé sous
pression, Magistretti résolut le délicat problème de la résistance des pieds
en les dotant d'une forme en S.

The sculptural "ABCD" system utilised individual fibreglass seat shells which could be either upholstered separately to form a chair or joined together and then upholstered to form two- or three-seater sofas.

Das skulptural wirkende Sitzmöbelsystem »ABCD« ist aus einzelnen Fiberglassitzschalen zusammengesetzt, die entweder, einzeln gepolstert, zum Sessel werden oder, miteinander verbunden, gepolsterte Zwei- oder Dreisitzer bilden.

Sculptural, le système « ABCD » faisait appel à des coquilles en fibre de verre qui pouvaient être rembourrées séparément pour former un fauteuil ou fixées ensemble pour constituer un canapé à deux ou trois places.

Pierre Paulin

ABCD, 1968

Textile-covered polyurethane foam-upholstered fibreglass seating shells on base with castors | Sitzschalen aus fiberglasverstärktem Kunststoff auf Rollen, Polsterung aus Polyurethanschaumstoff mit Stoffbezug | Coquilles en fibre de verre, rembourrage en mousse de polyuréthane recouverte de tissu, roulettes

ARTIFORT,
MAASTRICHT,
FROM C. 1968

◄ Pierre Paulin
ABCD chair, 1968

ARTIFORT,
MAASTRICHT,
FROM C. 1968

Pierre Paulin

Tongue, Model No. 577, 1967

Fabric-covered foam-upholstered tubular steel frame | Rahmen aus Stahlrohr, Schaumstoffpolsterung, mit Stoffbezug | Châssis en tube d'acier, rembourrage en mousse recouverte de tissu

ARTIFORT, MAASTRICHT, FROM 1967 TO PRESENT

▼ Artifort advertising photograph, c. 1967

The model No. 577, sometimes referred to as the "Tongue" because of its lingual form, rests directly on the floor allowing the user to assume a relaxed and informal posture.

Die Schale des Modells Nr. 577, das wegen seiner Form manchmal auch »Tongue« (Zunge) genannt wird, steht direkt auf dem Boden und erlaubt den Sitzenden eine bequeme, entspannte Haltung.

Le modèle n° 577, parfois appelé « Tongue » (langue) à cause de sa forme, repose directement sur le sol afin de permettre à son utilisateur de prendre une position totalement détendue.

Through the use of visually unified, abstract sculptural forms, Paulin's chairs are pleasing in appearance. They are also extremely comfortable due to their ergonomics and the extent to which they allow the user freedom of movement.

Mit ihren optisch einheitlichen, abstrakt skulpturalen Formen bieten Paulins Stühle einen ansprechenden Anblick. Zugleich sind sie durch ihre Ergonomie und ihre Proportionen und weil sie den Sitzenden in seiner Bewegungsfreiheit nicht einschränken, äußerst bequem.

Les formes sculpturales abstraites et très unifiées des sièges de Paulin les rendent agréables à regarder. Ils sont également très confortables grâce à leur ergonomie et à leur respect de la liberté de mouvement.

Pierre Paulin

Model No. 560, 1963

Fabric-covered latex-foam upholstered tubular steel frame with springing | Rahmen aus Stahlrohr mit Federung, Polsterung aus Latexschaumstoff, mit Stoffbezug | Châssis en tube d'acier, rembourrage en mousse recouverte de tissu, suspension à ressorts

ARTIFORT, MAASTRICHT, FROM C. 1963 TO PRESENT

◄ Pierre Paulin
Model No. 437, 1959

ARTIFORT, MAASTRICHT

Pierre Paulin

Model No. 545, 1963

Vinyl-covered latex-foam upholstered moulded plywood seating elements attached to brass-plated flat steel frame | Sitzschale und Kopflehne aus geformtem Schichtholz, Latexschaum-stoffpolsterung mit Vinylbezug, Fuß aus messingbeschichtetem Stahl | Éléments du siège en contre-plaqué moulé et rembourré de mousse de latex recouverte de vinyle, châssis en acier plat laitonné

ARTIFORT,
MAASTRICHT,
c. 1963–1969

While the chair No. 545 has a powerful sculptural presence, its three separate seat sections, which appear to float one above the other, provide it with a visual lightness. The even more sculptural "Ribbon" chair No. 582 is perhaps one of the most comfortable chairs ever designed. Its bold cradling form allows the user to assume a variety of positions while retaining the necessary support.

Dem kraftvoll skulpturalen Erscheinen des Sessels Nr. 545 wird durch die drei übereinander angeordneten Sitz- bzw. Rückenschalen eine optische Leichtigkeit verliehen. Der vielleicht noch skulpturalere »Ribbon«-Sessel Nr. 582 ist vielleicht eines der bequemsten Sitzmöbel, das je entworfen wurde. Seine kühne wiegende Form erlaubt dem Sitzenden, eine Vielfalt von Positionen einzunehmen, ohne den notwendigen Halt zu verlieren.

Pierre Paulin

*Ribbon, Model
No. 582, 1965*

*Tensioned rubber
sheet over bent
tubular metal frame
with textile-covered
latex-foam upholstery
on lacquered wood
base | Gestell aus
gebogenem Metall-
rohr, mit Gummi-
plane bespannt,
gepolstert mit
Latexschaum auf
lackiertem Holz,
Stoffbezug | Feuille de
caoutchouc tendue
sur un châssis en tube
métallique cintré,
rembourrage en
mousse de latex
recouverte de tissu,
piètement en bois
laqué*

ARTIFORT,
MAASTRICHT, FROM
C. 1965 TO PRESENT

La forte présence plastique du fauteuil n° 545 ne nuit pas à sa légèreté apparente grâce à l'articulation du siège en trois parties qui semblent en suspension l'une au-dessus de l'autre. Plus sculptural encore, le fauteuil « Ribbon » n° 582 est l'un des sièges les plus confortables jamais dessinés. Son audacieuse forme cintrée offre toute une gamme de positions en assurant toujours un excellent soutien.

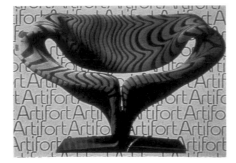

◀ Artifort ad-
vertising photo-
graph showing
Ribbon chair,
Model No. 582,
c. 1965

Olivier Mourgue

Djinn chaise longue,
1965

Stretch fabric-covered,
polyurethane foam-
upholstered, bent
tubular steel frame |
Rahmen aus geboge-
nem Stahlrohr, Pol-
sterung aus Polyure-
thanschaumstoff, mit
Stretchgewebebezug |
Châssis en tube
d'acier cintré, rem-
bourrage en mousse
de polyuréthane
recouverte de stretch

AIRBORNE INTER-
NATIONAL,
MONTREUIL-SOUS-
BOIS, 1963–1976

Used in Stanley Kubrick's film, *2001: A Space Odyssey*, the "Djinn" series'
title was derived from a spirit in Islamic mythology that can assume human
or animal form and control men with its supernatural powers. During the
1960s, the emerging popular interest in Eastern mysticism influenced the
decorative arts in Europe and America. The low height of this seating mir-
rors the informal lifestyle of the period.

Die »Djinn«-Sitzmöbelserie war in Stanley Kubricks Film »2001: Odyssee
im Weltraum« zu sehen; ihren Namen verdankt sie einem Geist aus der
Islamischen Mythologie, der abwechselnd Menschen- und Tiergestalt annehmen
kann und die Menschen mit seiner übernatürlichen Macht beherrscht. Während
der 60er Jahre hat das damals aufkommende und sich verbreitende Interesse an
orientalischem und fernöstlichem Mystizismus die dekorativen Künste in Europa
und Amerika beeinflußt. In der niedrigen Sitzhöhe dieser Möbel spiegelt sich der
informelle Lebensstil dieser Jahre.

◀ Scene from the
film *2001: A Space*
Odyssey by Stanley
Kubrick, 1968

Utilisée dans le film de Stanley Kubrick *2001, l'odyssée de l'espace*, la série
« Djinn » doit son nom à ces génies des pays islamiques qui peuvent
prendre des formes humaines ou animales pour exercer leur pouvoir sur-
naturel sur les hommes. Au cours des années 60, un regain d'intérêt pour
le mysticisme oriental influença les arts décoratifs en Europe comme en
Amérique. La faible hauteur de ces sièges rappelle le style de vie décontracté
de cette époque.

Olivier Mourgue

Djinn series, 1965

Fabric-covered poly-
urethane foam-uphol-
stered, bent tubular
steel frames | Geboge-
nes Stahlrohr, Poly-
urethanschaumstoff,
Stoffbezug | Châssis
en tube d'acier cintré,
rembourrage en
mousse de polyuré-
thane recouverte de
tissu

Olivier Mourgue

Bouloum, 1968

Foam-upholstered
tubular steel frame or
gel-coated moulded
fibreglass shell |
Rahmen aus Stahl-
rohr, Schaumstoff
oder: geformter, fiber-
glasverstärkter Kunst-
stoff mit Gelversiege-
lung | Châssis en tube
d'acier cintré, rem-
bourrage en mousse
de polyuréthane ou
coquille en fibre de
verre moulée enduite

ARCONAS, MISSISS-
AUGA, ONTARIO,
FROM C. 1968 TO
PRESENT

The "Bouloum", with its anthropomorphic form, was named after a child-hood friend of Mourgue's. The designer took this "characterful" seat with him when he travelled, photographed it in various situations and even wrote anecdotes about it. A weatherproof version was also available for outdoor use.

Die »Bouloum«-Sitzliege mit ihrer anthropomorphen Formgebung wurde nach einem Freund aus Mourgues Kindheit benannt. Der Designer nahm diese aus-drucksvolle Sitzgelegenheit mit auf seine Reisen und photographierte sie in den verschiedensten Umgebungen, schrieb sogar kleine Geschichten darüber. Für den Gebrauch im Freien war auch eine wetterfeste Version lieferbar.

Le nom de ce « Bouloum » anthropomorphe rappelle celui d'un ami d'enfance du designer. Mourgue a réalisé des reportages sur ce siège qu'il emportait avec lui dans ses voyages et a même écrit des anecdotes à son sujet. Une version résistant aux intempéries était disponible pour l'usage extérieur.

Poul Volther

*Corona, Model
No. EJ 605, 1961*

Chromed steel frame
with fabric-covered
latex-foam uphol-
stered moulded
plywood seat and
back elements |
Rahmen aus Stahl,
verchromt, Sitz- und
Rückenschalen aus
geformtem Schicht-
holz, Polsterung aus
Latexschaumstoff mit
Stoffbezug | Châssis
en acier chromé, siège
et dossier en contre-
plaqué cintré, rem-
bourrés de néoprène
et recouverts de tissu
ou de cuir

ERIC JØRGENSEN,
COPENHAGEN, FROM
C. 1961–1992

The floating elliptical elements of this chair are reminiscent of time-lapse
photographs of solar eclipses – thus its name, "Corona". It is an extremely
comfortable and high-quality example of Scandinavian design.
*Die fließenden elliptischen Formen dieses Sessels erinnern an Zeitraffer-
photographien einer Sonnenfinsternis – daher der Name »Corona«. Er ist ein
Beispiel für den hohen Sitzkomfort und die außergewöhnliche Qualität des
skandinavischen Designs.*
Les éléments elliptiques flottants de ce fauteuil rappellent les séquences de
photographies d'éclipses solaires, d'où son nom « Corona ». C'est un
exemple extrêmement confortable de design scandinave de haute qualité.

Verner Panton

Pantower,
1968–1969

Textile-covered poly-
urethane foam-uphol-
stered frame | Poly-
urethanschaumstoff,
Stoffbezug | Mousse
de polyuréthane
recouverte de tissu

The "Pantower" and Panton's related room design for the 1970 "Visiona II" exhibition held by Bayer AG demonstrate the contemporary interest in micro-environments. Seating came to be seen in some quarters in the late 1960s not so much as "equipment for living" but as apparatus for interactive play.

Der »Pantower« und Pantons verwandte Raumgestaltung für die »Visiona II«-Ausstellung, die 1970 von der Bayer AG veranstaltet wurde, demonstrieren das zeitgenössische Interesse an Wohnlandschaften. Sitze galten während der 60er

▲ **Verner Panton**
Room Installation
for the "Visiona II"
exhibition by Bayer
AG, Cologne, 1970

Jahre in bestimmten Kreisen nicht als »Wohnmöbel«, sondern zunehmend als Geräte für interaktive Spiele.

Le modèle « Pantower » est la contribution de Panton à l'exposition « Visiona » organisée en 1970 par Bayer AG. Elle témoigne de l'intérêt de l'époque pour les micro-environnements. Un siège était considéré dans certains cercles de la fin des années 60, non pas tant comme un « équipement pour la maison », mais comme un support de relations interactives.

Roberto Sebastian Matta

Malitte, 1966

Textile-covered polyurethane foam block construction | Blöcke aus Polyurethanschaumstoff, mit Stoffbezug | Blocs de mousse de polyuréthane recouverts de tissu

GAVINA, BOLOGNA, 1966–1968, KNOLL INTERNATIONAL, NEW YORK, 1968–1974

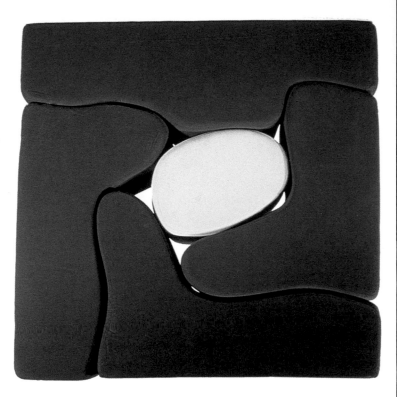

▲ Knoll advertising photograph, c. 1970

This seating system was designed by the architect and surrealist painter, Roberto Matta, to function as a sculptural wall when not in use – an innovation particularly well-suited to the minimalist interiors that became increasingly popular in the 1960s. Utilising low-tech manufacturing methods, the "Malitte" was intended for high-volume production.

Dieses Sitzmöbelsystem wurde von Roberto Matta, Architekt und surrealistischer Maler, so entworfen, daß es als skulpturale Wand dienen kann, wenn es nicht in Gebrauch ist – ein innovativer Einfall, der zu den minimalistischen Interieurs paßte, die in den 60er Jahren sehr beliebt waren. Mit einfachen Mitteln herstellbar, eignete sich »Malitte« für die Produktion in großen Stückzahlen.

Ce système de sièges fut conçu par l'architecte et peintre surréaliste Roberto Matta pour servir de mur-sculpture lorsqu'il n'était pas utilisé. Cette idée était bien adaptée aux intérieurs minimalistes de plus en plus à la mode pendant les années 60. Requérant des procédés de fabrication sommaires, le modèle « Malitte » était conçu pour la production en série.

Throughout his career, Prina has actively researched the application of plastics in industrial design. His "Sess Longue", also known as the "Skulptur" sofa, does not compromise comfort for aesthetics and reflects the sculptural tendency in 1960s' design which found its best expression in synthetic materials.

Während seiner gesamten Laufbahn als Designer hat Prina die Anwendungs-möglichkeiten von Kunststoffen im Industriedesign intensiv erforscht. »Sess Longue«, auch als »Skulptur«-Sofa bekannt, opfert den Sitzkomfort nicht der Ästhetik und reflektiert die skulpturalen Tendenzen im Design der 6oer Jahre, die in synthetischen Materialien ihren überzeugendsten Ausdruck fanden.

Au cours de sa carrière, Prina n'a jamais cessé de faire des recherches sur les possibilités d'utilisation de matières plastiques dans le design industriel. La « Sess Longue », aussi appelée canapé « Skulptur », n'accepte aucun compromis entre le confort et l'esthétique, et reflète les tendances sculpturales du design des années 60, qui trouvèrent leur meilleur moyen d' expression dans les matériaux synthétiques.

Nani Prina

Sess Longue, 1968

Textile-covered polyurethane foam | Polyurethanschaum-stoff mit Stoffbezug | Mousse de polyuré-thane recouverte de tissu

SORMANI, AROSIO, COMO, FROM C. 1968

Verner Panton

Upholstered seating system, 1963

Fabric-covered latex-foam upholstered construction on metal castors | Sitzschalen auf Metallrollen, mit Latexschaumstoff-polsterung und Stoff-bezug | Châssis métallique sur roulettes, rembour-rage de mousse de latex recouverte de tissu

STORZ + PALMER, COPENHAGEN, FROM C. 1963

Panton believed that when arranged next to one another, chairs should create "a kind of chair-landscape, which refuses to be just functional".
(A.L. Morgan, *Contemporary Designers*, St. James Press, London 1985, p. 471)
Panton war davon überzeugt, daß Stühle, wenn man sie nebeneinander arrangiert, »eine Art von Stuhllandschaft bilden müßten, die mehr bietet als bloße Funktionalität«.
(A.L. Morgan, »Contemporary Designers«, St. James Press, London 1985, S. 471)
Panton pensait que ses créations, une fois rapprochées les unes des autres, devaient créer une « sorte de paysage de sièges qui ne soit pas purement fonctionnel. »
(A.l. Morgan, *Contemporary Designers*, St. James Press, Londres, 1985, p. 471)

The "Bobo" chair's block-like polyurethane foam construction does not require an internal supporting structure. Boeri undoubtedly gained valuable experience in the use of foam while she was head of interiors and furnishing at Marco Zanuso's studio.

Der Block aus Polyurethanschaumstoff, aus dem »Bobo« besteht, braucht kein tragendes Gestell mehr. Boeri hat wertvolle Erfahrungen im Umgang mit Schaumstoff gesammelt, als sie in Marco Zanusos Atelier für Innenausstattung und Möbeldesign verantwortlich war.

La construction en blocs de mousse de polyuréthane du fauteuil « Bobo » ne nécessitait pas de structure interne. Boeri avait certainement acquis une bonne expérience de la mousse lorsqu'elle était responsable des aménagements intérieurs et du mobilier dans l'agence de Marco Zanuso.

Cini Boeri

Bobo, 1967

Textile-covered polyurethane foam-block construction | Block aus Polyurethanschaumstoff, mit Stoffbezug | Blocs de mousse de polyuréthane recouverts de tissu

ARFLEX, GUISSANO, MILAN, FROM 1967 TO PRESENT

◄Arflex advertising photograph, c. 1967

Gaetano Pesce

**Donna, Model
Nos. Up 5 & Up 6,
1969**

Stretch fabric-covered
moulded
polyurethane foam |
Geformter Polyure-
thanschaumstoff mit
Stretchgewebebezug |
Mousse de
polyuréthane moulée
recouverte de tissu
stretch

C & B ITALIA,
NOVEDRATE, COMO,
1969–1973 (LATER
TO BECOME B & B
ITALIA)

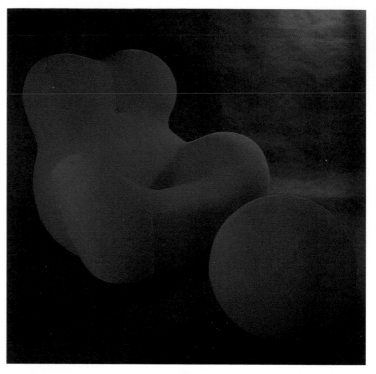

▶ C & B Italia series
of photographs
showing Up 5 being
unwrapped

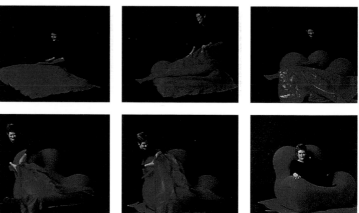

Compressed and vacuum-packed in PVC wrappers, the "Up Series" literally bounced into life when unwrapped. Described by Pesce as "transformation" furniture, these iconoclastic designs turned the act of purchasing a chair into a "happening".

Zusammengepreßt und in PVC-Folie vakuumverpackt, sprangen die Möbel der »Up Series« buchstäblich ins Leben, wenn sie ausgepackt wurden. Pesce hat sie auch als Transformations-Möbel bezeichnet; dieses ikonoklastische Design machte den Akt des Stuhleinkaufs zu einem »Happening«.

Comprimés et livrés dans un emballage sous vide, les sièges de la série « Up » prenaient littéralement vie au déballage. Désignés par Pesce comme mobilier « à transformation », ces modèles iconoclastes faisaient du simple acte d'achat d'un siège une sorte de happening.

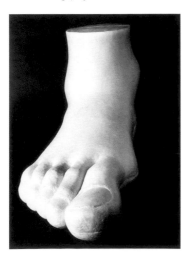

Gaetano Pesce

Up Series, 1969

Stretch fabric-covered moulded polyurethane foam | Geformter Polyurethanschaumstoff, mit Stretchgewebebezug | Mousse de polyuréthane moulée recouverte de tissu stretch

C & B ITALIA,
NOVEDRATE, COMO
(LATER TO BECOME
B & B ITALIA),
1970–1973

◄ **Gaetano Pesce**
Up 7, 1969

C & B ITALIA,
NOVEDRATE, COMO,
1970–1973

Roger Dean

Sea Urchin, 1968

Textile-covered polyurethane foam structure | Polyurethanschaumstoff mit Stoffbezug | Mousse de polyuréthane recouverte de tissu

HILLE INTERNATIONAL, LONDON, FROM 1968

The "Sea Urchin" was one of the first polyurethane foam chairs which adapted completely to the contours of the user. The rights to the design were bought by Hille who developed it in conjunction with Dunlop.

»Sea Urchin« war eines der ersten Sitzmöbel aus Polyurethanschaumstoff, die sich völlig an die Gestalt des Sitzenden anpaßten. Die Rechte an diesem Design wurden von der Firma Hille erworben, die es dann in Zusammenarbeit mit der Firma Dunlop produzierte.

Le « Sea Urchin » fut l'un des premiers fauteuils en mousse de polyuréthane à s'adapter étroitement aux formes de son utilisateur. Les droits de ce modèle furent acquis par Hille qui développa ensuite sa production en coopération avec Dunlop.

Giovanni
Travasa

Palla, Model
No. 827, 1966

*Woven rattan
construction |
Rattangeflecht |
Rotin tressé*

VITTORIO BONACINA
& C., LURAGO
D'ERBA, COMO,
FROM 1966 TO
PRESENT

Travasa utilised a traditional material – woven rattan – to create a contemporary form. The "Palla's" simple, almost elemental shape gives the once humble "basket chair" a poetic and sculptural strength.

Travasa verwendete einen traditionellen Werkstoff – Rattangeflecht –, um eine zeitgenössische Form zu schaffen. Die einfache, fast elementare Formgebung von "Palla" gibt dem traditionell einfachen Typus des Korbstuhls eine wieder poetische und skulpturale Ausdruckskraft.

Travasa fait ici appel à un matériau traditionnel – le rotin tressé – pour élaborer une forme contemporaine. Les contours simples, presque élémentaires du « Palla » donnent à l'humble « fauteuil d'osier » classique une puissance poétique et sculpturale.

Peter Raacke

Papp, 1967

Painted cardboard construction | Karton, lackiert | Carton peint

PAPP-FALTMÖBEL
ELLEN RAACKE,
WOLFGANG/HANAU,
FROM C. 1967

From a range of cardboard furniture items that included modular seating, storage units and tables, the "Papp" chair was one of the first designs to explore the possibilities of cardboard seating.

Der »Papp«-Stuhl ist Teil einer Möbelserie aus Karton, zu der Regalelemente, Sitzmöbel und Tische gehören. Es ist einer der ersten Entwürfe, mit denen erprobt wurde, welche Möglichkeiten Karton zur Herstellung von Sitzmöbeln bietet.

Appartenant à une gamme de meubles en carton qui comprenait des sièges modulaires, des rangements et des tables, le fauteuil « Papp » fut l'un des premiers à expérimenter les possibilités du carton dans le domaine du mobilier.

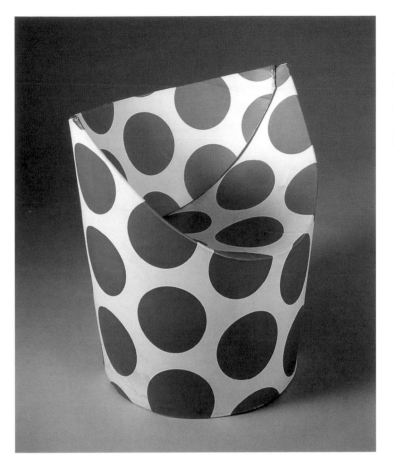

Peter Murdoch

Spotty, 1963

Polyethylene-coated, laminated paperboard construction | Laminierter Karton, mit Polyethylenbeschichtung | Papier cartonné enduit de polyéthylène

INTERNATIONAL PAPER, 1964–1965

Murdoch's polka-dot child's chair "Spotty" is an icon of the Pop era. Its low production costs and inherent disposability were ideally suited to the demands of the mass consumer market.

Murdochs Kinderstuhl »Spotty« wurde mit seinem Punktmuster zu einer Ikone der Pop-Ära. Niedrige Produktionskosten und seine universelle Verwendbarkeit machten ihn zum idealen Produkt für den Massenkonsum.

Ce siège d'enfant à pois, dessiné par Murdoch, est un symbole de la période Pop. Son faible coût de fabrication et le fait qu'il était jetable répondaient idéalement aux attentes du marché de la grande consommation.

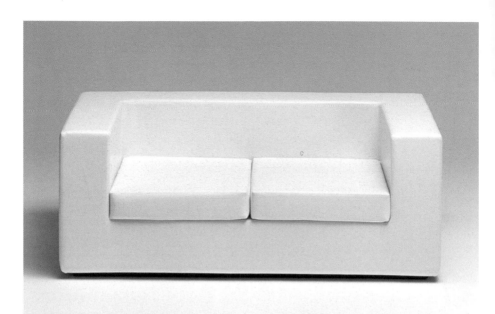

Willie Landels

Throw-away, 1965

Vinyl or leather-covered block polyurethane foam construction | Block aus Polyurethanschaumstoff mit Vinyl- bzw. Lederbezug | Mousse de polyuréthane recouverte de vinyle ou de cuir

ZANOTTA, MILAN, FROM 1966 TO PRESENT

The "Throw-away" sofa and matching chair were an inexpensive seating solution that relied on low-tech manufacturing methods. Implicit in its title is the "use it today, sling it tomorrow" ethos of the 1960s. Kinsman's "F Range" seating used a similar foam construction and was also covered in "wet-look" vinyl – a material that epitomises the decade's mockery of "good taste".

Das »Throw-away«-Sofa und der dazu passende Sessel waren preiswerte Sitzlösungen, die durch einfache Produktionsverfahren ermöglicht wurden. Der Name des Möbels bezieht sich direkt auf die 6oer Jahre-Mentalität des »Einmal brauchen und dann weg damit«. Kinsmans »F Range«-Sitzmöbel bestehen aus Schaumstoffblöcken und feuchtschimmernden Vinylbezügen – das Material, mit dem sich die 6oer über den »guten Geschmack« lustig machten.

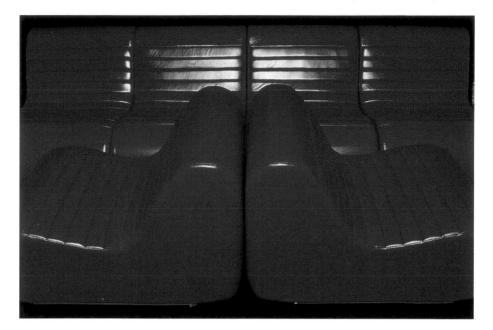

Le canapé « Throw-away » et son fauteuil assorti étaient proposés à un prix attractif en raison de procédés de fabrication très simples. Son nom sans équivoque « À jeter » rappelle son époque. La série « F Range» de Kinsman utilisait une structure en mousse identique et était également recouverte de vinyle luisant, matériaux qui, dans les années 60, se moquaient plaisamment du « bon goût».

Rodney Kinsman

F Range, 1966

Vinyl-covered polyurethane foam construction with linking zip device | Mit Reißverschluß verbundene Blöcke aus Polyurethanschaumstoff mit Vinylbezug | Mousse de polyuréthane recouverte de vinyle, fermeture à glissière

OMK DESIGNS, LONDON, FROM c. 1966

Cut into a wave-like form from a single block of polyurethane foam, the "Superonda" is exceptionally lightweight and easy to move. It can be configured in several ways – either as a chaise longue, sofa or divan – and is a highly interactive design, functioning more as a plaything than as a serious seating solution.

»Superonda«, hergestellt aus Polyurethanschaumstoffblöcken, die in wellenartige Formen geschnitten sind, ist außergewöhnlich leicht und mühelos zu bewegen. Das Möbel kann auf verschiedene Weise aufgestellt werden, als Liege, als Sofa oder als Diwan – ein sehr interaktiver Entwurf, eigentlich mehr Spielzeug als seriöses Sitzmöbel.

Découpé en forme de vague dans un bloc de mousse de polyuréthane, le « Superonda » est d'un poids exceptionnellement léger et donc facile à déplacer. Il offre plusieurs configurations – chaise longue, canapé ou divan. Très convivial, il fonctionne davantage comme un jouet que comme une proposition sérieuse de mobilier.

Archizoom Associati

Superonda, 1966

Vinyl-covered polyurethane foam-block construction | Konstruktion aus Polyurethanschaum-stoff mit Vinylbezug | Blocs de mousse de poyuréthane recou-verts de vinyle

POLTRONOVA, MON-TALE, PISTOIA, FROM 1966 TO PRESENT

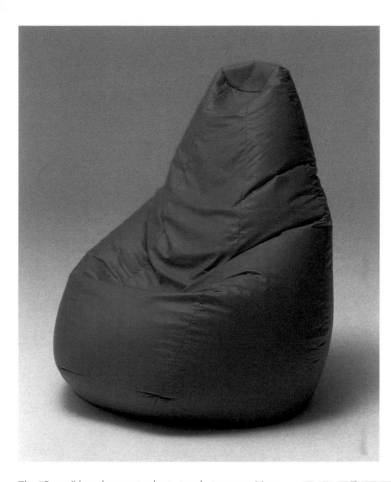

Piero Gatti, Cesare Paolini & Franco Teodoro

Sacco, 1968

Vinyl bag containing semi-expanded polystyrene pellets | Sack aus Kunstleder, Füllung aus Polystyrol-Kugeln | Sac de vinyle rempli de billes de polystyrène semi-expansé

ZANOTTA, MILAN, FROM 1968 TO PRESENT

◄◄ Zanotta photograph showing Piero Gatti, Cesare Paolini & Franco Teodoro sitting on Saccos, 1968

▼ Working drawing of Sacco's cover, c. 1968

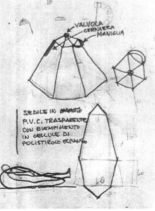

The "Sacco" beanbag seat adapts to whatever position the user assumes. The designers initially proposed a fluid-filled envelope, but excessive weight eventually led to the inspired choice of polystyrene beads.

Das Sackmöbel »Sacco« paßt seine Form der Position des Nutzers an. Die Designer hatten ursprünglich eine Füllung mit Flüssigkeit vorgeschlagen; das aber hätte zu übermäßigem Gewicht geführt, und so kam man schließlich auf den genialen Einfall, den Sitzsack mit Polystyrol-Kugeln zu füllen.

Le fauteuil-sac « Sacco » s'adapte à toutes les positions de l'utilisateur. Les designers avaient pensé initialement le remplir de liquide mais le poids excessif de cette solution lui fit préférer les billes de polystyrène.

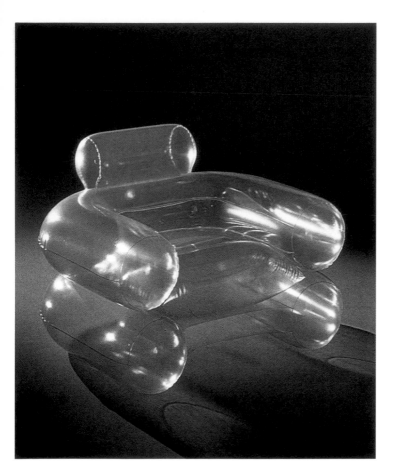

Gionatan De Pas, Donato D'Urbino, Paolo Lomazzi & Carla Scolari

Blow, 1967

Radio-frequency welded PVC (polyvinylchloride) | Hochfrequenzverschweißtes PVC (Polyvinylchlorid) | PVC soudé électroniquement (chlorure de polyvinyle)

ZANOTTA, MILAN, 1968–1969 & 1988–1992

◄◄ Designers of Blow at the Zanotta Stand, Eurodomus 3, Turin

▼ Working drawing of Blow chair, c. 1967

The first mass-produced inflatable chair in Italy, the "Blow" chair is an icon of 1960s' popular culture. Its inherent expendability dismissed the traditional associations of furniture with high cost and permanence.

»*Blow*«, *der erste aufblasbare Sessel aus Italien, der in Serie produziert wurde, ist eine Ikone der Popkultur der 60er Jahre. Dieses Sitzmöbel, auf schnellen Verschleiß angelegt, verabschiedet sich von der traditionellen Vorstellung, daß Möbel teuer und haltbar sein müssen.*

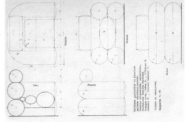

Premier siège gonflable produit en Italie, le fauteuil « Blow » est un icone de la culture populaire des années 60. Il balayait d'un coup l'idée traditionnelle selon laquelle un meuble devait être cher et durable.

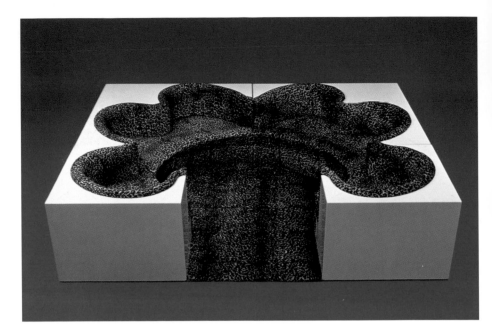

Archizoom Associati

Safari, 1968

Fibreglass frame with internal textile-covered latex foam upholstery | Rahmen aus fiberglasverstärktem Kunststoff, integrierte Polsterung aus Latexschaumstoff mit Stoffbezug | Châssis en fibre de verre, rembourrage intérieur en mousse de latex recouverte de tissu

POLTRONOVA, MONTALE, PISTOIA, FROM 1968

The "Safari" is a modular "livingscape" which, through its use of fake leopard skin and its flower-shaped form, revels in kitsch while mocking the conventional wisdom that "Good Design" equals good taste.

»Safari« bildet eine modulhafte Wohnlandschaft und schwelgt durch die Verwendung von imitiertem Leopardenfell und die Blumenform im Kitsch – ein Spott auf die Binsenweisheit, daß »gutes Design« das gleiche sei wie »guter Geschmack«.

Le « Safari » est un « espace de vie » modulaire qui, avec son faux léopard et sa forme de fleur, prend le parti du kitsch. Il se moque du préjugé selon lequel « Good Design » signifierait « bon goût ».

▶ Contemporary photograph showing Safari, c. 1968

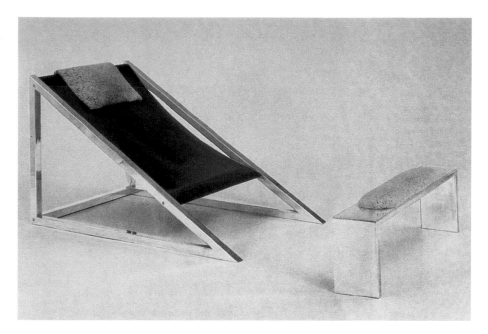

The "Mies" chair is another example of Italian Radical design that attempts to strip away the "pretensions" of Modernism. While the design is primarily concerned with making ironic comment, the rubber sling seat, which remains taut when not in use, is an innovative functional feature.

Der »Mies«-Stuhl ist ein weiteres Beispiel für das »Radical Design« in Italien, das aufräumen wollte mit den Prätentionen der Moderne. Das Design konzentriert sich vor allem auf den ironischen Kommentar, dennoch ist die Sitzbespannung aus Gummi, der nach Gebrauch in die straff gespannte Position zurückkehrt, eine funktionale Innovation.

La chaise longue « Mies » est un nouvel exemple d'un certain design radical italien tentant d'échapper aux prétentions du modernisme. Si ce modèle a essentiellement pour objectif la délivrance d'un message ironique, son siège suspendu en caoutchouc, qui reste tendu au repos, est une nouveauté fonctionnelle.

Archizoom Associati

Mies, 1969

Chromed steel frame with rubber sling seat | Rahmen aus Stahl, verchromt, Sitzbespannung aus Gummi | Châssis en acier chromé, siège suspendu en caoutchouc

POLTRONOVA, MONTALE, PISTOIA, FROM 1969

◄ Poltronova advertising photograph, c. 1969

Allen Jones

Chair-Sculpture,
1969

Partially clad
mannequin
construction with
leather-covered seat
cushion | Halbnackte
Schaufensterpuppen,
lederbezogener Sitz |
Mannequin
partiellement habillé,
coussins de siège en
cuir

ALLEN JONES,
LONDON

The artist, Allen Jones, has created various "furniture-sculptures" incorporating scantily-clad female mannequins. Inspired by popular culture rather than "high art", these pieces typify Pop Art. Although functional, they must be considered fine art rather than design.

Der Künstler Allen Jones hat verschiedene »Möbel-Skulpturen« geschaffen, in die er spärlich bekleidete Schaufensterpuppen einbezog. Inspiriert eher durch die Alltagskultur als durch »hohe Kunst«, sind diese Entwürfe ein Stück Pop-Art. Sie erfüllen ihren Zweck, müssen aber doch als Kunstwerke und weniger als »Design« betrachtet werden.

L'artiste Allen Jones a créé de nombreux « meubles-sculptures » à partir de mannequins féminins. Plus inspirés de culture populaire que de « grand art », ces modèles se rattachent au Pop Art. Malgré leur fonctionnalisme, ils relèvent davantage de la création artistique que du design.

Studio Simon

Omaggio ad Andy Warhol, 1973

Silk-screen printed recycled paint drum with loose textile-covered upholstered seat cushion | Recycelte Farbeimer mit Seidensiebdruck, lose Sitzkissen mit Stoffbezug | Bidon de peinture recyclé sérigraphié, coussin de siège rembourré et recouvert de tissu

SIMON INTERNATIONAL FOR GAVINA, BOLOGNA, FROM 1973 TO PRESENT

Making direct reference to Andy Warhol's *Campbell's Soup Cans* (1962), these stools exemplify many of the characteristics of Pop identified by Richard Hamilton: "Popular, Transient, Expendable, Low Cost, Young, Witty, Sexy, Gimmicky, Glamorous, Big Business". (Richard Hamilton, *Collected Words 1953–1982*, Thames and Hudson, London 1982, p.148–149)

Diese Hocker, die direkt auf Andy Warhols »Campbell's Soup Cans« (1962) an-spielen, zeigen viele der Eigenschaften, die Richard Hamilton als charakteristisch für Pop bezeichnet hat: »Populär, flüchtig, entbehrlich, billig, jung, geistreich, sexy, witzig-verspielt, auffällig, Big Business.«

Référence directe aux *Campbell's Soup Cans* d'Andy Warhol (1962), ces tabourets illustrent de multiples caractéristiques du Pop tel que le présentait Richard Hamilton : « Populaire, transitoire, consommable, bon marché, jeune, drôle, sexy, astucieux, séduisant, une bonne affaire. »

Kazuhide Takahama

Kazuki, 1968

Lacquered plywood frame with fabric seat covering | Rahmen aus Schichtholz, lackiert, Sitzfläche mit Stoffbezug | Châssis en contre-plaqué laqué, siège recouvert de tissu

SIMON INTERNATIONAL FOR GAVINA, BOLOGNA, FROM 1969 TO PRESENT

▼ **Kazuhide Takahama**
Saghi chairs, 1971

SIMON INTERNATIONAL FOR GAVINA, BOLOGNA

Influenced by the ancient Japanese tradition, Takahama lacquered the surfaces of his "Kazuki" chair. Its manufacturer, Gavina, was the first to exploit this technique within the modern industrial process.

Beeinflußt durch überlieferte japanische Traditionen, lackierte Takahama die Oberflächen seines »Kazuki«-Stuhls. Gavina war der erste Hersteller, der diese Technik in der modernen Industriefertigung einsetzte.

Influencé par l'ancienne tradition japonaise, Takahama avait laqué les surfaces de ce « Kazuki ». Son fabricant, Gavina, fut le premier à intégrer cette technique à un processus industriel moderne.

Kazuhide Takahama

Mantilla, 1973

Moulded polyurethane foam with interchangeable covering on plywood base | Basis aus Schichtholz, geformter Polyurethanschaumstoff mit auswechselbarem Bezug | Mousse de polyuréthane moulée, recouvrement interchangeable, base en contre-plaqué

SIMON INTERNATIONAL FOR GAVINA, BOLOGNA, FROM 1974 TO PRESENT

▼ **Kazuhide Takahama**
Gaja chairs, 1969

SIMON INTERNATIONAL FOR GAVINA, BOLOGNA

The "Mantilla" sofa incorporated a thoroughly novel concept – a replaceable blanket-like covering. Not only practical, this feature allowed greater freedom in the modification of interiors.

Das Sofa »Mantilla« verfolgt ein völlig neues Konzept – den auswechselbaren, wie ein Überwurf wirkenden Bezug. Neben den praktischen Vorteilen schafft dies eine größere Freiheit bei der Umgestaltung von Innenräumen.

Le canapé « Mantilla » appliquait un concept totalement nouveau, celui d'un recouvrement amovible sous forme de couverture. Non seulement pratique, cette idée permettait également une plus grande liberté dans l'aménagement des espaces intérieurs.

419

Roberto Sebastian Matta

MAgriTTA, 1970

Acrylic textile-covered methacrylate frame with polyurethane foam upholstery | Rahmen aus Methacryl, Polyurethanschaumstoffpolsterung, mit Acrylstoffbezug | Châssis en méthacrylate, rembourrage en mousse de polyuréthane recouverte de tissu acrylique

SIMON INTERNATIONAL FOR GAVINA, BOLOGNA, FROM C. 1971 TO PRESENT

▼ **Marion Baruch**
Ron Ron seat, 1972

SIMON INTERNATIONAL FOR GAVINA, BOLOGNA, FROM C. 1972

The "MAgriTTA" chair was inspired by the work of the Surrealist painter, René Magritte – the bowler hat and apple being his "trademarks".

Der »MAgriTTA«-Stuhl ist inspiriert durch das Werk des surrealistischen Malers René Magritte, zu dessen »Markenzeichen« der Bowler und der Apfel wurden.

Ce siège « MAgriTTA » est directement inspiré de l'œuvre du peintre surréaliste René Magritte, qui représenta souvent le chapeau melon et la pomme dans ses tableaux.

Roberto
Sebastian
Matta

Margarita, 1970

*Cast bronze form
with sheep skin |
Bronzeguß mit
Schaffell | Forme en
bronze, fourrure
d'agneau*

SIMON
INTERNATIONAL FOR
GAVINA, BOLOGNA,
FROM 1971 TO
PRESENT

This quasi-throne is a bronze casting of a manipulated metal drum and has
been described as a "counterfeit ready-made". "Margarita" is part of
Gavina's "Ultramobile" series which attempted to bring "the poetics of the
unexpected" into furniture design. (Virgilio Vercelloni, *The Adventure of
Design: Gavina*, Jaca Book, Milan 1987, p. 131)

*Das bearbeitete Metallfaß dieses Quasi-Throns ist aus Bronzeguß und wurde als
»Pseudo-Ready-made« bezeichnet. »Margarita« gehört zu Gavinas Serie
»Ultramobile«, mit der er »die Poesie des Unerwarteten« ins Möbeldesign ein-
führen wollte.*

Ce quasi-trône, réalisé en fonte de bronze à partir d'un récipient cylindrique
en métal, a été qualifié de «faux ready-made». «Margarita» appartient à la
série «Ultramobiles» de Gavina, qui voulait insuffler «la poésie de l'inat-
tendu» dans le design de mobilier.

Gionatan De Pas, Donato D'Urbino & Paolo Lomazzi

Joe, 1970

Leather or stretch fabric-covered moulded polyurethane foam | Geformter Polyurethanschaumstoff, mit Leder oder Stretchgewebe bezogen | Mousse de polyuréthane moulée recouverte de cuir ou de tissu stretch

POLTRONOVA, MONTALE, PISTOIA, FROM 1971 TO PRESENT

Named after the baseball legend Joe DiMaggio, this gigantic glove was inspired by the oversized and out-of-context sculptures of Claes Oldenburg. The form of the "Joe" chair can also be seen as an ironic comment on the proliferation of reissued Bauhaus furniture covered with high-priced glove leather.

Dieser riesenhafte Handschuh, nach dem legendären Baseballspieler Joe DiMaggio benannt, wurde inspiriert durch die überdimensionalen und verfremdeten Skulpturen von Claes Oldenburg. Die Gestaltung des »Joe«-Sessels kann auch als ein ironischer Kommentar zur neuerlichen Konjunktur reeditierter Bauhaus-Möbel verstanden werden, die mit teurem Handschuhleder bezogen wurden.

Nommé d'après le joueur de base-ball légendaire Joe DiMaggio, cet énorme gant s'inspire des sculptures géantes hors contexte de Claes Oldenburg. La forme du fauteuil « Joe » peut également être analysée comme un commentaire ironique de la prolifération des rééditions de meubles du Bauhaus, qui étaient recouverts de cuir fin.

This sectional sofa was constructed of self-skinning polyurethane foam elements which could be linked together to form, in theory, a seat of unlimited length. Its snaking form gave the design an inherent flexibility and this undoubtedly contributed to its commercial success.

Dieses Sofa wird aus Polyurethan-Integralschaumstoffelementen zusammengestellt, theoretisch läßt sich eine Sitzfläche unbegrenzter Länge bilden. Die geschwungene Form gab dem Entwurf eine besondere eigene Flexibilität, die zweifellos zum Markterfolg des Sofas beigetragen hat.

Ce canapé modulaire se compose d'éléments en mousse de polyuréthane surfacé que l'on pouvait assembler pour former, en théorie, un siège de longueur illimitée. Sa forme serpentine lui donne une souplesse naturelle qui a sans aucun doute contribué à son succès commercial.

Cini Boeri

Serpentone, 1971

Self-skinning polyurethane foam structure | Polyurethan-Integralschaumstoff | Structure en mousse de polyuréthane

ARFLEX, GIUSSANO, MILAN, FROM C. 1971

Rodolfo Bonetto

Melaina, 1970

Single-form moulded fibreglass-reinforced polyester | Einteilige fiberglasverstärkte Polyesterschale | Polyester renforcé de fibre de verre et moulé d'une pièce

DRIADE, FOSSADELLO
DI CAORSO,
PIACENZA,
FROM 1970

Bonetto's single-piece "Melaina" is a reworking of a traditional tub chair while Stoppino's "Alessia" explores the potential of a reversed cantilever. Through elegant Italian designs such as these, the perception of plastics changed in the 1970s – they came to be seen as noble, rather than cheap materials. Both designs demonstrate Driade's commitment to state-of-the-art technology and were exhibited at the 1972 "Design a Plastické Hmoty", Prague.

Bonetto hat seinen aus einem Stück geformten Plastikstuhl »Melaina« aus der Form des traditionellen Wannensitzes abgeleitet. Stoppinos »Alessia« hingegen experimentiert mit den Möglichkeiten eines umgekehrten Freischwinger-Gestells. Elegante Designs aus Italien wie diese beiden trugen dazu bei, daß sich in den 70er Jahren die Einstellung zu Plastik änderte. Kunststoffe galten nicht länger als

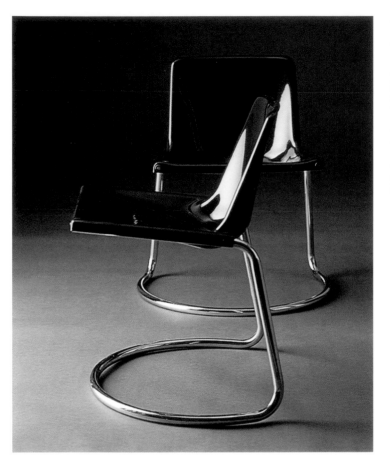

Giotto Stoppino

Alessia, 1970

Chromed tubular
steel frame with
fibreglass-reinforced
polyester seat | Gestell
aus verchromtem
Stahlrohr, Sitzschale
aus fiberglasver-
stärktem Polyester |
Châssis en tube
d'acier, siège en
polyester renforcé de
fibre de verre

DRIADE, FOSSADELLO
DI CAORSO,
PIACENZA,
FROM 1970

billig, sondern durchaus als »edle« Werkstoffe. Beide Entwürfe zeigen die
Konzentration des Herstellers Driade auf fortgeschrittenste Techniken; 1972
wurden beide Modelle in Prag auf der Ausstellung »Design a Plastické Hmoty«
präsentiert.

Fabriqué d'une seule pièce, le « Melaina » est l'adaptation d'un fauteuil gon-
dole traditionnel tandis que le modèle « Alessia » de Stoppino explore les
possibilités du cantilever inversé. Ce sont des créations italiennes de cette
élégance qui modifièrent la perception des matières plastiques au cours des
années 70, dorénavant considérées comme des matériaux presque nobles et
non seulement bon marché. Ces deux modèles illustrent l'intérêt de Driade
pour les technologies avant-gardistes et furent exposés en 1972 à Prague
lors de la manifestation « Design a Plastické Hmoty ».

Vico Magistretti

Gaudí, 1970

Compression-
moulded "Reglar"
fibreglass-reinforced
polyester |
Formgepreßtes, fiber-
glasverstärktes
»Reglar«-Polyester |
Polyester « Reglar »
renforcé de fibre de
verre et moulé sous
pression

ARTEMIDE, MILAN,
FROM 1970 TO
PRESENT

▼ **Vico Magistretti**
Gaudí & Vicario
chairs, 1970

ARTEMIDE, MILAN,
FROM 1971 TO
PRESENT

The "Gaudí" and "Vicario" evolved out of Magistretti's earlier "Selene" chair. Because the arms are integrated into the single-piece construction, perforations were required at the inner corners of the seat.

Den »Gaudí«- und den »Vicario«-Stuhl hat Magistretti aus dem »Selene«-Stuhl entwickelt. Da die Armlehnen in die einteilige Konstruktion integriert sind, waren Aussparungen an den hinteren Ecken der Sitzflächen notwendig.

Les modèles « Gaudí » et « Vicario » ont été développés à partir d'un siège antérieur de Magistretti, le « Selene ». Moulé d'une seule pièce, y compris les accoudoirs, il fallut prévoir des perforations dans la courbure intérieure du siège pour des raisons techniques.

Achille Castiglioni

Primate, 1970

"Baydur" frame on polystyrene base with vinyl-covered polyurethane foam sections and chromed tubular steel connecting element | Rahmen aus »Baydur«-Kunststoff auf Polyestersockel, Polyurethanschaumstoffposterung mit Vinylbezug, Verbindungsbügel aus Stahlrohr, verchromt | Châssis en « Baydur », base en polystyrène, éléments rembourrés de mousse de polyuréthane recouverte de vinyle, élément de connexion en tube d'acier chromé

ZANOTTA, MILAN, FROM 1970 TO PRESENT

Castiglioni's work is epitomised by experimental forms that are fundamentally inspired by function. His "Primate", the first mass-produced kneeling stool, was born out of ergonomic considerations and the desire for a more healthful sitting position.

Experimentelle, von der Funktion inspirierte Formen sind typisch für Castiglionis Werk. »Primate« ist der erste in Serie produzierte Kniehocker. Seine Form wurde aus ergonomischen Erwägungen entwickelt; er sollte eine gesündere Sitzhaltung ermöglichen.

Le travail de Castiglioni se caractérise essentiellement par des formes expérimentales qui s'inspirent d'une analyse approfondie de la fonction. Le « Primate », premier siège de ce type à être produit en grand série, répond à des considérations ergonomiques et au désir de trouver une position assise plus saine.

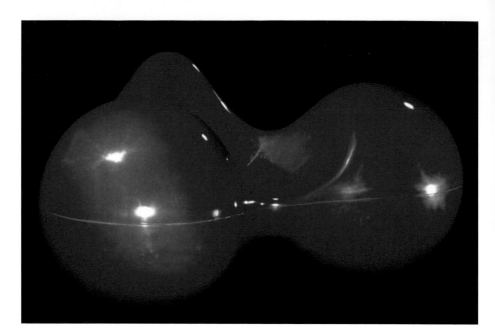

Eero Aarnio

Tomato, 1971

Moulded fibreglass-reinforced polyester structure | Geformtes, fiberglasverstärktes Polyester | Polyester moulé renforcé de fibre de verre

ASKO, LAHTI, 1968–C. 1980 (REISSUED BY ADELTA INTERNATIONAL, FINLAND C/O FINLANDCONTACT DINSLAKEN, FROM 1991)

The "Tomato" is perhaps Aarnio's most iconoclastic design for seating and was conceived for both indoor and outdoor use. Like his earlier "Globe" and "Pastille" chairs, its globular form visually accentuates the gleaming surface qualities of moulded fibreglass-reinforced polyester.

»Tomato«, vielleicht Aarnios radikalster Sitzmöbelentwurf, wurde für Innenräume und Außenbereiche entwickelt. Wie bei den früheren »Globe«- und »Pastille«-Sesseln unterstreicht die kugelige Form die optische Wirkung der glänzenden Oberflächen von geformtem, fiberglasverstärktem Polyester.

Le « Tomato » est sans aucun doute le projet de siège le plus audacieux de Aarnio. Il fut conçu aussi bien pour un usage intérieur qu'extérieur. Comme pour les modèles précédents « Globe » et « Pastille », sa forme globuleuse accentue les reflets de la lumière sur une structure en polyester renforcé de fibre de verre.

Luigi Colani

Zocker (Sitzgerät Colani), 1971–1972

Rotationally moulded polyethylene | Polyethylen, Rotationssinterverfahren | Polyéthylène mis en forme par rotation

TOP SYSTEM
BURKHARD LÜBKE,
GÜTERSLOH,
1973–1982

▼ Luigi Colani testing the Sitzgerät Colani, c. 1972

Initially, Colani designed a child's version of this "sitting tool" with its integrated seat and desk. This multifunctional, ergonomically inspired design could either be straddled or used in a conventional sitting position.

Zunächst hatte Colani eine Kinderversion dieses »Sitzwerkzeugs« mit integriertem Sitz und Pult entworfen. Auf diesem auf Multifunktionalität und Ergonomie ausgelegten Modell kann man entweder in konventioneller Haltung oder rittlings wie in einem Sattel sitzen.

Colani produisit d'abord une version pour enfants de ce tabouret à siège et plan de travail intégrés. Modèle ergonomique multifonctionnel, il permettait de s'asseoir à califourchon ou de manière plus conventionnelle.

Piero Gilardi

Massolo (Porfido),
1974

Moulded "Guflex"
polyurethane foam
with "Guflex"
lacquered finish |
Geformter »Guflex«-
Polyurethanschaum,
mit »Guflex«-
Lackierung | Mousse
de polyuréthane
« Guflex », finition de
surface en laque
« Guflex »

GUFRAM,
BALANGERO, TURIN,
FROM 1974 TO
PRESENT

Gilardi's polyurethane foam design modelled into the form of a gigantic slab
of porphyry demonstrates the influence of sculptor Claes Oldenburg on
Italian Radical designers associated with the Anti-Design movement. With
its incised lettering, "Massolo" intentionally mocks the funereal associations of the natural material it imitates.

Gilardis Entwurf aus Polyurethanschaumstoff, der wie eine riesige Porphyrplatte
geformt ist, demonstriert den Einfluß des Bildhauers Claes Oldenburg auf das
italienische Radical-Design, das mit der Anti-Design-Bewegung verbunden wird.
Mit der »eingravierten« Inschrift ironisiert »Massolo« die düsteren Friedhofs-
assoziationen, die sich mit dem nachgeahmten Material verbinden.

Ce siège en mousse de polyuréthane imitant une dalle de porphyre
témoigne de l'influence du sculpteur Claes Oldenburg sur les designers
radicaux italiens appartenant au mouvement de l'anti-design. Avec ces
lettres incisées, le « Massolo » se moque volontairement des évocations
funéraires qu'il suscite.

Studio 65

Capitello, 1971

*Self-skinning moulded polyurethane foam |
Geformter Polyurethan-Integralschaum |
Mousse de polyuréthane moulée*

GUFRAM,
BALANGERO, TURIN,
FROM 1971 TO
PRESENT

Predicting the work of Post-Modern classicists, such as Robert Venturi and Hans Hollein, the "Capitello" is utterly untruthful to the materials it employs. While the design appears extremely hard, in reality the moulded polyurethane foam is surprisingly soft. The original prototype was made up by Piero Gilardi, the designer of other out-of-context designs manufactured by Gufram.

Der »Capitello« nimmt Arbeiten von Klassikern der Postmoderne wie Robert Venturi und Hans Hollein vorweg und hält wie diese überhaupt nichts von Materialtreue. Optisch wirkt der Entwurf sehr hart, in Wirklichkeit aber erweist sich der geformte Polyurethanschaumstoff als überraschend weich. Den Prototyp hat Piero Gilardi geschaffen, von dem auch andere verfremdete Entwürfe für Gufram stammen.

Annonçant les recherches de postmodernistes comme Robert Venturi et Hans Hollein, le « Capitello » manque totalement de respect envers les matériaux qu'il emploie. Ce siège qui a l'air si ferme est en réalité étonnamment mou. Le prototype d'origine fut réalisé par Piero Gilardi, designer de nombreux modèles singuliers fabriqués par Gufram.

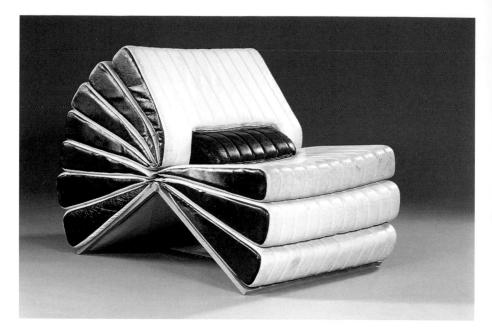

**Gruppo DAM
(Designers
Associati Milan)**

Libro, 1970

*Aluminium and
canvas frame with
vinyl-covered
polyurethane foam
folding elements |
Rahmen aus Alu-
minium und Segel-
tuch, Faltelemente
aus Polyurethan-
schaumstoff, Vinyl-
bezug | Châssis en
aluminium et toile,
éléments mobiles en
mousse de
polyuréthane
recouverte de vinyle*

GRUPPO
INDUSTRIALE
BUSNELLI, MEDA,
FROM C. 1970

The "Libro's" form was inspired, as its name suggests, by an opened book. The ten page-like seat sections pivot around a central element and can be flipped over to provide sitting positions of differing heights. The choice of two-tone ribbed vinyl upholstery was probably inspired by 1950s' kitsch furnishings.

*Die Formgebung des »Libro« ist, wie der Name sagt, von einem aufgeschla-
genen Buch inspiriert. Die zehn seitenähnlichen Sitzelemente können um ein
zentrales Element »geblättert« und übereinandergelegt werden, so daß
Sitzgelegenheiten mit verschiedenen Höhen entstehen. Möglicherweise spielt die
Auswahl der zweifarbig bezogenen Vinylpolster auf die kitschigen Möbel der 50er
Jahre an.*

La forme du « Libro » est inspirée comme son nom l'indique, de celle d'un livre ouvert. Ses dix « pages-coussins » pivotent autour d'un axe central et peuvent être feuilletées pour proposer différentes hauteurs de siège. Le choix du vinyle piqué à deux tons est probablement inspiré du mobilier kitsch des années 50.

Named after the actress Marilyn Monroe, Studio 65's sofa pays homage to Salvador Dalí's earlier "Mae West" sofa of 1936 and as such, can be viewed as an early example of Redesign. With its anti-establishment connotations, Surrealism was highly influential to the 1960s' and 1970s' Anti-Design movement. Inspiration for this quintessential Pop design must also have come from Andy Warhol's series of silkscreens.

Dieses Sofa des Studio 65 ist nach der Schauspielerin Marilyn Monroe benannt, zugleich ist es eine Hommage an Salvador Dalís »Mae West«-Sofa von 1936 und kann damit als frühes Beispiel für ein Redesign betrachtet werden. Mit seinen gegen das Establishment gerichteten Anspielungen hatte der Surrealismus großen Einfluß auf die Anti-Design-Bewegung der 6oer und 7oer Jahre. Auch Andy Warhols Siebdruckserien werden Anregungen für diesen unverfälscht poppigen Entwurf geliefert haben.

Nommé en souvenir de l'actrice Marilyn Monroe, le canapé du Studio 65 est un hommage au sofa « Mae West » de Salvador Dalí (1936) et constitue ainsi l'un des premiers exemples de redesign. Apprécié pour ses prises de positions contre l'establishment, le surréalisme exerça une forte influence sur le mouvement anti-design des années 60 et 70. Le design purement pop de ce siège a pu également s'inspirer des sérigraphies d'Andy Warhol.

Studio 65

Marilyn, 1972

Stretch fabric-covered moulded poly-urethane foam | Ge-formter Polyurethan-schaumstoff, mit Bezug aus Stretch-gewebe | Mousse de polyuréthane moulée recouverte de stretch

GUFRAM, BALANGERO, TURIN, FROM 1972 TO PRESENT

Verner Panton

Sitting Wheel, 1974

Fabric-covered foam-upholstered construction | Schaumstoff-polsterung und Stoffbezug | Mousse recouverte de tissu

(PROTOTYPE)
VERNER PANTON

▼ **Designer Unknown**
Inflatable PVC seating unit, 1968

MOBILIER INTERNATIONAL, FRANCE, FROM 1968

This prototype disturbs the traditional notions of a chair. Through designs like this, Panton attempted "to encourage people to use their fantasy and make their surroundings more exciting". (A. L. Morgan, *Contemporary Designers*, St. James Press, London 1985, p. 471)
Dieser Prototyp bringt alle traditionellen Vorstellungen darüber, wie ein Stuhl zu sein hat, durcheinander. Mit Entwürfen wie diesen versuchte Panton, »die Menschen zu ermutigen, ihre Phantasie zu benutzen und ihre Umgebung aufregender zu gestalten«.
Ce prototype dérange l'idée traditionnelle que l'on se fait d'un siège. Par de telles créations, Panton s'efforçait « d'encourager les gens à se servir de leur imagination et à rendre leur environnement plus excitant. »

Gruppo Strum

Pratone, 1966–1970

Self-skinning moulded polyurethane foam | Geformter Polyurethan-Integral-schaumstoff | Mousse de polyuréthane moulée

GUFRAM,
BALANGERO, TURIN,
FROM 1971 TO
PRESENT

▼ Paolo Ruffi
La Cova (The Nest),
1973

POLTRONOVA,
MONTALE, PISTOIA,
FROM 1973

In 1963, Gruppo Strum was founded in Turin and its radical ambition was the creation of "instrumental architecture", hence its title. "Pratone" is a contesting design that invites different modes of interaction. *Gruppo Strum wurde 1963 in Turin gegründet; das mit radikalem Ehrgeiz verfolgte Ziel der Gruppe war die Schaffung einer »instrumentellen Architektur«, daher der Name. »Pratone« ist ein provozierender Entwurf, der zu ganz verschiedenen Möglichkeiten der Benutzung einlädt.* En 1963, se crée à Turin le Gruppo Strum dont l'ambition était la création « d'une architecture instrumentale ». « Pratone » est un projet contestataire qui invite à différents modes d'échanges.

Gaetano Pesce

Sit Down, 1975–1976

Plywood frame with
polyurethane foam-
filled, Dacron-quilted
cover | Rahmen aus
Schichtholz, mit Poly-
urethanschaumstoff-
polsterung ausge-
gossen, gesteppter
Dacron-Bezug |
Châssis en contre-
plaqué, mousse de
polyuréthane,
couverture piquée en
dacron

CASSINA, MEDA,
MILAN, FROM 1976
TO PRESENT

The quilted cover of the "Sit Down" chair acted as a mould for the polyurethane foam which was poured into it. This innovative construction meant that high tooling costs were avoided, and due to the hands-on nature of the process, there was the possibility for slight variations in each chair.

Die gesteppten Bezüge des Sessels »Sit Down« dienten als Form für den Polyurethanschaumstoff, der einfach in sie hineingegossen wurde. Mit diesem neuartigen Herstellungsverfahren konnten hohe Maschinenkosten eingespart werden. Die Fertigung von Hand führt dazu, daß kein Sessel dem anderen völlig gleicht.

La housse piquée du fauteuil « Sit Down » servait de moule à la mousse de polyuréthane qui était versée directement à l'intérieur. Ce type de fabrication novateur éliminait le coût d'utilisation des machines-outils et, par son caractère artisanal et manuel, autorisait de légères variations d'un modèle à l'autre.

Gruppo
A.R.D.I.T.I.

Memoria, 1972

Dacron-covered polyurethane foam with internal airtight layer to provide adjustable air cavity with solid base | Polyurethanschaumstoff mit Dacron-Bezug, integrierte Luftkammer mit Ventilregulierung, fester Sockel | Mousse de polyuréthane recouverte de dacron, cavité à air interne de volume réglable, base massive

CASSINA, MEDA,
MILAN, FROM 1972

▼ **Gunnar Aagaard Andersen**
"Portrait of a Chesterfield Chair of My Mother's", 1964

GUNNAR ANDERSEN
AT THE DANSK
POLYTHER INDUSTRI,
FREDERIKSSUND

The printed textile of this design implies the imprint of a human form. The shape of the "Memoria" chair adjusted itself to the user by means of a valve which controlled the amount of air in its internal cavity.

Der bedruckte Bezugstoff des »Memoria«-Sessels läßt den angedeuteten Abdruck einer menschlichen Gestalt erkennen. Der Benutzer kann die Form des Stuhls seinen Bedürfnissen anpassen, indem er ein Ventil bedient, mit dem die im Innern des Sessels befindliche Luftmenge reguliert werden kann.

Le tissu imprimé de ce siège « Memoria » reproduit une forme humaine. Le fauteuil s'adaptait de lui-même à la morphologie de son utilisateur au moyen d'une valve de contrôle du volume d'air.

MULTI CHAIR
scale 1:10 TAV.5

The "Multi" chair's two upholstered elements can either be used separately or together. Connected by means of leather and metal hooks, the design can be configured to provide a variety of sitting positions. The adaptability of furniture as well as living spaces was Joe Colombo's primary goal in design.

Die beiden Elemente des »Multi«-Sessels können einzeln oder zusammen verwendet werden. Mit Lederriemen und Metallhaken zusammengehalten, lassen sich die Elemente immer wieder neu zu einer Vielzahl von Sitzgelegenheiten kombinieren. Die Flexibilität von Möbeln und Wohnräumen war Joe Colombos Hauptziel bei seiner Entwurfsarbeit.

Les deux éléments rembourrés du fauteuil « Multi » peuvent s'utiliser séparément ou ensemble. Réunis par des crochets en métal et en cuir, ils offrent de multiples possibilités de configuration. L'adaptabilité du mobilier et des lieux de vie constituaient l'objectif primordial de Joe Colombo en matière de design.

Joe Colombo

Multi chair, 1970

Stretch fabric-covered polyurethane foam cushions with metal fittings and leather straps | Kissen aus Polyurethanschaumstoff, mit Stretchgewebe bezogen, Metallbeschläge und Lederriemen | Coussins en mousse de polyuréthane recouverte de tissu stretch, garnitures métalliques, sangles de cuir

SORMANI, AROSIO, COMO, FROM 1970

◄ Joe Colombo
Views of an interior with Roto-living Unit, Cabriolet-Bed, Additional Living System and Multi chairs, c. 1970

Mario Bellini

Le Bambole, 1972

Polyurethane foam parts of differing densities held together by textile covering on rigid polyurethane core and internal tubular metal base | Rahmen aus Stahlrohr, starrem Polyurethanschaumstoff in verschiedenen Dichten, mit Stoffbezug | Éléments de mousse de polyuréthane de densités variées maintenus par une housse textile, base en polyuréthane et châssis en tube métallique

B & B ITALIA,
NOVEDRATE, COMO,
FROM 1972 TO
PRESENT

▼ B & B Italia
advertisement,
c. 1972

The "Le Bambole" series comprised approximately ten pieces and predicted the 1970s' predilection for soft foam seating. Different densities of foam were used in each piece to obtain the required structural rigidity.
Zur »Le Bambole«-Serie gehörten etwa zehn Modelle, die alle zeigen, welche Vorliebe man in den 70er Jahren für weiche Schaumstoffpolstermöbel hatte. Für jedes Modell wurde Schaumstoff unterschiedlicher Dichte benutzt, um die jeweilige Formfestigkeit zu erlangen.
La série « Le Bambole » comptait environ dix pièces et annonçait la prédilection des années 70 pour les sièges mous. Pour chaque modèle, différentes densités de mousse permettaient d'obtenir la rigidité nécessaire.

Enzo Mari

Sof Sof, 1971

*Painted metal rod frame with textile-covered polyurethane foam cushion |
Rahmen aus Metallstäben, lackiert, Kissen aus Polyurethanschaumstoff, mit Stoffbezug | Châssis en tige de métal peinte, coussin en mousse de polyuréthane recouverte de tissu*

DRIADE, FOSSADELLO DI CAORSO, PIACENZA, FROM 1972

▼ The frame and seat cushion of Sof Sof

Enzo Mari's "Sof Sof" chair has a simple welded rod frame which is padded with a single removable cushion. The design anticipates the trend in the 1970s towards lower-tech, less expensive methods of production.

Enzo Maris Stuhl »Sof Sof« hat ein einfaches Gestell aus verschweißten Metallstäben und ist mit einem losen Kissen gepolstert. Der Entwurf zeigt den Trend der 70er Jahre, preiswerte Low-Tech-Produkte zu entwickeln.

Le siège « Sof Sof » de Mari est soutenu par un simple cadre en tige métallique soudée, sur lequel repose un coussin amovible. Le design anticipe la tendance des années 70 à privilégier des méthodes de production moins technologiques et moins coûteuses.

Arata Isozaki

Marilyn, 1972

*Bent laminated wood
and solid beech frame
with leather-covered
upholstered seat |
Rahmen aus gebogo
nem, laminiertem
Holz und massiver
Buche, Sitzfläche
gepolstert, mit
Lederbezug | Châssis
en bois laminé cintré
et hêtre massif, siège
en cuir rembourré*

ICF VIMODROME,
ITALY, FROM C. 1972
(REISSUED BY TENDO
COMPANY, TENDO,
FROM 1983 TO
PRESENT)

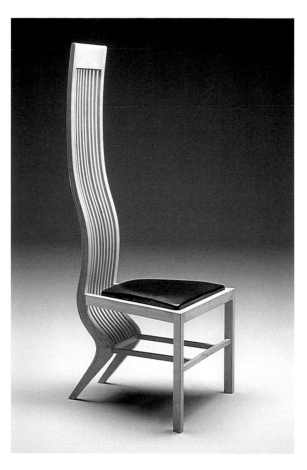

Primarily known for his work as an architect, Isozaki became closely associated with Memphis in the 1980s. Presaging Post-Modernism, the "Marilyn" chair of 1972 was inspired by the work of Charles Rennie Mackintosh who was in turn influenced by Japanese design.
Isozaki hat sich vor allem einen Namen als Architekt gemacht. In den 8oer Jahren stand er in enger Verbindung zur Memphis-Bewegung. Der Stuhl »Marilyn«, der die Postmoderne vorwegzunehmen scheint, wurde angeregt durch die Arbeiten von Charles Rennie Mackintosh, der sich wiederum von japanischem Kunsthandwerk inspirieren ließ.
Essentiellement connu pour son œuvre d'architecte, Isozaki s'associa aux recherches de Memphis dans les années 8o. Annonçant le postmodernisme, le siège « Marilyn », qui date de 1972, s'inspire de l'œuvre de Charles Rennie Mackintosh, lui-même très influencé par le design japonais.

Vico Magistretti

Golem, 1970

*Lacquered wood
frame with leather-
covered upholstered
seat | Rahmen aus
Holz, lackiert, Sitz-
fläche gepolstert, mit
Lederbezug | Châssis
en bois laqué, siège en
cuir rembourré*

CARLO POGGI, PAVIA,
FROM 1970 TO
PRESENT

The "Golem" chair, with its high-back and lacquered surfaces, is
Magistretti's homage to the work of Charles Rennie Mackintosh. Its
elegant, Japanese-inspired form, has a powerful presence.

*Der Stuhl »Golem« ist mit seiner hohen Rückenlehne und den lackierten
Oberflächen Magistrettis Hommage an das Werk von Charles Rennie
Mackintosh. Die elegante, vom japanischen Kunsthandwerk inspirierte Form
hat eine ausdrucksstarke Präsenz.*

Le « Golem » avec son dossier surdimensionné et ses surfaces laquées,
est un hommage de Magistretti à Charles Rennie Mackintosh. Sa forme
élégante, très imposante est d'inspiration japonaise.

Mario Bellini

Cab, Model No. 412, 1976

Enamelled steel frame with zip-fastening saddle-stitched leather covering | Rahmen aus Stahl, einbrennlackiert, Bezug aus sattelvernähtem Kernleder, mit Montagereiß-verschlüssen | Châssis en acier émaillé recouvert de cuir cousu façon sellier et zippé

CASSINA, MEDA, MILAN, FROM 1977 TO PRESENT

▼ **Mario Bellini**
Cab sofa, 1982

CASSINA, MEDA, MILAN, FROM 1982 TO PRESENT

The leather upholstery of the "Cab" chair zips directly onto the skeletal steel frame and functions as a supporting material. Its high-quality saddle stitching attests to Italy's tradition of producing fine leatherwork.
Der Lederbezug des Stuhls »Cab« wird über das Stahlgestell gezogen und hat, mit Montagereißverschlüssen befestigt, auch tragende Funktion. Die hochwertige Sattelnähung zeugt vom traditionellen Qualitätsstandard italienischer Lederverarbeitung.

Le rembourrage en cuir de la chaise « Cab » se fixe directement sur le châssis métallique par un système de fermeture à glissière et remplit également une fonction de soutien. Sa haute qualité de réalisation façon sellier témoigne de la tradition italienne de la maroquinerie de luxe.

Mario Bellini

Break, Model No. 401, 1976

Polyurethane foam-upholstered sheet-steel frame with removable leather-covers and feather filled cushion on ABS feet | Rahmen aus Stahlblech, Polsterung aus Polyurethanschaumstoff, abnehmbarer Lederbezug, Sitzkissen mit Federfüllung, Füße aus ABS-Kunststoff | Châssis en tôle d'acier rembourrée de mousse de polyuréthane, recouvrement en cuir amovible, coussin en plume, piètement en ABS

CASSINA, MEDA, MILAN, FROM 1976 TO PRESENT

▼ **Mario Bellini**
Model No. 685, 1973

CASSINA, MEDA, MILAN

Designed the same year as the "Cab", the "Break" chair utilised a similar removable leather covering. Designs such as these epitomise high-end Italian furniture of the 1970s.

Der Sessel »Break«, im selben Jahr wie »Cab« entstanden, hat einen ganz ähnlichen abnehmbaren Lederbezug. Entwürfe wie diese sind typisch für das obere Preissegment italienischer Möbel aus den 70er Jahren.

Conçu la même année que le « Cab », le fauteuil « Break » utilise le cuir de la même façon. Ces modèles illustrent la création de mobilier italien haut de gamme dans les années 70.

Gae Aulenti

Aulenti Collection,
Model No. 54A, 1975

Epoxy-coated rolled-formed steel frame, moulded laminated wood seat, uphol-stered in polyurethane foam, smooth uphol-stered back and front |
Rahmen aus form-gewalztem Stahl, Beschichtung aus Epoxidharz, Sitzfläche aus geformtem Schichtholz mit Polsterung aus Poly-urethanschaumstoff |
Châssis en acier plié gainé époxy, siège en contre-plaqué, rem-bourrage en mousse de polyuréthane

KNOLL INTERNA-TIONAL, NEW YORK, FROM 1975 TO PRESENT

▼ **Gae Aulenti**
Model No. 54-S 1, 1977

KNOLL INTERNA-TIONAL, NEW YORK, FROM 1977 TO PRESENT

With their composed Classical forms, the "Aulenti Collection" chairs possess distinct architectural quali-ties. Designed for the contract market, they received a Design Centre Stuttgart Award in 1977.

Die Sitzmöbel der »Aulenti Collection« besitzen durch ihre klassische Formgebung eine ausgeprägte architektonische Qualität. 1977 wurden die für den Büromöbelmarkt konzi-pierten Möbel mit einer Auszeichnung des Stuttgarter Design-Zentrums prämiert.

De formes classiques, les sièges de l' « Aulenti Collection » possèdent des qualités architecturales remarquables. Conçus pour le marché de l'équipement de bureau, ils reçu-rent le prix du Design Centre de Stuttgart en 1977.

Andrew Ivar
Morrison &
Bruce Hannah

Model No. 2328,
1970

Cast aluminium and
steel frame with tex-
tile-covered polyure-
thane foam uphol-
stered seat and back |
Rahmen aus Gußalu-
minium und Stahl,
Sitzfläche und
Rückenlehne mit
Polyurethanschaum-
stoffpolsterung,
Stoffbezug | Châssis
en fonte d'aluminium,
siège et dossier rem-
bourrés en mousse de
polyuréthane recou-
verte de tissu

KNOLL INTERNA-
TIONAL, NEW YORK,
FROM 1973

▼ Andrew Ivar
Morrison & Bruce
Hannah
Secretarial chair,
1970

Hannah and Morrison's two guiding principles in chair
design were that all corners should be rounded and that
a minimal amount of materials should be used. Here,
this approach produced a lyrical clarity of form.
Hannah und Morrison ließen sich beim Stuhldesign von
zwei Prinzipien leiten: Alle Ecken sollen abgerundet und
der Materialaufwand minimiert werden. Die Befolgung die-
ser Regeln führte hier zu einer lyrischen Klarheit der Form.
Pour Morrison et Hannah, tous les angles d'un siège
devaient être arrondis et il fallait n'utiliser que le minimum de matériaux. Cette conception aboutit ici à une
clarté formelle non dénuée d'un certain lyrisme.

Paolo Deganello & Gilberto Corretti

Archizoom Uno, 1973

Chromed tubular steel frame with textile-covered upholstered seat, back and armrests | Rahmen aus Stahlrohr, verchromt, Sitzfläche, Rücken- und Armlehnen gepolstert und mit Stoffbezug | Châssis en tube d'acier chromé, siège, dossier et accoudoirs rembourrés et recouverts de tissu

MARCATRÉ, MISINTO, MILAN, FROM 1973

▼ Paolo Deganello & Gilberto Corretti
Archizoom Due, 1973

MARCATRÉ, MISINTO, MILAN, FROM 1973

Deganello and Corretti, both founding members of Archizoom Associati, named their series of office chairs after this Radical Design group. "Archizoom Uno" introduced a forward-looking aesthetic to the workplace.
Deganello und Corretti, beide Gründungsmitglieder von Archizoom Associati, einer Gruppe des Radical-Design, benannten ihre Bürostuhlserie nach dieser Gruppe. »Archizoom Uno« brachte eine zukunftweisende Ästhetik an den Arbeitsplatz.
Deganello et Corretti, membres fondateurs d'Archizoom Associati, donnèrent le nom de ce groupe radical à leur série de sièges de bureau. « Archizoom Uno » introduisit une esthétique progressiste sur le lieu de travail.

Yrjö Kukkapuro

Fysio, 1978

Aluminium frame, seat and armrest of form-pressed birch shavings, varnished sections, detachable upholstery, chromed steel fittings, enamelled tilt mechanism | Rahmen aus Aluminium, Sitz und Armstützen aus formgepreßter Birkenspanplatte, teilweise furniert, abnehmbares Polster, Chromstahlbeschläge, emaillierte Kippvorrichtung | Châssis en aluminium, siège et accoudoirs en copeaux de bouleau compressés, rembourrage amovible, surfaces vernies, mécanisme d'inclinaison émaillé

AVARTE, HELSINKI, FROM 1978 TO PRESENT

▼ William Stumpf
Ergon, 1970–1976

Like Stumpf's earlier "Ergon" office chair, the "Fysio's" form was dictated by anthropometrics. For increased adjustability it incorporated height and tilt mechanisms.
Wie bei Stumpfs früherem Bürostuhl »Ergon« war auch das Design für den »Fysio« von ergonomischen Fragen bestimmt. Zur bequemen Bedienung lassen sich Sitzhöhe und Neigungswinkel an nur einem Hebel einstellen.
Comme le siège de bureau antérieur de Stumpf «Ergon», la forme du «Fysio» était dictée par des recherches anthropométriques. Il était réglable en hauteur et inclinable.

Richard Sapper

Sapper Collection,
1978–1979

Enamelled aluminium
frame and base with
"Plastisol" armrests
and a supporting
rubber-covered nylon
mesh with leather-
covered polyurethane
foam upholstery |
Rahmen und Unter-
gestell aus einbrenn-
lackiertem Alumi-
nium, Armlehnen aus
»Plastisol«, Sitzschale
aus gummibeschich-
tetem Nylongewebe,
Polyurethan-
schaumstoffpolste-
rung mit Lederbezug |
Châssis et piètement
en aluminium émaillé,
accoudoirs en « Plasti-
sol », rembourrage en
mousse de polyuré-
thane recouverte d'un
tulle de nylon
caoutchouté et de cuir

KNOLL INTER-
NATIONAL, NEW
YORK, FROM 1979

▼ **Richard Sapper**
Sapper Collection
sled base chair,
1978–1979

The "Sapper Collection" was one of the first executive
seating programmes. Sapper initially worked as a designer for Mercedes-Benz and his office chairs are
highly reminiscent of automotive seating.
Die »Sapper Collection« war eines der ersten Sitzmöbel-
programme für die Vorstandsetage. Sapper arbeitete
zunächst als Designer für Mercedes-Benz, und seine
Bürostühle erinnern sehr stark an Autositze.
La « Sapper Collection » fut l'un des premiers en-
sembles spécialement destinés aux bureaux de direction. Sapper avait travaillé pour Mercedes-Benz et ses
premières créations rappellent fortement les sièges
d'automobile.

Fred Scott

Supporto, 1979

Polished aluminium frame with gas-cylinderheight-mechanism and textile-covered foam-upholstered seat and back sections | *Rahmen aus poliertem Aluminium, mit Gasdruckmechanismus höhenverstellbar, Sitzfläche und Rückenlehne mit Schaumstoffpolsterung und Stoffbezug* | *Châssis en aluminium poli, réglage de la hauteur par amortisseur à gaz, siège et dossier rembourrés recouverts de tissu*

HILLE
INTERNATIONAL CO.,
LONDON, FROM
1979 TO PRESENT

▼ Hille photograph
showing the
articulation of the
Supporto's back

The "Supporto's" form was dictated by ergonomic considerations. During development, Hille undertook scientific research and interviews with testers of pre-production models.

Die Form des Bürosessels »Supporto« wurde von ergonomischen Erwägungen bestimmt. Hille begleitete die Entwicklungsphase durch ein wissenschaftliches Forschungsprogramm und befragte Testpersonen vor der Produktion zu ihren Erfahrungen mit den Testmodellen.

La forme du siège « Supporto » répond à des préoccupations ergonomiques. Au cours de sa mise au point, Hille entreprit des recherches scientifiques et interrogea les essayeurs des modèles avant la mise en production.

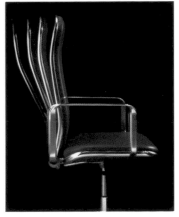

Ettore Sottsass

**Synthesis 45,
1970–1971**

*Injection-moulded
ABS height-adjustable
frame and base with
textile-covered
polyurethane foam-
upholstered seat and
back | Höhenverstell-
barer Rahmen und
Fuß aus spritzguß-
geformtem ABS-
Kunststoff, Sitzfläche
und Rückenlehne mit
Polyurethanschaum-
stoffpolsterung und
Stoffbezug | Châssis
réglable et piètement
en plastique ABS
moulé par injection,
réglage de la hauteur,
siège et dossier en
mousse de
polyuréthane
recouverte de tissu*

OLIVETTI, MILAN,
FROM C. 1973 TO
PRESENT

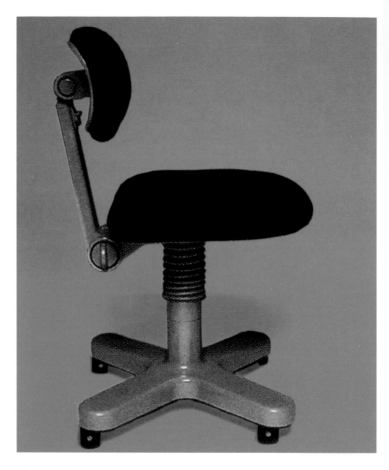

The "Synthesis 45" chair was one of a number of designs for the office environment designed by Sottsass for Olivetti. Like his "Valentine" typewriter,
this brightly coloured chair was intended to appeal to a more youthful
market.

*Der Stuhl »Synthesis 45« war einer von vielen Büromöbelentwürfen, die Sottsass
für Olivetti geschaffen hat. Seine leuchtende Farbe sollte wie die Schreib-
maschine »Valentine« ein jüngeres Publikum ansprechen.*

La chaise « Synthesis 45 » est l'une des nombreuses créations pour l'équipement du bureau que Sottsass proposa à Olivetti. Comme sa machine à
écrire « Valentine », cette chaise de couleur vive était censée plaire à un
marché plus jeune.

Emilio Ambasz
& Giancarlo
Piretti

Vertebra, 1977

Tubular steel frame, cast aluminium base, self-skinning urethane coating, leather-covered foam-upholstered seat and back | Rahmen aus Stahlrohr, Gußaluminiumfuß, Beschichtung aus Urethan-Integralschaumstoff, Sitzfläche und Rückenlehne mit Schaumstoffpolsterung und Lederbezug | Châssis en tube d'acier, piètement en fonte d'aluminium, gainage d'uréthane, siège et dossier en mousse recouverte de cuir

CASTELLI, OZZANO
DELL'EMILIA,
BOLOGNA, FROM
1977 TO PRESENT,
AND KRUEG, GREEN
BAY, WISCONSIN,
FROM 1977 TO
PRESENT

Utilising a system of counter springs, the "Vertebra", with its tilting seat and flexible back, was the first office chair to respond automatically to the body's movements.

Durch sein System gegenläufiger Federn, dem Kippmechanismus und der flexiblen Rückenlehne war der »Vertebra« der erste Bürostuhl, der den Bewegungen des Sitzenden automatisch folgte.

Avec son système de suspension à ressorts la « Vertebra » à siège et dossier inclinables est le premier siège de bureau à s'adapter automatiquement aux mouvements du corps.

Geoffrey Harcourt

Cleopatra, Model No. 248, 1973

Stretch fabric-covered polyurethane foam-upholstered tubular steel frame on metal castors | Rahmen aus Stahlrohr auf Metallrollen, Polsterung aus Polyurethanschaumstoff mit Bezug aus Stretchgewebe | Châssis en tube d'acier, rembourrage en mousse de polyuréthane recouverte de tissu stretch, roulettes

ARTIFORT, MAASTRICHT, FROM 1973 TO PRESENT

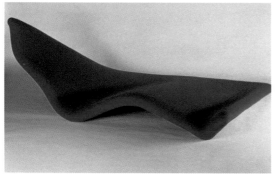

▲ **Floris van den Broecke**
Chairpiece, 1970–1974

(PROTOTYPE)
FLORIS VAN DEN BROECKE, LONDON

Harcourt began designing seating for Artifort in 1962. Since then, the firm has produced more than twenty of his designs – the "Cleopatra" being one of the best known. This chaise longue, which pays homage to Paulin's earlier designs, is a highly abstract and sculptural reworking of a traditional form.

Seit 1962 entwirft Harcourt für die Firma Artifort. Seitdem hat dieser Hersteller über zwanzig seiner Modelle produziert; das Sofa »Cleopatra« ist sicherlich das bekannteste. Die sehr abstrakte und skulpturale Form des Sofas ist eine Hommage an Paulins frühere Entwürfe.

Harcourt commença à dessiner des sièges pour Artifort en 1962. Depuis, cette firme a fabriqué plus d'une vingtaine de ses projets, le « Cleopatra » étant l'un des plus connus. Cette chaise longue, qui rend hommage aux précédentes créations de Paulin, s'inspire d'une forme traditionnelle. Elle est proche de l'abstraction et de la sculpture.

Paulin's chair model No. F598 was intended primarily for the contract market. The simplicity of the design, with its two side elements forming the legs, allows the floor underneath be easily cleaned, making the chair particularly suitable for office reception areas, airports and hotel foyers.

Paulins Sessel Modell Nr. F598 war vor allem für öffentliche Gebäude konzipiert. Der Entwurf ist durch seine zwei Seitenelemente, die zugleich die Füße bilden, sehr einfach aufgebaut und erleichtert damit das Säubern des Fußbodens unter dem Sessel. Damit ist er besonders für Empfangsbereiche in Bürohäusern, für Flughafenlobbys und Hotelfoyers geeignet.

Ce fauteuil n° F598 était destiné à l'origine au marché du mobilier de bureau. La simplicité de sa conception – les deux éléments latéraux forment les pieds – permet de nettoyer facilement le sol sans déplacer le siège : une solution idéale pour les halls de réception, les aéroports et les hôtels.

Pierre Paulin

Model No. F598,
1973

Stretch fabric-covered polyurethane foam-upholstered tubular steel frame with springing and aluminium glides | Rahmen aus Stahlrohr mit Federung und Aluminiumgleitern, Polsterung aus Polyurethanschaumstoff, mit Bezug aus Stretchgewebe | Châssis en tube d'acier, rembourrage en mousse de polyuréthane recouverte de tissu stretch, suspension à ressort, glissières en aluminium

ARTIFORT,
MAASTRICHT, FROM
1973 TO PRESENT

Frank O. Gehry

Wiggle, 1972

Laminated cardboard
construction |
Konstruktion aus
verleimtem
Wellkarton | Carton
contrecollé

JACK BROGAN, USA
1972–1973
(REISSUED BY VITRA,
FROM 1992 AS
WIGGLE SIDE CHAIR)

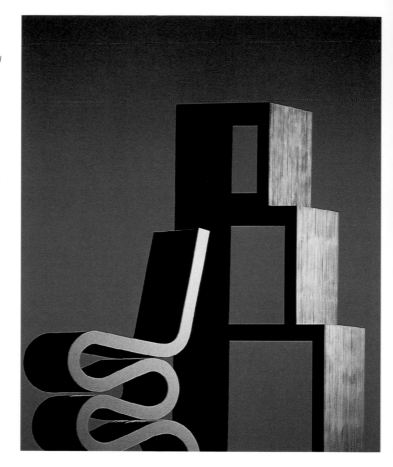

The "Easy Edges" series comprised fourteen pieces of cardboard furniture.
To increase the strength and resilience of their constructions, the layers of
cardboard were laminated at right angles to one another. Initially conceived
as low-cost furniture, these designs were so immediately successful, that
Gehry withdrew them from production after only three months, fearing that
his ascendancy as a popular furniture designer would distract him from
realising his potential as an architect.

Zur Serie »Easy Edges« gehörten vierzehn verschiedene Möbel aus Wellkarton. Um Tragkraft und Widerstandsfähigkeit dieser Konstruktionen zu erhöhen, wurden die Kartonschichten im rechten Winkel zueinander verleimt. Konzipiert als Billigmöbel, waren diese Entwürfe sofort so erfolgreich, daß Gehry sie nach nur drei Monaten aus der Produktion zurückzog. Er fürchtete, daß seine Karriere als populärer Möbeldesigner ihn daran hindern würde, seine Möglichkeiten als Architekt zu realisieren.

La série « Easy Edges » comprenait quatorze éléments en carton. Pour accroître la résistance et la rigidité de la construction, les couches de carton contrecollées étaient découpées verticalement dans l'épaisseur. Conçus au départ comme des meubles bon marché, leur succès immédiat poussa Gehry à arrêter leur production au bout de trois mois, tant il craignait que cette réussite ne l'empêche de poursuivre son œuvre d'architecte.

Frank O. Gehry

Easy Edges rocking chair, 1972

Laminated cardboard construction | Konstruktion aus verleimtem Wellkarton | Carton contrecollé

JACK BROGAN, USA 1972–1973 (REISSUED BY CHIRU, LOS ANGELES, FROM 1982)

D. T. Amat

Indiana, 1975

Chromed tubular
steel frame with
woven cane seat and
back | Rahmen aus
Stahlrohr, Sitzfläche
und Rückenlehne aus
Rohrgeflecht | Châssis
en tube d'acier
chromé, siège et
dossier en jonc tressé

AMAT, MARTORELL,
BARCELONA, FROM
C. 1975 TO PRESENT

The "Indiana" chair was created by the in-house design team of the
Barcelona-based manufacturer, Amat. It is a subtle reworking of a traditional
Spanish café chair and, with its elegant understated form, predicts the ap-
proach of many Spanish furniture designers in the 1980s.
*Der Stuhl »Indiana« ist ein Entwurf des Designerteams von Amat, ein in
Barcelona ansässiger Hersteller. Die Formgebung des Stuhls beruht auf einem
traditionellen spanischen Café-Stuhl und weist mit seinem eleganten
Understatement auf das spanische Möbeldesign der 8oer Jahre voraus.*
Ce fauteuil fut créé par l'équipe de design du fabricant catalan, Amat.
Subtile adaptation d'une chaise traditionnelle de café espagnol, ce modèle
aux formes discrètes et élégantes anticipe l'approche de nombreux
designers espagnols des années 80.

Achille Castiglioni

Irma, Model No. 2280, 1979

Stove-enamelled tubular steel frame with nylon seat and back upholstered in smooth leather | Rahmen aus einbrennlackiertem Stahlrohr, Sitzfläche und Rückenlehne aus Nylon mit weichem Lederbezug | Châssis en tube d'acier émaillé au four, siège en nylon et dossier en cuir légèrement rembourré

ZANOTTA, MILAN, FROM 1979 TO PRESENT

It is a tribute to Achille Castiglioni's unquestionable skill that he is able to produce such sophisticated forms as the "Irma" chair through the subtle manipulation of relatively simple constructional techniques.

Der Stuhl »Irma« zeugt von Achille Castiglionis unbestreitbarem Geschick, durch subtile Veränderungen verhältnismäßig einfacher konstruktiver Details zu äußerst raffinierten Formen zu gelangen.

C'est le mérite de Castiglioni d'avoir su créer des formes aussi raffinées que cette chaise « Irma » par une manipulation ingénieuse de techniques de construction relativement simples.

Carlo Scarpa

Model No. 783, 1977

Walnut frame with leather seat and back| Rahmen aus Walnußholz, Sitzfläche und Rückenlehne aus Lederbespannung | Châssis en noyer, siège et dossier en cuir

BERNINI, CARATE BRIANZA, MILAN, FROM 1977 TO PRESENT

▼ **Tobia & Afra Scarpa**
Africa chair, 1975

B & B ITALIA, NOVE-DRATE, COMO

Both Carlo Scarpa's chair model No. 783 and De Pas, D'Urbino and Lomazzi's "Linda" chair reflect the move away from plastics as the materials of choice in the mid-1970s. The return to natural materials and vernacular types indicated an increasing ecological awareness and a preference for humanising design – a trend instigated by the Oil Crisis and the rise of environmental pressure groups.

Sowohl Carlo Scarpas Stuhl Modell Nr. 783 als auch der Stuhl »Linda« von De Pas, D'Urbino und Lomazzi zeigen, daß Mitte der 70er Jahre Kunststoffe ihre Bedeutung als bevorzugtes Material verlieren. Die Rückkehr zu natürlichen

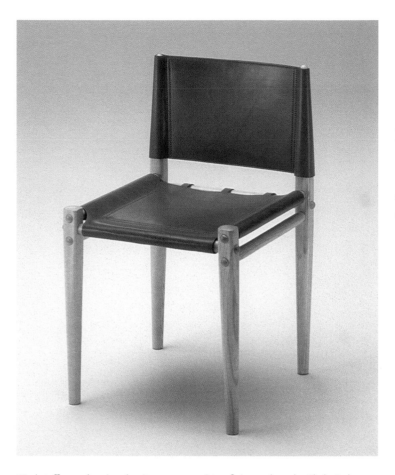

Gionatan De Pas, Donato D'Urbino & Paolo Lomazzi

Linda, 1975

Beech frame with leather seat and back | Rahmen aus Buche, Sitzfläche und Rückenlehne aus Lederbespannung | Châssis en hêtre, siège et dossier en cuir

ZANOTTA, MILAN, FROM C. 1975 TO PRESENT

Werkstoffen und regionalen Formen verweist auf ein wachsendes ökologisches Bewußtsein und auch auf die neue Vorliebe für benutzerfreundliche Entwürfe – Trends, die mit der Ölkrise und dem Druck der Umweltgruppen zusammenhingen.

Le modèle n° 783 de Carlo Scarpa et le siège « Linda » de De Pas, D'Urbino et Lomazzi témoignent de l'abandon des matières plastiques par de nombreux designers à partir du milieu des années 70. Le retour aux matériaux traditionnels et aux modèles vernaculaires traduisait une prise en compte croissante de l'écologie et une préférence pour un design plus humain, tendance qui s'accéléra avec la crise du pétrole et la montée en puissance des groupes de défense de l'environnement.

Enzo Mari

Box, 1975–1976

Injection-moulded polypropylene seat and back with tubular metal collapsible frame | Rahmen aus Stahlrohr (demontierbar), Sitzfläche und Rückenlehne aus spritzgußgeformtem Polypropylen | Siège et dossier en polypropylène moulé par injection, châssis pliant en tube de métal

CASTELLI, OZZANO DELL'EMILIA, BOLOGNA, FROM 1976 (REISSUED BY DRIADE, FOSSADELLO DI CAORSO, PIACENZA, FROM 1996)

▼ Early Anonima Castelli version of Box chair with canvas back, 1976

When dismantled, the components of this highly rational design can be easily packed into a flat box, hence its title. Only recently reissued, the "Box" chair originally had a canvas back.

Zerlegt können die Elemente dieses hochrationellen Entwurfs ohne Mühe in eine flache Schachtel gepackt werden – wie der Name signalisiert. Der Stuhl »Box« wurde vor kurzem reeditiert, ursprünglich bestand die Rückenlehne aus Leinenbespannung.

Démontés, les éléments qui composent ce modèle rationnel peuvent facilement se ranger à plat dans une boîte. Rééditée récemment, la chaise « Box » possédait à l'origine un dossier en toile.

Omkstak, 1971

Tubular steel frame with epoxy-coated pressed sheet steel seat and back | Rahmen aus Stahlrohr, Sitzfläche und Rückenlehne aus gepreßtem und epoxidbeschichtetem Stahlblech | Châssis en tube d'acier, siège et dossier en tôle d'acier estampée, gainage époxy

BIEFFEPLAST,
CASELLE DI
SELVAZZANO, FROM
1972 TO PRESENT

The "Omkstak" stacking chair epitomises the High-Tech style of the 1970s. It is a highly rational design suitable for large-scale production and was conceived for both indoor and outdoor use.

Der Stapelstuhl »Omkstak« verkörpert den High-Tech-Stil der 70er Jahre. Der rationelle Entwurf eignet sich für die Serienproduktion; er läßt sich in Innenräumen und im Außenbereich verwenden.

Le modèle « Omkstak » empilable incarne le style high-tech des années 70. Très rationnel, il est adapté à une production en grande série et s'utilise aussi bien à l'intérieur qu'à l'extérieur.

Giandomenico Belotti

Spaghetti, 1979

Tubular steel frame
with PVC strips
forming seat and
back | Rahmen aus
Stahlrohr, Sitzfläche
und Rückenlehne aus
gespannten PVC-
Schnüren | Châssis en
tube d'acier, siège et
dossier en corde de
PVC

ALIAS, GRUMELLO
DEL MONTE,
BERGAMO, FROM
1979 TO PRESENT

Originally entitled the "Odessa" chair, Belotti's design was rechristened while it was being exhibited in New York. Its new title, "Spaghetti", refers to the pasta-like strips of PVC used in its construction. Like many of Belotti's other furniture designs, it is based on an earlier existing type.

Dieser Stuhl hieß ursprünglich »Odessa«, wurde aber während einer Ausstellung in New York umbenannt. Der neue Name, »Spaghetti«, bezieht sich auf die dünnen Plastikschnüre aus PVC, die für Sitzfläche und Rückenlehne verwendet wurden. Wie bei vielen seiner Entwürfe knüpft Belotti auch hier an bestehende Formen an.

Appelée au départ « Odessa », cette création de Belotti changea de nom lors de son exposition à New York. Sa nouvelle appellation, « Spaghetti », se réfère aux bandeaux de PVC utilisé pour sa construction. Comme beaucoup d'autres projets de mobilier de Berlotti, elle s'inspire d'un modèle existant.

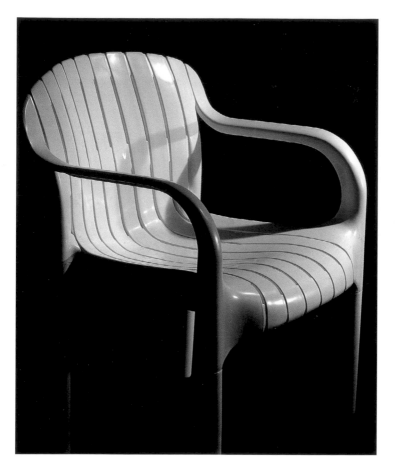

Pierre Paulin

Dangari, 1978

Injection-moulded
"Ultra Resin" (laden
polypropylene resin) |
Spritzgußgeformtes
»Ultra-Harz«
(speziell behandeltes
Polypropylenharz) |
«Ultra Résine»
(résine de
polypropylène
chargée) moulée par
injection

SAUVAGNAT
ALLIBERT GROUPE,
SASSENAGE, FROM
1978 TO PRESENT

The "Dangari" is Allibert's best-selling chair. Allibert is the market-leader in the vast garden seating sector and employs state-of-the-art technology to mass-produce "monobloc" fabricated seating in phenomenal quantities.

Der »Dangari« ist der meistverkaufte Stuhl der Firma Allibert und Marktführer auf dem Gartenmöbelsektor. Für die Herstellung des »Monoblock«-Sitzsystems werden modernste Massenproduktionstechniken genutzt.

Le « Dangari » est le siège Allibert qui se vend le mieux. Allibert occupe une place prépondérante dans le vaste secteur des meubles de jardin et réussit à appliquer la technologie d'art de pointe à la production massive de sièges « monobloc » fabriqués industriellement.

John Makepeace

Ebony Gothic, 1978

Carved ebony frame
with woven nickel
silver seat and back
sections | Rahmen
aus handgearbeite-
tem Ebenholz,
Sitzfläche und
Rückenlehne aus
Rohrgeflecht | Châssis
en ébène sculptée,
siège et dossier en
jonc tressé

JOHN MAKEPEACE,
PARNHAM

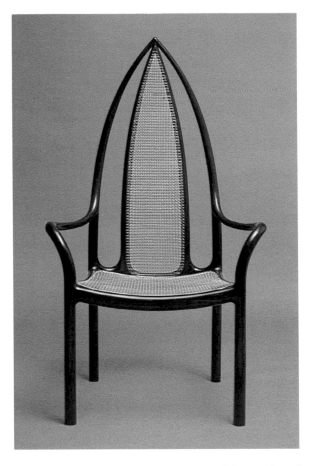

Makepeace, the most prominent exponent of the British Craft Revival, drew inspiration from Gothic and Art Nouveau sources for this exquisitely carved design which incorporates over two thousand pieces of ebony. Like Makepeace's chair, Castle's "Chair with Sports Coat" employs extraordinarily labour-intensive methods of production. He, however, often prefers to display his technical virtuosity through highly detailed carved illusionistic forms.

Makepeace, der bekannteste Exponent des »British Craft Revival«, zog Inspiration aus den Quellen von Neogotik und Jugendstil. Die handwerklich hochwertige Qualität dieses Entwurfs zeigt sich in den über zweitausend Ebenholzteilen, aus denen sich dieser Stuhl zusammensetzt. Wie Makepeace hat auch Castle für die Herstellung seines Stuhls eine außergewöhnlich arbeits-

Wendell Castle

Chair with Sports Coat, 1978

Carved solid maple
form | Aus massivem
Ahornholz | Érable
massif sculpté

WENDELL CASTLE,
SCOTTSVILLE, NEW
YORK

▼ Wendell Castle
Two-Seater settee,
1975

WENDELL CASTLE,
ROCHESTER, NEW
YORK

intensive Fertigungsweise gewählt. Seine handwerklich
perfekten Arbeiten zeichnen sich durch detailgenaue
Schnitzereien aus, die illusionäre Formen bilden.
Makepeace, le plus influent défenseur du « British Craft
Revival », s'inspire des styles gothique et Art nouveau
dans ce modèle d'un travail remarquable, qui fait appel
à plus de deux mille morceaux d'ébène. Le siège de
Castle utilise aussi des méthodes de fabrication exigeant un temps considérable. Le designer préfère cependant souvent montrer sa virtuosité technique dans
des formes bizarres et très sculptées.

Jan Ekselius

Jan, c. 1970

Stretch velour-cover-
ed, polyurethane
foam-upholstered,
bent tubular metal
frame with welded
steel springing |
Rahmen aus geboge-
nem Stahlrohr,
Federung aus
verschweißtem Stahl-
draht, Polsterung aus
Polyurethanschaum-
stoff, Stretchvelour-
bezug | Châssis en
tube de métal cintré,
suspension en acier
soudé, rembourrage
en mousse de poly-
uréthane recouverte
de velours stretch

STENDIG, NEW YORK,
FROM C. 1970

Jan Ekselius moulded the polyurethane foam directly onto this chair's internal steel springing. A removable zippered slipcover fits over the whole frame
to give the chair its remarkably sinuous contour. Etienne-Henri Martin's
"Chauffeuse 1500" has a less visually complicated form. The cantilevered
seat section of this design facilitates some flexibility and, with its
polyurethane foam upholstery, provides a great deal of comfort.

*Jan Ekselius schäumte den Polyurethanschaumstoff direkt auf die Stahlfederung
dieses Sessels. Ein abnehmbarer Bezug mit Reißverschluß wird über das ganze
ausgeschäumte Gestell gezogen und gibt dem Sessel seine markant wellenför-
mige Silhouette. Etienne-Henri Martins »Chauffeuse 1500« hat eine visuell*

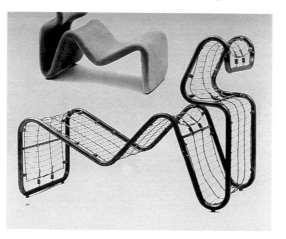

► The internal
sprung frame of the
Jan chaise

weniger anspruchsvolle Form. *Die freischwingende Sitzfläche gibt diesem Entwurf eine gewisse Flexibilität, zusammen mit der Polsterung aus Polyurethanschaumstoff sorgt dies für hohen Sitzkomfort.*

Jan Ekselius moulait directement la forme en polyuréthane sur la suspension à ressorts d'acier de cette chaise longue. Une housse munie d'une fermeture à glissière recouvre l'ensemble et donne à ce siège son étonnant aspect sinueux. La « Chauffeuse 1500 » d'Etienne-Henri Martin présente une forme moins complexe. Le siège en porte à faux assure une certaine souplesse tandis que le rembourrage en mousse polyuréthane garantit un grand confort.

Etienne-Henri Martin

Chauffeuse 1500, 1970–1971

Stretch-fabric covered polyurethane foam-upholstered tubular steel frame | Rahmen aus Stahlrohr, Polsterung aus Polyurethanschaumstoff, mit Stretchgewebebezug | Châssis en tube de métal, rembourrage en mousse de polyuréthane recouverte de tissu stretch

C.S.T.N. MANGAU
ATAL, FROM C. 1971

Verner Panton

*Sisters
Emmenthaler, 1979*

Fabric-covered
polyurethane-
upholstered frame on
enamelled metal
base | Rahmen mit
Polsterung aus Poly-
urethanschaumstoff,
mit Stoffbezug,
einbrennlackierte
Metallsockelplatten |
Châssis rembourré en
mousse de polyuré-
thane recouverte de
tissu, piètement en
métal

CASSINA, MEDA,
MILAN, FROM 1980

▼ **Verner Panton**
Mrs. Emmenthaler
chaise longue, 1979

CASSINA, MEDA,
MILAN, FROM 1980

Having produced landmark plastic chairs with abstracted organic forms in the 1960s, both Panton and Aarnio turned their attentions to more figurative forms constructed of polyurethane foam in the 1970s. The unusual titles of Panton's "Sisters Emmenthaler" sofa and "Mrs. Emmenthaler" chaise longue reflect and enhance the designs' anthropomorphism. Like Panton, Aarnio was also interested in creating designs with a strong and identifiable character. He achieved this through the emphatic and humorous zoomorphism of the "Pony" chair.

Nachdem sie in den 60er Jahren wegweisende Kunststoff-stühle aus abstrakten, organischen Formen entworfen hatten, wendeten Panton und Aarnio ihre Aufmerksamkeit in den 70er Jahren bildhafteren Formen zu, die sie aus Polyurethanschaumstoff schufen. »Sisters Emmenthaler« und »Mrs. Emmenthaler«, die ungewöhnlichen Namen für

Eero Aarnio

Ponies, c. 1970

Velour-covered
poyurethane foam
forms | Formen aus
Polyurethanschaum-
stoff mit Velour-
bezug | Formes en
mousse de
polyuréthane,
recouvertes de velours

STENDIG, NEW YORK,
FROM C. 1970

*Sofa und Liegesessel, spiegeln den Anthropomorphismus des Designs wider und
betonen ihn. Wie Panton kam es auch Aarnio darauf an, einprägsame und wie-
dererkennbare Entwürfe zu schaffen. Er erreichte dies durch den offensichtlichen
und augenzwinkernden Zoomorphismus des »Pony«-Stuhls.*

Créateurs de sièges historiques en plastique aux formes organiques
abstraites dans les années 60, Panton et Aarnio s'intéressèrent à des
formes plus construites en mousse de polyuréthane dix ans plus tard. Les
noms étranges du canapé et de la chaise longue de Panton rappellent et
accentuent l'anthropomorphisme de ces sièges. Aarnio chercha également
à créer des modèles de caractère marquant et identifiable. Il y réussit à
travers le zoomorphisme du siège « Pony ».

▶ **Verner Panton**
System 1-2-3 linking
chairs, 1973

FRITZ HANSEN,
ALLERØD, FROM 1973

▲ **Verner Panton**
System 1-2-3 arm-
chair, 1973

FRITZ HANSEN,
ALLERØD, FROM 1973

▲ **Verner Panton**
System 1-2-3 chair
with castors, 1973

FRITZ HANSEN,
ALLERØD, FROM 1973

Verner Panton

System 1-2-3, 1973

Textile-covered foam-
upholstered tubular
steel frames with
chromed tubular steel
arms and metal
bases | Rahmen und
Armlehnen aus Stahl-
rohr, Schaumstoff-
polsterung mit
Stoffbezug, Metall-
sockel | Châssis en
tube d'acier,
accoudoirs en acier
chromé, piètement
métallique,
rembourrage en
mousse recouverte de
tissu

FRITZ HANSEN,
ALLERØD, FROM 1973

Like his earlier stacking chair and
"S" chair, Panton's "System 1-2-3"
utilises a cantilevered form. This
seating, however, was developed as
a multifunctional programme –
chairs could be linked and a variety
of options were available for both
domestic and contract use.

*Wie für seinen älteren Stapelstuhl
und »S«-Stuhl verwendet Panton
auch für das »System 1-2-3« eine
freischwingende Konstruktion. Das
Sitzmöbelsystem ist als multifunktionales Programm konzipiert: Die Stühle können verbunden werden, und eine Vielzahl von Optionen steht für die Nutzung im häuslichen Bereich oder als Büromöbel
zur Verfügung.*

De même que ses précédents siège empilable et siège « S », le « Système 1-2-3 » de Panton se
sert d'un porte-à-faux. Ce principe fut développé sur une ligne multifonctionnelle avec des
chaises qui pouvaient être réunies en banquette et offraient diverses options. Elles s'adressaient
aussi bien au marché de la maison qu'à celui du bureau.

Gerd Lange

Flex 2000, 1973–1974

Solid beech legs with
moulded plywood side
sections and injection-
moulded polypropy-
lene seating section |
Stuhlbeine aus
Buche, seitliche Ver-
strebungen aus
geformtem Poly-
propylen | Pieds en
hêtre massif, côtés en
contre-plaqué moulé,
siège en polypropylène
moulé par injection

GEBRÜDER THONET,
FRANKENBERG,
FROM 1976 TO
PRESENT

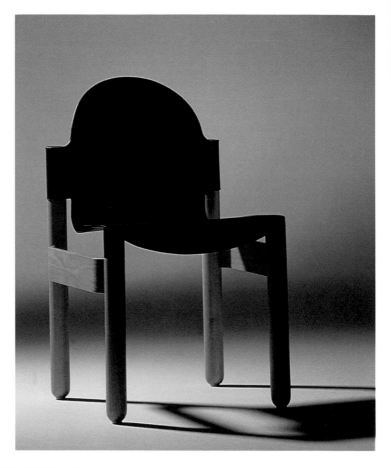

▼ **David Rowland**
Sof-Tech chair, 1979

THONET
INDUSTRIES, USA

Combining formal simplicity with persuasive technological reasoning, the "Flex" chair is a comfortable,
multipurpose seating solution. Lange was awarded the
"Gute Form" prize in 1969 for his chair designs.
*»Flex«, der formale Einfachheit mit überzeugender tech-
nischer Rationalität verbindet, ist ein bequemer Vielzweck-
stuhl. 1969 wurde er mit dem Bundespreis »Gute Form«
ausgezeichnet.*
Associant la simplicité formelle à une réflexion techno-
logique convaincante, la chaise « Flex » est à la fois
confortable et multifonctionnelle. Elle a reçu le prix
« Gute Form » en 1969.

Stefan Wewerka

Model No. B1, 1979

Lacquered wood
frame with textile-
covered upholstered
seat | Rahmen aus
Holz, lackiert,
Sitzfläche gepolstert,
mit Stoffbezug |
Châssis en bois laqué,
siège rembourré
recouvert de tissu

TECTA, LAUENFÖRDE,
FROM 1979 TO
PRESENT

▼ Stefan Wewerka
(top right) with D2
chair and ottoman,
1982

The asymmetry of the model No. B1 is intended to facilitate several sitting positions. The design's prototype was developed from a chair-sculpture by Wewerka that comprised two different chair halves.

Die Asymmetrie des Modells Nr. B1 hat den Zweck, verschiedene Sitzhaltungen zu ermöglichen. Der Prototyp des Entwurfs wurde aus einer Stuhlskulptur von Wewerka entwickelt, die zwei unterschiedliche Stuhlhälften vereint.

L'asymétrie du modèle n° B1 lui permet d'offrir plusieurs positions assises. Le prototype fut mis au point d'après une sculpture de Wewerka constituée de deux moitiés de chaises différentes.

Alessandro Mendini

Redesigned Thonet chair, 1979

Existing chair with applied decoration | Serienstuhl mit Dekor | Siège existant, décor appliqué

STUDIO ALCHIMIA, MILAN, FROM 1979

▼ **Alessandro Mendini**
Redesigned Superleggera, 1978

STUDIO ALCHIMIA, MILAN, FROM 1978

Believing that Modern Design had reached the end of its natural life and that designers could no longer create innovative designs in respect of what had gone before, Mendini "redesigned" acknowledged classics such as Breuer's "Wassily" chair. In doing so, he attempted to demonstrate that, among other things, the intellectual content of a design can be derived solely from applied decoration.

Ausgehend von der Überzeugung, daß das Design der Moderne einen Endpunkt erreicht habe und die Designer nicht mehr innovativ sein könnten, angesichts all dessen, was bereits realisiert wurde, schuf Mendini Redesigns von anerkannten Klassikern, wie z. B. von Breuers »Wassily«-

Alessandro Mendini

Redesigned Wassily armchair, 1978

Existing chair with applied decoration | Serienstuhl mit appliziertem Dekor | Siège existant, décor appliqué

STUDIO ALCHIMIA, MILAN, FROM 1978

Stuhl. Indem er dies tat, wollte er unter anderem auch de-monstrieren, daß ein Entwurf allein durch applizierten Dekor intellektuellen Gehalt gewinnen kann.

Persuadé que le design moderne en était arrivé à la fin de son existence et que les designers ne pouvaient plus innover par rapport à tout ce qui avait été réalisé aupa-ravant, Mendini «redessina» des classiques reconnus comme le fauteuil «Wassily» de Breuer. Ce faisant, il tentait de démontrer, entre autres, que le contenu intel-lectuel d'un style de design peut provenir d'un simple décor appliqué.

▲ Alessandro Mendini
Redesigned 4860 with a faux-marble finish, 1978

STUDIO ALCHIMIA, MILAN, FROM 1978

Alessandro Mendini

Proust's armchair,
1978

Existing chair with hand-painted decoration | Alter Sesseltyp mit hand-gemaltem Dekor | Fauteuil existant, décor peint à la main

STUDIO ALCHIMIA, MILAN, FROM 1978 (REISSUED BY CAPPELLINI, AROSIO)

Redesign or Banal Design attempted to address the intellectual and cultural void which was perceived to exist in the mass-design of industrialised society. The banality of existing objects was emphasised by applying bright colours and quirky decoration to them, such as "Proust's" armchair and the "Kandissi" sofa. Studio Alchimia heralded the end of Modernism's "prohibitionism" and the rebirth of a symbolic language in design.

Redesign bzw. das Banal-Design versuchte, die intellektuelle und kulturelle Leere vorzuführen, die man im Massendesign der Industriegesellschaft zu finden glaubte. Die Banalität vorhandener Objekte wurde mit hellen Farben und schrillen Dekors unterstrichen, so etwa beim »Proust«-Sessel oder dem »Kandissi«-Sofa. Studio Alchimia verkündete das Ende des Prohibitionismus der Moderne und die Wiedergeburt einer symbolischen Sprache im Design.

Le redesign ou le design banal tentèrent de combler le vide intellectuel et culturel que l'on pouvait percevoir dans le design de masse conçu pour la société industrialisée. La banalité des objets existants était soulignée par des couleurs vives ou d'étranges décors appliqués, comme pour ce fauteuil « Proust » ou ce canapé « Kandissi ». Le Studio Alchimia annonçait la fin de la « prohibition » moderniste et la renaissance d'un langage symbolique dans le design.

Alessandro Mendini

Kandissi, 1978

Sofa with applied painted wood cut-out decoration | Sofa mit ausgesägtem und appliziertem Dekor | Canapé avec application d'un décor découpé

STUDIO ALCHIMIA, MILAN, FROM 1978

Ettore Sottsass

Seggiolina, 1980

Formica-faced seat
and back with
chromed tubular
metal legs | Sitzfläche
und Ruckenlehne aus
Holz mit Furnier aus
Plastik, Stuhlbeine
aus Stahlrohr,
verchromt | Siège et
dossier plaqués de
formica, pieds
tubulaires en métal
chromé

STUDIO ALCHIMIA,
MILAN, FROM 1980

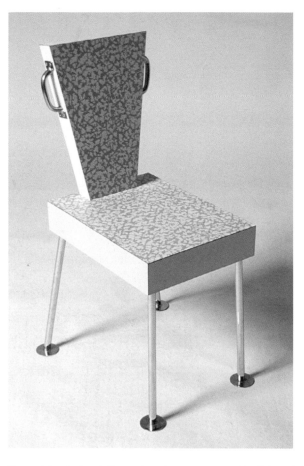

Comprising industrially produced components, this dining chair was intended as an ironic comment on design. Through its use of plastic laminates, a medium strongly associated with 1950s' kitsch, this chair can be
seen as an antecedent of later Memphis designs.

Dieser Eßzimmerstuhl besteht aus Fertigprodukten und war als ironischer
Kommentar zum Design intendiert. Mit der Verwendung von Plastiklaminat,
einem Material, das sehr eng mit dem Kitsch der 50er Jahre verbunden ist, kann
dieser Stuhl als Vorläufer des späteren Memphis-Designs betrachtet werden.

Faite d'éléments produits industriellement, cette chaise de salle à manger
se voulait un commentaire ironique sur le design. Par son recours au
plastique stratifié, matériau fortement associé au kitsch des années 50,
elle annonce les projets de Memphis.

The Viennese architect, Hans Hollein, is one of the best-known exponents of Post-Modernism. His bold "Art Deco meets Pop" furniture designs express the playful exuberance of the style.

Der Wiener Architekt Hans Hollein ist einer der bekanntesten Vertreter der Postmoderne. Seine kühnen Möbelentwürfe unter dem Motto »Art Deco meets Pop« belegen den spielerischen Überschwang der Postmoderne.

L'architecte viennois Hans Hollein est l'un des représentants les plus connus du postmodernisme. Ses projets de meubles « Quand Art déco et Art pop se rencontrent » expriment l'exubérance joyeuse du style.

Hans Hollein

Mitzi, Model
No. D90, 1981

Textile-covered polyurethane-upholstered wood frame with blonde root-wood veneered base | *Rahmen aus Holz, Polsterung aus Polyurethan, mit Stoffbezug, Sockel mit hellem Wurzelholz furniert |* Châssis en bois rembourré de mousse de polyuréthane recouverte de tissu, base plaquée de loupe blonde

POLTRONOVA, MONTALE, PISTOIA, FROM 1981 TO PRESENT

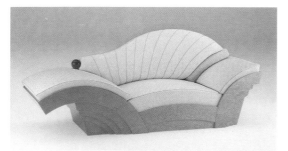

◄ **Hans Hollein**
Marilyn, Model
No. DL 190, 1981

POLTRONOVA, MONTALE, PISTOIA, FROM 1981 TO PRESENT

Stefan Wewerka

Einschwinger, Model No. B5, 1982

Chromed tubular steel frame with textile-covered upholstered seat and backrail | Rahmen aus Stahlrohr, verchromt, Sitzfläche und Rückenlehne gepolstert und mit Stoffbezug | Châssis en tube d'acier cintré, siège et dosseret rembourrés

TECTA, LAUENFÖRDE, FROM 1982 TO PRESENT

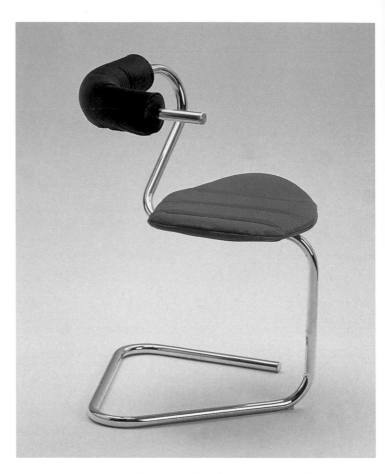

▼ Stefan Wewerka
Model No. D2, 1982

TECTA, LAUENFÖRDE, FROM 1982 TO PRESENT

Probably inspired by Silvio Coppola's similarly constructed "Gru" chair of 1970, the "Einschwinger's" asymmetrical frame is constructed from a single piece of tubular steel 3.2 m in length, bent into six equal angles.

Angeregt durch Silvio Coppolas ähnlich gebauten »Gru«-Stuhl von 1970 ist der asymmetrische Rahmen dieses »Einschwingers« mit sechs gleichen Winkeln aus einem einzigen Stück Stahlrohr von 3,20 m Länge gebogen.

Probablement inspirée par la chaise « Gru » de Silvio Coppola (1970), l'ossature asymétrique de ce modèle « Einschwinger » fait appel à un unique tube d'acier de 3,2 m de long, cintré selon six angles égaux.

Michele De Lucchi

First, 1983

Tubular steel frame with painted wood seat, back and armrests | Gestell aus lackiertem Stahlrohr, Armlehnen, Sitz und Rückenlehne aus lackiertem Holz | Châssis en tube d'acier, siège, dossier et accoudoirs en bois

MEMPHIS, MILAN, FROM 1983 TO PRESENT

▼ Memphis graphics for the First chair, c. 1983

The playful formal vocabulary of the "First" chair symbolises the electronic age and embodies the Post-Modern belief that the communication of meanings and values is the paramount concern of design.

Die spielerische Formensprache des Stuhls »First« spiegelt das Elektronikzeitalter wider und demonstriert die postmoderne Überzeugung, daß die eigentliche Aufgabe von Design in der Kommunikation von Bedeutungen und Werten liegt.

Le vocabulaire formel ludique de la chaise « First » symbolise l'âge de l'électronique et incarne la conviction postmoderne selon laquelle la communication des significations et des valeurs est l'objet essentiel du design.

483

Michele De Lucchi

Lido, 1982

Plastic laminate-faced wood frame with textile-covered upholstery | Rahmen aus Holz, mit Plastiklaminat, Polsterung mit Stoffbezug | Châssis en bois plaqué de plastique stratifié, rembourrage recouvert de tissu

MEMPHIS, MILAN, FROM 1982 TO PRESENT

Borrowing ornamental devices from previous decorative styles, Memphis successfully popularised Anti-Design and thereby contributed to its general acceptance within the furniture industry. Producing brightly coloured, fanciful furniture that ran against the accepted tenets of "Good Design", Memphis designers used decoration for its own sake in an attempt to establish a new visual design language.

Die Designergruppe Memphis, die in ihren Entwürfen ornamentale Details früherer Stilrichtungen verarbeitete, machte das Anti-Design populär und trug damit zu seiner breiten Akzeptanz innerhalb der Möbelindustrie bei. Die Designer von Memphis schufen leuchtend bunte, phantasievolle Möbel, die sich nicht um die Regeln von »Gutem Design« kümmerten, und sie nutzten, um zu einer neuen, visuellen Designsprache zu gelangen, das Dekor um des Dekors willen.

▶ Peter Shire
Bel Air, 1982

MEMPHIS, MILAN

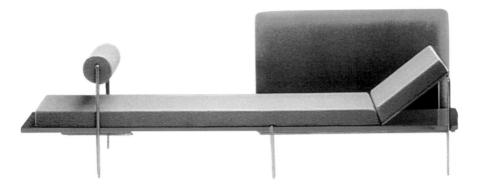

Empruntant des ornements à divers styles décoratifs antérieurs, Memphis popularisa avec succès l'anti-design et du coup, contribua à le par l'Industrie du mobilier. Réalisant des meubles amusants et de couleurs vives, à l'opposé des principes du « Good Design », les designers de Memphis se servaient du décor pour lui-même afin de trouver un nouveau langage visuel.

Andrea Branzi

Century, 1982

Painted tubular steel and varnished wood frame with textile-covered foam upholstery and wheels | Rahmen aus lackiertem Stahlrohr und furniertem Holz, Schaumstoffpolsterung, mit Stoffbezug, Rollen | Châssis en tube d'acier et bois verni, rembourrage en mousse recouverte de tissu, roulettes

MEMPHIS, MILAN, FROM 1982 TO PRESENT

◄ **George Sowden**
Oberoy covered in cotton fabric designed by Nathalie du Pasquier, 1981

MEMPHIS, MILAN

Ettore Sottsass

Teodora, 1986–1987

*Plastic laminate
veneered wood frame
with moulded perspex
back | Rahmen aus
Holz, mit Furnier aus
Plastiklaminat
Rückenlehne aus
geformtem Plexiglas |
Châssis en bois
plaqué de plastique
lamifié, dossier en
Perspex moulé*

VITRA, BASLE, FROM
1987 TO PRESENT

▼ **Ettore Sottsass**
Carabo, 1989

ZANOTTA, MILAN,
FROM 1989 TO
PRESENT

The "Teodora's" elegance and visual lightness is rarely seen in furniture of the Memphis school. The "Royal" chaise, however, epitomises Memphis design through the monumentality of its elemental construction, use of plastic laminates and highly patterned textiles. The "Teodora" is produced in a limited edition by Vitra who, like other established manufacturers, fund the production of some anti-rational furniture for reasons mainly to do with publicity.

Die Eleganz und optische Leichtigkeit des Stuhls »Teodora« findet sich bei den Möbeln der Memphis-Schule nicht sehr häufig. Die Liege »Royal« demonstriert charakteristisches Memphis-Design durch die Monu-

486

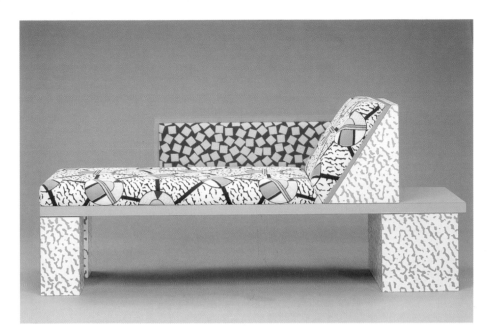

mentalität der einzelnen Elemente, durch die Verwendung von Plastiklaminaten und durch stark gemusterte Bezüge. »Teodora« wird in einer begrenzten Auflage von Vitra produziert; dieser und einige andere Hersteller finanzieren die Produktion von ausgewählten anti-rationalen Möbelentwürfen aus Gründen der Publicity.

L'élégance du petit « Teodora » et sa légèreté visuelle sont rares dans la production de l'école Memphis. La chaise longue « Royal », incarne quant à elle le style Memphis dans la monumentalité de sa construction, l'utilisation du plastique lamifié, et de tissus à larges motifs. Le « Teodora » est produit en série limitée par Vitra qui, comme d'autres importants fabricants, a soutenu la production de meubles antirationnels pour des raisons essentiellement publicitaires.

Nathalie du Pasquier

Royal, 1983

Plastic laminated-faced wood frame with fabric-covered upholstery (fabric used on cushion and armrest designed by George Sowden) | Gestell aus Holz, mit Plastiklaminat beschichtet, gepolstert und mit Stoff bezogen (Polsterstoff für Kissen und Armlehne entworfen von George Sowden) | Châssis en bois plaqué de plastique lamifié, rembourrage recouvert de tissu (tissus créés par George Sowden)

MEMPHIS, MILAN, FROM 1983 TO PRESENT

Robert Venturi

Grandmother, 1984

*Textile-covered poly-
urethane-upholstered
wood frame |
Rahmen aus Holz,
Polsterung aus Poly-
urethanschaumstoff,
mit Stoffbezug |
Châssis en bois, rem-
bourrage en mousse
de polyuréthane
recouverte de tissu*

KNOLL INTER-
NATIONAL, NEW
YORK, FROM 1984

▶ **Robert Venturi**
Venturi Collection,
1984

KNOLL INTER-
NATIONAL, NEW
YORK, FROM 1984

Deriving inspiration for the decoration and overall form of this collection from historic styles, Venturi emphasised the two-dimensionality of the chairs' surfaces with screen printing that could be described as Neo-Pop. His cartoonizing of ornament from the past typifies the Post-Modern style and can be seen as a response to Charles Jencks' rallying cry for double coding, mixed references and hybrid themes in design.

Seine Inspiration für Dekor und Gesamtgestaltung dieser Kollektion fand Venturi in historischen Stilen, er betonte die Zweidimensionalität der Oberflächen seiner Stühle mit Siebdrucken, die als »Neo-Pop« bezeichnet werden können. Im Stil der Postmoderne karikiert er Formen vergangener Epochen, was wiederum als Antwort auf Charles Jencks' Forderung nach einer doppelten Kodierung, nach einer Mischung von Bezügen und Themen zu verstehen ist.

Recherchant son inspiration formelle et décorative dans des styles historiques, Venturi soulignait l'aspect plat et lisse de la surface de ses sièges par des sérigraphies que l'on pourrait qualifier de « Neo-Pop ». Cette caricature d'ornements du passé caractérise le style postmoderne et répond aux appels de Charles Jencks en faveur d'un second degré, de références mixtes et de thèmes hybrides dans le design.

Robert Venturi

Art Deco & Sheraton,
1984

Silk-screen printed,
moulded plywood
construction | Aus
formgebogenem
Schichtholz, Sieb-
druckdekors | Contre-
plaqué moulé et
sérigraphié

KNOLL INTER-
NATIONAL, NEW
YORK, FROM 1984

► **Robert Venturi**
Queen Anne, 1984

KNOLL INTER-
NATIONAL, NEW
YORK, FROM 1984

◄ **Robert Venturi**
Chippendale, 1984

KNOLL INTER-
NATIONAL, NEW
YORK, FROM 1984

Riccardo Dalisi

Pavone, 1986

Nickel-plated and enamelled steel frame | Konstruktion aus Stahl, vernickelt und einbrennlackiert | Structure en acier émaillé et nickelé

ZANOTTA, MILAN, FROM 1986

▼ **Riccardo Dalisi**
Mariposa, 1989

ZANOTTA, MILAN, FROM 1989

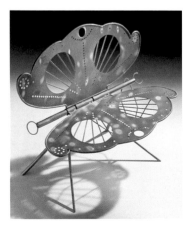

Riccardo Dalisi and Alessandro Mendini are regarded as pioneers of Anti-Design. They were founding members of "Global Tools" which was established in 1973 to "stimulate free development of individual creativity". Their later "Pavone" and "Zabro" designs, which form part of Zanotta's Edizioni range, demonstrate their interest in crafted artifacts that display the artistic imprint of their creators.

Riccardo Dalisi and Alessandro Mendini gelten als Pioniere des Anti-Designs. Sie gründeten 1973 »Global Tools«, um »die freie Entwicklung individueller Kreativität zu stimulieren«. Die Stühle »Pavone« und »Zabro«, Entwürfe, die später entstanden und zur Kollektion von Zanotta Edizioni

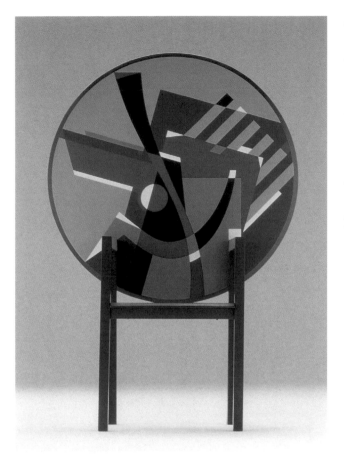

Alessandro Mendini

Zabro, 1984

Lacquered wood
construction with
hand-painted
decoration and
leather-upholstered
armrests |
Konstruktion aus
Holz, lackiert,
handgemaltes Dekor,
Armlehnen gepolstert
und mit Lederbezug |
Bois laqué, décor
peint à la main,
accoudoirs en cuir
rembourré

ZANOTTA, MILAN,
FROM 1984 TO
PRESENT

gehören, zeigen ihr Interesse an handwerklichen Artefakten, die die künstlerische Kreativität ihrer Schöpfer zur Schau stellen.

Riccardo Dalisi et Alessandro Mendini sont considérés comme des pionniers de l'anti-design. Ils fondèrent « Global Tools » en 1973 « pour stimuler le développement libre de la créativité individuelle. » Leur modèles ultérieurs, « Pavone » et « Zabro », qui font partie de la gamme Edizioni de Zanotta, illustrent leur intérêt pour des techniques artisanales qui mettent en valeur le talent artistique des créateurs.

**Stefano
Casciani**

Albertina, 1983–1984

Plywood frame on
brushed steel legs
with fabric-covered
polyurethane foam
upholstery | Rahmen
aus Schichtholz auf
mattierten Stahl-
füßen, Polsterung aus
Polyurethanschaum-
stoff mit Stoffbezug |
Châssis en contre-
plaqué, pieds en acier
brossé, rembourrage
en mousse de poly-
uréthane recouverte
de tissu

ZANOTTA, MILAN,
FROM 1984 TO
PRESENT

Despite their rather unconventional appearance due to their primary-coloured textile coverings, Stefano Casciani's "Albertina" range and Ettore Sottsass' "Westside Collection" are essentially rationally conceived seating series suitable for large-scale production. Relatively simple techniques are used in the manufacture of their block-like foam constructions. The playful and energetic vocabulary of these chairs which liberates colour, divorces geometrical forms and deforms structure, was no doubt intended to relieve the dullness of office reception areas.

Trotz ihrer recht unkonventionellen Erscheinung, die von den in Grundfarben gehaltenen Stoffbezügen herrührt, sind Stefano Cascianis »Albertina«- und Ettore Sottsass' »Westside«-Kollektionen rationell konzipierte Sitzmöbelserien für die Massenproduktion. Ihre blockartige Bauweise aus Schaumstoff erlaubt den Einsatz relativ einfacher Herstellungstechniken. Die spielerische und energische Gestaltung dieser Stühle, die den Farben freien Raum läßt, sich von geometrischen Formen löst und Strukturen deformiert, sollte ohne Zweifel Büro-Empfangsbereiche von ihrer Langeweile befreien.

Malgré leur apparence peu conventionnelle due à leur recouvrage en tissus de couleurs primaires, la gamme «Albertina» de Stefano Casciani et la «Westside Collection» de Sottsass sont à la base des sièges rationnels conçus pour une production en grande série. Leur construction en blocs de mousse fait appel à des techniques relativement simples. L'expression énergique et enjouée de ces fauteuils aux couleurs franches fait éclater les formes géométriques et oublier les structures. Ils voulaient dissiper l'atmosphère ennuyeuse des halls de réception des entreprises.

Ettore Sottsass

Westside Collection,
1983

Textile-covered,
polyurethane foam-
upholstered steel
frame with painted
legs | Rahmen aus
Stahl, Polsterung aus
Polyurethanschaum-
stoff mit Stoffbezug,
Füße lackiert | Châssis
en contre-plaqué,
pieds peints, rem-
bourrage en mousse
de polyuréthane
recouverte de tissu

KNOLL
INTERNATIONAL,
NEW YORK, FROM
1983

Paolo Deganello

AEO, Model No. 650, 1973

Lacquered steel frame and fibreglass-reinforced polyamide "Duratan" base with fabric sleeve and fabric-covered polyurethane foam and polyester padded cushion | Rahmen aus Stahl, lackiert, auf fiberglasverstärktem »Duratan«-Polyamidfuß, Stoffüberzug, Sitzkissen aus Polyurethanschaumstoff mit Polyestereinlagen und Stoffbezug | Châssis en acier laqué, base en polyamide « Duratan » renforcé de fibre de verre, housse en tissu, coussin en mousse de polyuréthane recouverte de tissu

CASSINA, MEDA, MILAN, FROM 1973 TO PRESENT

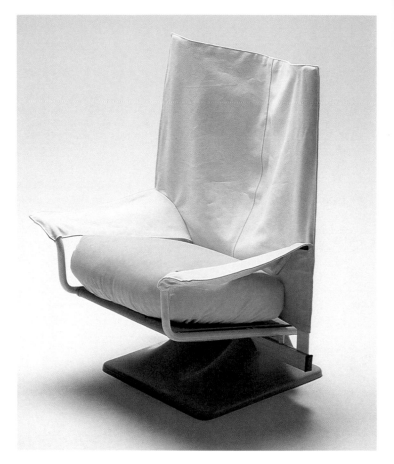

During the 1970s, Deganello, like many of his Radical counterparts in the 1960s, designed innovative seating within the constraints of the industrial process. The "AEO" can be collapsed for easier transportation.

Während der 70er Jahre schuf Deganello, wie viele seiner Kollegen des Radical-Design in den 60er Jahren, innovative Sitzmöbel innerhalb der Beschränkungen des industriellen Fertigungsprozesses. Der Stuhl »AEO« läßt sich zum einfacheren Transport auseinandernehmen.

Pendant les années 70, Deganello, comme beaucoup de ses collègues radicaux des années 60, dessina des sièges révolutionnaires tout en respectant les contraintes de la fabrication industrielle. Le modèle « AEO » se plie pour se transporter plus aisément.

Paolo Deganello

Torso, Model No. 654, 1982

Steel frame with elastic webbing, fabric-covered polyurethane foam and polyester padding upholstery | Rahmen aus Stahl mit elastischem Gurtband, Polsterung aus Polyurethanschaumstoff und Polyestereinlagen mit Stoffbezug | Châssis en acier, rembourrage en mousse de polyuréthane recouverte de tissu et gainage élastique, garnissages en polyester

CASSINA, MEDA, MILAN, FROM 1982 TO PRESENT

▼ Paolo Deganello
Working drawing of Torso, 1982

Deganello's "Torso" series promotes user-participation through the interchangeability of its parts which can be configured in a variety of ways. Its distinctive asymmetrical shape and colour options were inspired by 1950s' design.

Deganellos »Torso«-Serie fördert die Kreativität der Benutzer, da sich die Sitzelemente austauschen und auf vielfältige Weise kombinieren lassen. In ihrer charakteristischen asymmetrischen Form und der Farbwahl ist sie vom Design der 50er Jahre inspiriert.

La gamme « Torso » de Deganello incite l'utilisateur à en modifier les formes grâce à différents éléments interchangeables. L'asymétrie volontaire et le choix des couleurs s'inspirent du design des années 50.

495

Toshiyuki Kita

Wink, 1976–1980

Steel frame, textile-covered polyurethane foam | Rahmen aus Stahl, Polsterung aus Polyurethanschaum-stoff | Châssis en acier, mousse de polyuréthane

CASSINA, MEDA, MILAN, FROM 1980 TO PRESENT

The articulated frame of the "Wink" took four years to develop and allows the design to be configured in a variety of comfortable positions. It was launched at the 1981 Milan Furniture Fair to great acclaim.

Die Entwicklung des verstellbaren Rahmens des »Wink«-Sessels nahm vier Jahre in Anspruch, doch nun läßt sich das Modell in eine Vielzahl bequemer Positionen bringen. Zur Mailänder Möbelmesse von 1981 wurde »Wink« unter großem Beifall auf den Markt gebracht.

Le châssis articulé du «Wink» a nécessité quatre années de recherches. Il permet une multiplicité de positions confortables. Son lancement à la Foire du meuble de Milan en 1981 fut largement salué.

Available in a number of versions, the "Veranda's" adjustable frame allows the footrest to be folded under the seat when not in use and the headrest to be folded down to provide a low-back if required. The design's lithe form belies the strength required to facilitate this degree of flexibility.

Das Sitzmöbel »Veranda« ist in einer großen Zahl von Varianten lieferbar. Es ist verstellbar konstruiert, so daß sich die Fußstütze, wenn sie nicht benutzt wird, unter den Sitz klappen läßt und die Kopfstütze nach hinten umgelegt werden kann, wenn man die Rückenlehne niedrig halten möchte. Die Leichtigkeit des Designs täuscht über die Stärke der Rahmenkonstruktion hinweg, die diese haben muß, um eine solche Flexibilität zu erreichen.

Disponible en plusieurs versions, le « Veranda » possède un châssis réglable qui permet de replier le repose-pied sous le siège ou de rabattre le haut du dossier pour obtenir un fauteuil plus bas. La souplesse apparente de la forme fait oublier la rigidité nécessaire pour aboutir à un tel degré de polyvalence.

Vico Magistretti

Veranda, 1983

Painted articulated tubular steel frame with textile-covered polyurethane foam upholstery | Rahmen aus Stahlrohr mit Gelenken, lackiert, Polster aus Polyurethanschaum, mit Stoff bezogen | Châssis en tube d'acier articulé peint, rembourrage en mousse de polyuréthane recouverte de tissu

CASSINA, MEDA, MILAN, FROM 1983 TO PRESENT

◄ **Vico Magistretti**
Cardigan sofa, 1986

CASSINA, MEDA, MILAN, FROM 1986

Vico Magistretti

Sindbad, 1981

*Lacquered beech
frame, upholstered in
polyurethane foam
and polyester padding,
textile or leather
covers | Rahmen aus
Buche, lackiert, Pol-
sterung aus Polyure-
thanschaumstoff und
Polyestereinlagen,
Leder- oder Stoff-
bezug | Châssis en
hêtre laqué, rem-
bourrage en mousse
de polyuréthane,
garnissage en poly-
ester, couverture en
tissu ou cuir*

CASSINA, MEDA,
MILAN, FROM 1981
TO PRESENT

Magistretti's idea of throwing a thick wool horse blanket over an upholstered armchair resulted in his design for the "Sindbad" series. Its apparent
simplicity gives the design a sense of warmth and informality.

*Magistrettis Idee, eine dicke wollene Pferdedecke einfach über einen gepolsterten
Sessel zu legen, führte ihn zum Entwurf der Sitzmöbelserie »Sindbad«. Seine
schlichte Erscheinung gibt dem Entwurf etwas Warmes und Zwangloses.*

« Sindbad » naquit de l'idée de Magistretti de jeter une épaisse couverture
de cheval en laine sur un fauteuil rembourré. Sa simplicité apparente donne
à ce modèle une expression de chaleur et de décontraction.

▶ **Vico Magistretti**
Sketch of Sindbad
sofa, 1981

Gaetano Pesce

I Feltri, 1987

Frame of stitched thick wool felt impregnated with thermosetting resin with felt seat supported by hemp stringing | Rahmen aus vernähtem Filz, mit Epoxidharz versteift, Sitzfläche aus Filz auf Hanfschnüren | Structure en feutre épais piqué imprégné de résine à chaud, siège en feutre reposant sur des cordes de chanvre

CASSINA, MEDA,
MILAN, FROM 1987
TO PRESENT

▼ Gaetano Pesce
Sketch of I Feltri
chair, c. 1987

"I Feltri" is one of several designs by Pesce that explores the possibilities of resin-impregnated textiles. By saturating felt with an epoxy resin, Pesce was able to produce a self-supporting structure.

Der Sessel »I Feltri« ist einer von mehreren Entwürfen Pesces, mit denen er die Möglichkeiten von harzgetränkten Textilien erprobte. Indem er den Filz mit Epoxidharz versteifte, konnte Pesce eine freitragende Form erzielen.

« I Feltri » est l'un des projets de Pesce qui expérimente les possibilités des textiles imprégnés de résine. En saturant le feutre d'une résine époxy, le designer réussit à créer une structure autoporteuse.

Gaetano Pesce

Pratt, 1983

Urethane injected
into a mould by hand
(nine stages from soft
to rigid) | Von Hand
in eine Form gespritz-
tes Polyurethanharz
(in neun Schichten,
von weich bis starr) |
Structure en uréthane
injectée dans un
moule par processus
manuel en neuf
étapes

GAETANO PESCE,
NEW YORK, FROM
1983

▼ **Gaetano Pesce**
Greene Street,
1984–1986

VITRA, BASLE, FROM
1986

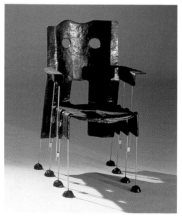

The "Pratt" chair is one of a series of nine chairs developed at the Pratt Institute, New York which explored the
structural properties of polyurethane resin of different
densities. Like many of Pesce's designs, it focuses on
the ambiguous relationship between art and industrial
production. His "Dalila" series of three chairs was designed to complement his "Sansone" table and intentionally invokes the soft forms of the female body.
»Pratt« gehört zu einer Serie von neun Stühlen, die am
New Yorker Pratt-Institut entwickelt wurden, wo man die
Struktureigenschaften von Polyurethanharz verschiedener
Dichte untersuchte. Wie bei vielen seiner Designs konzentriert sich Pesce auch mit dieser Serie auf die vieldeutigen

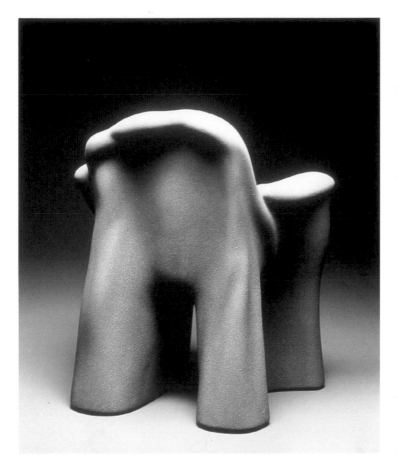

Gaetano Pesce

Dalila, 1980

Epoxy-coated, moulded rigid polyurethane foam | Geformter und ausgehärteter Polyurethanschaumstoff mit Epoxidharzbeschichtung | Mousse de polyuréthane rigide, enduit époxy

CASSINA, MEDA, MILAN, FROM 1980

▼ **Gaetano Pesce**
Tramonto a New York, 1980

CASSINA, MEDA, MILAN, FROM 1980 TO PRESENT

Beziehungen zwischen Kunst und industrieller Produktion. Die drei Stühle der »Dalila«-Serie entstanden als Ergänzung zu dem Tisch »Sansone«. Sie erinnern an die weichen Formen eines Frauenkörpers.

Le fauteuil « Pratt » fait partie d'une série de neuf sièges mis au point au Pratt Institute de New York pour explorer les propriétés structurelles d'une résine de polyuréthane de différentes densités. Comme beaucoup des créations de Pesce, ce modèle met l'accent sur la relation ambiguë entre l'art et la production industrielle. Sa série « Dalila » de trois sièges fut dessinée pour accompagner sa table « Sansone » et évoque volontairement les formes douces du corps féminin.

Ron Arad

Rover, 1981

Tubular steel frame supporting a salvaged Rover 2000 car seat |
Rahmen aus Stahl- rohr, darauf ein recycelter Autositz aus einem Rover 2000 |
Châssis en tube d'acier, siège de récupération de Rover 2000

ONE OFF, LONDON, FROM 1981

▼ Jean Prouvé
Prototype of ad- justable chair, 1924

This "ready-made" design utilises a salvaged car seat and a frame executed from scaffolding – a favourite medium of the High-Tech style. Its rough-and- ready appearance characterises the work of the British avantgarde in the 1980s.

Design als Ready-made: Ein gebrauchter Autositz in einem Rahmen aus Gerüstteilen – ein beliebter Werkstoff des High-Tech-Stils. Der improvisierte Eindruck ist typisch für die Arbeiten der britischen Avantgarde der 80er Jahre.

Ce modèle ready-made utilise un siège de voiture récupéré et un châssis fait de morceaux d'échafau- dage, l'un des matériaux préféré du style high-tech. Son aspect brut et improvisé caractérise les travaux de l'avant-garde britannique au cours des années 80.

Stiletto (Frank Schreiner)

Consumer's Rest,
1983

Zinc-plated cut-and-bent supermarket trolley with plastic liner | Einkaufswagen, zersägt, gebogen und verzinkt, mit Plastik-auflage | Chariot de supermarché en acier zingué, découpé et cintré, garniture plastique

STILETTO STUDIOS,
BERLIN, FROM 1984
(REISSUED BY
BRÜDER SIEGEL,
LEIPHEIM, FROM
1990 TO PRESENT)

▼ Stiletto (Frank
Schreiner)
Short Rest child's
chair, 1983

STILETTO STUDIOS,
BERLIN, FROM 1984
(REISSUED BY
BRÜDER SIEGEL,
LEIPHEIM, FROM
1990 TO PRESENT)

This "ready-made" chair, produced in a limited edition of 100, is a wry comment on consumerism. The function of this everyday object has been transformed and through this process, so has its cultural status.

Dieser Ready-made-Stuhl wurde in einer einmaligen Auflage von 100 Exemplaren hergestellt als sarkastischer Kommentar auf den Konsumrausch. Die Funktion des Gebrauchsgegenstandes hat sich gewandelt und in diesem Prozeß auch seine kulturelle Bedeutung.

Ce fauteuil ready-made, produit à 100 exemplaires, est un commentaire désabusé sur la société de consommation. La fonction de cet objet quotidien a été transformée, acquérant du coup un statut culturel.

Till Behrens

Kreuzschwinger®,
1983

*Chromed or epoxy-
coated stainless steel
and steel wire
construction | Draht
in Edelstahl oder
Normalstahl,
verchromt oder
pulverbeschichtet | Fil
d'acier inoxydable ou
d'acier ordinaire,
chromé ou pulvérisé*

SCHLUBACH,
GRIEBEN, BRANDEN-
BURG, FROM
1992 TO PRESENT

▼ **Till Behrens**
Kreuzschwinger®
(armchair), 1983

SCHLUBACH,
GRIEBEN, BRANDEN-
BURG, FROM
1992 TO PRESENT
1983 TO PRESENT

The stackable filigree "Kreuzschwinger"® is an innovation without precedent. Its cross-piece allows the sitter
to swing gently to and fro; it invites one to adopt a dy-
namic sitting posture but is simultaneously mentally
and physically relaxing. Attachable seat and arm cushions enhance seating comfort. The aesthetically pleasing "Schalenschwinger" is unusually comfortable as well
as being stackable.

*Der stapelbare filigrane Kreuzschwinger® ist Innovation
ohne Vorbild. Sein Schwingkreuz läßt den Sitzenden sanft
nach vorne und hinten schwingen und lädt zu einer dyna-
mischen Sitzhaltung ein, die zugleich physisch und psy-
chisch entspannt. Anklemmbare Sitz- und Lehnenkissen*

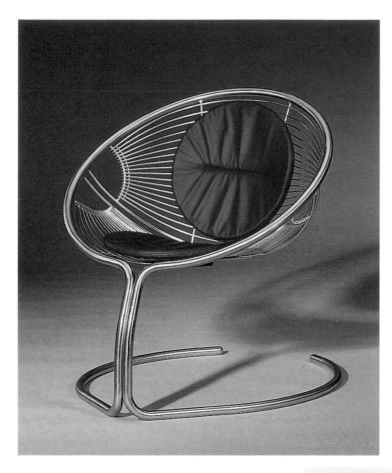

Till Behrens

Schalenschwinger,
1992

Titanium-coated
tubular steel and
steelwire construc-
tion| Rohr und
Drähte aus Edelstahl,
titanisiert | Tube et
fils d'acier inoxydable
titané

HINRICH PRAEFCKE,
WEISSACH,
HANS GRIMBERG –
EDELSTAHL, ESSEN,
FROM 1992 TO
PRESENT

▼ **Till Behrens**
Schalenschwinger,
1992

HINRICH PRAEFCKE,
WEISSACH,
HANS GRIMBERG –
EDELSTAHL, ESSEN,
FROM 1992 TO
PRESENT

steigern den hohen Sitzkomfort. Der ästhetisch anspruchs-
volle Schalenschwinger ist ein ungewöhnlich bequemes und
auch stapelbares Möbel.

Le siège filigrané empilable «Kreuzschwinger»® est une
création sans précédant. Le piètement croisé permet de
se balancer légèrement d'avant en arrière, invitant ainsi
à une posture dynamique, relaxante à la fois pour le
corps et pour l'esprit. Des coussins amovibles parachè-
vent le grand confort d'utilisation de ce modèle. Le
siège «Schalenschwinger», à l'esthétique raffinée, est
un meuble étonnamment confortable qui peut également être empilé.

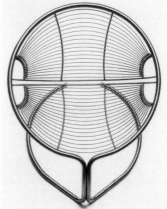

Mario Botta

Seconda, 1982

Epoxy-coated steel
frame with perforated
sheet steel seat and
expanded
polyurethane back-
rest | Rahmen aus
Stahl mit Epoxidharz-
beschichtung, Sitz-
fläche aus perforier-
tem Stahlblech,
Rückenlehne aus
aufgeschäumtem
Polyurethan | Châssis
en acier, gainage
époxy, siège en tôle
d'acier perforée,
dosseret en
polyuréthane expansé

ALIAS, GRUMELLO
DEL MONTE,
BERGAMO, FROM
1982 TO PRESENT

▼ Mario Botta
Quinta, 1985

ALIAS, GRUMELLO
DEL MONTE,
BERGAMO, FROM
1985 TO PRESENT

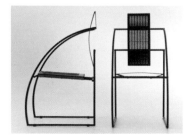

Having evolved stylistically from 1970s' High-Tech,
Botta's "Seconda" chair and Kinsman's "Vienna" chair
epitomise the "Matt Black" style of the 1980s. Arising in
part as a reaction against the decorative excesses of
Anti-Design movements such as Memphis, this type of
furniture attempted to express a rationalist aesthetic.
*Stilistisch aus dem High-Tech der 70er Jahre entwickelt,
verkörpern Bottas »Seconda«- und Kinsmans »Vienna«-
Stuhl den »Mattschwarzen Stil« der 80er Jahre. Entwürfe
dieser Art, die auch einer Gegenbewegung zum Anti-Design
à la Memphis mit seinen Dekorexzessen entspringen, sollten eine rationalistische Ästhetik zum Ausdruck bringen.*

Rodney Kinsman

Vienna, 1984

Chromed tubular steel frame with leather-covered foam-upholstered seat and back | Rahmen aus Stahlrohr, verchromt, Sitzfläche und Rückenlehne mit Schaumstoff-polsterung und Lederbezug | Châssis en tube d'acier cintré, siège et dossier en mousse recouverte de cuir

OMK DESIGN, LONDON, FROM 1984 TO PRESENT

▼ **Rodney Kinsman**
Tokyo, 1985

OMK DESIGN, LONDON, FROM 1985 TO PRESENT

Issus du high-tech des années 70, le fauteuil « Seconda » de Botta et le « Vienna » de Kinsman incarnent le style « Matt Black » des années 80. Né, pour une part, de la réaction contre les excès décoratifs des mouvements de l'anti-design comme Memphis, ce type de mobilier voulait exprimer une esthétique rationaliste.

Philippe Starck

Costes, 1982

Enamelled tubular steel frame with bent mahogany-faced plywood back and leather-covered foam-upholstered seat | Rahmen aus Stahlrohr, emailliert, Rückenlehne aus geformtem Schichtholz mit Mahagonifurnier, Sitzfläche aus Schaumstoff, gepolstert, mit Lederbezug | Châssis en tube d'acier émaillé, dossier en contreplaqué cintré, placage d'acajou, siège rembourré en mousse recouverte de cuir

DRIADE, FOSSADELLO
DI CAORSO,
PIACENZA, FROM
1985 TO PRESENT

One of Starck's best-known designs, the "Costes" was originally designed for the Café Costes in Paris. It was designed with three legs so that waiters at the café would trip up only half as many times as usual.

»Costes«, einer von Starcks bekanntesten Entwürfen, wurde ursprünglich für das gleichnamige Café in Paris entworfen. Der Stuhl wurde mit nur drei Beinen konzipiert, damit die Kellner im Café nur halb so oft stolperten wie gewöhnlich.

▶ **Philippe Starck**
Pratfall, 1982

DRIADE, FOSSADELLO
DI CAORSO,
PIACENZA, FROM
1985 TO PRESENT

L'une des créations les plus célèbres de Starck, le « Costes » fut à l'origine conçu pour le Café Costes, à Paris. Grâce à ses trois pieds au lieu de quatre, les serveurs avaient deux fois moins de chances de le bousculer.

Philippe Starck

Ed Archer, 1986

Leather-upholstered
tubular steel frame
with aluminium leg |
Rahmen aus Stahl-
rohr mit Lederbezug,
Aluminiumfuß |
Châssis en tube
d'acier, cuir
rembourré, pied en
aluminium

DRIADE, FOSSADELLO
DI CAORSO,
PIACENZA, FROM
1987 TO PRESENT

▼ **Philippe Starck**
J. (Serie Lang), 1986

DRIADE, FOSSADELLO
DI CAORSO,
PIACENZA, FROM
1987 TO PRESENT

During the 1980s Starck designed a plethora of chairs, each with a character-provoking name. "Ed Archer" is one of the most elegant of these designs which were intended for small to medium-scale production.

In den 80er Jahren entwarf Starck eine große Zahl von Stühlen und gab jedem Modell einen seinem Charakter entsprechenden Namen. »Ed Archer« ist einer der elegantesten dieser Entwürfe, die für die Produktion in kleiner oder mittelgroßer Serie gedacht waren.

Pendant les années 80, Starck dessina une pléthore de sièges, chacun portant un nom provocant. « Ed Archer » est l'une de ses créations les plus élégantes, conçue pour une production en petite ou moyenne série.

Mario Bellini & Dieter Thiel

Imago, 1984

Aluminium frame, leather-covered polyurethane foam upholstery, double castors | Rahmen aus Aluminium auf Doppelrollen, Polsterung aus Polyurethanschaumstoff mit Lederbezug | Châssis en aluminium, rembourrage en mousse de polyuréthane recouverte de cuir, doubles roulettes

VITRA, BASLE, FROM 1984 TO PRESENT

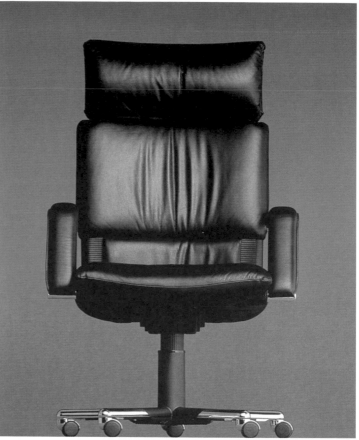

▼ Mario Bellini & Dieter Thiel
Persona office chair, 1984

VITRA, BASLE, FROM 1984 TO PRESENT

Developed from the earlier "Persona" collection and the more luxurious "Imago" series, the "Figura" programme includes not only a basic operator's chair, a conference chair and sled-base chairs, but also executive and tandem seating options. The "Figura" office chairs move automatically with the body to provide anatomical support as well as the freedom of movement necessary for comfort.

Zur Sitzmöbelserie »Figura«, einer Weiterentwicklung der Kollektion »Persona« und der luxuriösen Serie »Imago«, gehören nicht nur das Basismodell eines Bürodrehstuhls, ein Konferenzstuhl und ein Modell auf Gleitfüßen, sondern auch Vorstandssessel und Doppelsitzer.

Mario Bellini & Dieter Thiel

Figura, 1985

Epoxy-coated metal frame, column and base with textile-covered polyurethane foam upholstery, height adjustment mechanism and castors | Höhen-verstellbarer Rahmen aus epoxidharzbe-schichtetem Metall auf Rollen, Polsterung aus Polyurethan-schaumstoff mit Stoffbezug | Châssis, colonne et piètement en métal, gainage époxy, rembourrage en mousse de polyuréthane recouverte de tissu, réglage de la hauteur, roulettes

VITRA, BASLE, FROM 1985 TO PRESENT

Die »Figura«-Bürostühle folgen automatisch den Bewegungen des Körpers und bieten damit sowohl anatomisch richtigen Halt wie auch die Bewegungsfreiheit, die für den Sitzkomfort entscheidend ist.

Issu de la ligne « Persona » et de la série « Imago » plus luxueuse, le programme « Figura » comprenait non seulement un fauteuil classique, une chaise de salle de conférences et des fauteuils sur pied-traîneau, mais également des modèles de direction et à monter en tandem. Le siège se déplace automatiquement avec le poids du corps pour offrir un soutien anatomique permanent et une grande liberté de mouvement.

Shiro Kuramata

Sing Sing Sing, 1985

Anodised tubular
metal frame with
wire-mesh seating
section | Rahmen aus
eloxiertem Stahlrohr,
Sitzfläche und
Rückenlehne aus
Drahtgeflecht |
Châssis tubulaire en
métal anodisé, siège
en treillis métallique

XO, PARIS, FROM
1985

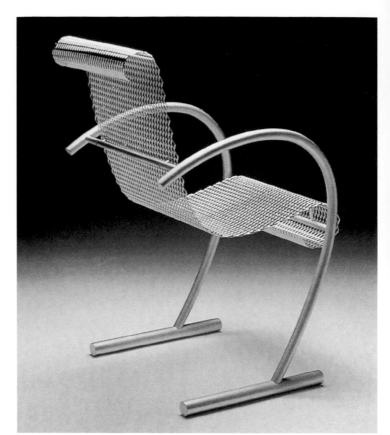

▶ **Shiro Kuramata**
Koko, 1986

XO, PARIS, FROM
1986

▶▶ **Shiro Kuramata**
Apple Honey, 1986

Shiro Kuramata

*How High the
Moon, 1986*

*Nickel-plated wire-
mesh construction |
Konstruktion aus
vernickeltem Streck-
metall | Treillis en
métal nickelé*

KUROSAKI, TOKYO,
FROM 1986
(REISSUED BY VITRA,
BASLE, FROM 1987
TO PRESENT)

▼ Shiro Kuramata
Begin the Beguine,
Homage to
Hoffmann, 1985

Through his intriguing choice of materials and graceful
use of proportions, Kuramata was able to express a
highly refined sense of space and lightness in his poetic
designs.
*Durch die faszinierende Materialauswahl und anmutig ge-
stalteten Proportionen zeigen diese poetischen Entwürfe
Kuramatas einen ausgeprägten Sinn für Raum und
Leichtigkeit.*
Par un choix étonnant de matériaux et une utilisation
élégante des proportions, Kuramata réussissait à exprimer un sens hautement raffiné de l'espace et de la
légèreté dans des créations poétiques.

Philippe Starck

Sarapis, 1985

Enamelled steel and
tubular steel
construction |
Einbrennlackierter
Stahl und Stahlrohr |
Acier émaillé et tube
d'acier

DRIADE, FOSSADELLO
DI CAORSO,
PIACENZA, FROM
1985 TO PRESENT

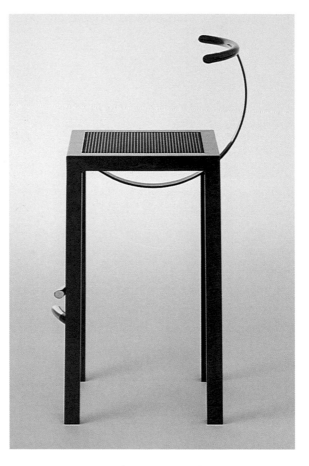

With its sprung steel backrest, "Sarapis" epitomises the
"Matt Black" style, but "Dr. Glob" was more commercially successful. Starck defends his use of plastic as
"the only real ecological answer".

*Mit seiner Rückenstütze aus federndem Stahl verkörpert
»Sarapis« den »Mattschwarzen Stil«, aber »Dr. Glob«
war der größere Markterfolg. Starck verteidigt die Verwendung von Kunststoff als »das ökologisch einzige Wahre«.*

Avec ce dosseret sur ressort, « Sarapis » incarne le style
« Matt Black ». Le modèle « Dr. Glob » a cependant
connu un plus grand succès commercial. Starck se fait
l'avocat du plastique qui, pour lui, est « la seule réponse
vraiment écologique ».

Philippe Starck

Dr. Glob, 1988

Tubular steel frame with polypropylene seat/front leg section | Rahmen aus Stahlrohr, Sitzfläche und vordere Stuhlbeine aus Polypropylen | Châssis en tube métallique, siège et pieds avant en polypropylène

KARTELL, NOVIGLIO, MILAN, FROM 1988 TO PRESENT

◄ Philippe Starck
Super Glob chairs, 1990

KARTELL, NOVIGLIO, MILAN, FROM 1990 TO PRESENT

◄◄ Philippe Starck
Hi Glob stools, 1990

KARTELL, NOVIGLIO, MILAN, FROM 1990 TO PRESENT

515

Maurizio Peregalli

Glasnost, 1988

Epoxy-painted square
tubular steel frame
with moulded
polyurethane seat and
back | Rahmen aus
Vierkant-Stahlrohr,
epoxidlackiert,
Sitzfläche und
Rückenlehne aus
geformtem
Polyurethan | Châssis
en tube d'acier de
section carrée,
peinture époxy, siège
et dossier en
polyuréthane

NOTO-ZEUS, MILAN,
FROM 1988 TO
PRESENT

▼ **Anna Anselmi**
Kite, 1985

BIEFFEPLAST,
CASELLE DI SELVAZ-
ZANO, FROM
1985 TO PRESENT

Peregalli established the Zeus gallery in Milan in 1984
and co-founded the manufacturing company, Noto. His
designs, such as "Glasnost", are characterised by the
use of simple geometric forms.
*Peregalli gründete 1984 die Galerie Zeus in Mailand und
war Mitgründer der Herstellerfirma Noto. Charakteristisch
für seine Entwürfe, wie hier beim Stuhl »Glasnost«, ist die
Verwendung einfacher geometrischer Formen.*
Peregalli fonda la galerie Zeus à Milan en 1984. Il est
également cofondateur du fabricant Noto. Ses projets,
comme le fauteuil « Glasnost », se caractérisent par des
formes géométriques simples.

Jorge Pensi

Toledo, 1986–1988

*Cast-aluminium
frame | Rahmen aus
Gußaluminium |
Fonte d'aluminium*

AMAT, MARTORELL,
BARCELONA, FROM
1989 TO PRESENT

The "Toledo" is a reworking of earlier designs used in Spanish open-air cafés. Its perforated ribs allude to antique armour, while its title refers to the city renowned for the sharpness of its steel sword blades.

»Toledo« ist eine Überarbeitung älterer Modelle, die in spanischen Straßencafés verwendet wurden. Seine perforierten Rippen erinnern an alte Rüstungen, der Name ist eine Anspielung auf die Stadt, die für die Schärfe ihrer Schwertklingen berühmt war.

Le « Toledo » est une interprétation de modèles antérieurs de chaises de cafés espagnols. Ses côtes perforées rappellent une armure ancienne. Son nom évoque la ville célèbre pour la finesse des lames de ses épées.

Charles Pollock

Penelope, 1982

Chromed tubular steel frame with steel wire-mesh seating section and rubber tubing | Rahmen aus Stahlrohr, verchromt, Sitzschale aus perforiertem Stahlblech, Gummischlauch | Châssis en tube d'acier chromé, coquille en treillis d'acier, gaines en caoutchouc

CASTELLI, OZZANO DELL'EMILIA, BOLOGNA, FROM 1982 TO PRESENT

Pollock worked in Nelson's office in the 1950s on the "Swagged Leg" series, which included the "MAA" with rubber shock mounts. This experience may have influenced his use of rubber tubing as shock absorbers on the "Penelope". The chair's metal mesh seat provides a great deal of breathability.

Pollock hat in den 50er Jahren im Büro von Nelson an der »Swagged Leg«-Serie gearbeitet, zu der auch der »MAA« mit Gummipuffern gehört. Diese Erfahrung mag ihn beim Entwurf des »Penelope«-Stuhls dazu angeregt haben, Gummischlauch als Stoßdämpfer zu verwenden. Die Sitzschale aus perforiertem Metallblech ist sehr atmungsaktiv.

Au cours des années 50, Pollock travailla dans l'agence de Nelson sur la série « Swagged Leg », qui comprenait le « MAA » monté sur amortisseurs en caoutchouc. Cette expérience a peut-être influencé son recours aux gaines de caoutchouc du « Penelope ». Ce siège en treillis métallique offre le maximum de respiration.

Vico Magistretti

Silver, 1989

Aluminium and tubular aluminium frame with injection-moulded polypropylene seat and back, plastic castors and swivelling mechanism | Drehbarer Rahmen aus Aluminium und Aluminiumrohr auf Plastikrollen, Sitzfläche und Rückenlehne aus spritzgußgeformtem Polypropylen | Châssis en aluminium et tube d'aluminium, siège et dossier en polypropylène moulé, mécanisme pivotant, roulettes

DE PADOVA, MILAN, FROM 1989 TO PRESENT

▼ **Vico Magistretti**
Silver II, stacking chair, 1989

DE PADOVA, MILAN, FROM 1989 TO PRESENT

Inspired by the form of an earlier Thonet chair designed by Breuer in 1925, the "Silver" was one of the first chair programmes designed specifically for home-office use.

Angeregt durch die Gestaltung eines Stuhls, den Breuer 1925 für Thonet entworfen hat, ist »Silver« eine der ersten Stuhlserien, die eigens für das häusliche Arbeitszimmer entworfen wurden.

Inspiré par la forme d'un fauteuil Thonet dessiné par Breuer en 1925, le « Silver » représente l'un des premiers programmes de sièges de bureau spécialement conçus pour la maison.

Niels Diffrient

Diffrient
Operational, 1980

Stamped steel frame with cast-aluminium base and column, textile covered moulded polyurethane foam-upholstered seat and back | Rahmen aus gepreßtem Stahl, Säule und Fuß aus Gußaluminium, Sitzschale und Rückenlehne aus geformtem Polyurethanschaumstoff und Stoffbezug | Châssis en acier estampé, colonne et piètement en fonte d'aluminium, siège et dossier en mousse de polyuréthane moulée recouverte de tissu

KNOLL INTERNATIONAL, NEW YORK, FROM 1980

▼ Niels Diffrient
Diffrient Executive Hi and Low office armchairs, 1980

KNOLL INTERNATIONAL, NEW YORK FROM 1980

This chair afforded much comfort through a high level of adaptation to the human body. According to Diffrient, "There is no perfect chair ... The best chair is still only good for a few hours, and then you ought to get up." *Dieser Stuhl bietet durch die Anpassung an den menschlichen Körper viel Sitzkomfort. Diffrient zufolge gibt es »keinen perfekten Stuhl ... Auch der beste Stuhl ist nur gut für ein paar Stunden, dann sollte man aufstehen.«* Le grand confort de ce fauteuil est dû à son degré élevé d'adaptabilité aux mouvements du corps humain. Selon Diffrient : « Le fauteuil parfait n'existe pas ... Le meilleur fauteuil ne l'est que pendant quelques heures. Ensuite vous devez quand même vous lever. »

William
Stumf &
Donald
Chadwick

Equa, 1984

*Aluminium frame,
moulded thermo-
plastic seat shell,
polyurethane foam |
Rahmen aus Alu-
minium, Sitz- und
Rückenschale aus
geformtem Thermo-
plast, Polyurethan-
schaumstoff | Châssis
en aluminium,
coquille de siège et
accoudoirs en
thermoplastique
moulé, mousse de
polyuréthane*

▼ Geoff Hollington
Hollington office
armchair, 1989

HERMAN MILLER
FURNITURE CO.,
MICHIGAN, FROM
1989 TO PRESENT

Developed from their earlier "Ergon", Stumpf and
Chadwick's "Equa" has a flexing back and provides even
greater comfort. The endurance of this design can be
linked to Stumpf's credo that, "Quality is everything".
*»Equa« von Stumpf und Chadwick, eine Weiterentwick-
lung ihres Modells »Ergon«, hat eine flexible Rückenlehne
und bietet darum noch größeren Sitzkomfort. Die Strapazierfähigkeit dieses Modells hat wohl etwas zu tun mit
Stumpfs Credo »Qualität ist alles«.*
Décliné à partir de l' « Ergon », l' « Equa » de Stumpf et
Chadwick possède un dossier flexible et offre un confort
encore supérieur. Sa solidité renvoie au credo de
Stumpf selon lequel « Tout est dans la qualité ».

Roy Fleetwood

Wing, 1988

Steel frame with leather-covered foam upholstery | Rahmen aus Stahl, Schaumstoffpolsterung mit Lederbezug | Châssis en acier, rembourrage en mousse recouverte de cuir

VITRA, BASLE, FROM 1988

The architect, Roy Fleetwood, adapts the construction techniques of High-Tech buildings and applies them to furniture design. The frame of his highly engineered "Wing" sofa resembles the span of a bridge, while its thrusting seat section is reminiscent of an aircraft wing. Martin Székely's "Pi" chaise longue also has a powerful engineering rhetoric. The oblique line of the back intersects the arc of the seat in a very graphic way – the "Pi's" profile appearing as though lifted directly off an engineering blueprint.

Der Architekt Roy Fleetwood setzt Konstruktionstechniken von High-Tech-Gebäuden entsprechend abgewandelt für das Möbeldesign ein. Der Rahmen des mit technischem Sachverstand konstruierten Sofas »Wing« ähnelt einem Brückenträger, die vorspringende Sitzfläche dagegen erinnert an die Tragfläche

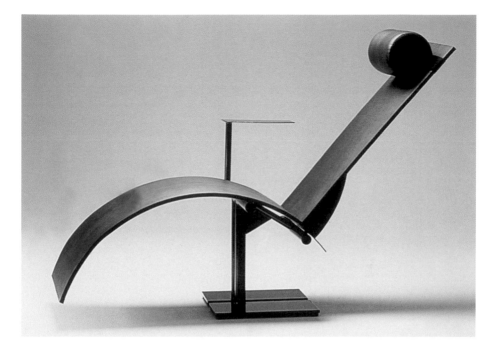

eines Flugzeugs. Auch Martin Székelys Liege »Pi« hat eine ausdrucksstarke Konstruktionstechnik. Auf graphische Weise schneidet die schräge Linie der Rückenlehne den Bogen der Sitzfläche. Man hat den Eindruck, als sei das Profil der Liege direkt der Konstruktionszeichnung eines Maschinenbauers entnommen. L'architecte Roy Fleetwood adapte les techniques de construction des immeubles high-tech pour les appliquer au design de mobilier. Le châssis complexe de ce canapé « Wing » fait penser à un tablier de pont et le profil de son dossier rappelle celui d'une aile d'avion. La chaise longue « Pi » de Martin Székely évoque également un travail de construction mécanique impressionnant. L'oblique du dossier coupe l'arc du siège de façon très graphique. Le profil de la chaise « Pi » semble provenir directement d'un schéma d'ingénieur.

Martin Székely

Chaise Pi, 1984

Painted moulded plywood, sheet metal and tubular metal frame with leather-covered foam-uphol-stered headrest | Rahmen aus geformtem Schicht-holz, Schichtholz, Stahlblech und Stahlrohr, lackiert, Kopfstütze aus Schaumstoff mit Lederbezug | Contre-plaqué moulé peint, contre-plaqué, châssis en tôle et tube de métal, repose-tête en mousse recouverte de cuir

NÉOTÙ, PARIS, FROM 1984

Frank O. Gehry

Little Beaver, 1980

Laminated cardboard construction | Konstruktion aus verleimter Wellpappe | Carton contrecollé

NEW CITY EDITIONS
FOR VITRA, BASLE,
FROM 1980

▼ Frank O. Gehry
Experimental Edges
(Little Beaver,
Carumba & Bubbles)
at the Fred
Hoffmann Gallery,
1987

Unlike his "Easy Edges" series, which was intended as low-cost seating suitable for mass-production, Gehry's "Experimental Edges" was conceived as a limited edition which explored the expressive qualities of corrugated cardboard. "Chair/Chair", also issued as limited edition "Art Furniture" by Vitra, was designed by the artist, Richard Artschwager. Its oversized proportions allow two people to sit side-by-side in relative comfort.

Anders als die Serie »Easy Edges«, die als preiswertes Sitzmöbelprogramm für die Großproduktion gedacht war, hat Gehry die Serie »Experimental Edges« für eine limitierte Auflage entworfen, mit der er die expressiven Qualitäten von

Richard
Artschwager

Chair/Chair,
1986—1987

Bent plywood and
laminated wood
frame with leather-
covered foam
upholstery | Rahmen
aus geformtem
Schichtholz und
laminiertem Holz,
Schaumstoffpolste-
rung mit Lederbezug |
Contre-plaqué cintré,
bois laminé,
rembourrage en
mousse recouverte de
cuir

VITRA, BASLE, FROM
1987 TO PRESENT

Wellpappe erforschen wollte. Den »Chair/Chair«, ebenfalls in limitierter Auflage
als »Kunst-Möbel« von Vitra vertrieben, hat der Künstler Richard Artschwager
entworfen. Mit seinen überdimensionalen Proportionen bietet er einigermaßen
bequem auch zwei Personen nebeneinander Platz.

À la différence de sa série « Easy Edges », qui se voulait un produit bon marché pour la production en grande série, celle des « Experimental Edges »
fut conçue pour une édition limitée et explorait les possibilités expressives
du carton ondulé. Le modèle « Chair/Chair », également fabriqué en petit
nombre (« mobilier d'art ») par Vitra, fut créé par l'artiste Richard
Artschwager. Ses proportions surdimensionnées permettent à deux
personnes de s'asseoir côte à côte dans un confort relatif.

Cini Boeri & Tomu Katayanagi

Ghost, 1987

Moulded glass construction | Konstruktion aus geformtem Glas | Verre moulé

FIAM, TAVULLIA, FROM 1987 TO PRESENT

The "Ghost" chair is uniquely formed from a single piece of moulded 12 mm thick glass which is toughened for additional strength. This completely transparent design comes close to realising Breuer's vision of a chair with an invisible form.

Der »Ghost«-Stuhl wird aus 12 mm dickem, gehärtetem Glas aus einem Stück geformt. Dieser völlig transparente Entwurf nähert sich Breuers Vision eines Stuhls mit unsichtbarer Form.

Le fauteuil « Ghost » est constitué d'une seule feuille de verre moulé renforcé de 12 mm d'épaisseur. Ce modèle entièrement transparent rappelle la vision de Breuer qui avait imaginé un siège sans forme visible.

Danny Lane

Etruscan, 1984

Forged mild steel frame with glass seat and back | Rahmen aus unlegiertem Stahl, geschmiedet, Sitzfläche und Rückenlehne aus Glas | Châssis en acier doux forgé, siège et dossier en verre

DANNY LANE,
LONDON, FROM
1984

▼ Danny Lane ·
Solomon chair, 1988

DANNY LANE,
LONDON, FROM
1988

The "Etruscan" chair uses glass expressively while demonstrating Lane's masterful handling of the material. The slab-like seat and back with their polished jagged edges oppose industrial uniformity.

Der Stuhl »Etruscan« nutzt die expressiven Qualitäten von Glas und zeigt Lanes meisterhaften Umgang mit diesem Material. Seine Sitzfläche und Rückenlehne in Baumscheibenform heben sich mit ihren schroffen, polierten Kanten gegen das Einerlei industrieller Formen ab.

La chaise « Etruscan » fait un usage très expressif du verre et révèle la maîtrise que Lane a de ce matériau. Le siège et le dossier aux bords déchiquetés mais polis contrastent avec l'uniformité des sièges industriels.

Tom Dixon

Kitchen, 1987

Welded mild steel
constructions
incorporating iron
frying pans and
ladles | *Konstruktion
aus unlegiertem Stahl
mit eingearbeiteten
Bratpfannen und
Schöpfkellen* | *Acier
doux forgé, avec
incorporation de
poêles à frire et de
louches*

SPACE, LONDON,
FROM 1987 TO
PRESENT

Working outside of the industrial process, Dixon explored the potential of spontaneous creativity in design.
His early designs, such as the "Kitchen" chair, incorporated "objets trouvés" which were welded together,
thus emphasising their rough-and-ready production
methods. Some of his later designs, such as the
"S" chair, have been adapted by established manufacturers for systemised production.

*Dixon arbeitet losgelöst vom industriellen Fertigungsprozeß
und erkundet Möglichkeiten spontaner Kreativität im
Design. Seine frühen Entwürfe, wie z. B. der »Kitchen«-
Stuhl, integrieren zusammengeschweißte »objets trouvés«,
womit das Improvisierte dieser Schaffensweise betont wird.
Einige seiner späteren Entwürfe, wie z. B. der »S«-Stuhl,
sind von etablierten Möbelfirmen an die Serienproduktion
angepaßt worden.*

En dehors de toute préoccupation industrielle, Dixon explore le potentiel de la créativité spontanée en matière
de design. Ses premières créations, comme cette chaise

▶ **Tom Dixon**
Felt upholstered S
chair, 1992

CAPPELLINI, AROSIO,
COMO, FROM
C. 1992 TO PRESENT

« Kitchen », incorporent des objets trouvés soudés ensemble et soulignent les très simples méthodes de production adoptées. Certaines de ses dernières œuvres comme la chaise « S » ont été adaptées par des fabricants pour pouvoir être fabriquées en série.

Tom Dixon

S chairs, 1988

Bent mild steel frame with either latex, rush or woven cane seating section | Rahmen aus unlegiertem Stahl, Bespannung aus Latex bzw. Binsen- oder Rohrgeflecht | Châssis en acier doux cintré, siège en jonc

SPACE, LONDON, FROM 1988 (REISSUED BY CAPPELLINI, AROSIO, COMO, FROM C. 1992 TO PRESENT)

Borek Sípek

Bambi, 1983

Enamelled tubular metal frame with brass fittings and sheer textile covering | Rahmen aus Stahlrohr, einbrennlackiert, Messingbeschläge, Rückenlehne mit Seidenbezug | Châssis en tube métallique émaillé, garnitures en laiton, tissu

NÉOTÙ, PARIS, FROM 1988

▼ **Borek Sípek**
Prokok, 1988

DRIADE, FOSSADELLO DI CAORSO, PIACENZA, FROM 1988

With its apparent structural instability and frail form, the "Bambi" is one of Sípek's most whimsical designs. He believes that it is "primitive" to consider functionalism the most important element of design.

Mit seiner offensichtlich instabilen und fragilen Konstruktion ist »Bambi« einer von Sípeks wunderlichsten Entwürfen. Er findet es »primitiv«, Funktionalität als das wichtigste Element eines Entwurfs zu betrachten.

Avec sa fragilité structurelle apparente et ses formes frêles, « Bambi » est l'une des créations les plus baroques de Sípek qui trouve « primaire » de considérer le fonctionnalisme comme le plus important élément du design.

Elisabeth
Garouste &
Mattia Bonetti

Prince Imperiale,
1985

Painted wood
construction with
Raffia | Konstruktion
aus bemaltem Holz
und Raffiabast | Bois
peint et raphia

NÉOTÙ, PARIS, FROM
1985

▼ Elisabeth
Garouste & Mattia
Bonetti
Barbare, 1981

NÉOTÙ, PARIS, FROM
1981

Garouste and Bonetti are among the leading "modern
barbarians" of the French Primitive movement. Their
designs are inspired by tribal art, chiefly African.
Garouste and Bonetti gehören zu den führenden »moder-
nen Barbaren« der französischen Primitivismus-Bewegung.
Aus der Stammeskunst, vor allem der afrikanischen, er-
halten sie ihre Anregungen für ihre äußerst detaillierten
Entwürfe.
Garouste et Bonetti font partie des « barbares modernes » les plus célèbres du mouvement primitiviste
français. Ses designs sont inspirés par l'art tribal,
principalement africain.

Shiro Kuramata

Indian Rhapsody,
1989

Tubular steel frames,
acrylic sheet back |
Rahmen aus Stahl-
rohr, Ruckenlehne aus
Acrylglas, Sitzfläche
gepolstert | Châssis en
tube d'acier, dossier
en acrylique, sièges
rembourrés

TOSH SASH CO.,
TOYKO, FROM 1989

Named after the central figure in Tennessee Williams' *A Streetcar Named Desire*, "Miss Blanche" possesses a poetic neo-romanticism with its fall of red paper roses suggesting, perhaps, the frailty of love.

Der Stuhl »Miss Blanche«, nach der Hauptfigur aus Tennessee Williams' Stück »Endstation Sehnsucht« benannt, zeigt mit seinen schwebenden roten Papierrosen einen poetischen Neo-Romantizismus, vielleicht ein Bild für die Flüchtigkeit der Liebe.

Nommé « Miss Blanche » d'après la célèbre pièce de Tennessee Williams *Un tramway nommé Désir*, ce siège « Miss Blanche » affiche un caractère poétique et néoromantique dans une pluie de roses en papier rouge suggérant, peut-être, la fragilité de l'amour.

Shiro Kuramata

Miss Blanche, 1989

*Paper flowers cast in
acrylic resin with
tubular aluminium
legs | Stuhlbeine aus
Aluminiumrohr,
Sitzschale aus Acryl
mit eingegossenen
Papierblumen | Pieds
en aluminium, siège,
dossier et accoudoirs
en résine acrylique
avec inclusion de
fleurs en papier*

KOKUYO, TOKYO,
FROM 1989

Jasper Morrison

Thinking Man's Chair, 1987

Painted tubular steel and flat steel bar construction | Rahmen aus Stahlrohr und Flachstahl, lackiert | Tube d'acier et lattes en acier plat peints

CAPPELLINI, AROSIO, COMO, FROM 1987 TO PRESENT

The "Thinking Man's Chair" was designed for both indoor and outdoor use. Constructed from a combination of welded tubular and flat steel, it was conceived for limited production. The circular discs on its arms act as supports for drinking glasses.

Der »Thinking Man's Chair« ist sowohl für den Gebrauch in Innenräumen als auch für den Außenbereich entworfen worden. Seine Konstruktion aus geschweißtem Flachstahl und Stahlrohr war für eine limitierte Produktion konzipiert. Die kreisförmigen Platten am Ende der Armlehnen bieten Abstellplatz für Trinkgläser.

Ce fauteuil bas est destiné à un usage intérieur ou extérieur. Combinant le tube et l'acier plat, il a été conçu pour une production limitée. Les disques en bout d'accoudoirs servent de plateaux pour les verres.

Ron Arad

Schizzo, 1989

Birch-faced, moulded plywood construction with tubular steel connections | Aus formgebogenem Schichtholz, Birkenholzoberfläche, Stahlrohrverbindungen | Contre-plaqué moulé, placage de bouleau, pièces d'assemblage en tube d'acier

VITRA, BASLE, FROM 1989 TO PRESENT

Sometimes referred to as the "Two in One" chair, the highly novel "Schizzo" is made up of two separate yet identical chairs which slot together to form a single entity. Both elements are functional whether they are split or joined.

Der innovative »Schizzo«, auch als »Two in One«-Stuhl bekannt, besteht aus zwei einzelnen, identischen Stühlen, die zusammengesteckt eine Einheit bilden. Ob einzeln oder zusammengeschoben, auf beiden Elementen kann man sitzen.

Parfois appelée « Two in One », cette très novatrice « Schizzo » se compose de deux chaises identiques mais indépendantes qui s'imbriquent pour ne former qu'un seul siège. Les deux éléments sont fonctionnels, qu'ils soient utilisés séparément ou ensemble.

Marc Newson

Felt, 1994

Fibreglass-reinforced polyester and anodised aluminium frame with textile upholstery | Konstruktion aus fiberglasverstärktem Polyester und eloxiertem Aluminium, Stoffpolsterung | Châssis en aluminium anodisé et polyester renforcé de fibre de verre, rembourrage textile

CAPPELLINI, AROSIO, COMO, FROM 1994 TO PRESENT

Marc Newson's designs are characterised by strong sculptural forms with an innate biomorphism. The form of his "Orgone" chaise is reminiscent of a surfboard – a testament to Newson's Australian origins – while his "Felt" chair has a powerful anthropomorphism. Sacrificing comfort to aesthetics, the "Lockheed Lounge" was influenced by the riveted structure of aircraft and stylistically reflects 1930s' streamlining. It is very expensive due to its laborious and time-consuming method of manufacture.

Typisch für Marc Newsons Entwürfe sind skulpturale, biomorphe Formen. Die Liege »Orgone« erinnert an die Form eines Surfbretts – ein Verweis auf Newsons Herkunft aus Australien. »Felt« dagegen hat etwas stark Anthropomorphes.

▶ **Marc Newson**
Orgone, 1991

CAPPELLINI, AROSIO, COMO, FROM 1991 TO PRESENT

»Lockheed Lounge«, von der genieteten Oberfläche eines Flugzeugs und der Stromlinienbegeisterung der 30er Jahre beeinflußt, opfert den Sitzkomfort der Ästhetik. Die Liege ist wegen der arbeitsintensiven und aufwendigen Herstellung sehr teuer.

Les créations de Marc Newson se caractérisent par des formes sculpturales affirmées qui intégrent des aspects biomorphiques. La forme de sa chaise longue « Orgone » rappelle une planche de surf – évocation des origines australiennes du designer – alors que son fauteuil « Felt » est presque anthropomorphique. Sacrifiant le confort à l'esthétique, la méridienne « Lockheed Lounge » s'inspire des constructions rivetées des avions et renvoie au style épuré des années 30. Les méthodes artisanales et le temps de fabrication qu'elle requiért en font un meuble très coûteux.

Marc Newson

MN-01 LC1,
Lockheed Lounge,
1985–1986

Fibreglass-reinforced polyester core covered in riveted sheet aluminium skin |
Kern aus fiberglasverstärktem Polyester, überzogen mit einer Haut aus genietetem Aluminiumblech |
Âme en polyester renforcé de fibre de verre et recouverte d'une peau de feuille d'aluminium riveté

IDÉE, TOKYO, FROM 1986 TO PRESENT

Philippe Starck

Lola Mundo, 1986

Ebonised wood seat
and folding back with
cast-aluminium legs
and rubber studs |
Sitzfläche und
klappbare Rücken-
lehne aus Holz,
schwarz gebeizt, Zier-
nägel mit Gummi-
köpfen, Stuhlbeine
aus Gußaluminium |
Sìège et dossier en
bois noirci, pieds en
fonte d'aluminium,
clous en caoutchouc

DRIADE, FOSSADELLO
DI CAORSO,
PIACENZA, FROM
1988 TO PRESENT

▶ **Philippe Starck**
Dr. Sonderbar, 1983

XO, PARIS, FROM
1983 TO PRESENT

◀ **Philippe Starck**
Von Vogelsang, 1984

DRIADE, FOSSADELLO
DI CAORSO, PIA-
CENZA, FROM 1985
TO PRESENT

Philippe Starck

Richard III, 1981

Moulded rigid
structural polyure-
thane form, painted
with polyurethane
enamel | Geformtes
und ausgehärtetes
Polyurethan,
beschichtet mit Lack
auf Polyurethanbasis |
Forme en polyuré-
thane rigide moulée,
peinte d'un émail
polyuréthane

BALERI, LALLIO,
BERGAMO, FROM
1981 TO PRESENT

Starck not only borrows references from previous decorative styles, he also imbues his designs with character through the use of clever and often humorous titles. The Louis XV-style cabriole legs of "Lola Mundo" are feminine while the visual solidity of "Richard III" is powerfully masculine.

Starck entlehnt nicht nur Elemente aus älteren dekorativen Stilen, sondern er gibt seinen Entwürfen auch Charakter durch hintersinnige, oft humorvolle Namen. »Lola Mundos«, im Louis-Quinze-Stil geschwungene Beine haben etwas sehr Feminines, der optisch massive »Richard III« dagegen wirkt kraftvoll und maskulin.

Starck emprunte ses références à des styles décoratifs antérieurs et enrichit ses modèles de noms astucieux, souvent drôles. Les pieds cambrés style Louis XV de la chaise « Lola Mundo » sont féminins à l'extrême alors que la massivité frontale du « Richard III » est puissamment masculine.

Aldo Rossi

Parigi, 1989

Enamelled tubular aluminium frame with leather-covered polyurethane foam upholstery | Rahmen aus Vierkantalumi-niumrohr, Polsterung aus Polyurethan-schaumstoff mit Lederbezug | Châssis en tube d'aluminium émaillé, rembourrage en mousse de poly-uréthane recouverte de cuir

UNIFOR, TURATE, FROM 1989 TO PRESENT

Rossi is one of the foremost exponents of the Post-Modern style but he eschews decorative embellishment in favour of quirky forms. Here, the formal geometry of his "Parigi" chair is visually disrupted by its disquieting tilt.

Rossi, ein Protagonist der Postmoderne, setzt nicht auf Dekor, sondern auf gewagte Formen, so z. B. beim Sessel »Parigi«, dessen starre Geometrie optisch gebrochen wird durch die beunruhigende Neigung.

Rossi est l'un des plus brillants représentants du style postmoderne mais n'en évite pas moins les ornements purement décoratifs au profit de formes bizarres. La géométrie de ce fauteuil « Parigi » est visuellement bousculée par une inclinaison dérangeante.

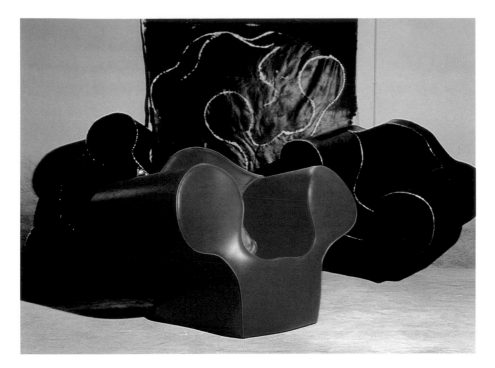

Possessing both structural integrity and narrative content, Arad's character-ful seat furniture powerfully conveys his interest in line and movement. He effects movement either physically, through the springing and/or rocking action of his chairs, or gesturally, through compelling a shift of visual attention across the highly graphic lines of his designs.

Arads charaktervolle Sitzmöbel weisen sowohl strukturelle Geschlossenheit als auch narrativen Gehalt auf, und sie zeigen sein Interesse an Linien und Bewegung. Letztere erzielt er entweder physikalisch, durch das Federn und/oder Schaukeln seiner Stühle, oder eher formal, indem er den Blick zwingt, den betont graphischen Linien seiner Entwürfe zu folgen.

Riches à la fois de leur forte intégrité structurelle et de leur contenu narratif, les sièges de Ron Arad montrent l'intérêt de leur designer pour la ligne et le mouvement. Il traduit le mouvement à la fois physiquement par des effets de ressort ou de balancement, et graphiquement en organisant le glisse-ment du regard sur les contours des formes.

Ron Arad

Big Easy Red Volume 1, 1989

Vinyl-upholstered, welded mild steel construction | Rahmen aus verschweißtem Stahlblech mit Vinylpolsterung | Acier doux soudé, rembourrage vinyle

ONE OFF, LONDON, FROM 1989

Ron Arad
After Spring / Before Summer, 1992

ONE OFF. LONDON, FROM 1992

Ron Arad
Creature Comfort, 1992

ONE OFF. LONDON, FROM 1992

Ron Arad
Doubletake, No Duckling No Swan, Soft in the Head, 1992

ONE OFF. LONDON, FROM 1992

Ron Arad
Up Like A Bear, 1992

ONE OFF. LONDON, FROM 1992

Oscar Tusquets Blanca

Gaulino, 1987

Stained oak frame with moulded plywood seat uphol stered in leather | Rahmen aus Eiche, gebeizt, Sitzfläche aus geformtem Schichtholz mit Lederbezug | Châssis en chêne teinté, siège en contre-plaqué moulé, légèrement rembourré et recouvert de cuir

CARLOS JANÉ CAMACHO, BARCELONA, FROM 1987 TO PRESENT

▼ Cover of Carlos Jané Camacho catalogue

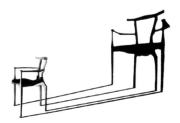

The form of the "Gaulino" evokes the gaunt silhouette of Cervantes' Don Quixote, giving the design a powerful Spanish character.

Die Gestalt des »Gaulino«-Stuhls läßt an die hagere Silhouette von Cervantes' Don Quixote denken, was diesem Entwurf einen ausdruckstarken spanischen Charakter verleiht.

Le « Gaulino » évoque la silhouette décharnée de Don Quichotte et donne à ce siège un caractère puissamment espagnol.

Roberto
Lazzeroni

Cigarra, 1988

*Carved cherry
construction |
Konstruktion aus
Kirschholz, ge-
schnitzt | Cerisier
sculpté*

CECCOTTI, CASCINA,
PISA, FROM
1988 TO PRESENT

▼ Roberto Lazzeroni
Chumbera Segunda

CECCOTTI, CASCINA,
PISA, FROM
1988 TO PRESENT

Lazzeroni 's elegant designs for Ceccotti, a firm which
prides itself on superlative craftsmanship, are based on
traditional forms which have been gently updated with a
subtle modernity.

*Lazzeronis elegante Entwürfe für Ceccotti, einen Hersteller,
der auf seine überragende Handwerkskunst stolz ist, basieren auf traditionellen Formen, die subtil und behutsam
modernisiert worden sind.*

Les élégants projets de Lazzeroni pour Ceccoti, fabricant qui se targue d'une qualité de fabrication exem-
plaire, reposent sur des formes traditionnelles réactuali-
sées d'un soupçon de modernité.

Design 134

Airport, 1989

Solid cherry frame with polished aluminium backrests | Untergestell aus massivem Kirschholz, Rückenlehnen aus poliertem Aluminium | Châssis en cerisier massif, dosserets en aluminium poli

IBRA, HOLBAEK, FROM 1989 TO PRESENT

Bjorli Lundin, Erling Christoffersen and Flemming Steen Jensen, having all graduated from the Danish Design School and the School of Architecture at the Royal Danish Academy of Fine Arts, established their own manufacturing company, Design 134, in 1989. Since then, they have exhibited widely and have gained considerable recognition for their often iconoclastic designs. Their "Airport" bench has a sculptural simplicity not usually associated with this type of furniture. Cortes's "Gracia" bench shares a similar clarity of form and was designed, like the "Airport", for short-term sitting only.

Bjorli Lundin, Erling Christoffersen und Flemming Steen Jensen, die alle in der Design- oder Architekturabteilung der Königlich Dänischen Hochschule der Bildenden Künste ihren Abschluß gemacht haben, gründeten 1989 die Firma Design 134. Seitdem haben sie sich an vielen Ausstellungen beteiligt und beträchtliche Anerkennung für ihre oft ikonoklastischen Entwürfe gefunden. Die »Airport«-Bank hat eine skulpturale Einfachheit, die für diesen Möbeltyp durchaus ungewöhnlich ist. Cortes' Bank »Gracia« besitzt eine ähnlich klare Formgebung und ist, wie die »Airport«-Bank auch, nur für kurzes Sitzen und Warten konzipiert.

Pepe Cortes

Gracia, 1991

Steel frame with beech-faced laminated wood seat and back | Rahmen aus Stahl, Sitzfläche und Rückenlehne aus laminiertem Holz mit Buchenfurnier | Châssis en acier, siège et dossier en bois laminé, placage de hêtre

PUNT MOBLES,
PATERNA, VALENCIA,
FROM 1991 TO
PRESENT

Bjorli Lundin, Erling Christoffersen et Flemming Steen Jensen, tous diplômés de l'École danoise de design et de l'école d'architecture de l'Académie royale danoise des beaux-arts, créèrent leur propre entreprise de fabrication, Design 134, en 1989. Depuis, ils ont beaucoup exposé et se sont fait remarquer pour des projets souvent iconoclastes. Leur banquette «Airport» présente une simplicité structurelle qui n'est pas courante dans ce type de meuble. Les bancs «Gracia» de Cortes offrent une lisibilité formelle similaire et sont conçus, comme «Airport», pour une occupation de durée limitée.

Hans Sangren Jakobsen & Inger Mosholt Nielsen

Spring, 1990

Steel frame with woven polyester sling seat | Rahmen aus Stahl, Sitzbespannung aus Polyestergewebe | Châssis en acier, siège tendu en polyester tissé

INTERIORS VIA
EUROPEAN DESIGN
TEAM, RANDERS,
FROM 1990 TO
PRESENT

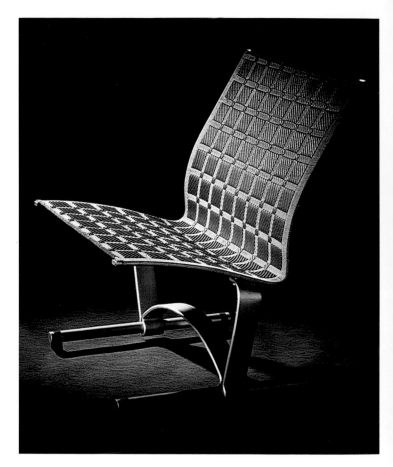

The "Spring" chair's construction is based on the so-called "active form principle". Fundamental to the design is a steel spring, the forces of which are held in balance solely by the textile covering.

Die Konstruktion des »Spring«-Stuhls basiert auf dem sogenannten »Aktivform-Prinzip«. Entscheidend für diesen Entwurf ist die gespannte Stahlfeder, die die Sitzbespannung in Form hält.

La construction de la chauffeuse « Spring » repose sur un « principe de forme active ». Le siège est constitué d'un ressort d'acier dont les forces sont maintenues en équilibre par un tissu en tension.

Antonio Citterio
& Glen Oliver
Löw

*Cittero Collection,
Model No. AC1, 1990*

*Tubular steel frame,
textile-covered poly-
urethane foam uphol-
stery, cast-aluminium
base | Rahmen aus
Stahl, Polsterung aus
Polyurethanschaum-
stoff mit Stoffbezug,
Fuß aus Gußalu-
minium | Châssis en
tube d'acier, rem-
bourrage en mousse
polyuréthane recou-
verte de tissu,
piètement en fonte
d'aluminium*

VITRA, BASLE, FROM
1990 TO PRESENT

▼ Antonio Citterio &
Glen Oliver Löw
T chair, 1990

VITRA, BASLE, FROM
1990 TO PRESENT

The AC1 provides anatomical support without reducing
freedom of movement. The programme offers a wide
variety of options including medium or high backrests
and a drafting chair.

*Der Bürostuhl AC1 bietet anatomisch korrekten Halt, ohne
die Bewegungsfreiheit einzuschränken. Zur Serie gehören
Modelle mit hohen bzw. mittelhohen Rückenlehnen und
ein Modell für den Zeichentisch.*

Le modèle AC1 procure un support anatomique qui ne
gêne pas la liberté de mouvement. Ce programme de
sièges propose une grande variété d'options à dossiers
hauts et bas, ainsi qu'un siège de dessinateur.

Roberto Lucci & Paolo Orlandini

SoHo, 1994

Injection-moulded thermo-plastic and tubular metal frame with removable seat and back, textile-covered moulded polyurethane-upholstered pads | Rahmen aus spritzgeformtem Thermoplast und Stahlrohr, Sitzfläche und Rückenlehne mit abnehmbaren Polstern aus Polyurethan mit Stoffbezug | Châssis en tube métallique et plastique moulé par injection, galettes de siège et de dossier amovibles et rembourrées de polyuréthane moulé recouvert de tissu

KNOLL INTERNA-
TIONAL, NEW YORK,
FROM 1994 TO
PRESENT

▶ **Dragomir Ivicevic**
Parachute chair,
1994

KNOLL INTERNA-
TIONAL, NEW YORK,
FROM 1994 TO
PRESENT

▶▶ **Dale Sahnstrom
& Michael McCoy**
Bulldog chair, 1990

KNOLL INTERNA-
TIONAL, NEW YORK,
FROM 1991 TO
PRESENT

Donald Chadwick & William Stumpf

Aeron, 1992

Recycled aluminium
and fibreglass-
reinforced polyester
frame and base with
polyester mesh seat
and back, on castors |
Rahmen aus recycel-
tem Aluminium und
fiberglasverstärktem
Polyester auf Rollen,
Sitzfläche und
Rückenlehne aus
Polyestergeflecht |
Châssis et piètement
en aluminium recyclé
et polyester renforcé
de fibre de verre, siège
et dossier en toile
polyester, roulettes

HERMAN MILLER
FURNITURE CO.,
ZEELAND,
MICHIGAN, FROM
1994 TO PRESENT

▼ Herman Miller's
developments in
office seating:
Ergon (1970–1976),
Equa (1984),
Aeron (1992)

The "Aeron" radically fulfils ergonomic, functional, anthro-
pometric and environmental considerations and represents state-of-the-art office seating. The low-cost "SoHo"
was developed for the small office/home-office market.
*Der »Aeron« erfüllt ergonomische, funktionale, anthropo-
metrische und ökologische Anforderungen und steht so für
die fortgeschrittensten Standards in der Büromöbelherstel-
lung. Der preiswerte »SoHo« wurde für das kleine Büro
oder private Arbeitszimmer entwickelt.*
Prenant en compte des considérations ergonomiques, fonctionnelles,
anthropométriques et écologiques, le modèle « Aeron » représente le
dernier cri en matière de siège de bureau. Moins coûteux, « SoHo » fut
mis au point pour le marché des petits bureaux ou du travail à domicile.

Pietro Arosio

Mirandolina, Model No. 2068, 1992

Stamped aluminium construction | Konstruktion aus gestanztem Aluminium | Aluminium estampé

ZANOTTA, MILAN, FROM 1992 TO PRESENT

▼ **Gijs Bakker**
DD17, chair with holes (maple), 1996

DROOG DESIGN, VOORBURG, FROM 1994 TO PRESENT

Formed from a single sheet of aluminium, the "Mirandolina" chair pays homage to earlier stamped metal chairs, such as Hans Coray's "Landi" chair of 1936. An armed version is also produced.

Der Stuhl »Mirandolina«, aus einem einzigen Stück Aluminiumblech geformt, ist eine Hommage an ältere Stühle aus gestanztem Metall, wie etwa Hans Corays »Landi«-Stuhl von 1936. Auch eine Version mit Armlehnen ist lieferbar.

Constituée d'une seule feuille d'aluminium, la chaise « Mirandolina » rend hommage à des modèles antérieurs en métal estampé, comme la « Landi » de Hans Coray (1936). Une version avec accoudoirs est également proposée.

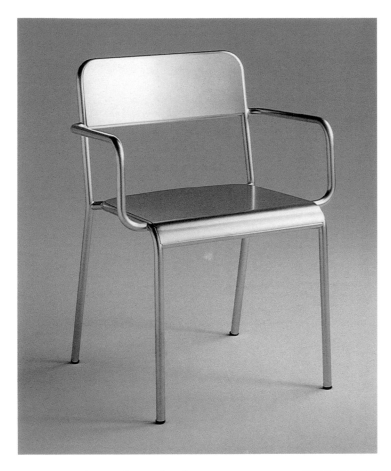

Piero Lissoni

Aprile, 1996

*Aluminium and
tubular aluminium
construction |
Konstruktion aus
Aluminiumrohr und
-blech | Aluminium et
tube d'aluminium*

CAPPELLINI, AROSIO,
COMO, FROM
1996 TO PRESENT

▼ Geoffrey
Hollington
MSc chair, 1994

SCP, LONDON, FROM
1995 TO PRESENT

Lissoni's "Aprile" armchair and Hollington's "MSc"
chair reflect the shift in the 1990s towards a more
austere approach to design which has given rise to
beautiful yet minimal forms.

*Lissonis Stuhl »Aprile« und Hollingtons Stuhl »MSc«
zeigen, wie das Design der 90er Jahre von strengen
Formen bestimmt wird; es entstehen elegante und zugleich minimalistische Entwürfe.*

Le petit fauteuil « Aprile » de Lissoni et la chaise
« MSc » de Hollington reflètent le glissement des
années 90 vers une approche du design plus austère
qui va donner naissance à de superbes formes minimalistes.

Riccardo Blumer

Laleggera,
1993–1996

Injection-moulded polyurethane frame veneered in maple | Konstruktion aus spritzgußgeformtem Polyurethan mit Ahornfurnier | Châssis en polyuréthane injecté, placage d'érable

ALIAS, GRUMELLO DEL MONTE, BERGAMO, FROM 1996

With its inner core of injected polyurethane which is then veneered in pale maple, the "Laleggera" chair is very light both in weight and in appearance. The elegance of this design epitomises the de-materialist aesthetic of the 1990s. Van Severen's chair, with its natural beech veneer, also displays this sense of restraint and purity yet in a more utilitarian way.

Mit seinem Kern aus spritzgußgeformtem Polyurethan, der dann mit hellem Ahornholz furniert wird, ist »Laleggera« sehr leicht, im Gewicht wie im Erscheinungsbild. Die Eleganz dieses Entwurfs verkörpert die dematerialisierte

Maarten Van Severen

No. 2, 1992

Beech-faced moulded plywood seating section on aluminium frame | Aluminium-gestell, Sitz aus geformtem Schicht-holz, Buchenholz-oberfläche | Châssis en aluminium, siège en contre-plaqué moulé, placage de hêtre

MAARTEN VAN
SEVEREN, GHENT,
FROM 1992 TO
PRESENT

▼ **Maarten Van Severen**
Aluminium chaise, 1996

MAARTEN VAN
SEVEREN, GHENT,
FROM 1996 TO
PRESENT

Ästhetik der 90er Jahre. Van Severens Stuhl repräsentiert mit seinem naturbelassenen Buchenholzfurnier diesen Sinn für Zurückhaltung und Reinheit durch sein sehr auf Funktion ausgerichtetes Design.

Avec sa structure en polyuréthane injecté plaquée d'érable pâle, la chaise « Laleggera » est aussi légère de poids que d'aspect. L'élégance de ce modèle incarne l'esthétique dématérialisée des années 90. La chaise de Van Severen, avec son placage de hêtre, diffuse le même sentiment de réserve et de pureté, mais d'une manière plus utilitaire.

Rodney Kinsman

Seville, 1991

Extruded anodised aluminium seat and beam sections with cast-aluminium floor-mounted supports | Sitz und Tragbalken aus strangepreßtem, eloxiertem Aluminium, verschraubbare Fußstützen aus Gußaluminium | Siège et poutrelle en aluminium extrudé anodisé, pieds à sceller en fonte d'aluminium

OMK DESIGN,
LONDON, FROM
1991 TO PRESENT

▼ **Rodney Kinsman**
Trax bench, 1988

OMK DESIGN,
LONDON, FROM
1988 TO PRESENT

Designed for the British pavilion at the 1992 Seville Expo, this "short-stay" public seating system utilises state-of-the-art aluminium extrusion technology in its manufacture.

Dieses Sitzsystem, für öffentliche Räume und kurze Aufenthalte konzipiert, war ein Entwurf für den britischen Pavillon auf der EXPO 1992 in Sevilla. Seine Konstruktion besteht aus ineinandergreifenden Gußaluminiumform-teilen.

Dessiné pour le pavillon britannique de l'Exposition universelle de Séville, en 1992, ce banc public est réalisé à partir de techniques avant-gardistes d'extrusion de l'aluminium.

Alfred Homann

*Ensemble, Model
No. B10, 1992*

*Moulded recyclable
plastic shell on bent
chrome-plated
tubular steel frame
with plastic "rocker-
toes" | Rahmen aus
gebogenem Stahlrohr,
verchromt, Sitzschale
aus recycelbarem
Kunststoff, Fußkap-
pen aus Plastik |
Coquille en plastique
recyclable moulé,
châssis en tube d'acier
cintré chromé, patins
en plastique*

FRITZ HANSEN,
ALLERØD, FROM
1992 TO PRESENT

Ergonomically conceived, the "Ensemble's" seat section is moulded in a specially developed recyclable plastic. Its innovative construction has air pockets inside the shell to provide a high degree of strength and flexibility.

Die ergonomisch gestaltete Sitzschale des Stuhls »Ensemble« wird aus einem eigens entwickelten recyclebaren Kunststoff geformt. Die in die Schale integrier-ten Lufttaschen – eine innovative Konstruktion – sorgen für hohe Sitzfestigkeit bei gleichzeitiger Elastizität.

De conception ergonomique, le siège de cet « Ensemble » est moulé dans un plastique recyclable spécial. À l'intérieur de la coquille, des poches d'air renforcent à la fois la rigidité et la souplesse.

Alfredo Arribas

J. Greystoke, 1990

Solid beech and anodised cast-aluminium frame with Alcantara-covered upholstered seat and back |
Rahmen aus Buche und eloxiertem Guß-aluminium, Sitzfläche und Rückenlehne gepolstert und mit Alcantarabezug |
Châssis en hêtre massif et fonte d'aluminium anodisée, siège et dossier en Alcantara rembourré

CARLOS JANÉ
CAMACHO,
BARCELONA, FROM
1990 TO PRESENT

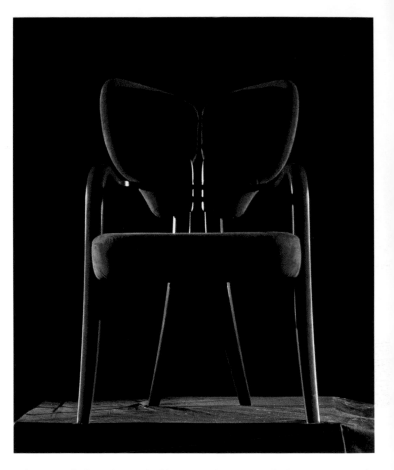

Taking its title from the Lord of the Apes, this design alludes to wild animal forms and is reminiscent of the earlier zoomorphic work of Carlo Mollino, particularly through the use of a bifurcated upholstered back.

Dieser Entwurf, dessen Name auf den Herrn der Affen (Tarzan) anspielt, erinnert mit seinen wilden animalischen Formen, insbesondere durch die zweigeteilte gepolsterte Rückenlehne, an die früheren zoomorphen Arbeiten von Carlo Mollino.

Avec un nom évoquant Tarzan, ce modèle rappelle des formes animales et les premières recherches zoomorphes de Carlo Mollino, en particulier avec son dossier rembourré en deux parties.

Luigi Serafini

Santa, 1992

*Tubular metal and brass frame with velvet-covered upholstered seat |
Rahmen aus Metallrohr und Messing, Sitzfläche gepolstert und mit Samtbezug |
Châssis en tube de métal et laiton, siège en velours rembourré*

SAWAYA & MORONI, MILAN, FROM 1992 TO PRESENT

▼ Luigi Serafini
Suspiral, 1986

SAWAYA & MORONI, MILAN, FROM 1986 TO PRESENT

"Santa" is typical of Serafini's playful, almost theatrical, designs hewn in mild steel. With its halo-like back, dark red velvet seat and title, this chair makes obvious reference to the Yuletide.

Der Stuhl »Santa« ist typisch für Serafinis spielerische, fast theatralische Entwürfe, die aus unlegiertem Stahl gearbeitet sind. Mit der an einen Heiligenschein erinnernden Rückenlehne und dem dunkelroten Samtbezug des Sitzpolsters bekommt dieser Stuhl etwas geradezu Weihnachtliches.

« Santa » est typique des créations en acier doux ludiques, presque théâtrales, de Serafini. Le dossier en forme d'auréole, le siège en velours rouge sombre et le nom rappellent l'époque de Noël.

559

Masanori Umeda

Getsuen, 1990

Fabric-covered polyurethane foam and Dacron-uphol-stered steel frame with carved wood details and plastic wheels | Rahmen aus Stahl mit Details aus geschnitztem Holz auf Plastikrollen, Polsterung aus Poly-urethanschaumstoff und Dacron mit Stoffbezug | Châssis en acier, rembourrage en mousse de poly-uréthane et dacron recouverts de tissu, éléments en bois sculpté, roues en plastique

EDRA, PERIGNANO, FROM 1990 TO PRESENT

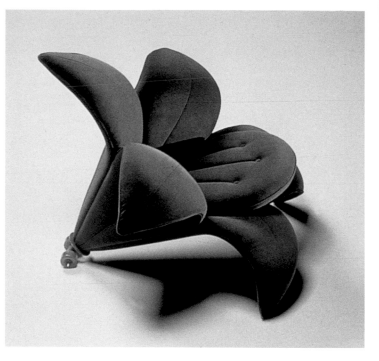

Claiming that, through its affluence, Japan has destroyed its own natural beauty, Umeda uses a variety of floral motifs in order to rediscover the roots of Japanese culture. Also influenced by Memphis, Umeda's designs can be seen as wry Post-Modern commentaries on the friction between the traditional and the contemporary.

Umeda glaubt, daß Japan durch seine Wohlstandsgesellschaft die natürliche Schönheit des Landes zerstört hat und verwendet deshalb eine Vielfalt von Blumenmotiven, um wieder zu den Wurzeln der japanischen Kultur zu gelangen. Beeinflußt auch durch das Memphis-Design, können Umedas Entwürfe als postmodern-ironische Kommentare zu den Gegensätzen zwischen Tradition und Gegenwart verstanden werden.

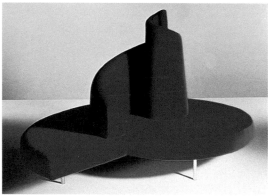

▲ Rocky Semprini & Mario Cananzi
Tatlin, 1989

EDRA, PERIGNANO, FROM 1989 TO PRESENT

Masanori
Umeda

Rose, 1990

*Fabric-covered
polyurethane foam
and Dacron-uphol-
stered steel frame
with carved wood
details and chromed
cast-aluminium legs |
Rahmen aus Stahl
mit Details aus
geschnitztem Holz,
Stuhlbeine aus
Gußaluminium,
verchromt, Polsterung
aus Polyurethan-
schaumstoff und
Dacron mit Stoff-
bezug | Châssis en
acier, rembourrage en
mousse de poly-
uréthane et dacron
recouverts de tissu,
éléments en bois
sculpté, pieds en fonte
d'aluminium
chromée*

EDRA, PERIGNANO,
FROM 1990 TO
PRESENT

Prétendant que, par sa richesse, le Japon a détruit sa beauté naturelle,
Umeda se sert de divers motifs floraux pour tenter de redécouvrir les
racines de la culture nippone. Influencées par Memphis, ses créations sont
également un commentaire ironique et postmoderne sur les frictions entre
le traditionnel et le contemporain.

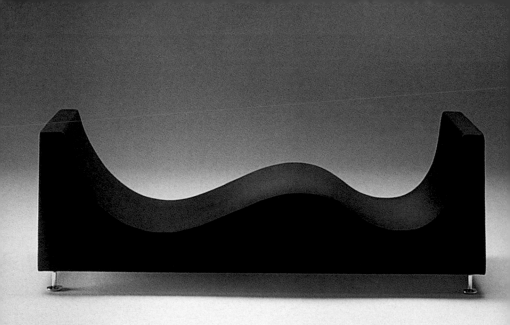

Jasper Morrison

Three, 1992

Aluminium frame with textile-covered polyurethane foam upholstery | Rahmen aus Aluminium, Polsterung aus Polyurethanschaumstoff mit Stoffbezug | Châssis en aluminium, rembourrage en mousse de polyuréthane recouverte de tissu

CAPPELLINI, AROSIO, COMO, FROM 1992 TO PRESENT

Although Morrison's designs for Cappellini, such as the "Three" sofa, are more expressive than those he does for Vitra, they retain a strong aesthetic purity derived from a rational approach to the manufacturing process. The seat of his Vitra sofa is set at an optimum height and the back section is sprung so as to assist the user getting up from it. A two-seater version of the sofa is also produced.

Obwohl Morrisons Entwürfe für Cappellini, wie z. B. das Sofa »Three«, expressiver sind als jene für Vitra, behalten sie doch ihre beeindruckende ästhetische Reinheit, die sich aus dem rationellen, vom Herstellungsverfahren ausgehenden Designansatz ergibt. Die Sitzfläche seines Sofas für Vitra hat die

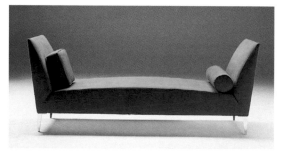

◄ **Jasper Morrison**
Day Bed, 1989

CAPPELLINI, AROSIO, COMO, FROM 1989 TO PRESENT

optimale Höhe, und die Rückenlehne ist gefedert, fast, als wolle er dem Sitzenden helfen, aufzustehen. Auch eine zweisitzige Version des Sofas wird produziert.

Bien que les projets de Morrison pour Cappellini, comme ce sofa « Three », soient plus expressifs que ses réalisations pour Vitra, ils conservent une pureté esthétique liée à une approche rationaliste du processus de fabrication. La hauteur du siège du sofa Vitra est optimale, et les ressorts du dossier aident l'utilisateur à se relever. Une variante à deux places est également proposée.

Jasper Morrison

Sofa, 1989–1991

Frame with flexible backrest upholstered in textile-covered polyurethane foam, with aluminium legs and loose upholstered seat cushions | Rahmen mit beweglicher Rückenlehne, Polsterung aus Polyurethanschaumstoff mit Stoffbezug, lose gepolsterte Sitzkissen, Füße aus Aluminium | Châssis avec dossier flexible, rembourrage en mousse de polyuréthane recouverte de tissu, pieds en aluminium, coussins rembourrés amovibles

VITRA, BASLE, FROM 1991 TO PRESENT

◄ Jasper Morrison
Benches, 1989–1991

VITRA, BASLE, FROM 1991 TO PRESENT

Jan Armgardt

Model No. JA43G,
1991

Iron frame with
laminated paper seat
section and wicker
back | Rahmen
aus Eisenstangen,
Sitzfläche aus
laminiertem Papier,
Rückenlehne aus
Weide | Châssis en fer,
siège en papier
contrecollé, dossier en
osier

KATZ-FLECHTMÖBEL,
NAGOLD, FROM
1991 TO PRESENT

▼ **Jan Armgardt**
Model No. JA46G,
1991

KATZ-FLECHTMÖBEL,
NAGOLD, FROM
1991 TO PRESENT

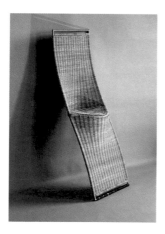

The resurgence of wicker in furniture design is mainly
due to its economical and ecological soundness.
Armgardt has produced a number of subtle designs
which utilise this natural material.

Die Renaissance der Korbmöbel hat vor allem damit zu
tun, daß dieses Material weder ökonomische noch ökolo-
gische Probleme macht. Armgardt hat eine ganze Reihe
eleganter Entwürfe geschaffen, die aus diesem natürlichen
Werkstoff gefertigt sind.

La résurgence du mobilier en osier est essentiellement
due à des raisons économiques et écologiques.
Armgardt a réalisé un certain nombre de modèles
raffinés qui font appel à ce matériau naturel.

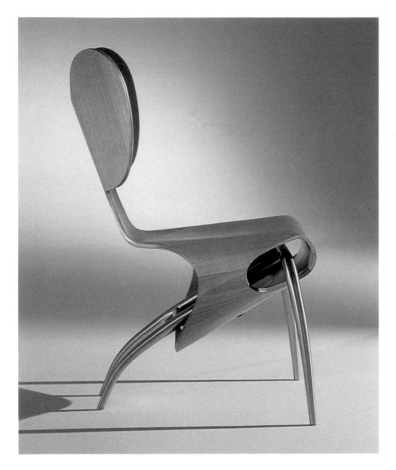

Ron Arad

Empty, 1993

Moulded plywood
seating section on
cast-aluminium base |
Rahmen aus
Gußaluminium,
Sitzschale aus
formgebogenem
Schichtholz | Siège en
contre-plaqué moulé,
piètement en fonte
d'aluminium

DRIADE, FOSSADELLO
DI CAORSO,
PIACENZA, FROM
1993

Arad is primarily concerned with the object/user relationship. While exploring these connections through novel forms, he communicates often double-coded symbolic meaning through a poetic rhetoric.

Arad beschäftigt sich vor allem mit dem Verhältnis zwischen Objekt und Benutzer. Und wenn er dieses Verhältnis mit einer neuen Formensprache erforscht, vermittelt er häufig doppelt kodierte symbolische Bedeutungen durch eine poetische Rhetorik.

Arad s'intéresse avant tout à la relation objet/utilisateur. Tout en explorant ces connexions à travers des formes nouvelles, il communique souvent une signification symbolique à double code à travers une rhétorique poétique.

Philippe Starck

Boom Rang, 1992

Polyurethane frame with steel inserts | Rahmen aus Polyurethan mit Stahleinlagen | Châssis en poly-uréthane, pièces insérées métalliques

DRIADE, FOSSADELLO
DI CAORSO,
PIACENZA, FROM
1992 TO PRESENT

▼ **Philippe Starck**
Royalton chair, 1991

DRIADE, FOSSADELLO
DI CAORSO, PIA-
CENZA, FROM 1991
TO PRESENT

The "Boom Rang" chair and "W.W. Stool" demonstrate the influence of "Soft Design" on Starck's work in the 1990s. His biomorphic forms have a visual, if not physical, softness that demand a tactile interaction. The "W.W. Stool" resembles a germinating rhizome, with the first shoot sprouting upwards to form the small backrest and the three roots delving down to form the legs.

Der Stuhl »Boom Rang« und der »W.W. Stool« demon-strieren den Einfluß des »Soft Design« auf Starcks Arbeiten der 90er Jahre. Seine biomorphen Formen haben eine

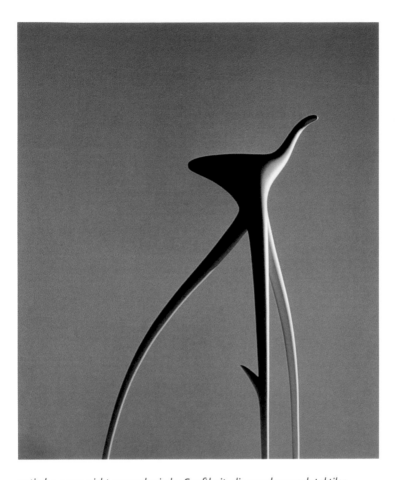

Philippe Starck

W.W. Stool, 1990

Lacquered sand-blasted cast-aluminium form | Aluminiumbandguß, lackiert und sandgestrahlt | Fonte d'aluminium laquée et sablée

VITRA, BASLE, FROM 1992 TO PRESENT

optische, wenn nicht sogar physische Sanftheit, die geradezu nach taktiler Kontaktaufnahme verlangt. »W.W. Stool« ähnelt einem keimenden Wurzelgeflecht, aus dem ein erster Trieb aus der kleinen Rückenlehne aufwärts sprießt; die drei Wurzeln, die nach unten drängen, bilden die Beine.

Le fauteuil « Boom Rang » et le modèle « W.W. Stool » illustrent l'influence du « Soft design » sur le travail de Starck au cours des années 90. Ses formes végétales affichent une douceur visuelle, voire physique, qui incite à l'expérience tactile. Le tabouret fait penser à un rhizome en pleine germination, une poussée formant le petit dosseret et les trois racines composant les pieds.

Frank O. Gehry

Powerplay,
1990–1992

Bent and woven
laminated wood
construction |
Konstruktion aus
gebogenen und
miteinander
verflochtenen,
laminierten
Holzstreifen | Bois
laminé cintré et tressé

KNOLL
INTERNATIONAL,
NEW YORK, FROM
1992 TO PRESENT

All previous important advances in the construction of plywood chairs depended on either a substructure or an intermediary structural support. The
innovative interwoven basket-like construction of Gehry's chairs, however,
is sufficiently strong to enable them to be self-supporting, while providing a
springiness for comfort. Newson's "Wooden Chair" is similarly constructed
from interlaced strips of steam-bent beech though it utilises horizontal
strengthening elements.

Alle vorangegangenen Fortschritte in der Bauweise von Schichtholzstühlen waren
von einer Unterkonstruktion oder von stützenden Elementen abhängig gewesen.
Der neuartige, korbähnlich geflochtene Aufbau von Gehrys Sesseln bietet jedoch
ausreichende Festigkeit, so daß die Konstruktion freitragend bleiben und federnd

Marc Newson

Wooden Chair, 1992

Bent beech heart-wood construction | Konstruktion aus gebogenem Buchenkernholz | Hêtre cintré

CAPPELLINI, AROSIO, COMO, FROM 1992 TO PRESENT

für Sitzkomfort sorgen kann. Newsons »Wooden Chair« ist ganz ähnlich aus verflochtenen, dampfgebogenen Buchenholzstreifen aufgebaut, allerdings werden hier horizontal verstärkende Streben eingesetzt.

L'ensemble des progrès réalisés dans la construction de sièges en contre-plaqué dépendaient jusqu'alors d'une structure rigide ou d'un soutien structurel intermédiaire. La construction tressée révolutionnaire des sièges de Gehry est suffisamment résistante pour être autoporteuse tout en offrant une souplesse qui assure un grand confort. La «Wooden Chair» de Newson est de construction similaire : ses lames de bois de hêtre cintré à la vapeur utilisent cependant des renforts horizontaux.

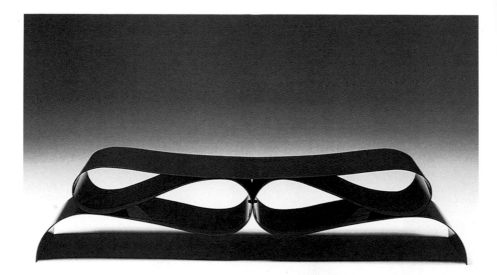

Agenore Fabbri

Nastro di Gala, 1991

Folded enamelled steel | Gefalteter emaillierter Stahl | Acier cintré émaillé

TECNO, MILAN, FROM 1991 TO PRESENT

Fabbri is primarily known for his work as an Expressionist artist and certainly his "Nastro di Gala" bench possesses distinct gestural qualities. He states, "If you manage to make an object which is functional and, in addition gives this sense … of happiness and play, then that's it." He also believes that designs should correspond to the age in which we live and express thoughts and ideas as well as function and beauty.

Fabbri hat sich hauptsächlich mit seinen expressionistischen Kunstwerken einen Namen gemacht, und so weist auch seine Sitzbank »Nastro di Gala« besondere gestische Qualitäten auf. Wenn es gelinge, so sagt er, »ein Objekt zu schaffen, das funktional ist und dazu noch diesen Eindruck von Glück und Spiel vermittelt, dann hat man es geschafft«. Seiner Meinung nach müssen Designmöbel etwas mit der Zeit zu tun haben, in der wir leben, und deren Ideen und Vorstellungen ebenso ausdrücken wie Funktionalität und Schönheit.

Fabbri est essentiellement connu pour son travail d'artiste expressionniste et son banc « Nastro di Gala » possède des qualités gestuelles remarquables. « Si vous arrivez à fabriquer un objet qui est fonctionnel et, de plus, donne cette impression … de bonheur et de jeu, vous y êtes! » dit-il. Il pense également que les meubles doivent correspondre à l'époque dans laquelle nous vivons et exprimer des pensées et des idées aussi bien qu'une fonction ou qu'une esthétique particulières.

Carlo Mo

Chip, 1991

Carved limed oak
seating section on
lacquered steel base |
Aus geschnitzter und
gekalkter Eiche,
Untergestell aus
Stahl, lackiert | Siège
en chêne enduit
sculpté, base en acier
laqué

TECNO, MILAN,
FROM 1991 TO
PRESENT

Known for his monumental Abstract-Expressionist sculptures, Mo believes there is no distinction between art and design, for both are dictated by form. "Chip" was inspired by African Art, of which Mo has a first-hand knowledge.

Mo, der für seine monumentalen abstrakt-expressionistischen Skulpturen bekannt ist, glaubt, daß es keinen Unterschied zwischen Kunst und Design gibt, da beide von der Form bestimmt sind. Der Lehnhocker »Chip« wurde von der afrikanischen Kunst inspiriert, die Mo aus eigener Anschauung kennt.

Connu pour ses sculptures expressionnistes abstraites monumentales, Mo pense qu'il n'existe pas de différences entre l'art et le design, car tous deux sont dictés par la forme. « Chip » s'inspire de l'art africain dont Mo possède une connaissance de première main.

Tom Dixon

Pylon, 1991

Painted welded steel
rod construction |
Konstruktion aus
verschweißten Stahl-
stäben, lackiert |
Construction en tige
d'acier soudée et
peinte

SPACE, LONDON,
FROM 1991 &
CAPPELLINI, AROSIO,
COMO, FROM
1992 TO PRESENT

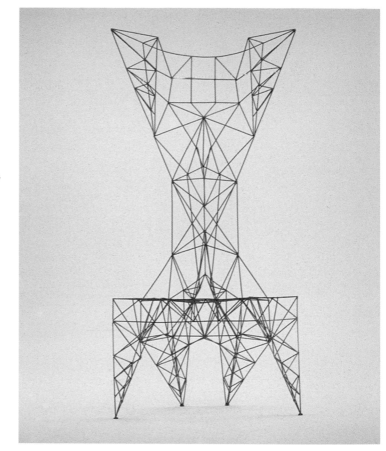

Dixon's "Pylon" chair is constructed of thin steel rods which, when welded together, give the structure sufficient strength to support even large people. Although this chair is manufactured entirely by hand, other designs by Dixon, such as "Bird 2", are more suited to industrial-type production. The bold shapes of his metal furniture translate well into upholstered forms.
Dixons »Pylon«-Stuhl besteht aus dünnen Stahlstäben, die, miteinander verschweißt, der Konstruktion so viel Festigkeit geben, daß sie auch schwere Menschen trägt. Dieser Stuhl wird völlig von Hand hergestellt. Andere Entwürfe Dixons, wie z. B. der »Bird 2«-Stuhl, sind dagegen für die industrielle Produktion geeignet. Die kühnen Formen seiner Metallmöbel lassen sich ausgezeichnet in gepolsterte Formen übertragen.

Tom Dixon

Bird 2, 1992

Textile-covered polyurethane foam-upholstered frame | Rahmen mit Polsterung aus Polyurethanschaumstoff und Stoffbezug | Châssis rembourré en mousse de polyuréthane recouverte de tissu

CAPPELLINI, AROSIO, COMO, FROM 1992 TO PRESENT

▼ **Tom Dixon**
Bird chaise longue, 1990

CAPPELLINI, AROSIO, COMO, FROM 1992 TO PRESENT

Le siège « Pylon » de Tom Dixon est construit en fines tiges d'acier qui, soudées ensemble, donnent à sa structure une résistance suffisante pour supporter le poids de n'importe quel utilisateur. Si ce siège est entièrement fabriqué à la main, d'autres modèles de Dixon, comme le « Bird 2 », sont mieux adaptés à une production industrielle. Les formes audacieuses de ses meubles en métal se traduisent bien en versions rembourrées.

Takenobu Igarashi

Zao, 1992

Cast-aluminium base with cast-iron seat | Untergestell aus Gußaluminium, Sitzfläche aus Gußeisen | Piètement en fonte d'aluminium, siège en fonte de fer

YAMADA SHOMEI
LIGHTING CO.,
TOKYO, FOR
CLASSICON,
MUNICH, FROM 1992
TO PRESENT

These stools have a restraint and minimalism that is reminiscent of Zen gardens. Their seats appear as fragile as crumpled tissue paper and seem to float like lily-pads, while the legs are suggestive of inverted branches.

Die Schlichtheit und der Minimalismus dieser Hocker erinnern an japanische Zen-Gärten. Ihre Sitzflächen wirken so zerbrechlich wie zerknülltes Seidenpapier und scheinen wie Lilienblätter zu schweben, während die Beine umgedrehten Astgabeln ähneln.

Ces tabourets discrets et minimalistes rappellent les jardins zen. Leurs sièges semblent fragiles, un peu comme du papier froissé ou une feuille de nénuphar sur un étang, tandis que les pieds suggèrent une fourche d'arbre renversée.

Unlike Igarashi's designs which are informed by nature and traditional Japanese culture, the "Unichair" by Hironen is inspired by science fiction and the popular consumer culture of contemporary Japan. Its spiked, mace-like design is suggestive of the Post-Punk apocalyptic forms of *Mad Max*.

Anders als Igarashis Entwürfe, die von der Natur und traditioneller japanischer Kunst geprägt sind, ließ sich Hironen für seinen »Unichair« von Science-fiction und der populären Konsumkultur des modernen Japan inspirieren. Dieser stachelige Entwurf erinnert an die Postpunk-Ästhetik von »Mad Max«.

À la différence des créations d'Igarashi, qui font référence à la nature et à la culture japonaise traditionnelle, l' « Unichair » de Hironen s'inspire de la science-fiction et de la culture de consommation populaire dans le Japon contemporain. Les protubérances de se siège évoquent l'univers apocalyptique de *Mad Max*.

Hironen

Unichair, 1993

Textile-covered polyurethane foam |
Polyurethanschaum-stoff mit Stoffbezug |
Mousse de polyuréthane recouverte de tissu

HIRONEN, TOKYO, FROM 1993 TO PRESENT

Vico Magistretti & Francesco Binfaré

Insica, 1992

Tubular steel frame with saddle-stitched leather seating section | Rahmen aus Stahlrohr, Sitzfläche aus vernähtem Leder | Châssis en tube d'acier, siège en cuir piqué sellier

DE PADOVA, MILAN, FROM 1992 TO PRESENT

With its saddle-form and colourful quilted lining, the "Insica" makes references to equestrianism with the intention of bringing associations of quality, sophistication and excitement to the design. It is primarily aimed at the burgeoning home-office market.

Mit seiner Sattelform und dem farbenfrohen, gesteppten Bezug spielt das Stuhlmodell »Insica« auf den Reitsport an, um Assoziationen zu Qualität, Weltläufigkeit und Nervenkitzel zu erzeugen. Der Stuhl zielt hauptsächlich auf den wachsenden Markt für Büromöbel für den privaten Bereich.

Avec sa forme de selle et son recouvrage passepoilé coloré, le fauteuil « Insica » évoque le sport équestre, symbole de qualité, de sophistication et de plaisir. Ce modèle est destiné au marché en plein développement du mobilier de bureau pour la maison.

William Sawaya

Patty Difusa, 1993

*Moulded mahogany-faced plywood frame with leather-covered upholstered seat |
Rahmen aus geformtem Schichtholz mit Mahagonifurnier, Sitzfläche gepolstert und mit Lederbezug |
Châssis en contre-plaqué moulé, placage d'acajou, siège en cuir rembourré*

SAWAYA & MORONI,
MILAN, FROM 1993
TO PRESENT

▼ William Sawaya
La Belle, 1991

SAWAYA & MORONI,
MILAN, FROM 1991
TO PRESENT

The remarkable form of this chair is representative of Sawaya & Moroni's virtuoso handling of materials and their willingness to create lyrical and fantastic designs mainly for the delight of a limited audience.

Die außergewöhnliche Form dieses Stuhls ist repräsentativ für Sawaya & Moronis virtuose Materialbehandlung und ihre Bereitschaft, zum Vergnügen eines kleinen Publikums lyrische und phantastische Entwürfe zu schaffen.

La forme remarquable de ce fauteuil est un bon exemple de la maîtrise virtuose de Sawaya & Moroni dans le traitement des matériaux ainsi que de leur volonté de créer des sièges lyriques et étonnants pour la plus grande satisfaction d'une clientèle restreinte.

Antonio Citterio

Compagnia delle Filippine, 1993

Beech frame with woven leather-covered polyurethane foam upholstery and aluminium sabots | Rahmen aus Buche, Polsterung aus Polyurethanschaumstoff Bezug aus geflochtenem Leder, Fußmanschetten aus Aluminium | Châssis en hêtre, rembourrage en mousse de polyuréthane recouverte de cuir tressé, sabots en aluminium

B & B ITALIA, NOVEDRATE, COMO, FROM 1993 TO PRESENT

Antonio Citterio is primarily known for his work in the office-seating sector – notably, the AC 1 and AC 2 programmes for Vitra. With this elegant range of woven leather chairs intended for the domestic market, he demonstrates his skill and versatility as a designer.

Antonio Citterio ist vor allem wegen seiner Entwürfe für den Büromöbelbereich bekannt, insbesondere mit den Serien AC 1 und AC 2 für Vitra hat er sich einen Namen gemacht. Mit dieser eleganten Kollektion von Sesseln mit Ledergeflecht, die für den häuslichen Bereich gedacht sind, demonstriert er sein Können und seine Vielseitigkeit als Designer.

Antonio Citterio est essentiellement connu pour son travail dans le secteur du mobilier de bureau, en particulier sur les programmes AC1 et AC2 créés pour Vitra. Cette gamme élégante de fauteuils en cuir tressé conçus pour la maison prouve la multiplicité de ses talents de designer.

Luca Meda

Riesiedo, 1990–1991

Walnut frame with woven straw seat | Rahmen aus Walnußholz, Sitzfläche aus Strohgeflecht | Châssis en noyer, siège et dossier en paille tressée

MOLTENI & C., GIUSSANO, FROM 1991 TO PRESENT

Like Ponti's "Superleggera", this chair by Luca Meda is a sensitive reworking of a vernacular type and is a design "without adjectives". The "Riesiedo's" rhetoric has a certain timelessness which precludes it from the evanescence of fashion.

Wie Pontis »Superleggera« ist auch dieser Stuhl von Luca Meda eine sensible Überarbeitung eines traditionellen Stuhltyps: ein Entwurf »ohne Adjektive«. Die Formensprache des »Riesiedo« hat eine gewisse Zeitlosigkeit, die diesen Stuhl vor der Flüchtigkeit der Moden schützt.

Comme la « Superleggera » de Ponti, ce fauteuil de Luca Meda est une déclinaison pleine de sensibilité d'un modèle vernaculaire et un bon exemple de design « sans adjectifs ». La rhétorique du « Riesiedo » présente un caractère assez intemporel qui le protège des phénomènes de mode évanescents.

Paolo Deganello

Re, 1991

*Enamelled steel frame with woven wicker seat and stitched leather back |
Rahmen aus Stahl, einbrennlackiert, Sitzfläche aus Weidengeflecht, Rückenlehne aus vernähtem Leder |
Châssis en acier émaillé, siège en jonc tressé, dossier en cuir cousu*

ZANOTTA, MILAN, FROM 1991 TO PRESENT

Deganello makes a point of separating the main elements of his chairs by constructing them in different materials and then playing their qualities off one against the other.

Deganello kommt es darauf an, bei seinen Stuhlentwürfen die einzelnen Bauteile sichtbar zu machen. Indem er sie mit unterschiedlichen Materialien gestaltet, können sie ihre Qualitäten gegeneinander ausspielen.

Deganello réussit à isoler les composantes de ses modèles en jouant de la variété des matériaux choisis.

Roberto Lazzeroni

Star Trek, 1994

Carved solid cherry frame with textile-covered upholstered seat and back | Rahmen aus massivem Kirschholz, Sitzfläche und Rückenlehne gepolstert und mit Stoffbezug | Châssis en cerisier massif sculpté, dossier et siège rembourrés

CECCOTTI, CASCINA, PISA, FROM 1994 TO PRESENT

Despite its title, which refers to the 1960s' television series, this chair is evocative of the expressive, anthropomorphic forms developed in Italy during the 1950s. It is one of the first upholstered designs produced by Ceccotti.

Trotz seines Namens, eine Anspielung auf eine TV-Serie der 60er Jahre, erinnert dieser Sessel an die ausdrucksvollen anthropomorphen Formen, die das italienische Design in den 50er Jahren entwickelt hat. Der Sessel gehört zu den ersten Polstermöbeln, die von Ceccotti produziert wurden.

Malgré son nom, qui renvoie aux feuilletons de télévision des années 60, ce fauteuil évoque plutôt les formes anthropomorphes expressives développées en Italie pendant les années 50. C'est l'un des premiers modèles rembourrés produits par Ceccotti.

Ross Lovegrove

M, 1994

*Textile-covered
moulded polyure-
thane foam-uphol-
stered frame on
tubular aluminium
legs | Rahmen mit
Polsterung aus
Polyurethanschaum-
stoff und Stoffbezug,
Füße aus Aluminium-
rohr | Châssis
rembourré en mousse
de polyuréthane
moulée et recouverte
de tissu, pieds en tube
d'aluminium*

MOROSO,
CAVALICCO, UDINE,
FROM 1994 TO
PRESENT

Lovegrove's designs are fundamentally informed by function, yet he skilfully and intuitively forms them into objects of sculptural beauty. The compelling aesthetic of this design is dictated by physical requirements – the M-shaped gully that runs along the top of the sofa acts as a comfortable hollow in which to rest one's arms.

Lovegroves Formgebung folgt der Funktion, aber er versteht es, seine Möbel mit Geschick und Intuition in Objekte von skulpturaler Schönheit zu verwandeln. Die bezwingende Ästhetik dieses Entwurfs wird vom Sitzkomfort bestimmt – so bietet die M-förmige Rinne, die das Polster umläuft, aufgelegten Armen eine bequeme Vertiefung.

Les créations de Lovegrove sont fondamentalement nourries de fonctionnalisme, ce qui ne l'empêche pas de les transformer avec beaucoup d'art et d'intuition en objets d'une grande beauté sculpturale. L'esthétique irrésistible de ce modèle est dictée par des arguments fonctionnels, la forme en gouttière des accoudoirs, par exemple, permettant de reposer confortablement le bras.

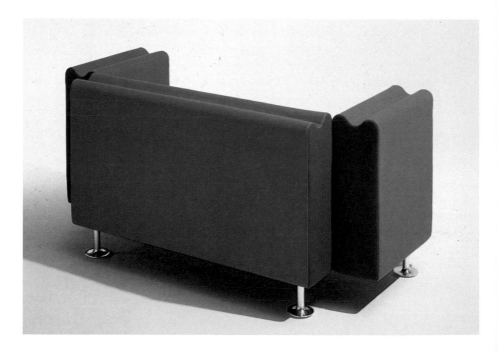

Jane Dillon's and Peter Wheeler's modular seating system "Multipla" has a strong sculptural quality. Its petal-like forms, enhanced by the use of muted yet rich colours, allow the chairs to readily form a rhythmical "chairscape".

Jane Dillons und Peter Wheelers modulares Sitzsystem »Multipla« hat ausdrucksvolle skulpturale Qualitäten. Die blütenblattähnlichen Formen, betont durch die Verwendung gedämpfter, doch satter Farben, ermöglichen es, daß die Sessel eine ungezwungene, rhythmische Sitzlandschaft bilden.

Ce système de sièges modulaires de Jane Dillon et Peter Wheeler présente de puissantes qualités sculpturales. Leurs formes en pétale, soulignées par des couleurs à la fois atténuées et riches, permettent à ces sièges de composer un paysage plein de rythme.

Jane Dillon & Peter Wheeler

Multipla, 1992

Steel frame with moulded polyurethane foam, Dacron upholstery and aluminium connections | Rahmen aus Stahl, Polsterung aus geformtem Polyurethanschaumstoff und Dacron, Verbindungselemente aus Aluminium | Châssis en acier, rembourrage en mousse de polyuréthane moulée et dacron, pièces d'assemblage en aluminium

KRON, MADRID, FROM 1992 TO PRESENT

Denis Santachiara

Mama, 1995

Textile-covered polyurethane foam-upholstered rocking frame with matching footstool | Schaukelgestell mit Polsterung aus Polyurethanschaumstoff und mit Stoffbezug, Fußhocker in passender Form | Châssis basculant rembourré en mousse de polyuréthane recouverte de tissu, repose-pied assorti

BALERI, LALLIO, BERGAMO, FROM 1995 TO PRESENT

Denis Santachiara's "Mama" is a novel interpretation of a rocking chair. With its pregnant form and egg-like ottoman, the design is full of maternal symbolism while its ample proportions and soft padding impart a comforting presence.

Denis Santachiaras Sessel »Mama« ist eine Neuinterpretation des Schaukelstuhls. Mit seiner bauchigen Form und dem eiähnlichen Fußhocker steckt der Entwurf voller Symbole der Mütterlichkeit, und seine ausladenden Proportionen sowie die weiche Polsterung haben etwas Tröstliches.

Le « Mama » de Denis Santachiara est une interprétation radicalement nouvelle du fauteuil à bascule. Avec ses rondeurs pleines et son pouf en forme d'œuf, ce modèle déborde de symbolisme maternel et procure, grâce à ses amples proportions et à son rembourrage mou, une présence confortable.

Since the 1980s, Branzi has been advocating a post-industrialist approach which maintains the importance of design for the individual. Although far removed stylistically from his earlier "neo-primitive" style and borrowing references from the Modern Movement, the "Niccola" is fundamentally a Post-Modern design.

Seit den 8oer Jahren propagiert Branzi eine postindustrielle Designtheorie, die die Bedeutung der Formgebung für das Individuum hervorhebt. Obwohl er sich stilistisch weit von seinem früheren »neo-primitiven« Stil entfernt hat und nun auch Anleihen bei der klassischen Moderne macht, ist der Sessel »Niccola« ein postmodernes Design.

Depuis les années 80, Branzi défend une approche postindustrielle qui prône l'importance du design pour l'individu. Bien que stylistiquement très éloigné de son style « néoprimitif » antérieur et empruntant ses références au mouvement moderniste, le « Niccola » est fondamentalement postmoderne.

Andrea Branzi

Niccola, 1992

Tubular steel frame with leather-covered polyurethane foam-upholstery, caned headrest and arm-rests | Rahmen aus Stahlrohr, Polsterung aus Polyurethan-schaumstoff, mit Lederbezug, Kopfstütze und Armlehnen mit Rohrumflechtung | Châssis en tube d'acier, siège et dossier rembourrés en mousse de polyuré-thane recouverte de cuir, repose-tête et accoudoirs cannés

ZANOTTA, MILAN, FROM 1992 TO PRESENT

Rolf Sachs

DJ Evolution, 1995

Solid maple
construction |
Konstruktion aus
Ahorn | Érable ᴍ ᴀᵢᵢ)

ᴵᴬGLIABUE, ITALY,
FROM 1995 TO
PRESENT

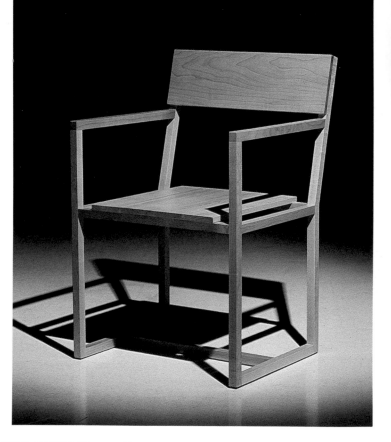

▼ Rolf Sachs
DJ Evolution series
for "Switch-Haus",
1995

TAGLIABUE, ITALY,
FROM 1995 TO
PRESENT

Rolf Sachs' designs are characterised by a minimalism
in which elemental geometric forms are repositioned
out of formal alignment and into poetic spatial arrangements. His "DJ Evolution" chair was designed specifically for his "Switch-Haus" – an environmentally conscious and energy-efficient building with a remarkable
compositional lightness which is widely marketed by a
German construction company.

*Rolf Sachs' Entwürfe sind von einem Minimalismus ge-
prägt, in dem elementare geometrische Formen aus traditionellen Verbindungen gelöst und in poetische räumliche
Arrangements übertragen werden. Sein Stuhl*

Rolf Sachs

Original, 1993

*MDF construction |
Aus MDF-Platten |
Construction en
médium*

(PROTOTYPE)
ROLF SACHS,
LONDON, FROM 1993

▼ **Rolf Sachs**
Ici Chère, 1995

ROLF SACHS,
LONDON, FROM 1995
TO PRESENT

»DJ Evolution« wurde eigens für sein Switch-Haus entworfen, ein ökologisches und energiesparendes Fertighaus von bemerkenswerter Leichtigkeit, das von einer deutschen Baugesellschaft vertrieben wird.

Les créations de Rolf Sachs se caractérisent par un minimalisme dans lequel des formes géométriques élémentaires sont détournées de leur alignement traditionnel et repositionnées dans l'espace de manière très poétique. Son fauteuil « DJ Evolution » a été spécialement dessiné pour sa « Switch-Haus », maison écologique d'une remarquable légèreté de composition et commercialisée par un constructeur allemand.

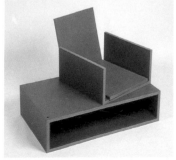

Jane Atfield

RCP2, 1992

Recycled plastic sheet construction |
Konstruktion aus recyceltem Plastik in Plattenform | Feuille de plastique recyclé

MADE OF WASTE,
LONDON, FROM
1992 TO PRESENT

Atfield's ecologically mindful "RCP2" chair utilizes sheets of recycled plastic to provide a colourful and materially radical seating solution.
Atfields hat für ihren umweltfreundlichen Stuhlentwurf »RCP2« Platten aus recyceltem Kunststoff verwendet und ein farbenfrohes und vom Werkstoff her revolutionäres Sitzmöbel geschaffen.
Solution colorée et radicale, la chaise écologique « RCP2 » d'Atfield est fabriquée à partir de feuilles de plastique recyclé.

The "Oritetsu" was conceived as "metal origami". It is sold in a flat sheet form which can then be easily bent into the required shape. Using a punch to stamp the perforations along the fold lines, Booth can mass-produce the chair without costly tooling.

Der Stuhl »Oritetsu« wurde als »Metall-Origami« konzipiert. Verkauft als flache Platte, kann er rasch und mühelos in die richtige Form gefaltet werden. Mit einem Prägestempel werden die Perforationen längs der Falzlinien gestanzt, so daß Booths Stuhl ohne aufwendige Maschinen industriell gefertigt werden kann.

La chaise «Oritetsu» a été conçue comme un «origami en métal». Elle est vendue sous forme d'une feuille plate qui peut facilement être pliée selon la forme requise. Avec ses perforations au poinçon le long des lignes de pliage, ce modèle pourrait être produit en série sans outillage particulier.

Sam Booth

Oritetsu, 1996

Epoxy-coated folded "Zinctec" (mild steel alloy with zinc coating) construction | Konstruktion aus einer gefalteten „Zinctec"-Platte (weiche Stahllegierung mit Zinnbeschichtung), expoxidbeschichtet | «Zinctec» (alliage d'acier doux zingué), gainage époxy

L. W. D., GLASGOW

Gaetano Pesce

Umbrella,
1992–1995

Tubular metal frame
with polypropylene
handle and feet and
polypropylene and
nylon seat | Rahmen
aus Metallrohr, Griff
und Füße aus Poly-
propylen, Sitzfläche
aus Polypropylen und
Nylon | Châssis en
tube métallique,
poignée et pieds en
polypropylène, siège
en polypropylène et
en nylon

ZERODISEGNO,
ALESSANDRIA, FROM
1995 TO PRESENT

▼ **Gaetano Pesce**
Seaweed armchair,
1991

PESCE, NEW YORK,
FROM 1991

Pesce continues to experiment with new forms and materials. His "Umbrella" chair is a lightweight, collapsible and highly portable design. It is transformed from a walking stick into a stable chair at the touch of a button. Pesce's "543 Broadway" has a captivating visual lightness due to the translucency of the epoxy resin used for its seat and back sections – the result of many years research into the remarkable properties of this medium. The spring-mounted feet which act as shock absorbers facilitate a pleasant rocking and rolling motion.

Pesce experimentiert mit neuen Formen und Materialien.
»Umbrella« ist ein Leichtgewicht unter den Stühlen, zu-

sammenklappbar und äußerst mobil. Auf Knopfdruck wird aus einem Spazierstock ein stabiler Stuhl. Pesces »543 Broadway« ist durch die Transparenz des Epoxidharzes von Sitz- und Rückenflächen von faszinierender visueller Leichtigkeit – das Ergebnis langjähriger Erforschung und Erprobung der bemerkenswerten Eigenschaften dieses Materials. Die gefederten Füße dienen als Stoßdämpfer und geben dem Sitzenden ein angenehm wiegendes und rollendes Gefühl.

Pesce poursuit ses expériences avec de nouvelles formes et de nouveaux matériaux. Sa chaise « Umbrella » est ultralégère, repliable et facilement portable. Elle passe de l'état de canne au statut de chaise par une simple pression sur un bouton. La « 543 Broadway » affiche une légèreté séduisante grâce à une résine époxy translucide pour le siège et le dossier, résultat de nombreuses années de recherche sur les propriétés remarquables de ce matériau. Les pieds montés sur ressorts jouant le rôle d'amortisseurs facilitent un léger et agréable effet de balancement et de roulement.

Gaetano Pesce

543 Broadway, 1993

Epoxy resin seat and back on stainless steel frame with nylon feet incorporating metal springs | Gestell aus rostfreiem Stahl, Sitz und Rückenlehne aus Epoxidharz, Nylonfüße mit Metallfedern | Châssis en acier inoxydable, siège et dossier en résine époxy, extrémités de pieds en nylon, ressorts en métal

BERNINI, CARATE BRIANZA, MILAN, FROM 1996 TO PRESENT

Christophe Pillet

Agatha Dreams,
1995

*Solid cherry
construction |
Konstruktion aus
Kirschholz | Cerisier
massif*

CECCOTTI, CASCINA,
PISA, FROM 1995 TO
PRESENT

Christophe Pillet is one of a new generation of "soft" designers who look to the organic rationalism of the Postwar years for inspiration. His beautiful and deeply humanising designs have a lightness of form, a subtlety of colour and a seductive rhythm. The silky smooth finish of his wooden "Agatha Dreams" chaise longue is wonderfully tactile, while his "Y's" chair revels in the textural qualities of its thick vinyl covering.

Christophe Pillet gehört zu einer neuen Generation von »weichen« Designern, die ihre Inspiration aus dem organischen Rationalismus der Nachkriegsjahre erhalten. Seine wunderschönen und außerordentlich benutzerfreundlichen Entwürfe vereinen Leichtigkeit der Formgebung, subtile Farbgebung und verführerischen Rhythmus. Die seidenglatte Oberfläche der Liege »Agatha Dreams«

▶ Christophe Pillet
So What, 1993

XO, PARIS, FROM
1993 TO PRESENT

◀ Christophe Pillet
Family Life, 1995

CAPPELLINI, AROSIO,
COMO, FROM
1995 TO PRESENT

hat wunderbar taktile Eigenschaften, der Stuhl »Y's« überzeugt dagegen durch die Qualität seines schweren
Vinylbezugs.

Christophe Pillet représente une nouvelle génération
de designers « soft » qui recherchent leur inspiration
dans le rationalisme organique de l'après-guerre. Ses
superbes créations possèdent une légèreté de forme,
une subtilité de couleurs et un rythme séduisant. La finition soyeuse de sa chaise longue « Agatha Dreams »
est merveilleusement tactile tandis que son fauteuil
« Y's » met en valeur les qualités de texture d'un épais
vinyle.

**Christophe
Pillet**

Y's, 1995

*Vinyl-covered
polyurethane foam-
upholstered seat shell
on swivelling cast-
aluminium base |
Sitzschale mit
Polsterung aus
Polyurethanschaum-
stoff mit Vinylbezug,
drehbarer Fuß aus
Gußaluminium |
Coquille rembourrée
en mousse de
polyuréthane
recouverte de vinyle,
piètement pivotant en
fonte d'aluminium*

CAPPELLINI, AROSIO,
COMO, FROM
1995 TO PRESENT

Tim Power

Chip, 1993–1995

Lacquered tubular aluminium frame with painted sandblasted glass seat and back | Rahmen aus Aluminiumrohr, lackiert, Sitzfläche und Rückenlehne aus eingefärbtem sandgestrahltem Glas | Châssis en tube d'aluminium laqué, siège et dossier en verre sablé et peint

ZERITALIA, S.
ANGELO IN LIZZOLA,
FROM 1995 TO
PRESENT

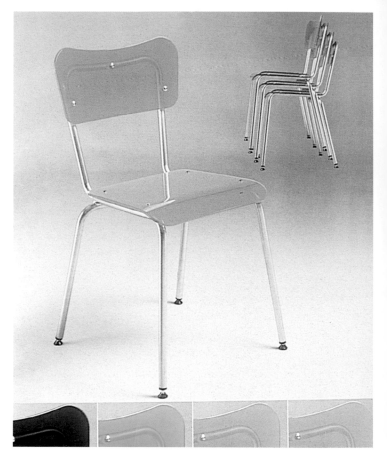

Most often glass is used expressively in chair design. With this example, however, it has been used in a highly rational manner. A mirrored version of the design is also produced.

Meistens wird der Werkstoff Glas im Stuhldesign auf sehr expressive Weise eingesetzt. In diesem Fall aber ist die Verwendung sehr kühl-rational. Dieser Stuhl wird auch in einer Version mit Spiegelglas produziert.

Le verre est la plupart du temps utilisé de manière expressive dans le design de sièges. Ici, cependant, il est mis en œuvre de façon très rationnelle. Une version en verre-miroir est également proposée.

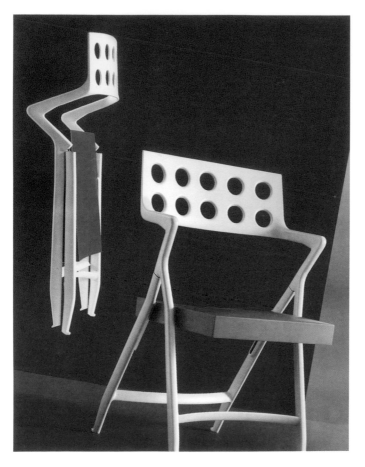

Antonio Citterio & Oliver Löw

Dolly, 1996

Injection-moulded
thermo-plastic
construction |
Konstruktion aus
spritzgußgeformtem
Thermoplast |
Thermoplastique
moulé par injection

KARTELL, NOVIGLIO,
MILAN, FROM
1996 TO PRESENT

Citterio and Löw's "Dolly", like their better-known designs for office seating, is an efficient solution. Utilising a minimal amount of material, this folding chair unusually incorporates integral armrests.

Der Stuhl »Dolly« von Citterio und Löw, besser bekannt für ihre Büromöbel-designs, ist eine zweckbezogene Lösung. Der Entwurf kommt mit einem Minimum an Material aus und hat dennoch, ungewöhnlich für einen Klappstuhl, integrierte Armlehnen.

Comme leurs créations les plus connues dans le domaine du siège de bureau, la « Dolly » de Citterio et Löw est une proposition efficace. N'utilisant que le minimum de matériau, cette chaise pliante possède – ce qui est rare –, des accoudoirs intégrés.

**Prospero
Rasulo**

Calea, 1996

*Polyurethane seat
and back section with
tubular steel frame |
Rahmen aus
Stahlrohr, Sitzfläche
und Rückenlehne aus
Polyurethan | Siège et
dossier en polyur-
éthane, châssis
tubulaire en acier*

ARFLEX, GIUSSANO,
MILAN, FROM
1996 TO PRESENT

The forward-looking "Calea" and "Novia" stacking
chairs reduce to a practicable minimum the amount of
materials necessary for their functions. Both express an
elegant de-materialist aesthetic which is persuasively
argued through an organic vocabulary of form.
*Die zukunftweisenden Stapelstühle »Calea« und »Novia«
beschränken das verwendete Material auf das funktional
notwendige Minimum. Beide zeigen eine elegante
materialreduzierte Ästhetik, die durch eine organische
Formensprache überzeugt.*

Gianni Pareschi
(Gruppo G14)

Novia, 1996

Beech-faced moulded plywood seat shell on lacquered tubular metal frame | Rahmen aus Metallrohr, lackiert, Sitzschale aus geformtem Schichtholz mit Buchenfurnier | Châssis en tube de métal laqué, coquille en contre-plaqué moulé, placage de hêtre

CIATTI, BADIA A
SETTIMO, FROM 1996
TO PRESENT

Ces chaises empilables assez futuristes réduisent pratiquement au minimum la quantité de matériau nécessaire à leur fabrication. Toutes deux expriment une esthétique élégante quasi dématérialisée et mise en scène de façon convaincante dans un langage de formes organiques.

Pascal Mourgue

Rio, 1991

Chromed tubular metal frame with lacquered plywood seat, back and lacquered wood front legs | Rahmen aus Stahlrohr, verchromt, Sitzfläche und Rückenlehne aus geformtem Schichtholz, lackiert, vordere Stuhlbeine aus Holz, lackiert | Châssis en tube de métal chromé, siège et dosseret en contreplaqué laqué, pieds antérieurs en bois laqué

ARTELANO, PARIS, FROM 1991 TO PRESENT

Sharing similar pared-down forms, both these chairs reflect the shift away from anti-rationalism. Whereas Maran's "Sinué" is intended for large-scale manufacture, Mourgue's "Rio" is better suited to lower-volume production.

Beide Stühle mit ihrer puristischen Formgebung zeigen ein Design, das sich vom Anti-Rationalismus fortentwickelt. Während Marans »Sinué« für die Serienproduktion gedacht ist, eignet sich Morgans »Rio« eher für kleine Auflagen.

Partageant des formes épurées similaires, ces deux petits fauteuils reflètent leur éloignement de l'antirationalisme. Si le modèle de Marco Maran « Sinué » est destiné à une production industrielle, le « Rio » de Mourgue est mieux adapté à une production en petite série.

Marco Maran

Sinué, 1995

Polypropylene seat and back on chromed tubular steel frame | Rahmen aus Stahlrohr, verchromt, Sitzfläche und Rückenlehne aus Polypropylen | Châssis en tube d'acier chromé, siège et dossier en polypropylène

FASEM, VICOPISANO, PISA, FROM 1995 TO PRESENT

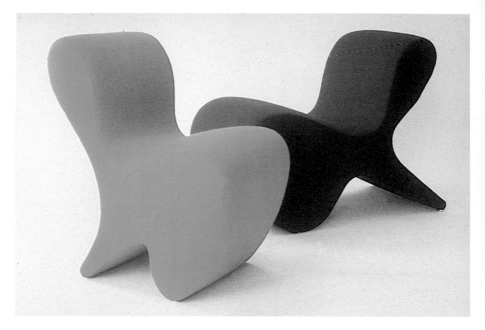

**James Davis &
David Walley**

*Chair 10 & Chair 9,
1996*

Textile-covered
polyurethane foam-
upholstered wood
frame | Rahmen aus
Holz, mit Polsterung
aus Polyurethan-
schaumstoff und
Stoffbezug | Châssis
en bois, rembourrage
en mousse de
polyuréthane
recouverte de tissu

YELLOW DIVA,
LONDON, FROM
1996 TO PRESENT

According to Davis and Walley, their work is driven by "a vibrant and revitalised modernism. Aesthetic form follows a re-evalued function where the 'furniture item' is seen as an object in space containing its own autonomous energy". Using similar abstract anthropomorphic forms, Gili's "Tonda" chair and ottoman look to the past rather than to the future, having been inspired by the "moderne" streamlined forms of the 1930s.

Wie Davis und Walley sagen, werden sie bei ihrer Arbeit von einem »vibrierenden und wiederbelebten Modernismus vorangetrieben. Die ästhetische Formensprache folgt einer neubewerteten Funktionalität, in deren Licht das Möbelstück als ein Objekt im Raum betrachtet wird, das eine eigene, autonome Energie

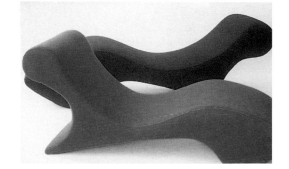

◄ James Davis &
David Walley
Chaise longue 3 &
Chaise longue 2,
1996

YELLOW DIVA,
LONDON, FROM
1996 TO PRESENT

Anna Gili

Tonda, 1991

*Textile-covered
polyurethane foam-
upholstered frame |
Rahmen mit
Polsterung aus Poly-
urethanschaumstoff
und Stoffbezug |
Châssis rembourré en
mousse de
polyuréthane
recouverte de tissu*

CAPPELLINI, AROSIO,
COMO, FROM 1991
TO PRESENT

besitzt.« Mit ganz ähnlichen, reduziert-anthropomorphen Formen weisen auch
Gilis Sessel »Tonda« und der dazugehörige Fußhocker eher zurück als in die
Zukunft, sind sie doch von der »modernen« Stromlinienbegeisterung der 30er
Jahre inspiriert.

Selon Davis et Walley, leur travail est animé par « un modernisme vibrant
et revitalisé. La forme esthétique répond à une fonction réévaluée dans
laquelle l'objet mobilier est considéré comme un objet dans l'espace, riche
de sa propre énergie interne. » Mettant en œuvre des formes abstraites
mais anthropomorphes similaires, le fauteuil « Tonda » de Gili et l'ottomane semblent regarder davantage vers le passé que vers le futur. Ils
s'inspirent des formes épurées « modernes » des années 30.

Francesco Binfaré

L'Homme et la Femme, 1996

Textile-covered polyurethane foam-upholstered metal and wood frame with steel supports | Rahmen aus Metall und Holz auf Stahl-stützen, Polsterung aus Polyurethan-schaumstoff mit Stoffbezug | Châssis en métal et bois rembourré en mousse de polyuréthane recouverte de tissu, supports en acier

EDRA, PERIGANO, PISA, FROM 1996 TO PRESENT

In 1960, Binfaré was appointed co-ordinator of Cassina's contemporary design collection, a post he held for many years. He also co-founded with Gaetano Pesce and Alessandro Mendini the Bracco di Ferro in 1962 and the Centre of Design and Communication in 1980. His sumptuous bed-like sofas for Edra have a monumental presence. Their larger-than-average size allows significant freedom of movement and, thereby, a wide range of uses. *1960 wurde Binfaré zum Kurator für Cassinas Sammlung zeitgenössischen Designs ernannt, eine Stellung, die er viele Jahre innehatte. Zusammen mit Gaetano Pesce und Alessandro Mendini gründete er 1962 die Bracco di Ferro und 1980 das Centre of Design and Communication. Seine luxuriösen bett-ähnlichen Sofas für Edra wirken monumental. Da sie größer sind als sonst üblich, erlauben sie Bewegungsfreiheit und eine vielseitige Nutzung.*

En 1960, Binfaré a été nommé coordinateur de la collection de design contemporain de Cassina, poste qu'il a occupé de nombreuses années. Il a également fondé, avec Gaetano Pesce et Alessandro Mendini, le Bracco di Ferro en 1962 et le Centre of Design and Communication en 1980. Ses somptueux canapés dessinés pour Edra possèdent une présence monumentale. Leurs larges dimensions donnent une grande liberté de mouvement et permettent du même coup de multiples utilisations.

Francesco Binfaré

Tangeri Bed, 1996

Velvet-covered polyurethane foam-upholstered metal and wood frame with chromed metal support and loose cushions | Rahmen aus Metall und Holz mit Stützen aus Metall, verchromt, Polsterung aus Polyurethanschaumstoff mit Samtbezug | Châssis en métal et bois rembourré en mousse de polyuréthane recouverte de tissu, supports en métal chromé et coussins amovibles

EDRA, PERIGANO, PISA, FROM 1996 TO PRESENT

◄ **Francesco Binfaré**
Angels, 1996

EDRA, PERIGANO, PISA, FROM 1996 TO PRESENT

Philippe Starck

Lord Yo, 1994

Injection-moulded polypropylene seat shell on tubular aluminium legs | Sitzschale aus spritz- gußgeformtem Polypropylen, Stuhlbeine aus Aluminiumrohr | Coquille en polypropylène moulé par injection, pieds en tube d'aluminium

DRIADE, FOSSADELLO
DI CAORSO,
PIACENZA, FROM
1994 TO PRESENT

▼ **Philippe Starck**
Olly Tango, 1994

DRIADE, FOSSADELLO
DI CAORSO,
PIACENZA

"Lord Yo" is essentially a plastic reworking of a tradi- tional tub chair. Together with "Miss Trip" and "Olly Tango", it marks a new maturity in Starck's work which has given rise to particularly elegant and rational forms. *»Lord Yo« ist der Neuentwurf eines traditionellen Röhren- sessels aus Plastik. Wie »Miss Trip« und »Olly Tango« repräsentiert es eine neue Reife in Starcks Schaffen, die zu eleganten und rationalen Formen geführt hat.* « Lord Yo » est essentiellement une réinterprétation en plastique du fauteuil en rotin traditionnel. Avec « Miss Trip » et « Olly Tango », il annonce une nouvelle matu- rité dans le travail de Starck, qui a donné naissance à des formes particulièrement élégantes et rationnelles.

Philippe Starck

Miss Trip, 1996

Injection-moulded polypropylene seat and laminated wood back on solid beech legs | Sitzfläche aus spritzgußgeformtem Polypropylen, Rückenlene aus laminiertem Holz, Stuhlbeine aus Buche | Siège en polypropylène moulé par injection, dossier en bois laminé, pieds en hêtre massif

KARTELL, NOVIGLIO, MILAN, FROM 1996 TO PRESENT

▲ **Philippe Starck**
Dr. No, 1996

KARTELL, NOVIGLIO, MILAN, FROM 1996 TO PRESENT

▲ **Philippe Starck**
Prince Aha, 1996

KARTELL, NOVIGLIO, MILAN, FROM 1996 TO PRESENT

Paolo Rizzatto

Young Lord, 1996

*Enamelled metal
frame with caned seat
and back on
swivelling base |
Drehbarer Rahmen
aus Metall, einbrenn-
lackiert, Sitzfläche
und Rückenlehne aus
Rohrgeflecht | Châssis
en métal émaillé,
siège et dossier
cannés, piètement
pivotant*

ALIAS, GRUMELLO
DEL MONTE,
BERGAMO, FROM
1996 TO PRESENT

"Young Lord" forms part of an extensive series of chairs and stools.
Intended for home-office use, the design's caning and quasi-traditional form
oppose the technocratic aesthetic of conventional office seating.

*Der Drehsessel »Young Lord« gehört zu einer größeren Sitzmöbelserie von
Stühlen und Hockern. Für die Benutzung im privaten Arbeitszimmer konzipiert,
stehen seine eher traditionelle Form und das verwendete Rohrgeflecht in Kontrast
zu der technokratischen Ästhetik konventioneller Büromöbel.*

« Young Lord » fait partie d'une gamme étendue de fauteuils et de tabourets. Conçus pour le marché du bureau à domicile, son cannage et ses
formes classiques s'opposent à l'esthétique technocratique des sièges de
bureau habituels.

Suitable for indoor and outdoor use, the structural "rightness" and visual coherence of "Armframe" and "Longframe" are the result of Meda's background in engineering.

Der Sessel »Armframe« und die Liege »Longframe« können in Innenräumen und im Außenbereich eingesetzt werden. Ihre konstruktive »Ehrlichkeit« und die optische Kohärenz verraten Medas ingenieurtechnische Ausbildung.

Conçues aussi bien pour la maison que pour l'extérieur, la justesse structurelle et la cohérence visuelle d' « Armframe » et de « Longframe » sont issues de l'expérience d'ingénieur de Meda.

Alberto Meda

Armframe, 1996

Polished cast-aluminium frame with nylon-mesh seating section | Rahmen aus Guß-aluminium, Sitzbespannung aus Nylongewebe | Châssis en fonte d'aluminium polie, siège en filet de nylon

ALIAS, GRUMELLO
DEL MONTE,
BERGAMO, FROM
1996 TO PRESENT

◄ **Alberto Meda**
Longframe, 1996

ALIAS, GRUMELLO
DEL MONTE,
BERGAMO, FROM
1996 TO PRESENT

Ross Lovegrove

Crop, 1996

Cherry-faced moulded plywood seat, chromed tubular steel base, polyurethane connectors | Sitzfläche aus geformtem Schichtholz mit Kirschholzfurnier, Stuhlbeine aus Stahlrohr, verchromt, Verbindungselemente aus Thermoplast | Siège en contreplaqué moulé, placage de cerisier, piètement en tube d'acier, fixations en thermoplastique

FASEM, VICOPISANO, PISA, FROM 1996 TO PRESENT

▼ **Ross Lovegrove**
Crop armchair, 1996

FASEM, VICOPISANO, PISA, FROM 1996 TO PRESENT

Ross Lovegrove

Bone, 1996

Carved maple frame
with stitched leather
saddle seat | Rahmen
aus Ahorn, Sitzfläche
aus vernähtem
Sattelleder | Châssis
en érable sculpté,
siège en cuir de selle
piqué

CECCOTTI, CASCINA,
PISA, FROM 1996 TO
PRESENT

The rhetoric of Lovegrove's "Crop" and "Bone" chairs is emotionally persuasive because it is expressed through a highly refined and seductive
organic vocabulary. His "Crop" armchair is remarkable for its single-form
seat shell with integral armrests.

Die Rhetorik von Lovegroves Stühlen »Crop« und »Bone« ist emotional über-
zeugend, weil sie sich in einem raffinierten und verführerisch-organischen
Vokabular ausdrückt. Bemerkenswert ist die aus einem Stück geformte
Sitzschale mit integrierten Armlehnen des Armlehnstuhls »Crop«.

La rhétorique de ces deux créations de Lovegrove convainc parce qu'elle
s'exprime dans un vocabulaire organique à la fois raffiné et séduisant. La
chaise « Crop » est remarquable pour son siège d'une seule pièce et ses
accoudoirs intégrés.

Ross Lovegrove

Magic, 1997

*Tubular aluminium
frame with moulded
polyurethane seating
section | Rahmen aus
Aluminiumrohr,
Sitzfläche aus
geformtem Poly-
urethan | Châssis en
tube d'aluminium,
siège en polyuréthane*

FASEM, VICOPISANO,
PISA, FROM 1997 TO
PRESENT

▼ **Ross Lovegrove**
Spider, 1997

DRIADE, FOSSADELLO
DI CAORSO,
PIACENZA, FROM
1997 TO PRESENT

Lovegrove believes that it is only through adopting a
Modern methodology that better-performing, more efficient and environmentally sound designs can be created. He perpetuates the ethos of "product morality"
through his beautiful, harmonious and holistically
derived tools for living which are intended to improve
the lives of and touch the souls of people.
*Lovegrove ist überzeugt, daß nur dann funktionalere, effi-
zientere und umweltbewußtere Entwürfe entstehen, wenn
man sich moderner Verfahrensweisen bedient. Mit seinen
schönen, harmonischen und ausgereiften Möbeln, die das*

Ross Lovegrove

FO8, 1992

*Rim-moulded
polyurethane seat
section on tubular
aluminium base with
nylon feet | Sitzschale
aus geformtem Poly-
urethan, Stuhlbeine
aus Aluminiumrohr
mit Nylonkappen |
Siège à rebord en
polyuréthane moulé
sur piètement en tube
d'aluminium, patins
en nylon*

CAPPELLINI, AROSIO,
COMO, FROM 1994
TO PRESENT

▼ Ross Lovegrove
Working drawing of
Fo8, 1992

*Leben der Menschen erleichtern und sie auch emotional
ansprechen sollen, hält er fest am Ethos der »Produkt-
moral«.*

Lovegrove pense que l'on ne peut créer un design plus
performant, plus efficace et plus respectueux de l'environnement qu'en adoptant une méthodologie moderne.
Il perpétue ainsi l'éthique de la « moralité du produit »
à travers des objets à vivre à la fois merveilleux, har-
monieux et holistiques, censés améliorer la vie et
toucher l'âme des gens.

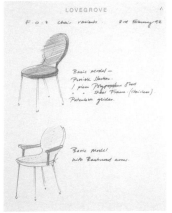

Photographic Credits Fotonachweis Crédits photographiques

L – left/links/
à gauche
C – centre/Mitte/
centre
R – right/rechts/
à droit
p. – page/Seite/
page

page 26 Main: Museum of Fine Arts, Boston – Charles Hitchcock Tyler Residuary Fund 27 Main: Haslam & Whiteway, London 27 Archival: Tecta, Lauenförde 28 Main: Museum Thonet – Gebrüder Thonet GmbH, Frankenberg 28 Archival: Museum Thonet – Gebrüder Thonet GmbH, Frankenberg 29 Main: Fiell International Ltd., London 29 Archival: Museum Thonet – Gebrüder Thonet GmbH, Frankenberg 30 Main: Museum Thonet – Gebrüder Thonet GmbH, Frankenberg 30 Archival: Museum Thonet – Gebrüder Thonet GmbH, Frankenberg 31 Main: Museum Thonet – Gebrüder Thonet GmbH, Frankenberg 32 Main: Haslam & Whiteway, London 34 Main: Haslam & Whiteway, London 34 Archival: Christie's Images, London 35 Main: Haslam & Whiteway, London 36 Main: Haslam & Whiteway, London 37 Main: Hancock Shaker Village, Pittsfield, MA (photo: Paul Rocheleau) 37 Archival: Hancock Shaker Village, Pittsfield, MA (photo: Paul Rocheleau) 38 Main: Laurent Sully-Jaulmes, Paris 39 Main: Barry Friedman, New York 40 Main: Det Danske Kunstindustriemuseum, Copenhagen 40 Archival: Deutsche Kunst und Dekoration, vol. VI, 1900, p. 589 41 Main: Sotheby's, London 41 Archival: Musée des Arts Decoratifs, Paris 42 Main: Musée des Arts Decoratifs, Paris 43 Main: Barry Friedman, New York 44 Main: Musée des Arts Decoratifs, Paris 44 Archival: Musée des Arts Decoratifs, Paris 45 Main: Torsten Bröhan, Düsseldorf 45 Archival: Barry Friedman, New York 46 Main: Barry Friedman, New York 47 Main: Sotheby's, London 47 Archival – L: Barry Friedman, New York 47 Archival – R: Barry Friedman, New York 48 Main: Christie's Images, London 49 Main: Torsten Bröhan, Düsseldorf 49 Archival: Nordenfjeldske Kunstindustrimuseum, Trondheim 50 Barry Friedman, New York 50 Archival: Dekorative Kunst, vol. VIII, 1901, p. 490 51 Main: Torsten Bröhan, Düsseldorf 51 Archival: Museum für Kunsthandwerk, Frankfurt am Main Collection, Munich 52 Main: Galerie Geitel, Berlin 53 Main: Private Collection, Munich (photo: S. R. Gnamm) 53 Archival: Private Collection, Munich (photo: S. R. Gnamm) 56 Main: Institut Mathildenhöhe Darmstadt, Darmstadt 55 Main: Institut Mathildenhöhe Darmstadt, Darmstadt 90 Main: Institut Mathildenhöhe Darmstadt, Darmstadt 56 Archival: Institut Mathildenhöhe Darmstadt, Darmstadt 57 Main: Hermann Muthesius, Das moderne Landhaus und seine innere Ausstattung, München 1905, p. 94 58 Main: Deutsche Kunst und Dekoration, vol. 11, 1902/1903, p. 292 59 Main: Haslam & Whiteway, London 60 Main: Private Collection, Munich (photo: S. R. Gnamm) 60 Archival – L: Barry Friedman, New York 60 Archival – R: Die Kunst, 1901, p. 347 61 Main: Private Collection, Munich (photo: S. R. Gnamm) 61 Archival: Barry Friedman, New York 62 Main: Deutsche Kunst und Dekoration, 10, 1902, p. 589 63 Main: Hunterian Art Gallery, University of Glasgow, Glasgow 64 Main: Fine Art Society, London 65 Main: Barry Friedman, New York 66 Main: Fischer Fine Art, Vienna 67 Main: Christie's Images, London 68 Main: Georg Kargi, Vienna 69 Main: Barry Friedman, New York 70 Main: Fischer Fine Art, Vienna 70 Archival – L: Historisches Museum der Stadt Wien, Vienna 70 Archival – R: Sotheby's, London 71 Main: Paul Asenbaum, Vienna 71 Archival: Fischer Fine Art, Vienna 72 Main: Sotheby's, London 72 Archival: Georg Kargi, Vienna 73 Main: Deutsche Kunst und Dekoration, vol. XVIII, 1906, p. 427 74 Main: Georg Kargi, Vienna 74 Archival: Sotheby's, London 75 Main: Sotheby's, London 75 Archival: The Studio, The Art Revival in Austria, London, 1906 76 Main: Georg Kargi, Vienna 76 Archival – L: Deutsche Kunst und Dekoration, XLI, 1917/1918 76 Archival – R: Barry Friedman, New York 77 Main: Sotheby's, London 78 Main: Sotheby's, London 78 Archival: Dr. Paul Asenbaum, Vienna 79 Main: Kunsthandel Thomas Berg, Bonn 79 Archival: Moderne Bauformen, VII., 1908, p. 370 80 Main: Christie's, New York 81 Main: David Rago Inc., Lambertville, New Jersey 81 Archival: L. & J. G. Stickley Inc., Manlins, NY 82 Main: Barry Friedman, New York 82 Archival: Torsten Bröhan, Düsseldorf 83 Main: Torsten Bröhan, Düsseldorf 84 Main: Christie's, New York 85 Main: Christie's, New York 86 Main: Christie's, New York 86 Archival – L: Cassina, Milan 86 Archival – R: Christie's, New York 87 Main: Christie's, New York 88 Main: Musée des Arts Decoratifs, Paris 89 Main: Sotheby's, London 89 Archival: Sotheby's, London 90 Main: Hunterian Art Gallery, University of Glasgow, Glasgow (photo: Anthony Oliver) 91 Main: Hunterian Art Gallery, University of Glasgow, Glasgow 92 Main: Tecta, Lauenförde 93 Main: Tecta, Lauenförde 93 Archival: Bildarchiv Foto Marburg 94 Main: Barry Friedman, New York 95 Main: Torsten Bröhan, Düsseldorf 96 Main: Barry Friedman, New York 96 Archival – L: Gustav Adolf Platz, Wohnräume der Gegenwart, Berlin 1933, p. IX 96 Archival – R: Barry Friedman, New York 97 Main: Barry Friedman, New York 98 Main: Barry Friedman, New York 98 Archival – L: Barry Friedman, New York 98 Archival – R: Barry Friedman, New York 99 Main: Christie's Images, London 99 Archival: Stiftung Bauhaus Dessau, Dessau 100 Main: Tecta, Lauenförde 100 Archival: Velhagen und Klasings Monatshefte, vol. III, 1927, p. 89 101 Main: Bauhaus-Archiv, Berlin 101 Archival: Kunstsammlungen zu Weimar, Weimar 102 Main: Bauhaus-Archiv, Berlin 102 Archival – L: Torsten Bröhan, Düsseldorf 102 Archival – R: Die Baubücher, vol. I, 1931, p. 41 103 Main: Torsten Bröhan, Düsseldorf (photo: Walter Klein) 103 Archival: Torsten Bröhan, Düsseldorf (photo: Walter Klein) 104 Main: Torsten Bröhan, Düsseldorf 104 Archival – L: Tecta, Lauenförde 104 Archival – R: Gustav Adolf Platz, Wohnräume der Gegenwart, Berlin 1933, p. 359 105 Main: Christie's, Amsterdam 105 Archival: Tecta, Lauenförde 106 Main: Stuhlmuseum Burg Beverungen, Beverungen 106 Archival: Innendekoration, 38, 1927, p. 449 107 Main: Stuhlmuseum Burg Beverungen, Beverungen 107 Archival: Stuhlmuseum Burg Beverungen, Beverungen 108 Main: Barry Friedman, New York 108 Archival – L: Ulrich Gronert, Kunsthandel, Berlin (photo: Lepkowski) 108 Archival – R: Gustav Adolf Platz, Wohnräume der Gegenwart, Berlin, 1933, p. 317 109 Main: De-

Photographic Credits | Fotonachweis | Crédits photographiques

signsammlung Ludewig, Berlin (photo: Lepkowski) 110 Main: Sotheby's, London 110 Archival – L: Tecta, Lauenförde 110 Archival – R: Gustav Adolf Platz, Wohnräume der Gegenwart, Berlin, 1933, p. 316 111 Main: Barry Friedman, New York 112 Main: Barry Friedman, New York 112 Archival – L: Tecta, Lauenförde 112 Archival – R: Innendekoration, 42, 1931, p. 254 113 Main: Fischer Fine Art, Vienna 113 Archival: Fischer Fine Art, Vienna 114 Main: Christie's, Amsterdam 114 Archival: Gustav Adolf Platz, Wohnräume der Gegenwart, Berlin, 1933, p. 313 115 Main: Barry Friedman, New York 115 Archival: Christie's, London 116 Main: Knoll International, New York 116 Archival: Knoll International, New York 117 Main: Knoll International, New York 117 Archival: Knoll International, New York 118 Main: Tecta, Lauenförde 118 Archival: Bauhaus-Archiv, Berlin (photo: Lepkowski) 119 Main: Tecta, Lauenförde 120 Main: Art et Décoration, vol. LVII, 1930, p. 31 121 , Main: Christie's, New York 121 Archival: Art et Décoration, vol. LVII, 1930, p. 55 122 Main: Sotheby's, London 123 Main: Ecart International, Paris 123 Archival: Art et Décoration, vol. LV, 1929, p . 177 124 Main: Musée des Arts Decoratifs, Paris 125 Main: Musée des Arts Decoratifs, Paris 126 Main: Barry Friedman, New York 126 Archival: Christie's, Monaco 127 Main: Sotheby's, London 127 Archival: Christie's, New York 128 Main: Sotheby's, London 128 Archival: Art et Décoration, vol. LVI, 1929, p. 10 129 Main: Christie's, New York 129 Archival: Sotheby's, London 130 Main: Cassina, Milan 130 Archival – Art et Décoration, vol. LVII, 1930, p. 41 130 Archival – R: Art et Décoration, vol. LVI, 1929, p. 181 131 Main: Kunsthandel Thomas Berg, Bonn 131 Archival: Charlotte Perriand 132 Main: Art et Décoration, vol. LVII, 1930, p. 34 132 Archival – L: L`art international d'aujourd'hui, Intérieurs, Paris, s. a. (1930), pl. 36 132 Archival – R: Cassina, Milan 133 Main: Fiell International Ltd., London (photo: Paul Chave) 133 Archival: Cassina, Milan 134 Main: Tecta, Lauenförde 134 Archival: Tecta, Lauenförde 135 Main: Tecta, Lauenförde 135 Archival: Tecta, Lauenförde 136 Main: Fischer Fine Art, Vienna 136 Archival: Fischer Fine Art, Vienna 137 Main: Barry Friedman, New York 137 Archival: Art et Décoration, vol. LVII, 1930, p. 59 138 Main: Benedikt Taschen Archiv, Cologne (photo: Jacques Vasseur) 138 Archival: Barry Friedman, New York 139 Main: Benedikt Taschen Archiv, Cologne (photo: Jacques Vasseur) 139 Archival: Art et Décoration, vol. LXI, 1932, p. 97 140 Main: Tecta, Lauenförde 140 Archival: Tecta, Lauenförde 141 Main: Tecta, Lauenförde 141 Archival: Tecta, Lauenförde 142 Main: Fischer Fine Art, Vienna 142 Archival: Stuhlmuseum Burg Beverungen, Beverungen 143 Main: Sotheby's, London 144 Main: Sotheby's, London 144 Archival: Victoria & Albert Museum, London 145 Main: ClassiCon, Munich 145 Archival – L: Private Collection, Brussels 145 Archival – R: ClassiCon, Munich 146 Main: ClassiCon, Munich 147 Main: ClassiCon, Munich 147 Archival: ClassiCon, Munich 148 Main: Art et Décoration, vol. LXI, 1932, p. 97 148 Archival: L'Art International d'aujourd'hui, Intérieurs, Paris, s. a. (1930), p. 39 149 Main: Barry Friedman, New York (photo: Richard P. Goodbody) 149 Archival: Christie's Images, London 150 Main: Formes Nouvelle, Paris 150 Archival: Art et Décoration, vol. LVII, 1930, p. 33 151 Main: Formes Nouvelle, Paris 151 Archival: Art et Décoration, vol. LXI, 1932, p. 102 152 Main: Zanotta, Milan 152 Archival: Zanotta, Milan 153 Main: Zanotta, Milan 153 Archival: Zanotta, Milan 154 Main: Zanotta, Milan 154 Archival – L: Zanotta, Milan 154 Archival – R: Zanotta, Milan 155 Main: Zanotta, Milan 155 Archival: Zanotta, Milan 156 Main: Barry Friedman, New York 157 Main: Barry Friedman, New York 157 Archival – L: Theodore M. Brown, The Work of G. Rietveld, Architect, A. W. Bruna & Zoon, Utrecht, 1958, p. 94 157 Archival – R: Barry Friedman, New York 158 Main: Christies, New York 159 Main: Bonhams, London 159 Archival: Barry Friedman, New York 160 Main: Fifty/50, New York 160 Archival: The Studio Year Book of Decorative Art, 1938, p. 74 161 Main: Fischer Fine Art, Vienna 161 Archival: Philadelphia Museum of Art (Purchased by COLLAB in honor of Cynthia W. Drayton and the Fiske Kimball Fund) 162 Main: Gordon Logie, Furniture from machines, London, 1947, p. 92, pl. 114 162 Archival – L: Artek, Helsinki 162 Archival – R: Artek, Helsinki 163 Main: Barry Friedman, New York 164 Main: Artek, Helsinki 164 Archival – L: Artek, Helsinki 165 Main: Artek, Helsinki 165 Archival: Artek, Helsinki 166 Main: Christies Images, London 166 Archival: Herbert Bayer, Das federnde Aluminium-Möbel, Wohnbedarf, Zürich 1934 167 Main: Fischer Fine Art, Vienna 167 Archival: Herbert Bayer, Das federnde Aluminium-Möbel, Wohnbedarf, Zürich, 1934 168 Main: Fischer Fine Art, Vienna 169 Main: Die Neue Sammlung, Staatliches Museum für angewandte Kunst, Munich 169 Archival: E. Nelson Exton & Frederic H. Littmann, Modern Furniture, London 1936, p. 38 170 Main: Haslam & Whiteway, London 170 Archival: The Museum of Modern Art, New York 171 Main: Museé des Arts Decoratifs, Montreal 172 Archival – Top: Barry Friedman, New York 172 Archival – Bottom: Barry Friedman, New York 173 Main: Fiell International Ltd., London (photo: Paul Chave) 174 Main: Fischer Fine Art, Vienna 174 Archival: Christies Images, London 175 Main: Christies Images, London 175 Archival: The Studio Year Book of Decorative Art, 1938, p. 124 176 Main: Rud Rasmussen Snedkerier, Copenhagen (photo: Schnakenburg & Brahl) 176 Archival: Rud Rasmussen Snedkerier, Copenhagen (photo: Schnakenburg & Brahl) 177 Main: Cranbrook Art Museum, Bloomfield Hills, MI 177 Archival: Cranbrook Art Museum, Bloomfield Hills, MI 178 Main: Haslam & Whiteway, London 179 Main: Fiell International Ltd., London – Collection of Sir Richard & Lady Rogers (photo: Paul Chave) 179 Archival – L: Maple & Co. Sales Catalogue, c.1925 179 Archival – R: Fiell International Ltd., London – Collection of Sir Richard & Lady Rogers (photo: Paul Chave) 180 Main: Rud Rasmussen Snedkerier, Copenhagen (photo: Ole Woldbye) 181 Main: Rud Rasmussen Snedkerier, Copenhagen 182 Main: Rud Rasmussen Snedkerier, Copenhagen 182 Archival: Rud Rasmussen Snedkerier, Copenhagen 183 Main:

Bernini, Milan **184** Main: Christies, New York **185** Main: Cooper-Hewitt, National Design Museum, Smithonian Inst./Art Resource, New York **185** Archival: Brooklyn Museum, New York **186** Main: Ecart SA, Paris **186** Archival: Barry Friedman, New York **187** Main: Stöhr Import-Export GmbH, Besigheim **187** Archival: Benedikt Taschen Archiv, Cologne **188** Main: Whitechapel Art Gallery, London **189** Main: Brighton Art Gallery & Museums, Brighton **189** Archival: The Art Institute of Chicago, Chicago (Gift of Mrs. Gilbert W. Chapman) **190** Main: Frank Lloyd Wright Foundation, Scottsdale, Arizona **191** Main: Christies, New York **191** Archival – L: Steelcase Strafor, Grand Rapids **191** Archival – R: Collection of the Public Museums of Grand Rapids, Grand Rapids **192** Main: Zanotta, Milan **192** Archival: Sotheby's, London **193** Main: Sotheby's, London **194** Archival – Top – L: »Organic Design in Home Furnishings« Catalogue, Museum of Modern Art, New York, 1940 **194** Archival – Top – R : »Organic Design in Home Furnishings« Catalogue, Museum ofMod-ern Art, New York, 1940 **194** Archival – Bottom: »Organic Design in Home Furnishings« Catalogue, Museum of Modern Art, New York, 1940 **195** Main: »Organic Design in Home Furnishings« Ca-talogue, Museum of Modern Art, New York, 1940 **195** Archival: »Organic Design in Home Furnishings« Ca-talogue, Museum of Modern Art, New York , 1940 **196** Main: Fiell International Ltd., London (photo: Peter Hodsoll) **196** Archival – L: Fifty/50, New York **196** Archival – R: Lucia Eames dba Eames Office, Venice, Cali-fornia (photo: Charles Eames) **197** Main: Fiell International Ltd., London (photo: Peter Hodsoll) **198** Main: Fischer Fine Art, Vienna **199** Main: Stuhlmuseum Burg Beverungen, Beverungen **199** Archival: Stuhlmuseum Burg Beverungen, Beverungen **200** Main: Museé des Arts Decoratifs, Montreal (Gift of Geoffrey N. Brad-field) (photo: Giles Rivest) **200** Archival: Knoll International, New York **201** Main: Artek, Helsinki **201** Archival: Artek, Helsinki **202** Main: W. Lusty & Sons Ltd., Chipping Campden **202** Archival: W. Lusty & Sons Ltd., Chipping Campden **203** Main: Museé des Arts Decoratifs, Paris **203** Archival: J. Royère Archives, Museé des Arts Decoratifs, Paris **204** Main: Race Furniture Ltd., Bourton-on-the-Water **205** Main: Race Furniture Ltd., Bourton-on-the-Water **205** Archival – L: Race Furniture Ltd., Bourton-on-the-Water **205** Archival – R: Race Furniture Ltd., Bourton-on-the-Water **206** Main: Fiell International Ltd., London (photo: James Barlow) **206** Archival: Fiell International Ltd., London (photo: James Barlow) **207** Main: Kohseki Co. Ltd., Kyoto **208** Main: Kohseki Co. Ltd., Kyoto **209** Main: Kohseki Co. Ltd., Kyoto **209** Archival: Kohseki Co. Ltd., Kyoto **210** Main: Carl Hansen, Odense **211** Main: P. P. Møbler, Allerød (photo: Schakenburg & Brahl) **212** Main: Fritz Hansen, Allerød **213** Main: P. P. Møbler, Allerød (photo: Schakenburg & Brahl) **213** Archival: Johannes Hansen, Allerød **214** Main: P. P. Møbler, Allerød (photo: Schakenburg & Brahl) **214** Archival: Fiell Interna-tional Ltd., London (photo: Paul Chave) **215** Main: Fritz Hansen, Allerød **215** Archival: Karl Andersson & Sohner, Huskvarna **216** Main: Lucia Eames dba Eames Office, Venice, California (photo: Charles Eames) **218** Main: Fischer Fine Art, Vienna **218** Archival – L: Fiell International Ltd., London (photo: Peter Hodsoll) **218** Archival – R: Lucia Eames dba Eames Office, Venice, California (photo: Charles Eames) **219** Main: Fiell Inter-national Ltd., London (photo: Paul Chave) **219** Archival: Herman Miller Inc., Zeeland, Michigan **220** Main: Treadway Gallery, Cincinnati **220** Archival: Museum of Modern Art, New York **221** Main: Bonhams, London **221** Archival: Museé des Arts Décoratifs, Montreal – Liliane & David M. Stewart Collection (photo: Richard P. Goodbody) **222** Main: Museé des Arts Décoratifs, Montreal – Gift of Fifty/50 (photo: Richard P. Good-body) **223** Main: J. G. Furniture Systems Inc., Quakertown **223** Archival: J. G. Furniture Systems Inc., Quaker-town **224** Main: Christina & Bruno Bischofberger Collection, Zurich **224** Archival: Mollino Archives, Faculty of Architecture, Turin (photo: Riccardo Moncalvo) **225** Main: Christina & Bruno Bischofberger Collection, Zurich **225** Archival: Mollino Archives, Faculty of Architecture, Turin **226** Main: Arflex, Milan **226** Archival: Zanotta, Milan **227** Main: Kohseki Co. Ltd., Kyoto **227** Archival: Kohseki Co. Ltd., Kyoto **228** Main: Museé des Arts Décoratifs, Montreal – Liliane & David M. Stewart Collection (photo: Mark Meachem) **228** Archival: Knoll International, New York **229** Main: Fiell International Ltd., London (photo: Peter Hodsoll) **229** Archival: Knoll International, New York **230** Main: David Rago Inc., Lambertville, New Jersey **230** Archival: Herman Miller Inc., Zeeland, Michigan **231** Main: 20th Century, Toronto **232** Main: Museé des Arts Décora-tifs, Montreal – Gift of Davis Pratt (photo: Richard P. Goodbody) **232** Archival: Museé des Arts Décoratifs, Montreal **233** Main: Museé des Arts Décoratifs, Montreal – Gift of Eva Zeisel (photo: Richard P. Goodbody) **233** Archival: Museé des Arts Décoratifs, Montreal **234** Main: Christies, New York **234** Archival: Museé des Arts Décoratifs, Montreal – Gift of Edward J. Wormley (photo: Mark Meachem) **235** Main: The Collection of the Public Museum of Grand Rapids, Grand Rapids **236** Main: Hille Ltd., Warrington, Cheshire **236** Archival: Hille Ltd., Warrington, Cheshire **237** Main: Bonhams, London **238** Main: Fritz Hansen, Allerød **239** Main: Fritz Hansen, Allerød **240** Main: P. P. Møbler, Allerød (photo: Schakenburg & Brahl) **240** Archival: Hans Wegner, Copenhagen **241** Main: P. P. Møbler, Allerød (photo: Schakenburg & Brahl) **241** Archival: Kohseki Co. Ltd., Kyoto **242** Main: Benedikt Taschen Archive, Cologne **242** Archival: Benedikt Taschen Archive, Cologne **243** Main: Det Danske Kunstindustrimuseum, Copenhagen **243** Archival: Fritz Hansen, Allerød **244** Main: Benedikt Taschen Archive, Cologne **244** Archival: Benedikt Taschen Archive, Cologne **245** Main: Benedikt Taschen Archive, Cologne **245** Archival: Galerie Artifical, Nuremberg **246** Main: Christies, New York **247** Main: Tecta, Lauenförde **248** Main: Cale Associates, London (photo: Schakenburg & Brahl) **248** Archival: Danish Design Centre, Copenhagen **249** Main: Fiell International Ltd., London (photo: Paul Chave) **249**

Photographic Credits | Fotonachweis | Crédits photographiques

Archival: Sotheby's, London **250** Main: Bonhams, London **250** Archival: Fiell International Ltd., London (photo: Peter Hodsoll) **251** Main: Fiell International Ltd., London (photo: Peter Hodsoll) **252** Main: ICF UK, London **252** Archival: Knoll International, New York **253** Main: Fiell International Ltd., London (photo: Peter Hodsoll) **254** Main: Knoll International, New York **254** Archival – L: Knoll International, New York **254** Archival – R: Knoll International, New York **255** Main: Fiell International Ltd., London (photo: Peter Hodsoll) **255** Archival: Knoll International, New York **256** Main: Fiell International Ltd., London (photo: Paul Chave) **257** Main: Museé des Arts Décoratifs, Montreal – Gift of George Nelson (photo: Richard P. Goodbody) **257** Archival: Herman Miller Inc., Zeeland, Michigan **258** Main: Knoll International, New York **258** Archival – L: Knoll International, New York **258** Archival–R: Knoll International, New York – Collection Don Petitt **259** Main: Fiell International Ltd., London (photo: Paul Chave) **259** Archival: Knoll International, New York **260** Main: Knoll International, New York **260** Archival: Fiell International Ltd., London (photo: Paul Chave) **261** Main: Fiell International Ltd., London (photo: Peter Hodsoll) **261** Archival: Herman Miller Inc., Zeeland, Michigan **262** Main: Herman Miller Inc., Zeeland, Michigan (photo: Earl Woods) **263** Main: Fifty/50, New York **263** Archival – L: Herman Miller Inc., Zeeland, Michigan **263** Archival – R: Herman Miller Inc., Zeeland, Michigan **264** Main: Fiell International Ltd., London (photo: Peter Hodsoll) **264** Archival: Herman Miller Inc., Zeeland, Michigan **265** Main: Fiell International Ltd., London (photo: Peter Hodsoll) **265** Archival: Herman Miller Inc., Zeeland, Michigan **266** Main: Artek, Helsinki **267** Main: Artery, New York **268** Main: Zanotta, Milan **269** Main: David Rago Inc., Lambertville, New Jersey **269** Archival: George Nelson, Chairs, Whitney Publications, New York, 1953, p. 142 **270** Main: Fiell International Ltd., London (photo: Paul Chave) **271** Main: Sotheby's, London **271** Archival: Hille Ltd., Warrington, Cheshire **272** Main: Fiell International Ltd., London (photo: Paul Chave) **273** Main: Race Furniture Ltd., Bourton-on-the-Water **273** Archival – L: Race Furniture Ltd., Bourton-on-the-Water **273** Archival – R: Race Furniture Ltd., Bourton-on-the-Water **274** Main: Fiell International Ltd., London (photo: Paul Chave) **274** Archival: Lucia Eames dba Eames Office, Venice, California (photo: Charles Eames) **275** Main: Fiell International Ltd., London (photo: Paul Chave) **275** Archival: Lucia Eames dba Eames Office, Venice, California (photo: Charles Eames) **276** Main: photo: Julius Shulman **277** Main: Herman Miller Inc., Zeeland, Michigan **277** Archival: Herman Miller Inc., Zeeland, Michigan **278** Main: Fiell International Ltd., London (photo: Peter Hodsoll) **278** Archival: Herman Miller Inc., Zeeland, Michigan (photo: William Sharpe – Effective Images) **279** Main: Herman Miller Inc., Zeeland, Michigan (photo: Earl Woods) **279** Archival – L: Lucia Eames dba Eames Office, Venice, California (photo: Charles Eames) **279** Archival – R: Herman Miller Inc., Zeeland, Michigan **280** Main: Herman Miller Inc., Zeeland, Michigan **280** Archival – L: Herman Miller Inc., Zeeland, Michigan **281** Main: Herman Miller Inc., Zeeland, Michigan (photo: Paul Chave) **281** Archival: Fritz Hansen, Allerød **282** Main: Fredericia Stolefabrik A/S, Fredericia **282** Archival: Fredericia Stolefabrik A/S, Fredericia **283** Main: Museé des Arts Décoratifs, Montreal – Gift of Geoffrey N. Bradfield (photo: Richard P. Goodbody) **283** Archival: Fritz Hansen, Allerød **284** Main: Fiell International Ltd., London (photo: Paul Chave) **284** Archival: Fritz Hansen, Allerød **285** Main: Fritz Hansen, Allerød **286** Main: Fritz Hansen, Allerød **286** Archival: Fritz Hansen, Allerød **287** Main: Fritz Hansen, Allerød **287** Archival – L: Fritz Hansen, Allerød **287** Archival – R: Treadway Gallery Inc., Cincinnati **288** Main: Fritz Hansen, Allerød **288** Archival: Whitechapel Art Gallery, London **289** Main: Museé des Arts Décoratifs, Montreal – Liliane & David Stewart Collection (photo: Richard P. Goodbody) **289** Archival: Cassina, Milan **290** Main: Tecno spa, Milan **290** Archival: Tecno spa, Milan **291** Main: Tecno spa, Milan **291** Archival: Tecno spa, Milan **292** Main: Arflex, Milan **292** Archival: Tecno spa, Milan **293** Main: Arflex, Milan **293** Archival: Arflex, Milan **294** Main: Arflex, Milan **294** Archival: Arflex, Milan **295** Main: Arflex, Milan **295** Archival: Arflex, Milan **296** Main: Arflex, Milan **296** Archival: Sotheby's, London **297** Main: Vittorio Bonacina & C., Lurago D'Erba **297** Archival: Vittorio Bonacina & C., Lurago D'Erba **298** Main: Christina & Bruno Bischofberger Collection, Zurich **298** Archival: Zanotta, Milan **299** Main: Christina & Bruno Bischof-berger Collection, Zurich **299** Archival: Christies Images, London **300** Main: Sotheby's, London **300** Archival: Mollino Archives, Faculty of Architecture, Turin **301** Main: Fifty/50, New York **301** Archival: Brooklyn Museum, New York **302** Main: Galerie Yves Gastou, Paris **302** Archival: SIM, Milan **303** Main: Sotheby's, London **303** Archival – L: SIM, Milan **303** Archival – R: Lillian Kiesler, New York **304** Main: Bernini, Milan **304** Archival – L: Gavina (Simon International), Bologna **304** Archival – R: Gavina (Simon International), Bologna **305** Main: Stuhlmuseum Burg Beverungen, Beverungen **306** Main: Fiell International Ltd., London (photo: Paul Chave) **306** Archival: Fifty/50, New York **307** Main: Fiell International Ltd., London (photo: Paul Chave) **308** Main: Fornasetti, Milan (photo: Michele Assante) **309** Main: Fiell International Ltd., London (photo: Paul Chave) **309** Archival: Fornasetti, Milan **310** Main: Zanotta, Milan **310** Archival – L: George Nelson, Chairs, Whitney Pub-lications, New York, 1953, p. 19 **311** Main: Zanotta, Milan **312** Main: Benedikt Taschen Archiv, Cologne **313** Main: Benedikt Taschen Archiv, Cologne **313** Archival: Verner Panton, Basle **314** Main: Verner Panton, Basle **315** Main: Fritz Hansen, Allerød **315** Archival: Verner Panton, Basle **316** Main: Museé des Arts Décoratifs, Paris (photo: L. Sully-Jaulmes) **317** Main: Museé des Arts Décoratifs, Paris (photo: L. Sully-Jaulmes) **318** Main: Zanotta, Milan **319** Main: Zanotta, Milan (photo: Masera) **319** Archival: Zanotta, Milan **320** Main: Museé des Arts Décoratifs, Montreal – Liliane & David Stewart Collection (photo:

Richard P. Goodbody) 320 Archival: Surreal Scales, Copenhagen 321 Main: Herman Miller Inc., Zeeland, Michigan (photo: Earl Woods) 322 Main: Christies, New York 322 Archival: Knoll International, New York 323 Main: Barry Friedman, New York 323 Archival: Fiell International Ltd., London (photo: Paul Chave) 324 Main: Howe Europe A/S, Middelfart 324 Archival: Howe Europe A/S, Middelfart 325 Main: Howe Europe A/ S, Middelfart 326 Archival – Top L: Hille Ltd., Warrington, Cheshire 326 Archival – Top C: Hille Ltd., Warrington, Cheshire 326 Archival – Top R: Hille Ltd., Warrington, Cheshire 326 Archival – Bottom: Hille Ltd., Warrington, Cheshire 327 Main: Fiell International Ltd., London (photo: Paul Chave) 328 Main: Lucia Eames dba Eames Office, Venice, California (photo: Charles Eames) 329 Main: Knoll International, New York 330 Main: Herman Miller Inc., Zeeland, Michigan 330 Archival: Herman Miller Inc., Zeeland, Michigan 331 Main: Herman Miller Inc., Zeeland, Michigan (photo: Earl Woods) 332 Main: Herman Miller Inc., Zeeland, Michigan 332 Archival – L: Herman Miller Inc., Zeeland, Michigan 332 Archival –R: Herman Miller Inc., Zeeland, Michigan (photo: Phil Schaafsma) 333 Main: Herman Miller Inc., Zeeland, Michigan (photo: Earl Woods) 334 Main: Herman Miller Inc., Zeeland, Michigan 334 Archival – L: Herman Miller Inc., Zeeland, Michigan 334 Archival – R: Herman Miller Inc., Zeeland, Michigan 335 Main: Knoll International, New York 336 Main: Zanotta, Milan (photo: Masera) 336 Archival: Zanotta, Milan (photo: Masera) 337 Main: Driade, Fossadello di Caorso 338 Main: Knoll International, New York 338 Archival: Knoll International, New York 339 Main: Herman Miller, Zeeland, Michigan 340 Main: Knoll International, New York 341 Main: Die Neue Sammlung, Staatliches Museum für angewandte Kunst, Munich (photo: Angela Bröhan) 342 Main: Whitechapel Art Gallery, London 343 Main: Fritz Hansen, Allerød 343 Archival: Fritz Hansen, Allerød 344 Main: Knoll International, New York 345 Main: B&B Italia, Novedrate 346 Main: Vitsoe, Eschborn 346 Archival: Vitsoe, Eschborn 347 Main: Fritz Hansen, Allerød 348 Main: B&B Italia, Novedrate 348 Archival: Cassina, Milan 349 Main: Cassina, Milan 349 Archival: Knoll International, New York 350 Main: Gavina (Simon International), Bologna 351 Main: Fiell International Ltd., London 352 Main: Bieffeplast, Caselle di Selvazzano 353 Main: Fischer Fine Art, Vienna 353 Archival: Kartell, Noviglio 354 Main: Fischer Fine Art, Vienna 355 Main: Zanotta, Milan 355 Archival: Whitechapel Art Gallery, London 356 Main: Danish Design Centre, Copenhagen 357 Main: Danish Design Centre, Copenhagen 358 Main: Benedikt Taschen Verlag Archiv, Cologne (photo: Clarissa Bruce) 359 Main: Fiell International Ltd., London 359 Archival: Avarte Oy, Helsinki 360 Main: Die Neue Sammlung, Staatliches Museum für angewandte Kunst, Munich 360 Archival: Flexform, Milan 361 Main: Fiell International Ltd., London (Bonhams, London) (photo: James Barlow) 362 Main: Kartell, Noviglio 363 Main: The Observer, London 364 Main: Museé des Arts Décoratifs, Montreal – Liliane & David Stewart Collection (photo: Richard P. Goodbody) 365 Main: Verner Panton, Basle 365 Archival: Fischer Fine Art, Vienna 366 Main: Fondation pour l'Architecture 367 Main: Adelta, Dinslaken 368 Main: Fiell International Ltd., London (photo: Paul Chave) 369 Main: Museé des Arts Décoratifs, Montreal – Gift of Nanette & Eric Brill (photo: Richard P. Goodbody) 369 Archival: Adelta, Dinslaken 370 Main: Museé des Arts Décoratifs, Montreal – Liliane & David Stewart Collection (photo: Giles Rivest) 371 Main: Saporiti Italia, Besnate 371 Archival: Saporiti Italia, Besnate 372 Main: Wendell Castle Inc., Scottsville, New York 372 Archival: Wendell Castle Inc., Scottsville, New York 373 Main: Wendell Castle Inc., Scottsville, New York 374 Main: Die Neue Sammlung, Staatliches Museum für angewandte Kunst, Munich 374 Archival: Wilhelm Bofinger KG, Ilsfield 375 Main: Galerie Objekt, Munich 376 Main: Die Neue Sammlung, Staatliches Museum für angewandte Kunst, Munich 376 Archival: Busnelli, Milan 377 Main: Fiell International Ltd., London (photo: Paul Chave) 378 Main: Whitechapel Art Gallery, London 379 Main: Cassina, Milan 380 Main: Verner Panton, Basle 381 Main: David Rago Inc., Lambertville, New Jersey 382 Main: Fiell International Ltd., London (Bonhams, London) (photo: James Barlow) 383 Main: Fiell International Ltd., London (photo: Paul Chave) 384 Main: Fiell International Ltd., London (photo: Paul Chave) 385 Main: Artifort, Lanaken 385 Archival: Artifort, Lanaken 386 Main: Fiell International Ltd., London (photo: Paul Chave) 386 Archival: Artifort, Lanaken 387 Main: Artifort, Lanaken 387 Archival: Fiell International Ltd., London (photo: Paul Chave) 388 Main: Fiell International Ltd., London (photo: Paul Chave) 389 Main: Fiell International Ltd., London 389 Archival: Artifort, Lanaken 390 Main: Whitechapel Art Gallery, London 390 Archival: Turner Entertainment Co., 1968 – All Rights Reserved 391 Main: Bonhams, London 392 Main: Arconas, Mississauga 393 Main: Fiell International Ltd., London (photo: Paul Chave) 394 Main: Verner Panton, Basle 396 Main: Museé des Arts Décoratifs, Montreal – Liliane & David Stewart Collection (photo: Richard P. Goodbody) 396 Archival: Knoll International, New York 397 Main: Die Neue Sammlung, Staatliches Museum für angewandte Kunst, Munich 398 Main: Verner Panton, Basle 399 Main: Arflex, Milan 399 Archival: Arflex, Milan 400 Main: B&B Italia, Novedrate 400 Archivals: B&B Italia, Novedrate 401 Main: B&B Italia, Novedrate 401 Archival: B&B Italia, Novedrate 402 Main: Hille Ltd., Warrington, Cheshire 403 Main: Vittorio Bonacina & C., Lurago d'Erba 404 Main: Kunstmuseum, Düsseldorf (photo: Walter Klein) 405 Main: Fiell International Ltd., London (photo: Peter Hodsoll) 405 Archival: Peter Murdoch, London 406 Main: Zanotta, Milan 407 Main: OMK Design Ltd., London 408 Main: Poltronova, Montale 409 Main: Poltronova, Montale 410 Main: Zanotta, Milan 411 Main: Zanotta, Milan 411 Archival: Zanotta, Milan 412 Main: Zanotta, Milan 413 Main: Zanotta, Milan 413 Archival: Zanotta, Milan 414 Main: Poltronova, Montale 414 Archival: Poltronova, Montale

Photographic Credits | Fotonachweis | Crédits photographiques

415 Main: Benedikt Taschen Verlag Archiv, Cologne (photo: Clarissa Bruce) 415 Archival: Poltronova, Montale 416 Main: Allen Jones, London 417 Main: Gavina (Simon International), Bologna 418 Main: Gavina (Simon International), Bologna 418 Archival: Gavina (Simon International), Bologna 419 Main: Gavina (Simon International), Bologna 419 Archival: Gavina (Simon International), Bologna 420 Main: Gavina (Simon International), Bologna 420 Archival: Gavina (Simon International), Bologna 421 Main: Gavina (Simon International), Bologna 422 Main: Poltronova, Montale 423 Main: Arflex, Milan 424 Main: Driade, Fossadello di Caorso 425 Main: Driade, Fossadello di Caorso 426 Main: Driade, Fossadello di Caorso 426 Main: Fiell International Ltd., London (photo: Paul Chave) 426 Archival: Artemide, Milan 427 Main: Zanotta, Milan 428 Main: Adelta, Dinslaken 429 Main: Christies Images, London 430 Main: Gufram, Balangero 431 Main: Gufram, Balangero 432 Main: Sotheby's, London 433 Main: Gufram, Balangero 434 Main: Verner Panton, Basle 435 Main: Gufram, Balangero 435 Archival: Poltronova, Montale 436 Main: Cassina, Milan 437 Main: Sotheby's, London 437 Archvial: Museé des Arts Décoratifs, Montreal – Liliane & David Stewart Collection (photo: Richard P. Goodbody) 440 Main: B&B Italia, Novedrate 440 Archival: B&B Italia, Novedrate 441 Main: Driade, Fossadello di Caorso 441 Archival: Driade, Fossadello di Caorso 442 Main: ICF, Vimodrone 443 Main: Vico Magistretti, Milan 444 Main: Fiell International Ltd., London (photo: Paul Chave) 444 Archival: Fiell International Ltd., London (photo: Paul Chave) 445 Main: Cassina, Milan 445 Archival: Cassina, Milan 446 Main: Knoll International, New York 446 Archival: Knoll International, New York 447 Main: Knoll International, New York 447 Archival: Knoll International, New York 448 Main: Marcatré, London 448 Archival: Marcatré, London 449 Main: Avarte Oy, Helsinki 449 Archival: Herman Miller Inc., Zeeland, Michigan (photo: Earl Woods) 450 Main: Knoll International, New York 450 Archival: Knoll International, New York 451 Main: Hille Ltd., Warrington, Cheshire 451 Archival: Hille Ltd., Warrington, Cheshire 452 Main: Olivetti, Milan (photo: Jean-Pierre Maurer) 453 Main: Kreug, Green Bay, Wisconsin 453 Archival: Kreug, Green Bay, Wisconsin 454 Main: Fiell International Ltd., London (photo: Paul Chave) 454 Archival: Floris van den Broecke, London 455 Main: Artifort, Lanaken 456 Main: Vitra AG, Basle 457 Main: Philadelphia Museum of Art, Philadelphia (Gift of Frank O. Gehry) 458 Main: HNB, London 459 Main: Zanotta, Milan 460 Main: Bernini spa, Carate Brianza 460 Archival: B&B Italia, Novedrate 461 Main: Zanotta, Milan 462 Main: Driade, Fossadello di Caorso 462 Archival: Castelli, Bologna 463 Main: OMK Design Ltd., London 463 Archival: OMK Design Ltd., London 464 Main: Alias, Grumello del Monte 465 Main: Sauvagnat Allibert, Sassenage 466 Main: John Makepeace, Beaminster 467 Main: Wendell Castle Inc., Scottsville, New York 467 Archival: Wendell Castle Inc., Scottsville, New York 468 Main: Stendig, New York 468 Archival: Stendig, New York 469 Main: Fiell International Ltd., London (photo: Paul Chave) 470 Main: Verner Panton, Basle 470 Archival: Verner Panton, Basle 471 Main: Stendig, New York 472 & 473 Main: Verner Panton, Basle 472 Archival – L: Verner Panton, Basle 472 Archival – R: Verner Panton, Basle 473 Archival: Verner Panton, Basle 474 Main: Museum Thonet–Gebrüder Thonet GmbH, Frankenburg 474 Archival: Cranbrook Academy, Bloomfield Hills (Thonet Industries, USA) 475 Main: Tecta, Lauenförde 475 Archival: Tecta, Lauenförde 476 Main: Alessandro Mendini, Milan 476 Archival: Alessandro Mendini, Milan 477 Main: Alessandro Mendini, Milan 477 Archival: Alessandro Mendini, Milan 478 Main: Alessandro Mendini, Milan 479 Main: Studio Alchimia, Milan 480 Main: Studio Alchimia, Milan 481 Main: Poltronova, Montale 481 Archival: Poltronova, Montale 482 Main: Tecta, Lauenförde 482 Archival: Tecta, Lauenförde 483 Main: Michele De Lucchi, Milan (photo: Studio Azzuro) 483 Archival: Memphis, Milan 484 Main: Memphis, Milan 484 Archival: Memphis, Milan 485 Main: Memphis, Milan 485 Archival: Memphis, Milan 486 Main: Vitra AG, Basle 486 Archival: Zanotta, Milan 487 Main: Memphis, Milan 488 Main: Knoll International, New York 488 Archival: Knoll International, New York 489 Main: Knoll International, New York 489 Archival – L: Knoll International, New York 489 Archival – R: Knoll International, New York 490 Main: Zanotta, Milan 490 Archival: Zanotta, Milan 491 Main: Zanotta, Milan (photo: Ramazzotti e Stucchi) 492 Main: Zanotta, Milan (photo: Ramazzotti e Stucchi) 493 Main: Knoll International, New York 494 Main: Cassina, Milan 495 Main: Cassina, Milan 495 Archival: Cassina, Milan 496 Main: Cassina, Milan 497 Main: Vico Magistretti, Milan (Cassina, Milan) 497 Archival: Vico Magistretti, Milan (Cassina, Milan) 498 Main: Vico Magistretti, Milan (Cassina, Milan) 498 Archival: Vico Magistretti, Milan (Cassina, Milan) 499 Main: Gaetano Pesce, New York (Cassina, Milan) 499 Archival: Gaetano Pesce, New York 500 Main: Gaetano Pesce, New York 500 Archival: Vitra AG, Basle 501 Main: Cassina, Milan 501 Archival: Cassina, Milan 502 Main: Fiell International Ltd., London (photo: Paul Chave) 502 Archival: Studio Year Book, 1932 503 Main: Stiletto Studios, Berlin (photo: Idris Koloziej) 503 Main: Stiletto Studios, Berlin (photo: Idris Koloziej) 504 Main: Archiv Till Behrens, Frankfurt am Main 504 Archival: Archiv Till Behrens, Frankfurt am Main 505 Main: Archiv Till Behrens, Frankfurt am Main 505 Archival: Archiv Till Behrens, Frankfurt am Main 506 Main: Alias, Grumello del Monte 506 Archival: Alias, Grumello del Monte 507 Main: OMK Design Ltd., London 507 Archival: OMK Design Ltd., London 508 Main: Driade, Fossadello di Caorso 508 Archival: Driade, Fossadello di Caorso 509 Main: Driade, Fossadello di Caorso 509 Archival: Driade, Fossadello di Caorso 510 Main: Vitra AG, Basle 510 Archival: Vitra AG, Basle (photo: Hans Hansen) 511 Main: Vitra AG, Basle 511 Archival: Vitra AG, Basle 512 Main: XO, Paris (photo: Hiroyuki Hirai) 512 Archival – L: XO, Paris (photo: Hiroyuki Hirai) 512 Archival – R: Hiroyuki Hirai, Toyko 513 Main: Vitra AG, Basle 513

Archival: Hiroyuki Hirai, Toyko **514** Main: Driade, Fossadello di Caorso **514** Archival: PWII International Ltd., London (photo: Paul Chave) **515** Main: Kartell, Noviglio **515** Archival L. Kartell, Noviglio **515** Archival – R: Kartell, Noviglio **516** Main: Noto-Zeus, Milan **516** Archival A biétteplast, Caselle di Selvazzano **517** Main: HNB, London **517** Archival: HNB, London **518** Main. Castelli, Ozzano Dell'Emilia **519** Main: De Padova, Milan **519** Archival: De Padova, Milan **rma** Main: Knoll International, New York **520** Archival: Knoll International, New York **521** Main: Herman Miller Inc., Zeeland, Michigan (photo: Nick Merrick Blessing & Dan Van Duine) **521** Archival: Herman Miller Inc., Zeeland, Michigan (photo: Effective Im-ages) **522** Main: Vitra AG, Basle **523** Main: Néotù, Paris **524** Main: Vitra AG, Basle **524** Archival: Fred Hoffmann Gallery, USA **525** Main: Vitra AG, Basle **526** Main: Fiam, Tavullia **527** Main: Bonhams, London (photo: Hanna Browne) **527** Archival: Danny Lane, London **528** Main: Space, London **529** Main: Space, London **529** Archival: Cappellini, Arosio **530** Main: Néotù, Paris **530** Archival: Driade, Fossadello di Caorso **531** Main: Néotù, Paris **531** Archival: Néotù, Paris **532** Main: Tosh Sash Co., Tokyo **533** Main: Keicki Tahara, Tokyo **534** Main: Cappellini, Arosio **535** Main: Vitra AG, Basle **536** Main: Cappellini, Arosio **536** Archival: Cappellini, Arosio **537** Main: Idée, Toyko (photo: Tom Vack) **538** Main: Driade, Fossadello di Caorso **538** Archival – L: XO, Paris **538** Archival – R: Driade, Fossadello di Caorso **539** Main: Baleri, Lallio **540** Main: Unifor, Turate **540** Archival: Unifor, Turate **541** Main: One Off Ltd., London **542** Top: One Off Ltd., London (photo: Christoph Kicherer) **542** Bottom: One Off Ltd., London (photo: Christoph Kicherer) **543** Top: One Off Ltd., London (photo: Christoph Kicherer) **543** Bottom: One Off Ltd., London (photo: Christoph Kicherer) **544** Main: Carlos Jané Camacho, Barcelona **544** Archival: Carlos Jané Camacho, Barcelona **545** Main: Ceccotti, Cascina **545** Archival: Ceccotti, Cascina **546** Main: Design 134 – Ibra, Holbaek **547** Main: Punt Mobles, Valencia **548** Main: Interiors VIA European Design Team, Randers **548** Archival: Interiors VIA European Design Team, Randers **549** Main: Vitra AG, Basle (photo: Hans Hansen) **549** Archival: Vitra AG, Basle (photo: Hans Hansen) **550** Main: Knoll International, New York **550** Archival – L: Knoll International, New York **550** Archival – R: Knoll International, New York **551** Main: Herman Miller Inc., Zeeland, Michigan (photo: Merrick, Nick, Hedrich-Blessing) **551** Archival: Herman Miller Inc., Zeeland, Michigan **552** Main: Zanotta, Milan **552** Archival: Droog Design Ltd., Voorburg **553** Main: Cappellini, Arosio **553** Archival: SCP Ltd., London **554** Main: Alias, Grumello del Monte **554** Archival: Alias, Grumello del Monte **555** Main: Viaduct Ltd., London **555** Archival: Viaduct Ltd., London **556** Main: OMK Designs Ltd., London **556** Archival: OMK Designs Ltd., London **557** Main: Fritz Hansen, Allerød (photo: Torsten Graae & Jens Bangbo) **558** Main: Carlos Jané Camacho, Barcelona **559** Main: Sawaya & Moroni, Milan (photo: Miro Zagnoli) **559** Archival: Sawaya & Moroni, Milan (photo: Marco Schillaci) **560** Main: Edra Mazzei, Perignano **560** Archival: Edra Mazzei, Perignano **561** Main: Edra Mazzei, Perignano **562** Main: Cappellini, Arosio **562** Archival: Cappellini, Arosio **563** Main: Vitra AG, Basle **563** Archival: Vitra AG, Basle **564** Main: Katz-Flechtmöbel, Nagold **564** Archival: Katz-Flechtmöbel, Nagold **565** Main: Driade, Fossadello di Caorso **566** Main: Driade, Fossadello di Caorso **566** Archival: Driade, Fossadello di Caorso **567** Main: Vitra AG, Basle (photo: Andreas Sütterlin) **568** Main: Knoll International, New York **569** Main: Cappellini, Arosio **570** Main: Tecno, Milan **571** Main: Tecno, Milan **572** Main: Cappellini, Arosio **573** Main: Cappellini, Arosio **573** Archival: Cappellini, Arosio **574** Main: ClassiCon GmbH, Munich **575** Main: Hironen, Toyko **576** Main: De Padova, Milan **577** Main: Sawaya & Moroni, Milan (photo: Santi Caleca) **577** Archival: Sawaya & Moroni, Milan (photo: Santi Caleca) **578** Main: B&B Italia, Novedrate **578** Archival: B&B Italia, Novedrate **579** Main: Molteni & C., Giussano **580** Main: Zanotta, Milan (photo: Marino Ramazzotti) **580** Archival: Zanotta, Milan (photo: Marino Ramazzotti) **581** Main: Ceccotti, Cascina **582** Main: Moroso, Cavalicco di Tavagnacco **583** Main: Kron, Madrid **584** Main: Baleri, Lallio **585** Main: Zanotta, Milan (photo: Marino Ramazzotti) **586** Main: Rolf Sachs, London **586** Archival: Rolf Sachs, London **587** Main: Rolf Sachs, London **587** Archival: Rolf Sachs, London **588** Main: Made of Waste, London **588** Archival: Made of Waste, London **589** Main: L. W.D., Glasgow **590** Main: Gaetano Pesce, New York **590** Archival: Gaetano Pesce, New York **591** Main: Bernini, Carate Brianza **592** Main: Ceccotti, Cascina **592** Archival – L: XO, Paris **592** Archival – R: Cappellini, Arosio **593** Main: Cappellini, Arosio **594** Main: Zeritalia, S. Angelo in Lizzola **595** Main: Kartell, Noviglio **596** Main: Arflex, Giussano **596** Archival: Arflex, Giussano **597** Main: Ciatti, Badia a Settimo **597** Main: Ciatti, Badia a Settimo **598** Main: Artelano, Paris **598** Archival: Artelano, Paris **599** Main: Fasem, Vicopisano **600** Main: Yellow Diva, London **600** Archival: Yellow Diva, London **601** Main: Cappellini, Arosio **602** Main: Edra Mazzei, Perigano **603** Main: Edra Mazzei, Perigano **603** Archival: Edra Mazzei, Perigano **604** Main: Driade, Fossadello di Caorso (photo: Tom Vack) **604** Archival: Driade, Fossadello di Caorso (photo: Tom Vack) **605** Main: Kartell, Milan (photo: Fabrizio Bergamo) **605** Archival – L: Kartell, Milan (photo: Fabrizio Bergamo) **605** Archival – R: Kartell, Milan (photo: Fabrizio Bergamo) **606** Main: Alias, Grumello del Monte **607** Main: Alias, Grumello del Monte **607** Archival: Alias, Grumello del Monte **608** Main: Studio X, London **608** Archival – L: Studio X, London **608** Archival – C: Studio X, London **608** Archival – R: Studio X, London **609** Main: Ceccotti, Cascina **610** Main: Fasem, Vicopisano **610** Archival: Driade, Fossadello di Caorso (photo: Tom Vack) **611** Main: Studio X, London **611** Archival: Studio X, London

Photographic Credits | Fotonachweis | Crédits photographiques